# THE WORD
## WITHIN THE WORD II

STUDENT EDITION

BY
MICHAEL CLAY THOMPSON
THOMAS MILTON KEMNITZ

JUNE 2015

**Royal Fireworks Press**
**Unionville, New York**

Royal Fireworks Press
PO Box 399
41 First Avenue
Unionville, NY 10988-0399
(845) 726-4444
fax: (845) 726-3824
email: mail@rfwp.com
website: rfwp.com

ISBN: 978-0-89824-914-9

Printed and bound in the United States of America on acid-free, recycled paper using soy-based inks and environmentally friendly cover coatings by the Royal Fireworks Printing Company of Unionville, New York.

Photographs and captions by Dr. Thomas Milton Kemnitz

# INTRODUCTION

As I described in my original introduction to this book twenty years ago, it took me two years to write it, getting up at 4 a.m. every morning and writing—on a good day—one page before going to class to teach English. The purpose of the book was to extend the vocabulary curriculum begun in *The Word Within the Word, Volume I*, and I first imagined that I would use the same lesson format, introducing 500 new stems, but that proved to be impossible. I already had used the majority of important stems, and the lessons of this book had to embrace a different format, although the focus continued to be on the massive interdisciplinary power of the Latin stems—a factor that makes this book, in essence, ten vocabulary books in one.

When I wrote this book, I scarcely imagined what it would become—a vocabulary text used in all states and many foreign countries, steadily revised to include new features and improvements with each succeeding edition. The reason, I think, that *The Word Within the Word* vocabulary curriculum has been so widely adopted is the inherent interdisciplinary nature of the stems. English is at its foundation a Germanic language, not a Romance language; its origin is not from Latin. But over the centuries, the academic strata of English have been infused with thousands of Latin-based words in every major discipline—so much so that academic English now feels like a Romance language. As a result, when students study the great base of stems in this curriculum, the stems make them better students in every subject. Students acquire a powerful vocabulary connection to the words of science, history, mathematics, Spanish (of course), and other courses. The stems are a kind of magic content that expand—once ingested—into an internal vocabulary comprehension engine. There is nothing else, so far as I know, like this content in intellectual life. It is truly power-learning at its most powerful, and it has a global academic effect.

And now, after many years, we arrive at this new enhanced edition of *The Word Within the Word, Volume II*. In this edition the original vocabulary knowledge is supplemented by a kind of book-within-the-book: superb photographs and essays by Dr. Thomas Milton Kemnitz, a historian by training and a photographer who took more than 100,000 photographs for this project. The new material focuses on the Roman Republic, as he explains in his introduction on the following page. You might, however, wonder if the focus of the text has been narrowed to history, when the central strength of the stems is that they are interdisciplinary. Indeed, we also could have created a science edition, if we had wanted to, with great effect. The most important observation is that the focus has not been narrowed. *The Word Within the Word* is just as interdisciplinary as it has always been, just as powerful a foundation for science or mathematics as it always was, but in addition to that, it now provides superior intellectual training that it never had before. It has acquired new vitamins, without losing any of its previous ability to make students stronger in every subject.

Let me explain. Unlike science or mathematics, Roman history is the actual background and source of academic English vocabulary. To study Rome *is* to study English vocabulary. To study Rome is, for any English speaker, to study yourself. Furthermore, there has been a renaissance in educational theory emphasizing the importance of nonfiction readings—what some movements refer to as informational or factual readings—and these new readings about Roman history and culture are perfect—a dream come true—for that purpose. In these advanced readings, students can discover what it is like to leave basic schoolbook prose behind and begin to read real, grown-up history. They can absorb the feel of real academic writing and apply it to their own nonfiction essays. This is exceptional training for the mind. The curricular focus is still on the stems; we do not even provide quizzes or questions for these historical readings because the emphasis is not on assessing them; it is on enjoying and absorbing them. They are a bonus. As you learn the stems, read Roman history too, and see the effect on vocabulary, reading power, writing style, and intellectual light.

Michael Clay Thompson

# INTRODUCTION TO THE ROMAN SECTIONS

This new edition of *The Word Within the Word, Volume II* has been revised to give you some insight into the Roman world. In this volume we have limited the topic to the Roman Republic, i.e., Rome until the assassination of Julius Caesar in 44 B.C.

We saw in the previous volume of *The Word Within the Word* that the Greeks were not only inordinately competitive but also highly creative. In the Romans we meet a people who were no less competitive than the Greeks but who were more organized, flexible, pragmatic, and practical. They lacked the Greek cultural sophistication, but they had a genius for finding solutions to problems.

In this period we are tracing the rise of Rome from a small, land-locked mud village in central Italy to the center of the civilized world. Rome created an empire that was larger in extent than any before or since in the West. From Scotland to Saudi Arabia, from North Africa to Turkey, Rome dominated the Western and Middle Eastern world—and maintained that dominance for half a millennium.

Rome is important to us in the first instance because it was the source of Latin, which is the foundation of so many English words. Rome was the vehicle by which most Greek culture was transmitted to us. The Roman government of the last centuries of the Republic was the model on which the American Founding Fathers based the United States Constitution, and Roman architecture was the model chosen for the buildings of the new American Republic.

This discussion of the Roman Republic is included for your enjoyment and edification, intended to broaden your education and to give you a wider understanding of the world from which our language derives. We hope that no one uses it as a basis for testing.

*The Word Within the Word* remains the premier text for developing English vocabulary, and we have not altered that aspect of this volume except to make some minor changes to improve your comprehension. The word lists and the activities are the same as in the previous edition. You should not be diverted by any of the discussion of ancient Rome from the fundamental purpose of this book, which is to increase your comprehension and to enhance your enjoyment of the English language.

Thomas Milton Kemnitz

| | | |
|---|---|---|
| • mal (bad) | malapropism | |
| • non (not) | nonplussed | |
| • post (after) | postlude | |
| • *archy* (government) | hierarchy | |
| • port (carry) | portly | |
| • inter (between) | interdiction | |
| • vid (look) | *vide* | |
| • omni (all) | omnibus | |
| • *mono* (one) | monolithic | |
| • *lith* (rock) | monolithic | |

| | | |
|---|---|---|
| • pond (weight) | imponderable | |
| • dict (say) | benediction | |
| • bene (good) | benediction | |
| • in (not) | incredulous | |
| • cred (believe) | incredulous | |
| • sci (know) | omniscient | |
| • *neo* (new) | neophyte | |
| • *phyte* (plant) | neophyte | |
| • uni (one) | unilateral | |
| • lat (side) | unilateral | |

**malapropism** (ludicrous misuse of a word) His malapropisms amused us.

**nonplussed** (perplexed) He was nonplussed by the unexpected question.

**postlude** (concluding section) It was a tragic postlude to her long life.

**hierarchy** (ranking) There must be a hierarchy of values.

**portly** (stout) The portly doorman carried himself gracefully.

**interdiction** (prohibition) The judge's interdiction stopped the construction.

**vide** (see) *Vide* Johnson's definition of politics on page 35.

**omnibus** (covering many things) The omnibus legislative bill passed.

**monolithic** (massive and uniform) The monolithic totalitarian society revolted.

**imponderable** (difficult to ponder) He tried to weigh the imponderable issue.

•   •   •

**benediction** (blessing) The grandfather's benediction made them happy.

**incredulous** (not believing) Her incredulous face revealed her mistrust.

**omniscient** (all-knowing) The story was told from an omniscient point of view.

**neophyte** (beginner) The graduate was a neophyte in the business world.

**unilateral** (one-sided) The unilateral decision required no conference.

Roman oil lamp

## As Used by Sir Walter Scott in *Ivanhoe*

| | After | these | **neophytes** | came | a | guard | of | warders. |
|---|---|---|---|---|---|---|---|---|
| **Parts of Speech:** | prep. | adj. | **n.** | v. | adj. | n. | prep. | n. |
| **Parts of Sentence:** | | | | AVP | | subj. | | |
| **Phrases:** | -----prepositional phrase----- | | | | | | --prep. phrase-- | |
| **Clauses:** | ----------------------------------independent clause---------------------------------- | | | | | | | |
| | one independent clause; a simple, declarative sentence | | | | | | | |

Here Sir Walter Scott uses the plural common noun *neophytes* as the object of a preposition, where the prepositional phrase modifies the verb. Notice how the subject and verb are reversed. The word *these* is a demonstrative adjective here. AVP means action verb predicate.

## Pronunciation

| | | | |
|---|---|---|---|
| **malapropism** | mal a PRO pism | **monolithic** | mono LITH ic |
| **nonplussed** | non PLUST | **imponderable** | im POND er ah ble |
| **postlude** | POST lood | **benediction** | beneh DICT shun |
| **hierarchy** | HI er arky | **incredulous** | in KRED ju luss |
| **portly** | PORT lee | **omniscient** | om NIH shunt |
| **interdiction** | in ter DICT shun | **neophyte** | NEE oh fite |
| *vide* | VIE dee | **unilateral** | yoo nih LAT eral |
| **omnibus** | OM nih bus | | |

## Spanish Cognates

English and Spanish are close relatives, as we see in these cognates:

| | | | |
|---|---|---|---|
| **incredulous** | incrédulo | **omniscient** | omnisciente |
| **interdiction** | interdicción | **omnibus** | ómnibus |
| **neophyte** | neófito | **benediction** | bendición |
| **monolithic** | monolítico | **hierarchy** | jerarquía |
| **unilateral** | unilateral | **imponderable** | imponderable |

1. A **Micropoem**: When we say that a beginner is a **neophyte**, we are comparing the beginner to a new (*neo*) plant (*phyte*) that has just pushed through the surface of the ground. In other words, to call a person a neophyte is to use a metaphor—only we often become so accustomed to using a word in its metaphorical sense that we forget that we are even doing so. The word *neophyte* is also a good example of the way we borrow words from various fields (in this case botany) for more general usage.

2. Why does the adjective **nonplussed** mean perplexed? In Latin it literally means no (*non*) more (*plus*). It is a plea for mercy! Please, no more, I am confused enough already! By the way, *nonplussed* is also sometimes spelled *nonplused*.

3. The adjective **monolithic** can refer to something made of stone, such as a large column formed from a single stone—as are some of the stones at Stonehenge. But we also use the word *monolithic* to refer to human societies. In 1989 Chinese students, massed in Tiananmen Square to protest for democratic reform, learned through bloodshed that their government intended to keep China monolithic: massively, totally uniform.

4. The noun **malapropism** is based on the character Mrs. Malaprop, created by Richard Brinsley Sheridan in his 1775 comedy *The Rivals*. It was Mrs. Malaprop's habit to misuse words in ridiculous fashion, usually confusing two words that sounded similar. Sheridan no doubt formed Mrs. Malaprop's name from the French *malapropos*, meaning badly suited to the purpose.

5. The verb *vide* is sometimes pronounced WEEday, and sometimes VYEdee, the latter being probably more common. It is rare in speech but is often used in formal academic writing to direct the reader's attention to a specific passage.

6. Please do not confuse the adjectives **incredible** (unbelievable) and **incredulous** (full of disbelief). If you witness an incredible phenomenon, such as a tornado, you will have an incredulous expression on your face.

7. A **Classic Word**: The adjective **portly** is often seen in the classics. In 1596 Shakespeare used it in *Romeo and Juliet*: "A bears him like a portly gentleman." (The *A* in Shakespeare's sentence is not a typo; it was shorthand for *he*.) Almost three hundred years later, in 1876, Mark Twain used *portly* to modify the same noun: "a fine, portly, middle-aged gentleman." Barrie described "two portly figures" in *Peter Pan*. In *Lord Jim* (1900), Joseph Conrad described a man "well set up, portly, and of conquering mien." But the most fun to be had with *portly* was by that American genius Herman Melville, who used *portly* to describe—what else—the whale! "The Fin-back," said Melville with his distinguished tongue in cheek, "resembles the right whale, but is of a less portly girth." The sperm whale, according to Melville, was also portly. Even the words themselves that Melville applied to the whale seemed to him to be necessarily portly: "Applied to any other creature than the Leviathan—to an ant or a flea—such portly terms might justly be deemed unwarrantably grandiloquent."

The myth of the founding of Rome is that the Trojan Aeneas escaped from Troy as it fell and made his way to Italy, where he founded a town called Lavinium. Four centuries later his descendants Romulus and Remus were cast out as infants and were saved by a she-wolf, who fed and cared for them. This particular bronze wolf dates back to the beginning of the fifth century B.C.; the two infants were a later addition. The lamp shows Aeneas leaving Troy with his father on his back and his son in hand. The Greeks in the Classical Age left tens of thousands of vases with wonderfully sharp images; much of what the Romans of the Republic left is far less distinct, and we have to puzzle out the meaning of images that are less clear. Frequently we have to look to other sources to be certain that our interpretation is correct. Often it is what the characters are holding or wearing or their juxtaposition that provides the evidence we need to interpret an image correctly.

# THE FOUNDING OF ROME
## Dr. Thomas Milton Kemnitz

Rome is the site of old settlements—far older than the legend of its founding by Romulus and Remus in 753 B.C. indicates. However, the ancient Romans believed the founding story of Romulus and Remus, as well as a chronology that Rome was ruled by seven kings before it became a republic in 509 B.C. Because the records of the city were destroyed by Gallic invaders in 387 B.C., the Romans knew little about their early history. The difficulty was that in 387, the Romans had no sense of history or its importance. The Greek Herodotus had begun to write history less than a century earlier, and the concept had not yet reached Rome, so when the records were destroyed, no one tried to recreate them. The legend of the founding of the Roman Republic in 509 B.C. might or (more likely) might not be accurate; the date gives Rome precedence by two years over Athens in the formation of that city's democracy. The interesting questions are how and why a little mud village in central Italy became the center of the greatest empire the West has ever known.

Rome's rise from a village of no consequence to the major power controlling all of the Italian peninsula was the result of a multitude of factors. First, the Roman belief structure was based on the family, clan, and community as more important than the individual. These beliefs produced men and women who were willing to sacrifice for the state, who thought in terms of their duty to larger entities rather than looking out for their own individual welfare. Second, the organization of the Republic fostered a small number of families and clans fighting for pre-eminence. Pre-eminence was gained by serving Rome. The Roman Republic was based on a constant striving for *auctoritas*, on having a prestige based on family eminence and individual achievement. The individual gained recognition through his service to the state, and that included administration as well as military service—Romans did not separate the two. Third, the Romans were remarkably pragmatic, flexible, undogmatic, and organized in their arrangements—particularly in comparison to those of their contemporaries; this enabled them to co-opt rather than conquer the people they defeated in battle. Fourth, the Romans did not give up.

The family/clan arrangement is crucial to understanding Rome; the head of the family (*paterfamilias*) ruled with complete authority over everyone in the family except his wife—women in Rome had some personal freedoms not generally enjoyed by women in the ancient world. Rome was effectively ruled by a small number of patrician families. The patrician *paterfamilias* played an especially important role because he was the head of a group of men and their families for which he was the patron, and they were his clients. Their obligation was to support him, his to provide for them. This relationship might include dozens or hundreds of clients. In Rome itself, the clients (*clientes*) would gather at the home of their patron (*patroni*) in the morning and accompany him to the Forum or the Senate or wherever his business took him. In a city without a police force, they were his personal safety; in a country without a safety net, he was their long-term security. There might be a difference in power, but their interests were mutual. The relationship was a matter of tradition, honor, and law; the patrons did not cheat or fail the clients. This patron/client relationship (*clientala*) was extremely important in Rome; it was often a hereditary bond that superseded family obligations. The Roman terms were *pietas* for the respect the clients owed to the patron and *fides* for the faithfulness both sides felt in carrying out their duties in the relationship. This sense of mutuality was fundamental to how Romans understood the world, and it would prove key to their ability to conquer it.

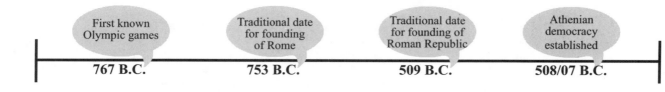

| First known Olympic games | Traditional date for founding of Rome | Traditional date for founding of Roman Republic | Athenian democracy established |
| --- | --- | --- | --- |
| 767 B.C. | 753 B.C. | 509 B.C. | 508/07 B.C. |

In each case below, one of the choices was really the word used by the author in the sentence provided. All of the choices can be found in the example words on the first page of this lesson. Your challenge is to decide which word the author used. This is not a test; it is more like a game because more than one word choice may work perfectly well. See if you can use your sensitivity and intuition to guess correctly which word the author used. You may use a dictionary.

1.  **From Herman Melville's *Billy Budd***

    He was _____, evincing a confusion.
    a. omnibus
    b. monolithic
    c. nonplussed
    d. omniscient

2.  **From Herman Melville's *Moby Dick***

    What things real are there, but _____ thoughts?
    a. omnibus
    b. imponderable
    c. incredulous
    d. unilateral

3.  **From Joseph Heller's *Catch-22***

    His ruddy _____ face softened with amusement.
    a. incredulous
    b. portly
    c. nonplussed
    d. monolithic

4.  **From E.L. Doctorow's *Ragtime***

    He talked incessantly in his European accent, with _____ he himself...laughed over.
    a. malapropisms
    b. imponderables
    c. neophytes
    d. benedictions

5.  **From John Milton's *Paradise Lost***

    Sternly he pronounced the rigid _____.
    a. hierarchy
    b. postlude
    c. interdiction
    d. benediction

Though it is a good thing to have a rich vocabulary, it is not a good thing to abuse that vocabulary by writing verbose, abstruse, sesquipedalian sentences. Those who overuse their vocabularies often do so at the expense of clarity. Translate the following showy, ponderous passage into graceful, direct English. Do not use slang, but do use words that seem familiar and comfortable.

UPON HEARING the omniscient judge issue his imponderable interdiction against omnibus legislation and monolithic government, the nonplussed, portly neophyte unilaterally pronounced a benediction, which included the following malapropism: "I have not begun to postlude remarks about such matters." This sentence formed a condign postlude to the day's events.

Lavinium in Roman legend is the city Aeneas founded after reaching Italy on his journey from Troy via Carthage. It is there that he deposited the Penates that he had carried from Troy. The Penates were worshipped privately as protectors of the individual household, particularly the larder and food stores. Villas had shrines with images of them—like the one pictured here—that were worshipped at family meals and on special occasions. The shrines were often in the atrium as well as in the areas where food was prepared or eaten. Offerings were made of small portions of food. The state as a whole worshipped the public Penates (*Penates Publici*). This state cult occupied a significant role as a focal point of Roman patriotism and nationalism. The Penates were related to Vesta, the goddess of the hearth—and of the city of Rome. This Penate is carrying a conucopia, or horn of plenty, as a symbol of abundance in his right hand, and he holds a libation bowl (like the Greek *phiale*) in his left hand.

### Reading Comprehension

1. In Translation 31, which of the following best expresses the main idea?
   a. Most judges do not know what they are talking about.
   b. Powerful governments need to be restrained by the people.
   c. A beginner was pleased that the judge stood up to big government.
   d. It is important to choose your words precisely.

2. The author's attitude in Translation 31 is best described as:
   a. The day's events had been ridiculous.
   b. Judges deserve more respect than they get.
   c. The neophyte should have kept quiet.
   d. The day's events had been important and meaningful.

### Analogies

3. **BENEDICTION : INTERDICTION ::**
   a. order : command
   b. blessing : judge
   c. Pope : judge
   d. church : prohibition

4. **IMPONDERABLE : NONPLUSSED ::**
   a. confusing : confused
   b. heavy : more
   c. impressive : noncombatant
   d. perplexed : difficult to ponder

### Antonyms

5. **INCREDULOUS :**
   a. incredible
   b. credulity
   c. omniscient
   d. gullible

6. **OMNIBUS :**
   a. taxicab
   b. narrow
   c. monolithic
   d. unilateral

The sanctuary for the household gods—a small alcove called a *lararium*—can be seen in many of the structures still standing in Pompeii and Herculaneum. The curved top was the *limus*, and the most sacred spot in the home was under the *limus*. It is from this association that we get the word *sublime* and its meaning. These household gods fell victim to the eruption of Vesuvius. The shape of the *lararium* can be seen more clearly on page 24.

**synthesis**

With which other word in List 31 do you think the adjective **nonplussed** has the most in common? Explain why you think the two words have something in common. Remember that your connection can be in any category at all.

**analysis**

Imagine that you decided to organize your values into a **hierarchy** so that you knew what was important to you. To begin, you would sort your values into categories in order to make better sense of them. What would be some of the main categories of values you would use?

**divergence**

List as many things as you can that might be described as **imponderable**. Remember to keep listing after the easy answers are exhausted so that you find some original and creative answers.

**convergence**

If you had to live in a **monolithic** society in which a tyrannical government demanded mass, uniform adherence to its ideas, which society would you choose? You may select any society you can think of, ancient or modern, fictional or historical. Explain your choice.

**application**

Use five or more of the words in List 31 to describe something or to make a statement.

**evaluation**

What criteria might a judge use to determine whether or not to issue an **interdiction** against building a toxic waste site in a populated area? List at least five criteria, and then rank them in order of importance.

**ethics**

Imagine that a strange virus was slowly giving you the power of **omniscience** but that you could still choose not to know certain things if you wished. What things, other than some of the obvious private matters in individuals' lives, would you choose not to know because you think it would not be ethical for you to know them?

**intuition**

You have just written a short story in which the character wakes with a start, a completely **incredulous** expression on his face. Why is he incredulous?

**emotion**

Is being **nonplussed** an emotion? Or is it not an emotion but simply a perception, more intellectual than affective? Explain.

### Neologist's Lexicon

Use the stems in this list to create a new word (neologism). Give the word, the pronunciation, the part of speech, the etymology, and the definition(s). Keep a record of the neologisms you create from list to list. Here are some examples:

**monoscient** (mo NO se ent) adj. [*mono* (one), *sci* (know)] 1. being fixed and obsessed with a single idea 2. so specialized as to know only one thing, while being ignorant of all else

**lithovidesis** (lith o vid EE sis) n. [*lith* (rock), *vid* (look)] 1. a look that turns one to stone, as the look of the Gorgon 2. the look of one whose name you have mispronounced

### Sesquipedalian Theater

Using at least one word from this week's list in every sentence, write a small one-act play. If circumstances allow, it would be good to perform the sesquipedalian play in class. Having a witty prop is a good idea. Use a pseudonym, or *nom de plume*, if you like. Emphasis should be on creativity and fun; feel free to be silly or absurd. As an example:

### Unidentified Flying Monoliths
#### by Michael Skellig

Scene: A small group of people are walking in the park. One is pulling a stuffed animal on a leash. One is bouncing a basketball and never stops or looks up throughout the play. One is chewing gum animatedly and stares wide-eyed at the audience the whole time.

One:  Look, in the imponderable sky! It is a bird, a plane, an unidentified flying monolith!

Two:  Monolith?? Oh no! I see, but I'm incredulous, but I see, but I'm incredulous!

One:  Be not nonplussed! Trust to the verification of your own eyes!

Three (looking up, agape): Oh my omnibus mind, my neophyte eyes! Can this vision be unilateral, or does all the world see what I see?

One and Two: *Vide, VIDE, VIDE*!! (They pronounce the word differently each time.)

One:  Oh hierarchy of truths! Oh benediction and postlude to nonplussed day! Oh omniscient visitors from afar! What interdictions have we broken, that you visit us??

Two:  Wait!

One:  Oh, my earthbound portliness! Oh, my . . .

Two:  Wait!

One:  Oh, OMNIBUS OMNISCIENT BENEDICTIONS AND INTERDICTIONS AND...

Two:  WAIT! Did you say "unidentified flying monolith"? That's no monolith! That's a monoPLANE, you neophyte! MONOPLANE! Ha!! What a malapropism!

One:  Monoplane? . . .

One:  Plane? . . .

One:  Malapropism? . . .

All (muttering): Ooohh nooo . . .

All stare blankly at audience.

*finis*

| | | | | | |
|---|---|---|---|---|---|
| • *hypo* | (under) | hypothecate | • contra | (against) | contravene |
| • *hetero* | (different) | heterodox | • ven | (come) | contravene |
| • *dox* | (opinion) | heterodox | • con | (together) | confluence |
| • pater | (father) | paterfamilias | • flu | (flow) | confluence |
| • put | (think) | putative | • circum | (around) | circumlocution |
| • ver | (true) | aver | • loqu | (talk) | circumlocution |
| • *mega* | (large) | megaton | • sol | (alone) | soliloquy |
| • sangui | (blood) | sangfroid | • moll | (soft) | mollify |
| • ego | (I) | alter ego | • fy | (make) | mollify |
| • alter | (other) | altercation | • greg | (group) | gregarious |
| • tion | (act or state) | altercation | • ous | (full of) | gregarious |

**hypothecate** (pledge as security) Hypothecate the land as security.

**heterodox** (unorthodox) He was criticized for his heterodox opinions.

**paterfamilias** (male head of family) Please consult with the paterfamilias.

**putative** (thought-to-be) He was the putative leader of the mafia.

**aver** (affirm or declare) He averred to the prosecutor that he had seen nothing.

**megaton** (force of a million tons of dynamite) A ten-megaton bomb exploded in the desert.

**sangfroid** (cold-blooded composure) She performs with cool sangfroid in emergencies.

**alter ego** (second self) She was not just a friend but an alter ego to me.

**altercation** (heated dispute) Talleyrand heard the noisy altercation in the streets.

**contravene** (go against) Do not contravene a command intentionally.

•   •   •

**confluence** (a flowing together) The U.S. is a confluence of many peoples and cultures.

**circumlocution** (talking in circles) His circumlocution of the issue rankled the audience.

**soliloquy** (speech to oneself) He roamed the kitchen in humorous soliloquy.

**mollify** (make soft) We need to mollify the client's resentment.

**gregarious** (sociable) The warm host had a gregarious personality.

## As Used by Henry James in *The American*

| | His | unconscious | sangfroid | was | boundless. |
|---|---|---|---|---|---|
| **Parts of Speech:** | adj. | adj. | **n.** | v. | adj. |
| **Parts of Sentence:** | | | subj. | LVP | S.C. |
| **Phrases:** | -----no prepositional, appositive, or verbal phrases----- | | | | |
| **Clauses:** | --------------------------------independent clause---------------------------------- | | | | |
| | one independent clause; a simple, declarative sentence | | | | |

Here Henry James uses the singular common noun *sangfroid* as the subject of the verb *was*; *was* is a linking verb that connects the subject *sangfroid* to the subject complement (S.C.) *boundless*. In this sentence, the word *his* is being used as a possessive adjective. LVP means linking verb predicate.

## Pronunciation

| | | | |
|---|---|---|---|
| **hypothecate** | hi POTH uh kate | **altercation** | alter KAY shun |
| **heterodox** | HETT er o dox | **contravene** | contra VEEN |
| **paterfamilias** | PAH ter fa ME lee us | **confluence** | KONN flu ence |
| **putative** | PYOO tah tiv | **circumlocution** | SIR cum lo KYOO shun |
| **aver** | ah VUR | **soliloquy** | so LIL o kwee |
| **megaton** | MEG a tun | **mollify** | MOLL ih fye |
| **sangfroid** | sahn FRWAH | **gregarious** | greh GAR ee us |
| **alter ego** | alter EE go | | |

## Spanish Cognates

| | | | |
|---|---|---|---|
| **heterodox** | heterodoxo | **putative** | putativo |
| **contravene** | contravención | **confluence** | confluencia |
| **soliloquy** | soliloquio | **gregarious** | gregario |
| **circumlocution** | circunlocución | **altercation** | altercado |

1.  The verb **mollify** does mean to make soft, but it does not apply to physical objects; we do not say that we mollify hard clay by kneading it. We mollify hard minds, hard feelings, anger. To mollify is to appease, to make soft the hard attitude of an intractable opinion.

2.  It is interesting to contrast the noun **circumlocution** with the verb **equivocate** and the noun **subterfuge**. Each of these words refers to a way of avoiding a straight answer, but each is different. Circumlocuting is talking (*locu*) in circles (*circum*), equivocating is giving equal (*equi*) voice (*voc*) to both sides of an issue while taking neither side, and a subterfuge is a trick or dodge that lets the speaker duck (*fug*: flee, *sub*: under) the question.

3.  If the adjective **putative** seems strange or alien at first, think of other words that also have the *put* (think) stem, such as **computer**, **reputation**, and **dispute**. A computer is a thinking machine (sort of), a reputation is what you have when people know you again (*re*), and a dispute is what happens when people do not think alike.

4.  The adjective **heterodox** can mean "of many opinions": the United States is a heterodox nation consisting of many different cultures. The word also can mean simply "not orthodox": a person's heterodox views can land him or her in trouble in a rigid society or group that does not tolerate divergent opinions.

5.  A **Classic Word**: We think of the word **soliloquy** as a technical term to use in describing famous scenes from Shakespearean plays. The phrases spill from one's memory: to be or not to be; tomorrow and tomorrow and tomorrow; here's yet some liquor left; I have no cause to spurn at Caesar but for the general, he would be crowned. And yet *soliloquy* has been a popular word for many modern novelists, especially in the nineteenth century. Hardy, Twain, Thoreau, Melville, Stowe, and the Brontës all used *soliloquy* in their works. In *Tom Sawyer*, Sid soliloquizes just audibly. At Walden Pond, Thoreau finds himself soliloquizing and talking to all the universe at the same time. Melville's Stubb soliloquizes at the try-works in *Moby Dick*. Harriet Beecher Stowe and Emily Brontë used *soliloquy* over and over. In *Uncle Tom's Cabin,* we find Andy cutting short Tom's soliloquy, Cassy stealing up on a soliloquy, and people in reveries soliloquizing to themselves as if by music. In *Wuthering Heights,* we find characters murmuring in soliloquy, half soliloquizing, indulging in a soliloquy of execrations, soliloquizing in an undertone of peevish displeasure, and soliloquizing on the length of the night as they look at their watches.

6.  The noun **sangfroid** is the French word for cold-bloodedness. It refers to not getting rattled, to keeping your cool, to being self-possessed, poised, in control of yourself, despite conditions that would leave some people shook up. Elvis Presley was all shook up and lacked sangfroid. In other words, this word is fun. (Yes, Elvis and I should have said "shaken up," but then the wink of the line would have been lost!)

7.  A **Micropoem**: The noun **confluence** contains a beautiful image of liquids streaming together, as when two rivers meet. This metaphorical word is often used to depict the flowing together of minds or of cultures.

Juno was one of the earliest Roman deities, along with Jupiter and Mars and others, but at Veii she was the patron deity of the city. When they took Veii, the Romans brought Veii's Juno to the Aventine Hill and established an independent cult just outside of the city walls. The Juno of Veii and other Italian cities was Juno Regina—the Queen—and represented youthfulness and vitality. The Romans would continue for centuries the practice of taking back to Rome the deities of the people they conquered.

# THE FOUNDATIONS OF ROME
## Dr. Thomas Milton Kemnitz

The *clientala* gave the Romans a model to use when they began to win battles with neighboring towns. It conditioned them to think of the losers not as the conquered but as potential clients—people with whom to form a mutually beneficial relationship based on each side serving the other. They did not enslave their neighbors the way the Spartans enslaved the Helots; the Romans co-opted them into their sphere. The Romans were extraordinarily flexible in making different arrangements for each locality they overwhelmed. In one city they would install an oligarchy favorable to their interests; another would be left autonomous with its institutions as they were before they lost to the Romans; a third would find itself more closely held, perhaps offered a form of Roman citizenship. In the ancient world, most cities had strict limits on who qualified as citizens—who received the benefits and privileges of citizenship—but the Romans seem to have had only one requirement: that an arrangement work. The long-term result was that Rome bound to itself the communities it conquered, made them allies, and increased its power in doing so. The multiplicity of arrangements would stand Rome in good stead in the centuries and wars to come.

The persistence of the Romans in military matters was also extraordinary. They were not deterred by a setback here or difficulties there. They remained flexible and inventive in their tactics and strategies. They persisted in fighting an enemy until they prevailed. Others might retire after taking casualties in an indecisive engagement or a loss, but not the Romans. They returned to the field with fresh troops and new leaders if necessary, but they continued to fight their enemies. Centuries passed in which the Romans sent an army into the field every year to do battle with people who were farther and farther away from Rome itself.

From the earliest years of the Republic, the Romans showed unusual flexibility in dealing with their citizens. The Republic was organized with a Senate that had 600 patrician members (*patricii*) and an Assembly (*comitia centuriata*) of all the citizens (*plebii*), who elected each year two consuls who were the government. Each consul had complete authority (*imperium*), which meant that one consul could veto the decisions or actions of the other. Voting in the Assembly was arranged by wealth, with the richest—the patricians—having the most votes and able to command the votes of their clients. The consuls, moreover, were nominated by the Senate, which nominated only patricians. This did not seem to be a good arrangement to the more than ninety percent of Romans who were not patricians, and the plebeians demanded changes. One mechanism by which they forced the patricians to deal with them was to bring the city to a standstill by withdrawing to a hill outside the walls of Rome and camping there until agreement was reached. The first alteration they insisted upon was the election of tribunes to protect them from arbitrary actions by the consuls and the other authorities. These Tribunes of the Plebs (*tribuni plebis*) would come to be an important part of the Roman government.

A huge problem for most of Roman history was debt; in the early years the problem was crushing because the Roman economy was agriculturally based and subject to repeated crop failures, famines, and plagues. If a debtor could not pay, the creditor was entitled to put the defaulter in chains and make him a serf for life. One of the protections the tribunes could offer was that the debtor at least would have time and due process before this enslavement occurred. The next thing the plebs wanted was a codification of the laws, and that, too, the patricians granted. But when the law was codified on twelve tablets, it was plain to the plebs just how few rights they had. Their agitation for more rights and protections continued, and amelioration was granted by the patricians as the years went by. The more affluent plebs were needed for the army, and Rome had to be stable for the army to leave the city to fight in places that were increasingly far away from the banks of the Tiber.

| First known Olympic games | Traditional date for founding of Rome | Traditional date for founding of Roman Republic | Athenian democracy established |
|---|---|---|---|
| **767 B.C.** | **753 B.C.** | **509 B.C.** | **508/07 B.C.** |

In each case below, one of the choices was really the word used by the author in the sentence provided. All of the choices can be found in the example words on the first page of this lesson. Your challenge is to decide which word the author used. This is not a test; it is more like a game because more than one word choice may work perfectly well. See if you can use your sensitivity and intuition to guess correctly which word the author used.

1. **From Henry James's *The American***

   He was not embarrassed, for his unconscious _____ was boundless.
   a. alter ego
   b. sangfroid
   c. confluence
   d. soliloquy

2. **From George Orwell's *1984***

   Suddenly the group broke up, and two of the men were in violent _____.
   a. paterfamilias
   b. confluence
   c. circumlocution
   d. altercation

3. **From Robert Penn Warren's *All the King's Men***

   "Pressure is a prettier word," I _____.
   a. averred
   b. hypothecated
   c. contravened
   d. mollified

4. **From Emily Brontë's *Wuthering Heights***

   I declined answering Mrs. Dean's question, which struck me as something _____.
   a. gregarious
   b. putative
   c. heterodox
   d. mollified

5. **From Jonathan Swift's *Gulliver's Travels***

   It put me to the pains of many _____ to give my master a right idea of what I spoke.
   a. circumlocutions
   b. altercations
   c. confluences
   d. soliloquies

Though it is a good thing to have a rich vocabulary, it is not a good thing to abuse that vocabulary by writing verbose, abstruse, sesquipedalian sentences. Those who overuse their vocabularies often do so at the expense of clarity. Translate the following showy, ponderous passage into graceful, direct English. Do not use slang, but do use words that seem familiar and comfortable.

WITH ADMIRABLE SANGFROID and without circumlocution, the omniscient paterfamilias, in order to achieve a confluence of heterodox viewpoints, and to avoid the need for mollifying the disputants, urged all present to avoid further altercations over warheads, megatons, and putative future doom. "Gregarious though you be," he averred, "confine your assertions to soliloquy or to your alter egos; do not contravene my unilateral interdiction against altercation. If you are nonplussed or incredulous, then please respect the hierarchy of family authority."

The idea of service to the state was ingrained in Romans and was reflected in many ways throughout Roman life. Pictured here is a household oil lamp. Winged Victory is shown holding a palm branch and a wreath with the inscription *OB CIVES SERVAT*—meaning to serve the citizens.

## Reading Comprehension

1. The author of Translation 32 does all of the following EXCEPT:
    a. describe a male head of household's interdiction
    b. describe a violent altercation
    c. describe someone speaking directly to others
    d. describe an interfamilial mollification

2. The author's attitude is best described as:
    a. It is good to be even-tempered and candid.
    b. A father should rule the household.
    c. Disagreement should be kept to oneself.
    d. Global dangers should not be discussed openly.

## Analogies

3. **MOLLIFY : ALTERCATION ::**
    a. mollusk : alternator
    b. soften : endurance
    c. soothe : dispute
    d. peace : violence

4. **SOLILOQUY : CIRCUMLOCUTION ::**
    a. orbit : sun
    b. solo : symphony
    c. mumble : periphrasis
    d. evasion : speech

## Antonyms

5. **HETERODOX :**
    a. doxology
    b. dogmatic
    c. heteromorphic
    d. unorthodox

6. **SANGFROID :**
    a. hot-tempered
    b. bloody
    c. acerbic
    d. cool

The myth of Curtius was the story of a selfless hero who sacrificed himself for Rome. In the myth, a widening chasm appeared in the Forum, along with the prophesy that it would continue to grow until Rome threw what it valued most into it. Marcus Curtius understood that it was the life of a brave Roman warrior that Rome held most dear, and in full armor he rode his horse into it, after which the chasm closed over him.

**synthesis**

What character in literature or mythology can you recall who behaves with **sangfroid** at a time of danger? Can you think of more than one character?

**divergence**

Think of the **soliloquies** you have with yourself, in which you scold yourself, remind yourself, encourage yourself. How many soliloquy topics can you think of that are common in your life? List as many soliloquy topics as you can.

**convergence**

Our planet is a **heterodox** place, containing many cultures with many customs. If you had to write a fifty-page typed research paper on one culture other than your own, what other culture would you choose, purely on the basis of interest? Why?

**ethics and evaluation**

Many people believe that it is usually right to behave lawfully, in accordance with legally constituted authority, but that sometimes, as Thoreau and Gandhi indicated, it is right to **contravene** even legally constituted authority if that authority requires you to engage in a crime against humanity. An obvious example of this idea is the war crimes trials held to prosecute Nazi war criminals, who often argued that they were simply obeying the commands of their superiors. The question is: Where do you draw the line between when it is wrong to disobey authority and wrong to obey authority? In creating an answer to this difficult but important question, remember that you must always create and employ intelligent criteria when you are trying to evaluate a difficult question.

**analysis**

**Altercations** do not normally erupt instantaneously but evolve from pleasant conversations into heated disputes. Think about this process, and list the stages of interaction that often lead from discussion to altercation.

**intuition, emotion, and imagination**

You are watching a play, and the **gregarious** protagonist is in the midst of a **soliloquy** characterized by an extreme emotion. What is the emotion, and what is the subject of the soliloquy? Use your intuition and imagination to form an elaborate version of the scene, and then describe it in detail.

**aesthetics and application**

If you were going to develop a poster to depict the effects of a twenty-**megaton** nuclear weapon, what colors would you use, and what would the primary image be?

Roman keys

### Neologist's Lexicon

Use the stems in this list to create a new word (neologism). Give the word, the pronunciation, the part of speech, the etymology, and the definition(s). Keep a record of the neologisms you create from list to list. Here are some examples:

**sanguiloquacious** (SAN gwe lo KWAY shus) adj. [*sangui* (blood), *loqu* (talk)] 1. excessive use of the adjective *bloody* 2. speaking in coarse, offensively explicit language

**heteromollidoxical** (HET er o moll i DOX i cal) adj. [*hetero* (different), *moll* (soft) *dox* (opinion)] 1. having many soft-headed or ill-founded opinions 2. pertaining to a society in which such views have wide acceptance

### Sesquipedalian Poetry

Using at least one word from this week's list in most lines, write a short poem. You may use regular meter, internal or end rhyme, or other poetic devices, or not! Here is a sample:

#### Cool Kid

megaton, megaton
anthropodynamo
cool kid, cool—if you ask me
confluent talent
my young alter ego
halt not your ego
go contravene limits
unorthodox and gregarious (precarious)
mollify my putative spirit of various altercations
with your soliloquies and

    c
      i
        r
      c
    u
  m

       locutions/talktome
willowtree will you grow
small spirit with your cool sangfroid
cool kid
cool

This is a *lararium* in a villa in Pompeii; it differs from many in that it has an altar, while most were built into the wall as an alcove with a shelf.

| | | | | | |
|---|---|---|---|---|---|
| • de | (down) | declaim | • non | (not) | *non sequitur* |
| • clam | (cry out) | declaim | • sequ | (follow) | *non sequitur* |
| • voc | (voice) | *sotto voce* | • ego | (I) | egocentric |
| • trans | (across) | translucent | • centri | (center) | egocentric |
| • luc | (light) | translucent | • loqu | (talk) | loquacious |
| • fort | (strong) | forte, *fortissimo* | • ous | (full of) | loquacious |
| • acr | (sharp) | acerbity | • sacro | (holy) | sacrosanct |
| • per | (through) | perambulate | • sanct | (holy) | sacrosanct |
| • ambul | (walk) | perambulate | • caco | (bad) | cacophony |
| • fid | (faith) | perfidy | • phon | (sound) | cacophony |
| • pugn | (fight) | impugn | • tang | (touch) | tangible |

**declaim** (speak rhetorically)  The pompous opponents declaimed vociferously.

**sotto voce** (in a low voice)  He tried to inform her, *sotto voce*, of the problem.

**translucent** (semitransparent)  The glass was translucent, not completely transparent.

**forte** (strong point)  Spelling is not his forte.

**fortissimo** (very loudly)  The orchestra played a thunderous *fortissimo* passage.

**acerbity** (sharpness of temper)  His constant acerbity was demoralizing.

**perambulate** (wander through)  The boy perambulated through the park.

**perfidy** (breach of faith)  We deplored the scoundrel's perfidious act.

**impugn** (attack as false)  Another witness impugned his testimony.

**non sequitur*** (an idea that does not follow)  The idea was a ludicrous *non sequitur*.

• • •

**egocentric** (self-centered)  His egocentric conversation became boring.

**loquacious** (talkative)  We avoided the loquacious chatterbox.

**sacrosanct** (sacred)  The second rule is sacrosanct and inviolable.

**cacophony** (bad noise)  We heard the cacophonous blaring of the horns in the street below.

**tangible** (touchable)  The nice office is a tangible benefit of the job.

*Foreign language terms are in italics unless they are familiar and widespread. We have been conservative about this, placing most in italics, but it is in part a matter of preference.

## As Used by Charles Dickens in *David Copperfield*

| | I | stood | amazed | at | the | revelation | of | all | this | **perfidy.** |
|---|---|---|---|---|---|---|---|---|---|---|
| **Parts of Speech:** | pron. | v. | adv. | prep. | adj. | n. | prep. | adj. | adj. | **n.** |
| **Parts of Sentence:** | subj. | AVP | | | | | | | | |

**Phrases:** -------prep. phrase------- -------prep. phrase------

**Clauses:** ----------------------------------independent clause----------------------------------
one independent clause; a simple, declarative sentence

Here Charles Dickens uses the singular common noun *perfidy* as the object of the preposition *of.* This sentence is a good reminder of how much we use prepositional phrases.

## Pronunciation

| | | | |
|---|---|---|---|
| **declaim** | dee KLAIM | **impugn** | im PYOON |
| *sotto voce* | sotto VO chay | *non sequitur* | non SEK wih tur |
| **translucent** | trans LOO sent | **egocentric** | ego SEN trik |
| **forte** | FORT | **loquacious** | lo KWAY shus |
| *fortissimo* | for TEE see mo | **sacrosanct** | SACK ro sankt |
| **acerbity** | ah SIR bih tee | **cacophony** | kah KOFF uh nee |
| **perambulate** | per AM byoo late | **tangible** | TANJ ih bul |
| **perfidy** | PURR fid ee | | |

## Spanish Cognates

| | | | |
|---|---|---|---|
| **translucent** | translúcido | **acerbity** | acerbidad |
| **perambulate** | perambulación | **perfidy** | perfidia |
| **loquacious** | loquaz | **sacrosanct** | sacrosanto |
| **cacophony** | cacofonía | **tangible** | tangible |

1.  The noun **forte**, when used to mean "strong point," should be pronounced FORT. The pronunciation FORtay is used for the musical term that means to play a musical passage with great strength. The FORtay passage is the forte of some orchestras. Since this is widely misunderstood, you may have to use the correct pronunciation with extra confidence.

2.  We often use the adjective **sacrosanct** in a sincere sense, as to describe the sacrosanct values of a religious faith. But we also use the word in an ironic sense, for the purpose of pointed humor, as when we tell a selfish person, "Excuse ME for touching your sacrosanct typewriter."

3.  A *non sequitur* is a pseudo-logical conclusion that a speaker draws but that actually does not follow from what has been said previously. In Eugene Ionesco's play *Rhinoceros*, characters completely misunderstand the relationships in logic and wind up with the following reasoning: All cats are mortal, and Socrates was mortal; therefore, Socrates was a cat. This, we will note, is a *non sequitur*. The correct relationship of a **syllogism** (for that is what the characters were trying to demonstrate) is as follows: All cats are mortal, and Schmerz is a cat; therefore, Schmerz is mortal.

    WRONG:      All A is C, and B is C; therefore, B is A.
    RIGHT:      All A is C, and B is A; therefore, B is C.

4.  The verb **declaim** is an interesting word. It combines the stems *de* (down) and *clam* (cry out), and the crying down to which it refers is pompous, dramatic, or highly emphatic rhetorical speech. In *A Separate Peace*, the students declaim their threats to enlist in the war with a grinding of teeth and a flashing of eyes. One of my favorite sentences using declaim is this one from Wilder's *The Bridge of San Luis Rey*: "and often until dawn they would remain there declaiming to one another the lordly conversation of Calderón."

5.  A **Classic Word**: Authors from Jonathan Swift in the early 1700s to John Knowles in the 1950s have found it helpful to distinguish between the **tangible** phenomena that we can touch and the **intangible** phenomena that we cannot touch but nevertheless recognize. In one of his voyages, Swift's Gulliver finds inhabitants condensing air into a dry, tangible substance. Melville describes Moby Dick's intangible malignity. Dickens, in *A Tale of Two Cities*, describes the intangible impurities of poverty and deprivation. Conrad explains that some facts are visible, tangible, and open to the senses. In *Ethan Frome*, Edith Wharton notes signs of Zeena's disfavor as intangible but disquieting. Classic authors have described tangible proofs of convalescence (Emily Brontë), the remoteness and intangibility of a minister (Hawthorne), the tangible, separate existence of a people (Stowe), the intangible tints of morning or evening (Thoreau), swinging and clawing at the intangible air (Twain), and looking for the call of the wild as though it were a tangible thing (London).

6.  A **Micropoem**: The adjective **egocentric** contains a striking geometric image of the self (*ego*) at the center (*centri*) of all other phenomena, which are revolving around it.

The walls of Rome built after 387 B.C. were twelve feet thick and twenty-four feet high—a formidable defensive barrier. The walls stood as a part of Rome's defenses for 800 years before they were breached by the barbarians. The fourteen roads that led to Rome all necessitated a gate to get through the walls into the city. In the bottom photo is the gate for the Appian Way, the oldest of Rome's major roads. When Pompey wanted to include elephants in his Triumph, he found that the gates were too small for the animals to pass through.

# THE SACK OF VEII AND ROME
## Dr. Thomas Milton Kemnitz

For the first half-century of the Republic, Rome sent a legion south or west to fight and ultimately to befriend the Latium towns nearby, and it was moderately successful. But eventually Rome had to deal with the Etruscans. It is probable that Rome's last king was Etruscan and that the Etruscans controlled Rome for many years before the founding of the Republic. The Etruscans had controlled much of central Italy from about 800 B.C. in a loose confederation of cities. With productive mines and an expertise in metallurgy, they traded lucratively with the Greeks and Carthaginians. Rome lay at the best crossing point on the Tiber between the northern and southern Etruscan territory. The Etruscan city nearest to Rome was Veii, only twelve miles away, and it presented a grave threat to Rome's independent existence. In the last years of the fifth century B.C., the Romans attacked Veii, which asked for help from its sister Etruscan cities. The nearby Etruscan city of Caere (only twenty miles distant from Rome), however, was already linked by treaty to Rome, which also drew strength from its alliances with the Latium cities. After a prolonged series of military engagements that may have lasted a decade, the Romans gained a foothold near Veii's city walls, cleared out the tunnels through which water fed into the city, and made their way through them to emerge inside the walls and thereby force the surrender of the inhabitants in 396. The Romans needed to end forever the threat Veii posed, so they demolished its walls and expelled most of its citizens. The Romans settled their citizens on Veii's agricultural land and thereby doubled the area they controlled. The patron god of Veii was Juno, queen of the goddesses, and the Romans took her back to their city and established her as one of the pantheon they worshipped; they would continue to assimilate the gods of cities they conquered into their pantheon as their area enlarged. Rome also quickly exploited Veii's Grotta Oscura quarry; for more than two centuries, this was the primary source of stone for large structures in Rome, including two bridges over the Tiber.

The destruction of Veii meant that the Romans were freed of a powerful threat from a nearby city, but soon they faced a more distant and formidable enemy. The Gauls had settled in northern Italy, and now they swept down the peninsula, plundering as they went. The Romans mustered an army of more than 10,000 men, the largest force they had ever assembled. But they were facing as many as 30,000 Gauls with a very mobile cavalry and long, slashing swords. Holding unweildly thrusting spears about eight feet long and defended by shields— round and about three feet in diameter for the wealthiest citizens, oval for the less prosperous—the Romans arrayed themselves in a phalanx, a solid line several men deep, much as the Greeks were using at that time. Protecting their rear was a river. The battle was fought eleven miles from Rome. The Gallic cavalry turned the Roman flanks, while their foot soldiers with long swords inflicted heavy casualties before the Romans could do any damage to the invaders. The Roman phalanx broke and ran; most of the Romans drowned in the river at their rear. There was no one left to defend the city, and the invaders plundered and razed Rome, destroying all of the records of the early years of Rome. When 200 years later the Romans began to wonder about the origins of their city, they had to rely on myths and try to create plausible stories.

In the aftermath of the destruction of Rome, the Romans had to see more effectively to their defense. One answer to that was to build massive city walls from blocks of stone they took from Veii's quarry. The Romans also began to alter their military, adopting a long sword in place of the unwieldy thrusting spear and increasing their body armor.

| Traditional date for founding of Roman Republic | Athenian democracy established | Peloponnesian Wars end | Rome conquers Veii | Rome sacked by Gauls |
|---|---|---|---|---|
| 509 B.C. | 508/07 B.C. | 404 B.C. | 396 B.C. | 387 B.C. |

In each case below, one of the choices was really the word used by the author in the sentence provided. All of the choices can be found in the example words on the first page of this lesson. Your challenge is to decide which word the author used. This is not a test; it is more like a game because more than one word choice may work perfectly well. See if you can use your sensitivity and intuition to guess correctly which word the author used.

1.   **From Harriet Beecher Stowe's *Uncle Tom's Cabin***

     His life is a logical result of his opinions, and mine is a complete _____.
     a. *fortissimo*
     b. perfidy
     c. cacophony
     d. *non sequitur*

2.   **From Nathaniel Hawthorne's *The House of the Seven Gables***

     The judge's smile seemed to operate on her _____ of heart like sunshine upon vinegar.
     a. acerbity
     b. perfidy
     c. *non sequitur*
     d. translucence

3.   **From Aldous Huxley's *Brave New World***

     With closed eyes...John was softly _____ to vacancy.
     a. impugning
     b. perambulating
     c. declaiming
     d. *sotto voce*

4.   **From James M. Barrie's *Peter Pan***

     They suddenly saw the _____ pirates bearing down upon them.
     a. perfidious
     b. translucent
     c. tangible
     d. egocentric

5.   **From Jack London's *The Call of the Wild***

     They were _____ skeletons.
     a. *fortissimo*
     b. *sotto voce*
     c. perambulating
     d. loquacious

Though it is a good thing to have a rich vocabulary, it is not a good thing to abuse that vocabulary by writing verbose, abstruse, sesquipedalian sentences. Those who overuse their vocabularies often do so at the expense of clarity. Translate the following showy, ponderous passage into graceful, direct English. Do not use slang, but do use words that seem familiar and comfortable.

STANDING BEFORE the translucent stained glass window, the loquacious conductor, knowing that *sotto voce* remarks were not his forte, declaimed with acerbity against the cacophony of the orchestra's *fortissimo* passage, impugning the musicians' integrity, accusing them of egocentric perfidy because of their performance of the sacrosanct Fifth Symphony. With ironic sangfroid, the neophyte bassoon player noted that this was a *non sequitur* and that the players had not wished to contravene the omniscient conductor's directions. She also remarked that musicians do not play for tangible rewards, but for the imponderable glories of the musical experience. Unilaterally, the incredulous bassoon player decided to resign and, rising from her stool, began to perambulate through the orchestra on her way to the exit.

Mars was the Roman god of war and the father of Romulus and Remus. He was an important god in the Roman panthenon because war was nearly a constant activity for the Romans during the years of the Republic. In the 465 years between the putative founding of the Republic and the assassination of Julius Caesar, Roman historians said that Rome was at war for 463 of them. Prowess in battle was valued by the Romans, and military skills were part of the education of their boys. Plutarch says of the elder Cato, "when the taste for [Greek] philosophy first sprang up in Rome, Cato was vexed at it and feared that the young men might become more eager to gain distinction by fluent speaking than by warlike exploits." This small figure of Mars was intended for a *lararium*.

### Reading Comprehension

1. Which of the following best expresses the main idea of Translation 33?
   a. A conductor suffered the insolence of a musician.
   b. A musician defended her dignity from an abusive conductor.
   c. An orchestra played Beethoven in lackluster fashion.
   d. Beginners often make serious mistakes.

2. With which statement would the author likely agree?
   a. You are obligated to accept the instructions of your superior.
   b. You must not be disruptive when your team depends on you.
   c. You are an individual, free to participate voluntarily in events or not.
   d. Sometimes discipline requires sacrifice.

### Analogies

3. **CACOPHONOUS : SOTTO VOCE ::**
   a. bad : good
   b. ululation : voice
   c. racket : whisper
   d. pandemonium : wine

4. **PERFIDY : SACROSANCT ::**
   a. break : rule
   b. faith : holy
   c. declaim : *fortissimo*
   d. treachery : sacred

### Antonyms

5. **TANGIBLE :**
   a. translucent
   b. solid
   c. ineffable
   d. incorporeal

6. **TRANSLUCENT :**
   a. black
   b. opaque
   c. dense
   d. intransitive

This is a small statue of an Etruscan warrior, now missing his sword and shield; the Etruscans went into battle equipped much like the Greek hoplite, and they probably fought in phalanx formation.

**synthesis**

We can use **perambulate** in its physical sense, as to perambulate through a park. But we can also use *perambulate* in a metaphorical sense. How many different experiences can you think of that might be metaphorically described by the verb *perambulate*?

**divergence and convergence**

Make a list of acts of **perfidy**, either fictitious or historical. One example from literature is Iago's deliberate destruction of Othello and Desdemona in Shakespeare's *Othello*. After you have made your list, choose the one you personally deplore most, and explain the reasons for your choice.

**evaluation**

Think of something that you have spent time doing and/or learning to do and that you regard as beneficial. Then make a list of two **tangible** benefits and two intangible benefits of this experience. When you are finished, rank the four benefits in order of importance. Is the chief benefit tangible or intangible? What criteria did you use to make your hierarchy of benefits?

**emotion**

After an unusual event happens, you tell your best friend about it, but your friend **impugns** your veracity. You sincerely aver that you are telling the truth, but your friend again impugns your veracity. How does this make you feel?

**aesthetics**

Are there any forms of **cacophony** that routinely detract from the quality of your life? Do they keep you awake, or keep you from studying, or keep you from thinking or talking? What are the sources of these noises?

**imagination and intuition**

In a dream, you suddenly find yourself in a monochrome world, where everything is one color. There you meet a unique being whose **forte** is a talent completely unknown to you previously. What color is the world, what is the being like, and what is his forte? Remember that *forte* is pronounced FORT unless it refers to music.

This small bronze jug is inscribed in Etruscan with the word *suthina*, meaning intended for a tomb. The Etruscans used a modified form of the Greek alphabet and were writing as early as 700 B.C. The Roman alphabet and numerals were derived from Etruscan models.

## Neologist's Lexicon

Use the stems in this list to create a new word (neologism). Give the word, the pronunciation, the part of speech, the etymology, and the definition(s). Keep a record of the neologisms you create from list to list. Here are some examples:

**sacrophonous** (sak RAW fun us) adj. [*sacro* (holy), *phon* (sound) *ous* (full of)]  1. sacred in sound, as the wind in the Grand Canyon  2. high-toned in language, as the speaking tone adopted for religious ceremonies

**egopugnant** (EE go PUG nant) adj. [*ego* (I), *pugn* (fight)]  1. being repulsive to others in one's essential personality  2. being repulsive to others as a result of one's inherent hostility or pugnacity

## Sesquipedalian Fiction

Using at least one word from this week's list in every sentence, write a short play, scene, or story. You may also use words from previous lists if you like. Feel free to be imaginative, silly, or absurd. Do not let your critical or judgmental faculties interfere with your creative ideas.

## Sesquipedalian Caption

Using words from this week's list, make up a phrase or sentence that you can use as the caption of a cartoon or drawing. For example, can you think of funny cartoons to draw for the following captions: Mort declaimed with acerbity against the cacophonous video game. Or: Perambulation, she learned, was not her forte. Write some captions of your own, and draw the cartoons or drawings.

## Sesquipedalian Poetry

Using at least one word from this week's list in almost every line, write a short poem. You may use regular meter, or end rhyme, or other poetic devices, or not! Here is a sample:

### Storm

translucent, blue scent, cloudless sky
    horizon high *sotto voce* intimation
ok, (loudless), here I come, sensation
    distant cacophonous rumbling cumulus
impugning this transitory serenity
    approaching *fortissimo*
lightning its forte like a short *non sequitur*
    perfidiously striking like Hecate our
sacrosanct evening, leaving
    only the tangible tangible:
    wet grass
    and puddles

Roman oil lamp

| | | | | | | |
|---|---|---|---|---|---|---|
| • dict | (say) | *obiter dictum* | • tort | (twist) | retort |
| • sequ | (follow) | obsequious | • nihil | (nothing) | nihilism |
| • bas | (low) | abase | • ism | (doctrine) | nihilism |
| • path | (feeling) | pathetic fallacy | • super | (over) | supersede |
| • muta | (change) | *mutatis mutandis* | • in | (not) | inanimate |
| • inter | (between) | interstices | • anim | (mind) | inanimate |
| • terr | (land) | *terra incognita* | • ob | (against) | obsequious |
| • cogn | (know) | *terra incognita* | • obit | (death) | *obiter dictum* |
| • sed | (sit) | sedate | • epi | (on) | epigram |
| • re | (again) | retort | • gram | (writing) | epigram |
| • tion | (act or state) | ratiocination | • de | (down) | condescend |

**obiter dictum** (passing remark)  I liked the judge's *obiter dictum* on politics.

**obsequious** (servilely following)  He's an obsequious, fawning flatterer; he is a toady.

**abase** (to lower)  You abase yourself when you always agree.

**pathetic fallacy** (ascribing feelings to things)  Example: It is a lonely sea tonight.

**ratiocination** (methodical thinking)  Her acute ratiocinations won the point.

**mutatis mutandis** (with necessary changes)  Type this letter, *mutatis mutandis*.

**interstice** (small space)  Wind blew through the wall's interstices, and the candle flickered.

**terra incognita** (unknown land)  He knew not the *terra incognita* of his own emotions.

**sedate** (calm)  The Count's sedate good manners charmed us all, alas.

**retort** (swift reply)  She was famous for her devastatingly witty retorts.

•     •     •

**nihilism** (belief in nothing)  The new convert forsook his former nihilism.

**supersede** (replace)  This procedure supersedes our former process.

**inanimate** (lifeless)  Inanimate objects tell no tales, but many animate objects have tails.

**condescend** (lower oneself)  His condescending remarks insulted the guest.

**epigram** (witty comment)  She enjoyed his spontaneously brilliant epigram on the topic.

**As Used by Joseph Heller in *Catch-22***

| On | the | landing | below | lived | the | **obsequious** | owners. |
|---|---|---|---|---|---|---|---|

**Parts of Speech:** prep. · adj. · n. · adj. · v. · adj. · **adj.** · n.

**Parts of Sentence:** AVP · · · · subj.

**Phrases:** -----------prep. phrase---------

**Clauses:** -----------------------------------independent clause-----------------------------------
one independent clause; a simple, declarative sentence

Here Joseph Heller uses the adjective *obsequious* to modify the singular common noun *owners*, which is the subject of the sentence, even though it is the last word.

## Pronunciation

| | | | |
|---|---|---|---|
| *obiter dictum* | OH bih ter DICT um | **sedate** | suh DATE |
| **obsequious** | ob SEE kwee us | **retort** | re TORT |
| **abase** | ah BASE | **nihilism** | NIE ill izm |
| **pathetic fallacy** | pah THET ik FAL a see | **supersede** | super SEED |
| **ratiocination** | rah shee ah sin AY shun | **inanimate** | in AN ih mutt |
| *mutatis mutandis* | myoo TAH tiss myoo TAND iss | **condescend** | KON dee SEND |
| **interstice** | in TURR stiss | **epigram** | EPP ih gram |
| *terra incognita* | TERR ah in kog NEE tah | | |

## Spanish Cognates

| | | | |
|---|---|---|---|
| **obsequious** | obsequioso | **interstice** | intersticio |
| **condescension** | condescendencia | **nihilism** | nihilismo |
| **epigram** | epigrama | **inanimate** | inanimado |
| **retort** | retorta | **ratiocination** | raciocinación |

Roman key

1. The verb **supersede** is a rarity; it is the only word I know of that ends in -**sede**. That is because it is not a combination of *super* (over) and *cede* (go), but of *super* and *sed* (sit). That which supersedes something else replaces it, and the image is of the new sitting above the old.

2. An **obsequious** person is a servile, fawning flatterer, such as Lex Luthor's toady in the Superman films. Yes sir, no sir, whatever you say sir. The obsequious toady follows (*sequ*) his master wherever the master leads.

3. In the age of satellites, it is less common than it once was to speak literally of a ***terra incognita***, an unknown land. Today, we more commonly use the term metaphorically, as to describe someone who does not know himself. Of course, the planets stand as a new *terra incognita* for humanity, and the next few centuries should be great and exciting ages of discovery.

4. A **Micropoem**: A **retort** is a reply so swift and effective that it can be thought of as a twisting (*tort*) back again (*re*) of the other person's remark. In a retort, you do not even give the poor opponent's remark time to land before you twist it back on him. Whack. Some of the loveliest retorts in English literature appear in the sonnet that Shakespeare writes to describe the meeting between Romeo and Juliet; clearly, part of the reason they fall in love is the matching of their minds in this brilliant volley of retorts. It must have been apparent to each of them that they had met someone unusual, capable of wit and quick thinking.

5. The verbs **condescend** and **abase** both suggest a lowering of the self, but the words are different in meaning. To condescend to someone is an insult to that person, suggesting that you regard yourself as above him or her but that you are lowering yourself to speak to someone in a low status, as though it were *infra dig* (beneath one's dignity) even to speak to someone so below you. To abase yourself is to degrade or humble yourself, leaving yourself in a lower status.

6. The **pathetic fallacy** does not acquire its name from the idea of something being pathetic—filled with **pathos**. Instead, the word refers to feelings (*path*) attributed to things that do not have feelings. And since things cannot both have and not have feelings, this is a logical contradiction. As human beings, we are full of feelings, and we often project our feelings onto the world. We see a mournful sea, a hopeful dawn, or a wrathful storm. In Shakespeare's *Julius Caesar*, Calpurnia implores Caesar not to go to the Senate because it has been a tempestuous night, filled with inexplicable wonders, and she is afraid of these omens. "When beggars die," Calpurnia tells Caesar, "there are no comets seen." To the Romans, such omens and warnings seemed a natural part of the interrelationship between human beings and the cosmos, but to us, they just seem to be examples of the pathetic fallacy. Of course, when we read a play, we do not think that way; instead, we practice what Coleridge called the "suspension of disbelief," imagining that everything we read is true.

Roman key

# A ROMAN HERO: MARCUS FURIUS CAMILLUS
## Dr. Thomas Milton Kemnitz

Marcus Furius Camillus was known in his day (c. 456–365 B.C.) as the Second Founder of Rome. It was he who devised the plan that led to the conquest of Veii and who led the revival of Rome after it was taken by the Gauls. He was a patrician of the Furii clan, who originally were from Tusculum generations before Camillus was born. His lifetime was marked not only by constant wars but also by extreme tension between the patricians of the Senate and the leading plebeians. The latter were demanding that one of the consuls come from their ranks rather than, as had always been the case, both from the patricians. The plebs were unhappy that men were being drafted into the service and that a war tax was imposed on the people. The patricians refused to agree, so for many years when Camillus was active, no consuls were elected; he was one of the elected tribunes numerous times.

Camillus became tribune for the second time two months before normal because two tribunes were forced to resign for losing a battle at Veii. The two were bitter personal enemies, and when the forces of one were attacked, he refused to ask his personal enemy for reinforcements, and the second refused to send troops unless the first asked for help. As a result, many Romans died, and the siege of Veii was temporarily lifted. The historian Livy tells us that when Camillus became tribune on this occasion, Rome was fighting four wars—at Veii, at Capena, at Falerii, and against the Volscians. During that year, the Romans won battles in all four wars, but it would be years before Camillus took Veii.

Two years later Camillus was the Roman commander fighting at Falerii. He won a battle against the Falerii army outside their city walls and then besieged the city. It appeared that the action would last a long time because the Faliscans were well-provisioned with food and had adequate water. However, the Faliscan schoolmaster took his charges—the sons of the leading men of Falerii—into the Roman camp and delivered the children to Camillus. Instead of seeing this as an opportunity to force Falerii to surrender, Camillus was outraged at the actions of the pedagogue. He ordered the master stripped of his clothes, had his hands bound, and gave the students rods to beat him with as they went back to the care of their parents. The Faliscans were so taken by this honorable gesture that they decided that it would be better to live in peace by the laws of the Romans than to continue under their own laws. They surrendered the city, and the Senate of Rome accepted the alliance, asking the Faliscans only to pay the Roman troops their year's wages. In a very few years, the Romans had considerably extended their territory, mainly through the leadership of Camillus.

The plebeians were not entirely happy with Camillus, though, because they got no chance to loot Falerii. Moreover, he later alienated many by opposing a plebeian plan to settle the land and city of Veii as a plebeian city. Eventually a plebeian tribune impeached Camillus for his handling of the spoils of Veii, and feeling was so high that it was clear Camillus would be convicted. According to Livy, when Camillus knew that he was about to take Veii, he sent a message to the Senate to say that the spoils would be far greater than any Rome had ever seen before and to ask the Senate how they should be handled; there was nothing dishonorable about how Camillus had behaved. Unwilling to accept an unjust verdict, Camillus left Rome, offering—according to Livy and Plutarch—a prayer to the gods that if he was suffering wrongly as an innocent man, the gods would make his ungrateful fellow Romans very soon feel the need for him. He was fined in his absence 15,000 ases—the coinage of Rome.

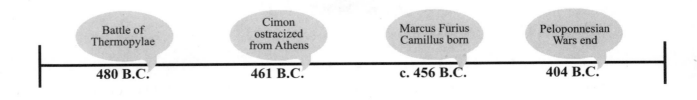

| Battle of Thermopylae | Cimon ostracized from Athens | Marcus Furius Camillus born | Peloponnesian Wars end |
|---|---|---|---|
| 480 B.C. | 461 B.C. | c. 456 B.C. | 404 B.C. |

# CAMILLUS, COMINIUS, AND MARCUS MANLIUS
## Dr. Thomas Milton Kemnitz

When the Gauls took Rome, Camillus's prayer was answered—his fellow countrymen needed him. He was an exile in the neighboring town of Ardea when Gallic foraging parties arrived to steal crops and plunder whatever they could. Camillus rallied the townspeople of Ardea and attacked the Gauls as they slept in drunken stupor; most were killed before they had time to defend themselves. The Roman stragglers camped at Veii inflicted a similar defeat upon the Etruscans who were pillaging Roman territory, and then yet another on a group from Tuscan. These Romans wanted Camillus to become their leader, but he would not take command without the authority of the Senate. At that time the remaining senators were barricaded in a defensible position on Capitoline Hill. A soldier named Pontius Cominius volunteered to make his way through the besieging army of Gauls and up the cliff face to the Tarpeian rock to get the agreement of the Senate to make Camillus commander. Cominius made it up; Camillus was appointed dictator, and Cominius made it down and back to Veii, whereupon Camillus was summoned from Ardea to Veii to take command of the Roman troops. In Cominius the Romans had a messenger hero to match the exploits of the Athenian Pheidippides, who before the battle of Marathon ran from Athens to Sparta and back.

The other unlikely heroes of this episode were the geese sacred to Juno. The starving Romans had not eaten the geese, for that might invite the wrath of the gods, so the geese were there to play their part in the story. The Gauls discovered the path Cominius had taken up and down the cliff face, and one moonless night they sent men up to take the Roman position. The invaders eluded the sentries and the dogs, but the geese were aroused and awakened the Romans. The Roman who responded in the most notable fashion was Marcus Manlius, who knocked the first invader over the edge of the cliff with a thrust of his shield and led in sending others falling to their deaths. Eventually the Romans threw down enough stones to force all of the invaders off the cliff, many of them fatally. The next morning the Romans threw their sentry on duty that night to his death down the very same cliff. Manlius was declared the hero of the hour, and each Roman gave him a portion of meager rations.

In Roman legend, Camillus played a decisive role in lifting the siege of Capitoline Hill and freeing Rome from the yoke of Gallic control. He is said to have defeated the Gauls in a pitched battle outside of the city and then gone on to defeat all of Rome's enemies in turn in the years after, to have never lost a battle, to have been pressed into service leading armies even as a very old man, and to have arranged for the people of Tusculum to seek Roman citizenship.

In his capacity as a leading patrician in the increasingly bitter battles between the plebeians and the patricians, Camillus prevented the plebeians from populating Veii. He also authored a great compromise that acceded to the plebeian demands that one of consuls each year should come from their ranks, rather than both coming from the patricians, as had been the case since the founding of the Republic.

Manlius was very jealous of Camillus's standing and thought that his leading role on Capitoline Hill should have accorded him the primary place in the Senate. He became bitter at his Senate colleagues, and although a patrician, he joined the plebs in advocating their position. He accused members of the Senate of stealing and hiding the Republic's gold from the people of Rome. Finally, he was ordered to show where the gold was hidden, and when he could not, he was tried and convicted of treason. In an irony that would not have been missed by Manlius, he was put to death by the Romans by being thrown from the Tarpeian rock—over the very same cliff where his outstanding act of heroism had taken place a few short years earlier.

| Rome conquers Veii | Rome sacked by Gauls | Marcus Furius Camillus dies | Alexander the Great born |
|---|---|---|---|
| 396 B.C. | 387 B.C. | 365 B.C. | 356 B.C. |

In each case below, one of the choices was really the word used by the author in the sentence provided. All of the choices can be found in the example words on the first page of this lesson. Your challenge is to decide which word the author used. This is not a test; it is more like a game because more than one word choice may work perfectly well. See if you can use your sensitivity and intuition to guess correctly which word the author used.

1. **From Thornton Wilder's *The Bridge of San Luis Rey***

   The frightened mother became meek and _____.
   a. sedate
   b. inanimate
   c. obsequious
   d. nihilistic

2. **From H.G. Wells's *The Invisible Man***

   I went and peered out through their _____.
   a. interstices
   b. ratiocinations
   c. epigrams
   d. *terra incognita*

3. **From Herman Melville's *Moby Dick***

   The plebeian herds crouch _____ before the tremendous centralization.
   a. obsequious
   b. inanimate
   c. abased
   d. superseded

4. **From Herman Melville's *Moby Dick***

   We know the sea to be an everlasting _____.
   a. *obiter dictum*
   b. *mutatis mutandis*
   c. pathetic fallacy
   d. *terra incognita*

5. **From Thomas Hardy's *The Mayor of Casterbridge***

   The usually _____ Farfrae was in the midst of the other dancers.
   a. inanimate
   b. sedate
   c. abased
   d. condescending

Though it is a good thing to have a rich vocabulary, it is not a good thing to abuse that vocabulary by writing verbose, abstruse, sesquipedalian sentences. Those who overuse their vocabularies often do so at the expense of clarity. Translate the following showy, ponderous passage into graceful, direct English. Do not use slang, but do use words that seem familiar and comfortable.

THE SEDATE, condescending villain glared at his loquacious, obsequious toady, who began to wish he could hide in one of the interstices in the wall. "My ratiocinations inform me," the nihilistic villain began, "that I must supersede my recent *obiter dictum* on your merits with a new epigram." The nonplussed toady could not retort. "Your inanimate brain," the villain averred, "is only one sign of your abased condition. The other is your continual use of the pathetic fallacy. Such logic I cannot abide. If your own intelligence is such *terra incognita* to you, then I will have to send notice of your dismissal, *mutatis mutandis*, to my scribe." The toady was heard to reply, *sotto voce*, that the villain would never declaim so to him again.

In the Imperial period, the Romans removed the Tarpeian rock and built over the cliff face.

## Reading Comprehension

1.  It can be inferred from Translation 34 that:
    a. Condescension is effective in controlling people.
    b. Speaking harshly to others is sometimes necessary.
    c. Being illogical is a good way to get into trouble.
    d. Loyalty must be earned.

2.  Translation 34 could best be described as:
    a. Two villains are forming a plot.
    b. An evil boss excoriates his employee.
    c. A toady is criticized for not doing what he was told.
    d. A rebellion is plotted against an unjust command.

## Analogies

*lower oneself   severly fdlowing*

3.  **CONDESCEND : OBSEQUIOUS ::**
    a. stoop : grovel
    b. land : ascend
    c. beg : command
    d. contact : obstruct

*witty coment   swift reply*

4.  **EPIGRAM : RETORT ::**
    a. letter : reply
    b. telegram : answer
    c. epithet : remove
    d. remark : rejoinder

## Antonyms

5.  **NIHILISM :**
    a. credulity
    b. obedience
    c. ratiocination
    d. disbelief

6.  **ABASE :**
    a. condescend
    b. elevate
    c. debase
    d. retort

The geese earned an enduring place in Roman iconography.

**synthesis**

List at least three characters from different novels who have in common the fact that they are either **condescending** or **obsequious**.

**application**

What might be a real-life situation in which the phrase *mutatis mutandis* would be appropriate? Obviously, the term is erudite enough that in many situations it would not be appropriate, so what do you imagine its appropriate use would be?

**imagination and intuition**

In a chapter of a science fiction novel, the protagonist, a Galactic Survey surgeon, is slipping silently and carefully through the purple mist of a planet with low gravity. Suddenly, she stumbles over an **inanimate** object that proves to be a discovery that revolutionizes human life on the planet. Describe the object, and explain its value.

**emotion**

What emotions do you associate with the word **sedate**? It might help to think of events that would leave you feeling calm and sedate. If you were writing screenplays, what would be the likely emotions associated with characters who could be described as sedate?

**aesthetics**

Pretend that you are going to make a film about a **nihilistic** villain, such as one of the exaggerated villains in the Superman or Batman cartoons. What symbolic colors, objects, and sounds will you include in your film to enhance the audience's abhorrence of the nihilism that the character possesses? Thinking about these artistic decisions will give you some insight into the careful planning that film directors and artistic crews go through. Sometimes directors spend millions of dollars solely on design elements, getting every color, shadow, and item of furniture right. In fact, in addition to writing a script, before filming they draw storyboards in which the angles and details of every shot are determined and graphically depicted in advance; in other words, they draw the movie before they film it! That's planning.

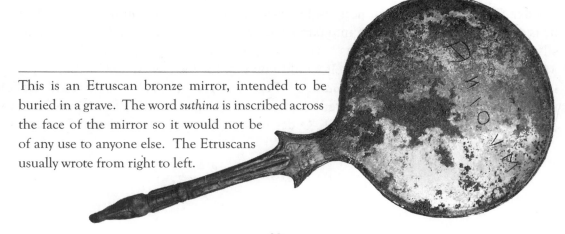

This is an Etruscan bronze mirror, intended to be buried in a grave. The word *suthina* is inscribed across the face of the mirror so it would not be of any use to anyone else. The Etruscans usually wrote from right to left.

## Neologist's Lexicon

Use the stems in this list to create a new word (neologism). Give the word, the pronunciation, the part of speech, the etymology, and the definition(s). Keep a record of the neologisms you create from list to list. Here are some examples:

**resequious** (ree SEEK we ous) adj. [*re* (again), *sequ* (follow), *ous* (full of)]  1. following someone around, even after being asked not to  2. following someone as he or she performs a duty that requires him or her to move back and forth

**epitort** (EH pih tort) n. [*epi* (on), *tort* (twist)]  1. a mechanical object that twists on, such as a soda bottle cap  2. an idea that is difficult for a person to accept, requiring great effort for those who would persuade

## Sesquipedalian Advertising

Using the words from this week's list, write a short advertisement. Feel free to make it silly or satirical. You might like to write a spoof on an ad you have heard. A sample:

### Alumiwipes, the Metal Towel of Tomorrow, Today!

Friends! Why abase yourself any longer by using old-fashioned paper towels? Now you too can have new, improved ALUMIWIPES, the aluminum towel that lasts forever! Are you tired of paper towel salesmen condescending to you? Are you tired of having the pathetic fallacy used on you as a sales ploy? Have you had enough of obsequious phone calls from towel representatives? Has your cleaning closet become a *terra incognita* of antiquated supplies and materials? Have you lost your sedate equanimity from the acerbic retorts of nihilistic towel salesmen? Do you anguish over the trees that lose their lives in the paper towel manufacturing process? Well, your happy day is here! Alumiwipes are made of inanimate metal! Alumiwipes have micro-interstices built in to catch all of the water, grime, and toxic substances, leaving your household surfaces CLEANER THAN THE DAY THEY WERE NEW! No need for ratiocination; buy Alumiwipes today. Buy one: that's all you'll ever need! How much would you pay for such an exciting home improvement product?

But wait! If you buy your Alumiwipe today, you also get *Mutatis Mutandis*, the pestogen that turns all of your household pests into benevolent creatures! Tired of having fleas in your carpet? Turn them into parakeets with *Mutatis Mutandis*! Tired of ants and silverfish in your kitchen cabinets? Turn them into plants and goldfish! It is easy, with *Mutatis Mutandis*! Now, how much would you pay for the AMAZING benefits you get from Alumiwipes and *Mutatis Mutandis*? Five hundred dollars? A thousand? Believe it or not, you get both of these incredible products for only NINETEEN NINETY-FIVE! That's NINETEEN NINETY-FIVE! Order today. Use your Command Card or VITA credit card number!

- *centri* (center) anthropocentric
- *gastro* (stomach) gastronome
- *auto* (self) autodidact
- *mono* (one) monism
- *ism* (doctrine) monism
- medi (middle) *in medias res*
- *anthropo* (man) lycanthrope
- *lykos* (wolf) lycanthrope
- ambi (both) circumambient
- fy (make) reify

- trans (across) transmogrify
- contra (against) *au contraire*
- viv (life) vivacious
- *helio* (sun) heliotropic
- *tropo* (turn) heliotropic
- ex (out) exculpate
- culp (blame) exculpate
- intro (into) introspective
- spec (look) introspective
- circum (around) circumvent

**anthropocentric** (man-centered) We believed in an anthropocentric cosmos.

**gastronome** (a gourmet or epicure) Try the gastronome's recipe for squid *a la mode*.

**autodidact** (self-taught person) His writing contains the tell-tale errors of the autodidact.

**monism** (doctrine that reality is one) Einstein's space-time is a scientific monism.

*in medias res* (in the middle of things) *The Odyssey,* by Homer, begins *in medias res*.

**lycanthrope** (werewolf) Jove's anger turned Lycaon into a howling lycanthrope.

**circumambient** (surrounding) Enjoy the circumambient breezes that waft over the deck.

**transmogrify** (change form) The hecklers were transmogrified into obsequious admirers.

**reify** (treat as real) To believe in the dark force is to reify the concept of evil.

*au contraire* (to the contrary) "*Au contraire!*" he exclaimed in protest.

•   •   •

**vivacious** (lively) His vivacious conversation entertained the group long into the night.

**circumvent** (get around) To circumvent this surgical procedure is dangerous.

**heliotropic** (sun-following) The sun-seeking tourists reminded him of heliotropic plants.

**exculpate** (free from blame) Fortunately, the jury exculpated the innocent girl.

**introspective** (inward looking) His introspective thoughts were too personal to share.

Roman keys

## As Used by L.M. Montgomery in *Anne of Green Gables*

| | The | big | eyes | were | full | of | spirit | and | **vivacity.** |
|---|---|---|---|---|---|---|---|---|---|
| **Parts of Speech:** | adj. | adj. | n. | v. | adj. | prep. | n. | conj. | **n.** |
| **Parts of Sentence:** | | | subj. | LVP | S.C. | | | | |
| **Phrases:** | | | | | | --------prepositional phrase-------- | | | |
| **Clauses:** | ----------------------------------independent clause------------------------------------ | | | | | | | | |
| | one independent clause; a simple, declarative sentence | | | | | | | | |

Here L.M. Montgomery uses the noun *vivacity* as one side of a compound object of preposition. This word appears in its adjective form, *vivacious*, on our list.

## Pronunciation

| | | | |
|---|---|---|---|
| **anthropocentric** | an thro po SENT rik | **reify** | REE if fy |
| **gastronome** | GAS tro nome | *au contraire* | OH kon TRAIR |
| **autodidact** | auto DIE dakt | **vivacious** | vie VAY shus |
| **monism** | MOAN ism | **circumvent** | sir come VENT |
| *in medias res* | in MAY dee as RACE | **heliotropic** | hee lee oh TRO pik |
| **lycanthrope** | LIE can thrope | **exculpate** | EX kul pate |
| **circumambient** | SIR come AM bee ent | **introspective** | intro SPEK tiv |
| **transmogrify** | trans MOG ri fie | | |

## Spanish Cognates

| | | | |
|---|---|---|---|
| **vivacious** | vivaz | **introspective** | instrospectivo |
| **heliotrope** | heliotropo | **monist** | monista |
| **exculpation** | exculpación | **anthropocentric** | antropocéntrico |
| **gastronome** | gastrónomo | | |

1. A **monism** is a metaphysical doctrine that holds that ultimate reality is one thing; an example is Einstein's space-time—the concept that all of reality is a single continuum of four-dimensional space-time, that nothing is really separate from or different in substance from anything else, and that the entire cosmos is actually a single, huge geometrical structure of four-dimensional space-time. This monism might be contrasted with a **dualism**, such as Descartes's idea that the universe contains both matter and mind and that the two are different. Descartes's dualism has been called the *mind/body dichotomy*. If you believe that everything in the universe is actually an idea in the mind of God, that is a monism.

2. Homer begins *The Odyssey* **in medias res**: Odysseus has left Troy after the events described in *The Iliad* and has not yet reached home.

3. A **Micropoem**: The adjective **heliotropic** is a botanical term, usually applied to plants that turn (*tropo*) to follow the sun (*helio*) on its daily path across the sky. We might occasionally use the word metaphorically and humorously to describe vacationing tourists flocking to the beaches, but the primary use of this word is scientific.

4. The adjective **anthropocentric** means centered (*centri*) around man (*anthropo*). We could say that human beings have believed in an anthropocentric cosmos, meaning that we often have the theological idea that we are special to the purpose of the universe, not just insignificant dots on a shrimpy planet around a commonplace star. We can also apply the word *anthropocentric* to the unfortunate man-centered ideas with which we rationalize our destruction of other species, such as the wholesale extinctions of species in the Amazon. We might also note that Western art seems more anthropocentric than Oriental art. Compare, for instance, the *Mona Lisa* to a Chinese landscape: the *Mona Lisa* shows us a big person and a little world, but the Chinese landscape shows us a balanced environment in which everything is in scale and harmony, each part contributing to the whole.

5. A **Classic Word**: Authors from Daniel Defoe in 1719 to George Orwell in 1945 have found **vivacious** [filled with (*ous*) life (*viv*)] to be a good word for describing a bright, animated, and lively character. We see this word in *Robinson Crusoe, Gulliver's Travels, Wuthering Heights, Jane Eyre, The Scarlet Letter, Uncle Tom's Cabin, Moby Dick, Walden, A Tale of Two Cities, Tom Sawyer, The Return of the Native, The Mayor of Casterbridge, The Red Badge of Courage,* and *Animal Farm*. In these books we find vivacity and sparkling sharpness in the eye, an exuberance of vivacity, the vivacity excited by rapid motion, an uncommon vivacity of intelligence, sham vivacity, and vivacity rebuked. Characters vivaciously cry, vivaciously wake, and vivaciously accost people. We see vivacious suffering, vivacious features, ordinary vivacious chat, vivacious fish and other vivacious denizens of the waters (Melville, of course), vivacious lilacs, vivacious voices, vivacious fun, and a vivacious Bacchanalian flame (Dickens). Orwell's Snowball "was a more vivacious pig than Napoleon." Melville's Flask is truly vivacious, tumultuous, and ostentatious. One of the most profound uses of *vivacious* is from Harriet Beecher Stowe: "when the bodily eyes are thus out of the lists, the spiritual eyes are uncommonly vivacious and perspicuous."

TUSCANIA .

. RIETI

APPENNINES

VATICAN
CITY
VEII . . FALERII
CAERE . . TIVOLI
CAPENA . . PALESTRINA
ROME
. TUSCULUM
LATIUM
LAVINIUM . FROSINONE . . ATINA
. APRILIA
ARDEA .
MARE . LATINA
TIRRENO CAMPANIA
GAETA .
NAPLES
HERCULANEUM .
. POMPEII

# ROME CONQUERS CENTRAL ITALY
## Dr. Thomas Milton Kemnitz

Early legends of Rome include tangled relations with the Sabines; those who lived south of the Tiber moved to Rome to become part of the growing city, and several of the early kings of Rome were Sabines. The remaining Sabines lived in the Appennine mountains to the north and east of Rome. They were small farmers—sturdy, thrifty, and industrious—much as the Romans were. In the seventh and sixth centuries B.C., the Romans and the Sabines fought each other on occasion. Immediately after the founding of the Republic in 509, the Sabines challenged the Romans and were decisively defeated, as they were again in 449. The Romans settled some of their people on Sabine land and subsumed the Sabines into the Roman Republic. Later Roman writers would speak of the Roman and Sabine customs as though they were the same. Many family names in Rome included the appellation *Sabinus*, indicating that the family was of Sabine origins.

In the 490s, the Romans fought a large battle with a league of Latium towns that may have been testing the limits of Roman power. The Romans won a notable victory and made peace on a basis of rough equality with the entire league of Latium towns. In the early years of the fifth century, the Latium towns and Rome shared a common threat in invaders from the Appennines. Besides the Sabines, the Volscians and Aequians invaded from highly defensible strongholds in the mountains, and the Latium towns needed Roman help, just as the Romans need Latium allies to deal with Veii, as well as the Sabines. In the last half of the century, the Romans could be more aggressive toward the Latium towns because the threat from the Sabines had diminished, and it was then that Rome was strong enough to make treaties that bound the other Latium cities individually to it. The alteration of status became clear when Rome conquered Veii and assumed control of all of the surrounding land without allocating areas to its Latium allies.

After Rome suffered its devastating defeat at the hands of the Gallic invaders, the Latin towns once again tried to assert themselves, but the Romans were quick to find solutions when the citizens of Tusculum became restive. Tusculum was a Latin city now entirely circled by Roman-held territory. Instead of beating the citizens into submission, the Romans in 381 B.C. offered them full citizenship as Romans together with continued control over their own local affairs. Roman citizenship gave the people of Tusculum rights equal to a Roman in Roman territory and hence was potentially very valuable to merchants and others, but their ability to participate in affairs in Rome was limited by distance and access, so they had no say in who was elected consul or tribune. From the Roman perspective, they had given away little and gained much.

By the 350s, the Romans had established themselves as the senior partner to the largest and most wealthy Latium towns. Then in 343, Rome received an appeal for help from towns in Campania, south of the Latium cities; the threat in this case came from the powerful Samnites, who occupied much of the eastern and southern Italian peninsula. Campania was rich agricultural land, which appealed to the Romans, who were still largely an agrarian society, and their positive response disconcerted the Latins, who now feared that the Romans might absorb them. The Campanians had second thoughts about dealing with the Romans. The Latium towns armed themselves to fight the Romans. At the battle of Trifanum in 340, the Romans decisively defeated the Campanians and thereafter took some of their rich northern farmlands for themselves; then they turned their attention to the Latins. By 338, the Romans had defeated the Latium towns. Thus in half a decade, Rome had asserted itself as the major power in central Italy; not half a century earlier, Rome had been sacked by the Gauls.

| Rome sacked by Gauls | Marcus Furius Camillus dies | Battle of Trifanum | Rome defeats Latium towns | Alexander invades Asia |
|---|---|---|---|---|
| 387 B.C. | 365 B.C. | 340 B.C. | 338 B.C. | 332 B.C. |

In each case below, one of the choices was really the word used by the author in the sentence provided. All of the choices can be found in the example words on the first page of this lesson. Your challenge is to decide which word the author used. This is not a test; it is more like a game because more than one word choice may work perfectly well. See if you can use your sensitivity and intuition to guess correctly which word the author used.

1.    **From Herman Melville's *Billy Budd***

The _____ air in the clearness of its serenity was like smooth white marble.
a. heliotropic
b. anthropocentric
c. circumambient
d. vivacious

2.    **From John Gardner's *Grendel***

The civilization he meant to build has _____ to a forest thick with traps.
a. reified
b. exculpated
c. circumvented
d. transmogrified

3.    **From John Gardner's *Grendel***

Importance is primarily _____ in its reference to the universe.
a. anthropocentric
b. *in medias res*
c. monistic
d. introspective

4.    **From Walter Scott's *Ivanhoe***

Gurth, knowing his master's irritable temper, attempted no _____ .
a. exculpation
b. introspection
c. circumvention
d. transmogrification

5.    **From Thornton Wilder's *The Bridge of San Luis Rey***

Her daughter scolded her for a(n) _____ and for making a cult of sorrow.
a. introspective
b. lycanthrope
c. monist
d. gastronome

Though it is a good thing to have a rich vocabulary, it is not a good thing to abuse that vocabulary by writing verbose, abstruse, sesquipedalian sentences. Those who overuse their vocabularies often do so at the expense of clarity. Translate the following showy, ponderous passage into graceful, direct English. Do not use slang, but do use words that seem familiar and comfortable.

AMIDST THE HELIOTROPIC VINES, the vivacious lycanthrope (a neophyte of the species and an autodidact in metamorphosis) was caught *in medias res* as she transmogrified cacophonously. An introspective, perambulating gastronome happened to look through the window—open to the circumambient breeze—but his anthropocentric world view (unlike Einstein's abstract monism) interfered with his ratiocinations and prevented him from realizing what he was seeing. We may exculpate the gastronome, however, for he did not circumvent the expected courtesies; *au contraire*: "Good day," he averred. The *sotto voce* growl of her retort left him incredulous.

*[handwritten annotations: sun-following, lively, werewolf, new, self-taught, change, in the middle of things, changed form, loudly, inward looking, wandering, surrounding, man-centered, doctrine, methodical thinking, free from blame, epicure, got around, on the contrary, stated, low, really, not believing]*

The relationship between Rome and the Latium towns was not simply a matter of war and conquest, but more a matter of trade and mutual advantage. Palestrina was a center of bronze working, specializing in the production of mirrors. This mirror is decorated with a scene from Homer's *Iliad* and shows Ajax arming, helped by Thetis while Alcumena plays a lyre. With the trade in Latium goods came a heavy dose of Greek culture and art, which became the dominant cultural influence on Rome.

## Reading Comprehension

1. In Translation 35, the author does all of the following EXCEPT:
   a. explain how the lycanthrope met the gastronome
   b. explain what the lycanthrope was doing when they met
   c. explain how the gastronome felt about the lycanthrope's response
   d. explain how the lycanthrope felt during transmogrification

2. It can be inferred from the passage that:
   a. Anthropocentrism can interfere with clear thinking.
   b. All lycanthropes are vivacious.
   c. Gastronomes are rarely courteous.
   d. Introspective people do more perambulating.

## Analogies

3. **TRANSMOGRIFY : LYCANTHROPE ::**
   *change form      werewolf*
   a. alter : modify
   b. evolve : chrysalis
   c. metamorphose : insect
   d. transpose : music

4. **CIRCUMVENT : CIRCUMAMBIENT ::**
   *get around      surrounding*
   a. evade : surrounding
   b. circumference : circumnavigate
   c. anthropocentrism : *mise-en-scène*
   d. introspection : autodidact

## Antonyms

5. **EXCULPATE :**
   *free from blame*
   a. accuse
   b. convict
   c. impeach
   d. imprison

6. **INTROSPECTIVE :**
   *inward looking*
   a. extroverted
   b. thoughtful
   c. meditative
   d. provident

The early Roman coins were bronze and were deliberately heavy. The largest coins here are the ases or aeses.

**synthesis**

Use any five words from List 35 in a single sentence.

**divergence and convergence**

People often **circumvent** rules, regulations, and traditions that they do not wish to observe or perhaps do not believe in. For example, people who organized the underground railroad in the early nineteenth century bravely circumvented the slavery laws, and did so at considerable personal risk. But we often see people circumvent rules solely for personal convenience or gain, as in the case of people who fail to declare portions of their income at tax time. First (divergent question), how many things can you think of that people do or could circumvent? List as many as you can. Second (convergent question), what is one example of a situation in which you would never circumvent the rules? Explain.

**intuition and imagination**

In a dream you find yourself a research botanist on a distant and little-explored planet. You can breathe the air. The planet is densely covered with **heliotropic** plants and vines. Unlike earth, this planet rotates once a minute, and all of the tall heliotropic vegetation around you leans far east every sixty seconds for the new sunrise, rises straight up as the sun reaches its zenith in fifteen seconds, and leans far west as the sun sets thirty seconds after it rose, only to rise again thirty seconds later. Tell us more about life on this planet. Aesthetic challenge: describe the most beautiful scene on the planet.

**emotion**

You are talking to your friend, who suddenly breaks into a hideous laugh, her face **transmogrified** into a frightful, twisted, glaring grin. She will not explain and will not stop laughing. How does this make you feel, as you stare into her transmogrified face?

**analysis**

Using a dictionary, carefully explain the differences between the etymology (origin), the grammar, and the best usage of the words **transmogrify** and **metamorphosis**.

When Rome began to issue coins, their value was determined by their weight rather than an amount stamped on them. That necessitated equipment like this to weigh the coins in every transaction.

## Neologist's Lexicon

Use the stems in this list to create a new word (neologism). Give the word, the pronunciation, the part of speech, the etymology, and the definition(s). Keep a record of the neologisms you create from list to list. Here are some examples:

**exism** (EX ism) n. [*ex* (out), *ism* (doctrine)] 1. the pathological addiction to the phrase "I'm outa here." 2. chronic and habitual staring at the doors and windows during conversation

**lykospection** (LIE ko speck shun) n. [*lykos* (wolf), *spect* (look), *tion* (act)] 1. girl-watching, especially at a beach or other holiday area 2. adopting the appearance and mannerisms of a ladies' man

## Sesquipedalian Poetry

Use the words from this week's list to write a poem. This time, try to intensify your poem with sound, even at the expense of meaning. In fact, you might enjoy writing a pure sound poem that has no intelligible meaning at all. If you do not worry about meaning, you can have fun with the euphony and cacophony of the sounds of the vowels and consonants. You can even do creative, experimental things with punctuation! For example:

### Autodidact

O, monism, moan, is he? No
gastronome; spent tricks and intricate
anthropocentrics, yes sir.  Come
circumambient am being into
vivacious . . . shucks lace life lazy fly
reify wholly transmogrify
*au contraire*! Circumvent.  Specks exculpate
rarely *in medias res*, and so
race to your auto you autodidact!
Did you act it out totally, Lycanthrope?
Hohoho, hopelessly circumvent helioptropes, sir.
Autodidact, invent
Yourself yourself yourself yrslf;:,.
NOW.

Roman key

sacrosanct     egocentric

perfidy     non sequitur     inanimate

loquacious     obsequious

perambulate     translucent     nihilism     tangible

malapropism     omnibus     epigram

interdiction     unilateral     exculpate

omniscient     incredulous     postlude

neophyte     benediction     retort     impugn

monolithic     imponderable     autodidact

heterodox     supersede     gregarious

altercation     soliloquy     cacophony

sangfroid     contravene     circumlocution

confluence     paterfamilias     heliotropic

pathetic     interstices     transmogrify

anthropocentric


Focus on the central concept of our learning:
the stems are our prize content.
The stems provide us with a vocabulary construction set.
The words are just examples and variations
to show us how the stem system works.
By knowing the stems, we can learn
the words in this book and thousands more.

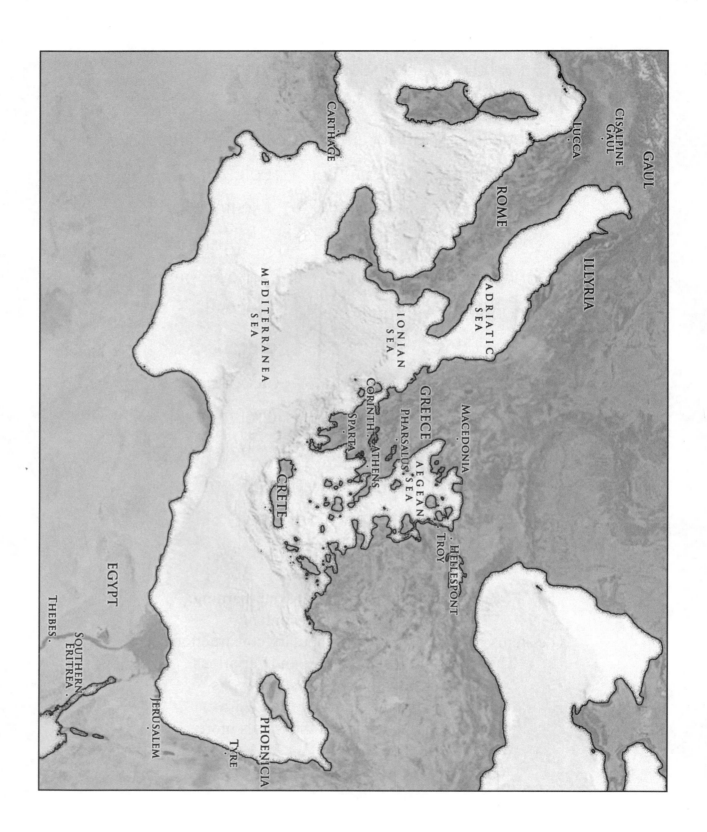

CARTHAGE

CISALPINE GAUL

LUCCA

GAUL

ROME

ILLYRIA

ADRIATIC SEA

MEDITERRANEA SEA

IONIAN SEA

GREECE

MACEDONIA

CORINTH
SPARTA
ATHENS
PHARSALUS
AEGEAN SEA

CRETE

TROY

HELLESPONT

EGYPT

THEBES

SOUTHERN ERITREA

JERUSALEM

TYRE

PHOENICIA

| | | | | | | |
|---|---|---|---|---|---|---|
| • pre | (before) | *a priori* | • ped | (foot) | sesquipedalian |
| • post | (after) | *a posteriori* | • sesqui | (one and a half) | sesquipedalian |
| • gen | (origin) | parthenogenesis | • sui | (self) | *sui generis* |
| • *partheno* | (virgin) | parthenogenesis | • cracy | (government) | plutocracy |
| • son | (sound) | assonance | • *pluto* | (wealth) | plutocracy |
| • ob | (against) | objurgation | • lin | (line) | delineate |
| • jur | (swear) | objurgation | • tomy | (cut) | dichotomy |
| • *demo* | (people) | demotic | • dicho | (in two parts) | dichotomy |
| • sopor | (sleep) | soporific | • phan | (appearance) | epiphany |
| • inter | (between) | internecine | • tort | (twist) | tortuous |
| • nec | (kill) | internecine | | | |

*a priori* (from theory) The theory was developed through deduction from principle, *a priori.*

*a posteriori* (from observation) The idea was reached inductively from evidence, *a posteriori.*

**parthenogenesis** (unfertilized birth) Athena was born by parthenogenesis from Zeus's forehead.

**assonance** (vowel repetition) Notice the assonance of the words *croon*, *duel*, and *tube*.

**objurgation** (rebuke) We read the teacher's red-penned objurgations on the term paper.

**demotic** (of the common people) We studied the demotic alleyway slang.

**soporific** (sleep-inducing) His soporific platitudes bored everyone in the audience.

**internecine** (mutually destructive) Their internecine wars doomed the barbarian tribes.

**sesquipedalian** (very long (words)) Having a sesquipedalian vocabulary is fun.

*sui generis* (unique) Her self-originated style was boldly *sui generis.*

•   •   •

**plutocracy** (government of the wealthy) The democracy degenerated into a plutocracy.

**delineate** (to outline) Please quickly delineate the features of your plan.

**dichotomy** (two-part division) Is there a clear dichotomy between the two choices?

**epiphany** (revelation) In a sudden epiphany, he saw the solution!

**tortuous** (twisting) The tortuous highway winds through the hills of West Virginia.

## As Used by Alfred Lansing in *Endurance*

|  | To reach | them | involved | a | **tortuous** | crawl. |
|---|---|---|---|---|---|---|
| **Parts of Speech:** | n. | pron. | v. | adj. | **adj.** | n. |
| **Parts of Sentence:** | --------subject ------ | | AVP | | | D.O. |
| **Phrases:** | --infinitive phrase--- | | | | | |
| **Clauses:** | ----------------------------------independent clause----------------------------------- | | | | | |
| | one independent clause; a simple, declarative sentence | | | | | |

Here Alfred Lansing uses the adjective *tortuous* to modify the singular common noun *crawl*.  Of course, *crawl* can also be a verb, but here it is a noun modified by an adjective and serving as the direct object of the action verb.

## Pronunciation

| | | | |
|---|---|---|---|
| *a priori* | AY pry OR eye | sesquipedalian | SESS kwi pe DAY lian |
| *a posteriori* | AY post ear ee OR eye | *sui generis* | swee JEN er iss |
| parthenogenesis | PAR then oh GEN eh sis | plutocracy | ploo TOCK ra see |
| assonance | AH son ance | delineate | de LIN ee ate |
| objurgation | ob jur GAY shun | dichotomy | die KOHT o me |
| demotic | deh MOHT ic | epiphany | ee PIFF a nee |
| soporific | soh pore IF ic | tortuous | TOR tyoo us |
| internecine | inter NEE seen | | |

## Spanish Cognates

| | | | |
|---|---|---|---|
| soporific | soporífico | introspective | instrospectivo |
| plutocracy | plutocracia | epiphany | epifanía |
| assonance | asonancia | tortuous | tortuoso |
| delineation | delineación | parthenogenesis | partenogénesis |

1. Philosophers often use the terms *a priori* (from before) and *a posteriori* (from afterward) when they discuss epistemology, the question of how we know things. *A priori* (*pre*: before) knowledge is knowledge that can be deduced from principles; it can be known prior to empirical verification. *A posteriori* (*post*: after) knowledge is knowledge that is dependent upon induction, reasoning after experience, and empirical verification. Some would say human freedom of mind is an *a priori* truth. The scientific method gives us many *a posteriori* truths.

2. A **Micropoem**: The adjective **sesquipedalian** is a humorous word that refers to words that are a foot and a half long! *Sesqui* means one and a half, and *ped* means foot! If you master the vocabulary in this course, you will have a sesquipedalian vocabulary.

3. Poets and novelists make frequent use of **assonance**, the repetition of vowel sounds. When Sandburg wrote "The voice of the last cricket/Across the first frost/Is one kind of goodbye," he used assonance on *across/frost* and *kind/bye* (*o* sound and *i* sound). Assonance is different from **consonance**, the repetition of consonant sounds. To make the cricket chirp, Sandburg used consonance on *voice/last/first/frost* (*s* sound). Both assonance and consonance are different from **alliteration**, the repetition of initial sounds, which Sandburg used on *first/frost* (*f* sound).

4. The term *sui generis*, like the word **unique**, is best used for things that are truly one of a kind. Something cannot be very unique. There are no degrees: it either is unique or it is not. Similarly, to be *sui generis* is to form a kind (*generis*) all by your self (*sui*).

5. The adjective **internecine** refers to mutual slaughter, as in a civil war. It comes from the Latin *inter* (between) and *necare* (to kill).

6. Some insects and algae are able to reproduce from an unfertilized egg or spore. This ability is known as **parthenogenesis**, after Athena, the Greek goddess of wisdom who was born from Zeus's forehead! Athena's temple in Athens is, of course, the Parthenon.

7. To **delineate** is to outline, but it is not to outline in the complete, systematic manner of a formal outline. Rather, to delineate is to sketch out in words the basic outline of something (*de*: down, *lin*: line). Delineation is brief analysis, rather than full formal analysis.

8. A **Classic Word**: The adjective **tortuous** is more commonly found in the classics than you might imagine. Harriet Beecher Stowe described how the red, muddy, turbid current flowed through the abrupt, tortuous windings of the Red River. In Dickens's *A Tale of Two Cities*, there is a tortuous, uphill thoroughfare. In Hardy's *The Mayor of Casterbridge*, there is a tortuous defile for carriages down the centre of the street. H.G. Wells's Martians are unearthly in their tortuous forms. In *Lord Jim*, Joseph Conrad even described policies as tortuous! Kipling's Kim found a tortuous and indirect person playing a hidden game. Fitzgerald, in *The Great Gatsby*, described superior couples holding each other tortuously.

# THE RISE OF ROME
## Dr. Thomas Milton Kemnitz

What made Rome great was not its rapid military victories over the Campanians and Latin towns, but the astonishingly generous arrangements that ended the hostilities in 338 B.C. None of the vanquished towns was forced to change its governance or its local leadership. The inhabitants of the Latin towns nearest to Rome were given Roman citizenship. Two of the larger towns a little farther away were allowed, with the loss of some of their territory, to assume full independence, a satisfying gesture that had more symbolic than actual meaning because they were entirely surrounded by Roman territory. The citizens of other Latin towns were made Roman citizens without voting rights except in local elections. In each case they were required in the event of war to raise troops for the common defense. In sum, what the Romans did was to turn former adversaries into Romans and thereby increase greatly their territory and power. And to cement their control, they established a series of defensive colonies of about 2,000 families each comprised of a mixture of Romans, Latins, and Campanians. These colonies were fortified, provided with cisterns for water, and laid out in straight streets intersecting on the perpendicular on the model established by Hippodamus of Miletus at Piraeus and exported by the Greeks to the towns they founded in Magna Graecia in southern Italy and Sicily.

These fortified colonies provided a first line of defence, and the Romans—particularly the newly-minted Romans—needed it, for what they had won most notably was the enmity of the powerful Samnites, who had much in common with the Sabines. The Romans suffered devastating military defeats in 321 and 315 B.C. at the hands of the Samnites. That led the Roman army to abandon the Greek phalanx system of men packed closely together and to adopt a more widely spaced maniple organization, with squares of men separated by space between them and the squares arranged three deep. They adopted as weapons a shorter sword and the javelin. They paid particular care to who was in the three lines and how they used new recruits—as advanced javelin throwers who then retreated to the rear. Their new organization proved effective in defeating the Samnites, who had been joined by the Etruscans to Rome's north. In 290 B.C., the Romans overcame the Samnites and gained control of much of the Italian peninsula, including for the first time towns east of the Appennines. Again, the Romans were lenient victors and made the Samnites Roman citizens without the right to vote.

Images of Samnite warriors from tomb paintings

Victory over the Samnites brought Roman territory into contact with the Magna Graecia towns in the south of Italy, and those towns were disturbed by the growing power of Rome. In the past, Carthage had represented the greatest threat to their way of life. Rome's new army system of legions first faced a trained Greek phalanx in the Pyrrhic War (280-275 B.C.). Pyrrhus of Epirus brought 25,000 troops and a score of war elephants to southern Italy to aid the cities of Magna Graecia against the Romans. He was disappointed in his expectation that the cities of Italy would support him; they stood by the Romans. The Romans narrowly lost two early battles against Pyrrhus but inflicted such high casualties that the term *Pyrrhic victory* came to mean one won at too high a cost. In 275 B.C., the Roman legions—having learned how to deal with Greek spearmen and war elephants—decisively defeated Pyrrhus and brought under their control the Greek cities in the south of Italy. During this war, some of the Etruscan towns to the north of Rome revolted and were crushed, erasing the Etruscans from those able to challenge Rome. Rome now controlled the entire Italian peninsula. Alexander had died fifty-eight years previously.

The next major involvement of Rome with Greece came against Queen Teuta. After the death of her husband in 230, she ruled much of Illyria as regent for her stepson. Queen Teuta used piracy as well as direct aggression as a means of advancing the interests of her kingdom against the neighboring states. Soon her Illyrian ships were intercepting and plundering Roman merchant vessels, and they began to disrupt the trade routes between Greece and Magna Graecia. The Romans felt threatened by Teuta's aggression, and the Senate sent two ambassadors to demand an end to all pirate expeditions and repayment for losses. Teuta told them that piracy was lawful in Illyria and that her government would not intervene. The Romans were less than properly respectful of the queen, and as a result one was killed and the other imprisoned.

Rome responded in 229 by sending a fleet of 200 ships, four legions, and cavalry. The Romans soon made one of Teutra's governors, Demetrius, an independent client of Rome with a large part of the queen's territory, and in 227 they forced her to accept peace on Rome's terms. They allowed her to keep a very small slice of land and her capital city, but the Illyrians were limited in where they could sail warships and were required to pay an annual tribute to Rome.

During the next decade, Demetrius began to assert himself, acquiring territory and playing a large part in Greek affairs. Finally Rome decided that he had become too large a threat in the Adriatic region, and they sent a fleet with more troops to correct the situation. They quickly routed Demetrius's troops, and he beat a hasty retreat to the court of Philip V of Macedonia.

| Rome defeats Latium towns | Alexander invades Asia | Samnite War | Rome finally defeats the Samnites | Rome defeats King Pyrrhus |
|---|---|---|---|---|
| 338 B.C. | 335 B.C. | 326-304 B.C. | 290 B.C. | 275 B.C. |

In each case below, one of the choices was really the word used by the author in the sentence provided. All of the choices can be found in the example words on the first page of this lesson. Your challenge is to decide which word the author used. This is not a test; it is more like a game because more than one word choice may work perfectly well. See if you can use your sensitivity and intuition to guess correctly which word the author used.

1.  **From Charlotte Brontë's *Jane Eyre***

    The heavy supper she had eaten produced a(n) _____ effect.
    a. soporific
    b. demotic
    c. internecine
    d. sesquipedalian

2.  **From Sylvia Plath's *The Bell Jar***

    His breath shaped _____ smoke signals in the gray air.
    a. demotic
    b. soporific
    c. tortuous
    d. *a priori*

3.  **From Mary Shelley's *Frankenstein***

    How ___ the wretch whom with such infinite pains and care I had endeavoured to form?
    a. dichotomize
    b. internecine
    c. delineate
    d. objurgate

4.  **From Rachel Carson's *Silent Spring***

    The greatest single factor in preventing insects from overwhelming the rest of the world is the _____ warfare which they carry out among themselves.
    a. internecine
    b. dichotomous
    c. tortuous
    d. *sui generis*

5.  **From Jack London's *White Fang***

    His arms [were] raised in _____.
    a. dichotomy
    b. assonance
    c. parthenogenesis
    d. objurgation

Roman oil lamp

Though it is a good thing to have a rich vocabulary, it is not a good thing to abuse that vocabulary by writing verbose, abstruse, sesquipedalian sentences. Those who overuse their vocabularies often do so at the expense of clarity. Translate the following showy, ponderous passage into graceful, direct English. Do not use slang, but do use words that seem familiar and comfortable.

AFTER TWENTY YEARS of perfidious, internecine civil conflict over language customs, the victorious, monolithic plutocracy formally rejected the demotic, heterodox slang (an assonant jargon known as *lunorap*) spoken on the lunar colony and issued an objurgation to the obsequious colonists, insisting on formal use of its own soporific, sesquipedalian language and tortuous logic in all official documents. Putative *a posteriori* knowledge, the omniscient government averred, would no longer be allowed to contradict official *a priori* truth. This unilateral interdiction (actually, it was an omnibus document that in a brief *obiter dictum* outlawed parthenogenesis) superseded all previous language edicts, delineated a dichotomy between sedate GOVSPEAK and loquacious COLSPEAK, and left the nonplussed colonists incredulous; but no cacophonous, acerbic altercation or nihilistic retort followed, and the gregarious colonists did not contravene the condescending edict, even though no effort was made by the government to mollify the colonists.

A Samnite helmet

## Reading Comprehension

1. In Translation 36, it can be inferred that:
   - a. GOVSPEAK is soporific and sesquipedalian.
   - b. GOVSPEAK is demotic, heterodox slang.
   - c. GOVSPEAK is the dialect spoken by most colonists.
   - d. GOVSPEAK is similar to COLSPEAK.

2. The author does all of the following EXCEPT:
   - a. describe the colonists' reaction to the government edict
   - b. describe the difference between the official and popular languages
   - c. describe the three types of colonists
   - d. describe the cause of the civil conflict

## Analogies

3. **A PRIORI : A POSTERIORI ::** *(handwritten: Theory   Observation)*
   - a. microscope : telescope
   - b. history : science fiction
   - c. theology : science
   - d. dreaming : exploration

4. **PLUTOCRACY : DEMOTIC ::**
   - a. aristocracy : popular
   - b. meritocracy : labor
   - c. oligarchy : monarchy
   - d. autocracy : heptarchy

## Antonyms

5. **ASSONANCE :**
   - a. alliteration
   - b. end rhyme
   - c. consonance
   - d. internal rhyme

6. **DICHOTOMY :**
   - a. unity
   - b. continuity
   - c. ambiguity
   - d. contiguity

King Pyrrhus, like many others, won some battles against the Romans but lost the war. He gave his name to the term *Pyrrhic victory*, meaning a victory won at too high a cost. As the Romans well knew, it was not the battle but the war that had to be won, and repeatedly they showed the capacity to think in longer terms and to win in the end.

### synthesis

Think of three examples of **internecine** conflict, and explain why you would describe them as internecine. Of course, all wars are to some extent mutually destructive, and yet we do not describe all wars as internecine. What is the difference between internecine wars and non-internecine wars?

### analysis

Can you form a **dichotomy** between *a priori* truths and *a posteriori* truths? Consider various ideas, facts, or principles that you consider to be true, and decide whether each one is an *a priori* truth or an *a posteriori* truth. As an example, Jefferson began the *Declaration of Independence* with an *a priori* statement: "We hold these truths to be self-evident . . . ." Find at least five truths of each kind.

### intuition

In a dream, you are on a difficult, **tortuous** path leading upwards through steep, rocky, evergreen wilderness. Finally, you climb through a layer of misty clouds into blue mountain summits, and you are completely surprised at what you find in front of you on the mossy boulders. What do you find?

### ethics

Consider the implications of living in a **plutocracy**. Then consider that a government could be an official plutocracy, officially requiring a high financial status of all officeholders, or it could be an unofficial plutocracy that does not officially require great wealth but through *de facto* means makes it impossible for anyone without great wealth to successfully seek office. What do you think are the most important ethical issues in plutocratic rule? From your study of history, what examples of plutocracy can you think of?

### divergence

The word **soporific** means sleep-inducing. Used literally, it can refer to a drug, but used with more humor, it can refer to something that is so boring (such as a bad lecture or program) that it puts people to sleep. Make a long, humorous list of soporifics you have endured.

A Samnite bronze belt

### Neologist's Lexicon

Use the stems in this list to create a new word (neologism). Give the word, the pronunciation, the part of speech, the etymology, and the definition(s). Keep a record of the neologisms you create from list to list. Here are some examples:

**sesquinecinary** (SESS kwee NEE sih nary) adj. [*sesqui* (one and a half), *nec* (kill)] 1. killing in a manner far beyond what is necessary (killing and a half) to terminate life, as Achilles's killing of Hector and dragging his body around the walls of Troy 2. obsessive use of the phrase "That kills me"; derived from J.D. Salinger's character Holden Caulfield in *The Catcher in the Rye*

**soporocracy** (sah pore AH cracy) n. [*sopor* (sleep), *cracy* (government)] 1. a government that is asleep to dangers and threats to the nation 2. a government led by individuals who are indifferent to, uninterested in, or uninformed about national affairs

### Sesquipedalian Dialogue

Use the words from List 36 to construct a short philosophical dialogue between two characters. Feel free to be playful or satirical. If you would like a paradigm for a philosophical dialogue, you might like to read one of the shorter *Dialogues* of Plato. As an example, here is a spoof of a Platonic dialogue. In the real dialogue, the conversation is between Socrates and Meno:

### Meanie

Sogreat and Meanie walk down a path and sit on a bench, looking out over a grove called *Countryday*.

Sogreat: Well, Meanie, this beautiful grove reminds me of your sesquipedalian speech yesterday. I must admit that I was quite impressed with your command of ideas. In fact, sometimes it seemed that your complexities are too intricate for me.

Meanie: Oh, Sogreat, you don't fool me with your *sui generis* ironies. I sense your silent objurgations lurking under the surface of your sentences.

Sogreat: No, Meanie, your ideas seemed to emerge fully grown, without the need for logical development, like Athena's parthenogenesis from the head of Zeus.

Meanie: Well, Sogreat, in a demotic society such as ours, we must lead people to epiphanies quickly, without the soporific details that make arguments (such as yours) so tortuous.

Sogreat: I see that you can delineate my faults succinctly, Meanie. I must agree that there is a sharp dichotomy between my tedious logic and your exciting insights. Tell me, Meanie, would you say that *a priori* thinking or *a posteriori* thinking is more likely to lead to knowledge of the truth?

Meanie: Oh, Sogreat, you can't catch me in one of your famous traps.

Sogreat: Meanie, you clever plutocrat, I see that our internecine arguments are accomplishing nothing. In fact, I seem to understand you less now than I did when we sat down!

*finis*

| | | | | | | |
|---|---|---|---|---|---|---|
| • *thanatos* | (death) | thanatopsis | • *syn* | (together) | synoptic | |
| • *opia* | (sight) | thanatopsis | • *ize* | (make) | lionize | |
| • vac | (empty) | vacuous | • sed | (sit) | assiduous, sedentary | |
| • ous | (full of) | vacuous | • sub | (under) | subterfuge | |
| • luc | (light) | lucubration | • fug | (flee) | subterfuge | |
| • ex | (out) | *ex cathedra* | • bon | (good) | *bon vivant* | |
| • man | (hand) | legerdemain | • viv | (life) | *bon vivant* | |
| • spir | (breathe) | suspiration | • *ine* | (nature of) | saturnine | |
| • *ism* | (doctrine) | nepotism | • **pusill** | (small) | pusillanimous | |
| • **nepo** | (nephew) | nepotism | • anim | (mind) | pusillanimous | |

**thanatopsis** (view of death)  We thoughtfully read the introvert's poetic thanatopsis.

**vacuous** (stupidly empty of ideas)  See the vacuous expression on his uninformed face.

**lucubration** (late studying)  His midnight lucubrations by candlelight tired him.

**ex cathedra** (from the throne)  The king pronounced, *ex cathedra*, his opinion.

**legerdemain** (sleight of hand)  His verbal legerdemain confused those who did not pay attention.

**suspiration** (deep sigh)  We endured his mournful suspirations over Lulu.

**nepotism** (favoritism to relatives)  Graft and nepotism weakened the government.

**synoptic** (general in view)  Read the synoptic gospels; view a synoptic chart.

**lionize** (treat as a celebrity)  Upon her return to the city, she was lionized by the joyful crowd.

**assiduous** (persevering)  His assiduous efforts to balance the budget finally paid off.

•       •       •

**subterfuge** (evasive dodge)  He ducked a question with a clever subterfuge.

**bon vivant** (indulger in luxury)  The wealthy *bon vivant* lived the good life in Hawaii.

**saturnine** (gloomy and remote)  Her saturnine personality caused her to lose friends.

**sedentary** (sitting)  Flagpole sitting is a notably sedentary occupation.

**pusillanimous** (small-minded)  The snub at the losing team was a low, pusillanimous act.

## As Used by Bram Stoker in *Dracula*

| | I | have | been | practicing | shorthand | very | **assiduously.** |
|---|---|---|---|---|---|---|---|
| **Parts of Speech:** | pron. | v. | v. | v. | n. | adv. | adv. |
| **Parts of Sentence:** | subj. | ------------AVP------------- | | | D.O. | | |
| **Phrases:** | ----no prepositional, appositive, or verbal phrases---- | | | | | | |
| **Clauses:** | --------------------------------independent clause---------------------------------- | | | | | | |
| | one independent clause; a simple, declarative sentence | | | | | | |

Bram Stoker uses the adverb *assiduously* to modify the present perfect action verb *have been practicing*. Notice that the adverb is modified by its own adverb, *very*.

## Pronunciation

| | | | |
|---|---|---|---|
| **thanatopsis** | thah na TOP siss | **lionize** | LIE on ize |
| **vacuous** | VACK yoo us | **assiduous** | ah SID yoo us |
| **lucubration** | loo kyoo BRAY shun | **subterfuge** | SUB tur fyooj |
| *ex cathedra* | ex cah THEE dra | *bon vivant* | bohn vee VAHN |
| **legerdemain** | LEJ ur de MAIN | **saturnine** | SAT ur nine |
| **suspiration** | suss pih RAY shun | **sedentary** | SED en tary |
| **nepotism** | NEH po tiz um | **pusillanimous** | pyoo si LAN ih muss |
| **synoptic** | sin OP tick | | |

## Spanish Cognates

| | | | |
|---|---|---|---|
| **vacuous** | vacuo | **nepotism** | nepotismo |
| **subterfuge** | suberfugio | **pusillanimous** | pusilánime |
| **assiduous** | asiduo | **lucubration** | lucubración |
| **sedentary** | sedentario | **synoptic** | sinóptico |

1.  The adjective **assiduous** has more in common with the word **sedentary** than first meets the eye. *Assiduous* traces back to the Latin *ad*: to, and *sedere*: to sit. In other words, being assiduous suggests that you are persevering because you sit there until the job is done! A sedentary job is one in which you are sitting down most of the day. One could have a sedentary job without necessarily being assiduous.

    **Assiduous** is a good **Classic Word**. In the writings of the Brontës, Stowe, Thoreau, Dickens, Wells, Conrad, and Wilder, we find characters proceeding assiduously with their occupations, assiduously giving reading lessons, knitting away assiduously, gnawing assiduously at the near foreleg of an enemy, being too assiduously engaged to talk, chewing betel assiduously, and cultivating the city assiduously for material. There are assiduous pupils, those who arrange cups and spoons with assiduous celerity, and those who are equally assiduous in every duty.

2.  Named after the Roman god Saturn, who is identified with the Greek god Cronus, the giant ringed planet is the second-largest planet in our solar system and the sixth from the sun. When we describe a person as **saturnine**, however, we suggest none of the beauty that is identified with the great ringed planet. Rather, we mean that, like Saturn, the person is remote, gloomy, and silent.

3.  The adjective **pusillanimous** is best regarded in light of its opposite, **magnanimous**. To be magnanimous is to be generous, brave, large, or great (*magn*) in spirit (*anim*). To be pusillanimous is to be small-minded, timid, or even cowardly.

4.  Popes and kings can make pronouncements ***ex cathedra***, literally from their thrones. We can still use this term, however, even when we are not actually describing magnates or potentates. If we wish to satirize someone who is behaving in a self-important, puffed-up manner, we can use *ex cathedra* to enhance the sense of irony: The little boy straddled the hobby horse and issued his instructions to his nursemaid, *ex cathedra*.

5.  The noun **lucubration** refers to laborious studying, especially writing done late at night. A poetic word, *lucubration* gives us the image of the writer leaning over his or her desk in the early hours of the morning, the soft light (*luc*) of the candle casting its glow on the newly written ideas. The Latin *lucubrare* meant to work by artificial light.

6.  A **Micropoem**: **Subterfuge** is an especially descriptive noun. It refers to the evasions we use to avoid being pinned down. You can evade a question with a subterfuge, as by distracting the questioner with an unrelated counter-question. The word contains a metaphorical image of what is happening: to use a subterfuge is to duck, to flee (*fug*) underneath (*sub*).

7.  The noun **thanatopsis** was coined by William Cullen Bryant for a poem musing on death. The word literally means a view (*opsis, opia*) of death (*thanatos*). There are some other interesting words that come to mind in light of Bryant's contribution. One is **thanatology**, the study of death, and another is **thanatophobia**, an abnormally great fear of death.

The Roman army fought in the Iberian peninsula during the Second Punic War. There they encountered the Celtiberian warriors, whose helmet style they adopted in what became known as the Montefortino type of Roman helmet (see page 218). They also adopted their opponents' shorter sword, which the Romans called the *gladius* and which became standard for the Roman army for centuries. For more then two centuries they used the oval shield the Celtiberian warrior depicted here is shown holding. This small figure was part of a gold clasp.

# THE CENTRAL MEDITERRANEAN
## Dr. Thomas Milton Kemnitz

In the centuries before the emergence of Rome as a major power, the central Mediterranean had been dominated by three major forces: the Etruscans, the Carthaginians, and the Greek colonies led by Syracuse. The Romans encountered first the Etruscans, who controlled much of central Italy. From about 800 B.C., the Etruscans organized themselves into loose confederations of cities. With productive mines and an expertise in metallurgy, they traded lucratively with the Greeks and Carthaginians. They came into conflict with Greek colonies in what is now southern France and along the west coast of Italy, and that led the Etruscans to ally themselves with Carthage. Gradually through the sixth and fifth centuries B.C. in a series of conflicts, the Etruscan sphere was circumscribed by more aggressive traders and by the power of the Greeks of Magna Graecia. At the beginning of the fourth century, the Romans managed to defeat the Etruscan city of Veii, and thereafter the Etruscans were never in a position on their own to mount a serious challenge to the Romans.

For several centuries, the two greatest cities of the central Mediterranean were Carthage and Syracuse. Carthage was the older city, founded about 813 or 814 B.C. by settlers from Tyre in Phoenicia. The Phoenicians were Canaanites and lived in what is now Lebanon. They were seafaring traders, and legend has it that a queen led a group west to establish Carthage. They picked an ideal spot where they could control trade between the east and west Mediterranean and where a fertile plain offered abundant harvests. The Phoenician city states had much the same structure as their contemporary Greek counterparts, and the Greeks and Phoenicians traded in relative harmony. Phoenician cities were conquered by the Persian Cyrus the Great in 539 B.C.—eleven years after he had conquered the Ionian cities to the north and west—and in the next century it is likely than many of Cyrus's new Phoenician subjects fled to Carthage and other still-independent Phoenician-founded cities in the west. A little more than two centuries after Cyrus the Great, Alexander the Great conquered Tyre after a long and difficult siege. He treated the inhabitants less than leniently, massacring many and selling the rest into slavery. Thus encouraged, the other Phoenician cities surrendered without resistance. The Phoenicians would never regain the prominence they had before Cyrus and then Alexander began the reduction of their autonomy. Now Carthage was the leading city of Phoenician origin in the ancient world.

Syracuse was founded by settlers from Corinth in 734 or 733 B.C. It had close ties to Sparta as well as Corinth. Situated on fertile ground on the east coast of Sicily, like Carthage it was in a good position to control trade in the Mediterranean. While Carthage was the principal port of a nexus of Phoenician cities in the Mediterranean, Syracuse was the primary city of a large number of colonies—known as Magna Graecia—founded by Greeks in Sicily and Italy. Urged on by Alcibiades in one of his power plays, the Athenians had sent a large fleet to attack Syracuse during the Peloponnesian War. The Spartans rendered material aid to Syracuse, and eventually the entire Athenian contingent perished in a disastrous defeat for Athens. As Syracuse grew and prospered, it came into conflict with Carthage, which controlled the western half of Sicily. Wars between the two raged for part of the fifth and almost all of the fourth century B.C.

Because Syracuse and Carthage saw the other as their primary foe, they were slow to recognize the growing power of Rome to their north. Only when the Romans had conquered the Samnites and reached the boot of Italy did they begin to touch directly on the interests of Syracuse and Carthage.

In each case below, one of the choices was really the word used by the author in the sentence provided. All of the choices can be found in the example words on the first page of this lesson. Your challenge is to decide which word the author used. This is not a test; it is more like a game because more than one word choice may work perfectly well. See if you can use your sensitivity and intuition to guess correctly which word the author used.

1.  **From Dava Sobel's *Longitude***

    And this was done through the application of some mathematical _____ called the Equation of Time.
    a. subterfuge
    b. legerdemain
    c. *bon vivant*
    d. thanatopsis

2.  **From Alfred Lansing's *Endurance***

    He was _____ wherever he went...knighted by his king.
    a. synoptic
    b. vacuous
    c. lionized
    d. sedentary

3.  **From Joseph Conrad's *Lord Jim***

    She chewed betel _____.
    a. assiduously
    b. *ex cathedra*
    c. synoptically
    d. pusillanimously

4.  **From William Shakespeare's *Hamlet***

    Hamlet described the "windy _____ of forced breath."
    a. legerdemain
    b. subterfuge
    c. lucubration
    d. suspiration

5.  **From Joseph Heller's *Catch-22***

    Now she sat resting in _____ indolence.
    a. saturnine
    b. vacuous
    c. pusillanimous
    d. assiduous

Though it is a good thing to have a rich vocabulary, it is not a good thing to abuse that vocabulary by writing verbose, abstruse, sesquipedalian sentences. Those who overuse their vocabularies often do so at the expense of clarity. Translate the following showy, ponderous passage into graceful, direct English. Do not use slang, but do use words that seem familiar and comfortable.

FIRST OBSEQUIOUSLY LIONIZED by the public and then accused of perfidious nepotism and egocentrism, the nonplussed plutocrat—with assiduous lucubration, frequent suspirations, and *sotto voce* epigrams— devoted himself to an introspective and saturnine thanatopsis. Without verbal legerdemain, circumlocution, or subterfuge, he delineated the pusillanimous and vacuous character of the sedentary *bon vivants*, portly gastronomes, putative autodidacts, and heterodox neophytes who had dared to impugn his *ex cathedra* synoptic ratiocinations. Condescendingly and with sedate sangfroid, he noted that he need not mollify the acerbity of the incredulous or exculpate himself from the specious charges of abased nihilists who—with their constant internecine cacophonous altercations—contravened every reasonable interdiction and declaimed with loquacious retorts and tortuous *non sequiturs* against every *obiter dictum*. "*Au contraire*," he averred in his postlude, "the soporific objurgations and demotic malapropisms of the gregarious masses trouble me not. As paterfamilias of the nation, I must allow nothing to supersede my *sui generis* sacrosanct *a priori* responsibilities. These matters are an imponderable *terra incognita* to those whose hierarchy of values begins and ends with the tangible." Then, in a sudden epiphany, he added, "One cannot expect lycanthropes to appreciate heliotropes; it is not their forte."

This is a tablet in Oscan, which was the language of the Samnites and which was usually written from right to left. The Samnites conquered Pompeii, where this inscription was found. Although the Romans took Pompeii from the Samnites and made all of the inhabitants citizens, some people still spoke and wrote Oscan in Pompeii when the eruption of Vesuvius destroyed it in 79 A.D. Some of the graffiti that has been found on the sides of buildings was written in Oscan.

**Reading Comprehension**

1. For Translation 37, which of the following does the passage suggest?
   a. Corrupt rulers manipulate the people.
   b. An educated populace is essential in a democracy.
   c. Public favor is an ephemeral phenomenon.
   d. Intellectuals make poor government officials.

2. The passage could best be described as:
   a. A thoughtful ruler stands by his principles.
   b. A plutocrat enriches himself from the public coffers.
   c. A tyrant ignores the voice of the people.
   d. Power corrupts, and absolute power corrupts absolutely.

**Analogies**

3. **LUCUBRATION : ASSIDUOUS ::**
   a. sedentary : sedate
   b. thanatopsis : mordant
   c. synopsis : verbose
   d. application : sedulous

4. **BON VIVANT : SATURNINE ::**
   a. legerdemain : confusing
   b. thanatopsis : subterfuge
   c. sedentary : flagpole
   d. monograph : synoptic

**Antonyms**

5. **VACUOUS :**
   a. cognizant
   b. fecund
   c. ignorant
   d. effusive

6. **BON VIVANT :**
   a. stoic
   b. epicurean
   c. ascetic
   d. eremite

This scene on an oil lamp shows gladiators awaiting a verdict. The Etruscans staged gladiatorial contests, and the Romans learned the practice from them.

**ethics**

    **Nepotism**, the corrupt practice of showing favoritism to friends and relatives, is almost universally regarded as unethical. For example, if a high governmental official appoints a close friend or family member to a desirable or lucrative position, the governmental official could be condemned and accused of nepotism (literally, nephew-ism). Specifically, what are the reasons why nepotism is unethical? Try to list several precise reasons why widespread nepotism could be harmful to a nation's well-being. It might help to remember that nepotism actually is widespread in many countries.

**imagination and intuition**

    You are a research scientist in a biological research station in a rainforest. For years, you have worked on the solution to a problem, and now you have it. For this solution, you will be **lionized** by the public, esteemed by the scientific community, and might receive the Nobel Prize. Describe your work in the rainforest, and explain your problem and its solution.

*write xceptance speech*

**synthesis**

    Use any ten of the words from List 37 in a single coherent paragraph. Humor is acceptable.

**emotion and analysis**

    In *Leaves of Grass*, Walt Whitman gives a new angle to the term **thanatopsis**. The smallest blade of grass, Whitman explains, shows that there is really no death. Whitman notes that many feel it is lucky to be born, but he says that it is just as lucky to die. Find a copy of *Leaves of Grass*, and examine these passages and others; then analyze Whitman's concept of no-death, and discuss your emotional response to Whitman's ideas. You might enjoy comparing Whitman's poem to Bryant's famous poem "Thanatopsis."

This Corinthian-style helmet was made in Apulia on the southeast coast of Italy in the area known as Magna Graecia. The repair on the top back is ancient and might have been made by the helmet's second owner.

## Neologist's Lexicon

Use the stems in this list to create a new word (neologism). Give the word, the pronunciation, the part of speech, the etymology, and the definition(s). Keep a record of the neologisms you create from list to list. Here are some examples:

**pusillopia** (PYOO sill OH pia) n. [*pusill* (small), *opia* (sight)] 1. a form of egocentrism in which the victim sees all other persons as smaller and less important than himself 2. chronic, pathological condescension

**fuganimism** (fyooj AN im ism) n. [*fug* (flee), *anim* (mind), *ism* (doctrine) 1. the tendency to avoid experiences that contain, or require the comprehension of, ideas 2. reflexive switching of the radio channel when the news comes on.

## Sesquipedalian Pet Commands

Using words from List 37 or previous lists, construct a series of commands useful for training a pet, such as a dog, raccoon, or chimpanzee. A few examples:

1. BE SEDENTARY! The pet will sit down and look silently into your eyes, waiting for the next instruction.

2. ESCHEW NEPOTISM! The pet will ignore his or her brothers and sisters and will come to you.

3. SUSPIRATE! The pet will look at you in a longing way and then emit a deep sigh, as of adoration. This command is best issued when the pet is hungry, just prior to feeding.

4. LIONIZE! At this command, the pet will manifest joy in your presence effusively, running back and forth, jumping up and down, and whining with glee.

## Sesquipedalian Poetry

Use the words from List 37 to create a poem. This time, work to establish interesting rhythms or metrical patterns. The whole poem does not have to be iambic, trochaic, dactylic, or anapestic, but try to control the fall of the syllables so that the rhythm is consonant with the meaning of the poem.

This theater mask was made in Sicily about 350 B.C. The Greek theater was a feature of life in Magna Graecia.

| | | | | | |
|---|---|---|---|---|---|
| • *log* | (reason) | syllogism | • *phobia* | (fear) | lyssophobia |
| • *nym* | (name) | metonymy | • *ideo* | (idea) | *idée fixe* |
| • *meta* | (change) | metonymy | • *schizo* | (divide) | schism |
| • *phor* | (carry) | anaphora | • *apo*\* | (up) | apotheosis |
| • *ize* | (make) | bowdlerize | • *theo* | (god) | apotheosis |
| • *loco* | (place) | *locus classicus* | • pre | (before) | precursor |
| • *re* | (again) | reiterate | • curs | (run) | precursor |
| • *de* | (down) | desultory | • *cosmo* | (universe) | cosmology |
| • *ambul* | (walk) | funambulist | • *eu* | (good) | euphony |
| • *funi* | (cord) | funambulist | • *phon* | (sound) | euphony |

**syllogism** (three-part deduction) Example: All A is B; C is A; therefore, C is B.

**metonymy** (association name) Example: The White House has announced a new policy.

**anaphora** (repetition in successive phrases) Dr. King used anaphora, repeating, "I have a dream."

**bowdlerize** (censor prudishly) We deplore the bowdlerization of great literature.

**locus classicus** (classical example) *The Iliad* is a *locus classicus* for the heroic ideal.

**reiterate** (repeat) It is needless to reiterate one's objections.

**desultory** (rambling) He gave a desultory, soporific lecture.

**funambulist** (tightrope walker) The speech was an act of political funambulism.

**lyssophobia** (fear of insanity) It was a family of schizophrenics and lyssophobiacs.

**idée fixe** (obsession) For Ahab, the whale was an *idée fixe*.

•     •     •

**schism** (division) A schism developed in the Democratic party.

**apotheosis** (raising to god status) We noted the public's apotheosis of the new champ.

**precursor** (forerunner) This unfortunate event was the precursor of the tragedy to come.

**cosmology** (study of the universe) The existence of the Big Bang is a cosmological question.

**euphony** (beautiful sound) Hear the soft euphony of the wind in the trees.

\*We introduce a new definition of *apo*.

**As Used by Herman Melville in *Moby Dick***

|  | Straight | up, | leaps | thy | **apotheosis!** |
|---|---|---|---|---|---|
| **Parts of Speech:** | adv. | adv. | v. | adj. | **n.** |
| **Parts of Sentence:** |  |  | AVP |  | subj. |
| **Phrases:** | ----no prepositional, appositive, or verbal phrases---- |
| **Clauses:** | ----------------------------------independent clause----------------------------------- |
|  | one independent clause; a simple, exclamatory sentence |

Here Herman Melville uses the noun *apotheosis* as the subject of the sentence. Notice that the subject comes after the verb, for effect.

## Pronunciation

| | | | |
|---|---|---|---|
| **syllogism** | SILL oh jiz um | **lyssophobia** | LISS oh FO bee ah |
| **metonymy** | meh TAHN o mee | ***idée fixe*** | EE day FEEKS |
| **anaphora** | ah NAFF o rah | **schism** | SIZZ um |
| **bowdlerize** | BOW dler ize | **apotheosis** | a POTH ee O siss |
| ***locus classicus*** | LO kuss KLASS ikuss | **precursor** | pre KURR sor |
| **reiterate** | ree IT er ate | **cosmology** | kozz MAH lo jee |
| **desultory** | DESS ul tory | **euphony** | YOO fo nee |
| **funambulist** | foo NAM byoo list | | |

## Spanish Cognates

| | | | |
|---|---|---|---|
| **reiteration** | reiteración | **anaphora** | anáfora |
| **schism** | cisma | **euphony** | eufonía |
| **syllogism** | silogismo | **precursor** | precursor |
| **apotheosis** | apoteosis | **metonomy** | metonimia |

1. In 1818 an English editor, Thomas Bowdler, published an expurgated edition of Shakespeare, removing passages that he found to be offensive. Today, we say a work has been **bowdlerized** when it has been prudishly censored.

2. The noun **metonymy** is actually composed of the Greek stems *meta*, which in this case means other, and *nym*, which means name. *Metonymy* is another name, a name exchanged for the usual name. When we say that the White House has announced a new policy, we do not mean that the building spoke; instead of saying that the President announced the policy, we say that the White House announced the policy, since the White House is an image that everyone associates with the President.

3. A **Micropoem**: A **desultory** speech or conversation is one that is not coherent or connected; it is random and aimless, wandering. It is lacking in structure, sequence, purpose. The word desultory comes from *de* (down) and *salire* (leap), the idea being that in speaking so aimlessly, you are jumping off the subject. One common reason for losing the theme is that one has no purpose or theme to care about.

   **Desultory** is also a good **Classic Word**. It is a word that Thomas Hardy especially loved and used in many of his novels in the 1870s and 1880s because it captured the aimlessness and lack of purpose that he found in the effete and decadent *fin de siecle*. Hardy described his characters' desultory ramblings, desultory chats, and desultory conversations. In *The Mayor of Casterbridge*, Hardy noted "the walk of the skilled countryman as distinct from the desultory shamble of the general labourer" and the "Saturday afternoon [that] slipped on thus desultorily."

4. The French term *idée fixe* means a fixed idea, a monomania, or an obsession. Ahab's *idée fixe* was Moby Dick. You would enjoy looking up the story of Berlioz, who used this term to describe his obsession with a beautiful woman—translated into a musical theme that pervades his masterpiece, *Symphonie Fantastique*.

5. A *locus classicus* is a literary passage that is a primary classical example of something, a passage that is typically cited as authoritative or illustrative. *The Iliad* is the *locus classicus* of martial heroism. Oedipus's arrogant inability to understand that he himself could be the source of evil in his city is the *locus classicus* for the Greek concept of hubris.

6. The word **syllogism** comes from the Greek *syllogismos*, a reckoning together or summing up. The stems are *syn* (together) and *logos* (word). In formal logic, a syllogism is a logical structure that contains two premises and a logical conclusion drawn from the two premises. First premise: All men are perplexed. Second premise: Socrates is a man. Conclusion: Therefore, Socrates is perplexed. Note that the truth of the conclusion is not assured if the premises are not true or if the reasoning is not logical. Examples of false syllogisms: All men have hair; Peggy Sue has hair; therefore, Peggy Sue is a man. Or: All planets have moons; pzx is a newly discovered planet; therefore, pzx must have moons.

# ROME AND CARTHAGE—THE PUNIC WARS (264–218)
## Dr. Thomas Milton Kemnitz

The Romans used the term *Punic* to refer to Carthage, a reference to the city's Phoenician origins. Rome and Carthage had cooperated in dealing with Pyrrhus in the early third century B.C., but the two soon found themselves dragged into a conflict in Sicily. Carthage was a thalassocratic state—a state founded on sea power like Athens. It had a large permanent navy, which was the occupation of the poor of the city. Its army was largely hired mercenaries, many from nearby Nubia. Rome had no navy at the outbreak of the Punic Wars.

The First Punic War was fought for control of Sicily. At the siege and battle of Agrigentum in 261, Roman legions inflicted a hard-won defeat on the Carthaginians attempting to hold the city as a vital part of its supply lines. As was usually the case, the Romans showed themselves willing to run high risks and take massive losses to prevail in the end. After this defeat on land, the Carthaginians attempted to fight the rest of the war at sea. The Romans lost an initial naval skirmish involving fewer than twenty ships on either side. The Romans copied a wrecked Carthaginian quinquereme—a ship with five banks of oars—and built many quinqueremes and some triremes—ships with three banks of oars like the older Greek vessels—and then they added a new piece of equipment, a *corvus*, a ladder-like gangplank attached to the prow on a pivot that could be hooked to enemy ships to allow the Romans to board them. The Romans won the Battle of Mylae decisively in 260 B.C., capturing fifty of the enemy's 130 ships; the *corvus* proved extremely effective in its first engagement. The Romans then bested the Carthaginians at a naval battle at Sardinia. The Carthaginians crucified the general who had lost at Agrigentum, Mylae, and Sardinia. Although the Romans lost a battle in Tunis, the First Punic War ended with Carthage signing a peace treaty that obliged it to evacuate Sicily and pay the Romans a large war indemnity.

In 238 B.C., Carthage was plunged into war with another enemy, and Rome took the opportunity to seize Sardinia and Corsica; Rome was now a naval power with off-shore territories to protect. Rome also dealt with the Illyrians to the east (in what is now Albania) across the Adriatic Sea in wars in 229 and 219 B.C. Rome began to engage in clearing the sea of pirates and of interfering in Greek affairs for the protection of its merchants.

Meanwhile the Carthaginians gained control over much of what is now southern and eastern Spain, formed an alliance with the Celts in the Po region of the Italian peninsula, and planned an invasion of Italy. Ever wary of potential threats, Rome attacked the Celts first in 225, and by 220 they had annexed the region. However, that did not stop the Carthaginians, and in 218 Hannibal led an army composed largely of Spanish mercenaries across the Alps with a sizeable cavalry and some war elephants—few of whom survived the crossing of the Alps. Once in Italy, his force was augmented by tens of thousands of Celtic mercenaries.

Hannibal was the greatest commander the Romans would meet, and he won two tremendous victories after he entered Italy. The first was at Trebia, where in late December a part of the Roman army was led by a consul to wade across a freezing stream to attack the enemy. Hannibal had laid a trap and ambushed the freezing Roman soldiers, killing more than half of them. The Roman army was divided into two parts under two consuls who did not get along, and half the army was not involved in this battle. The next year Hannibal laid a trap for another impetuous consul and half the Roman army, and again he was successful, though once again half the Roman army was unaffected. Thereafter the Romans turned to the generalship of Quintus Fabius Maximus, who developed a strategy of harassing the Carthaginians without engaging in a pitched battle. This is known as the *Fabian strategy*.

| First Punic War begins | First Punic War ends | Rome takes Sardinia and Corsica | Rome attacks the Celts | Rome annexes Cisalpine Gaul | Hannibal invades Italy |
|---|---|---|---|---|---|
| **264 B.C.** | **241 B.C.** | **238 B.C.** | **225 B.C.** | **220 B.C.** | **218 B.C.** |

In each case below, one of the choices was really the word used by the author in the sentence provided. All of the choices can be found in the example words on the first page of this lesson. Your challenge is to decide which word the author used. This is not a test; it is more like a game because more than one word choice may work perfectly well. See if you can use your sensitivity and intuition to guess correctly which word the author used.

1.  **From E.M. Forster's *A Passage to India***

    The crowds of Hindus began a _____ move back into town.
    a. euphonic
    b. desultory
    c. bowdlerized
    d. reiterated

2.  **From Robert Louis Stevenson's *Treasure Island***

    "Rout the house out!" _____ Pew, striking with his stick upon the road.
    a. bowdlerized
    b. precursor
    c. euphony
    d. reiterated

3.  **From Nathaniel Hawthorne's *The Scarlet Letter***

    [He was] so _____ by worshipping admirers.
    a. apotheosized
    b. reiterated
    c. bowdlerized
    d. schism

4.  **From Henry David Thoreau's *Walden***

    The tortoise and the frog are among the _____ and heralds of this season.
    a. funambulists
    b. schisms
    c. precursors
    d. euphonies

5.  **From Jonathan Swift's *Gulliver's Travels***

    Gulliver spoke of "our wars by sea and by land, of our _____ in religion."
    a. precursors
    b. schisms
    c. cosmologies
    d. *locus classicus*

Though it is a good thing to have a rich vocabulary, it is not a good thing to abuse that vocabulary by writing verbose, abstruse, sesquipedalian sentences. Those who overuse their vocabularies often do so at the expense of clarity. Translate the following showy, ponderous passage into graceful, direct English. Do not use slang, but do use words that seem familiar and comfortable.

THE FOURTEENTH-CENTURY COSMOLOGIST, a precursor of contemporary astrophysicists, deduced through careful (though specious) syllogisms that the heavenly spheres made a celestial music as they coursed through the translucent vapors of the imponderable cosmos. This Euphony of the Spheres became an *idée fixe* for the poor scientist (whose lectures were notoriously desultory and were filled with obscure metonymy, boring anaphora, and superfluous reiterations).

Insanity in the cosmologist's family had given him an acute saturnine lyssophobia, which proved to be prophetic: reading a bowdlerized old copy of Lucretius's *De Rerum Natura*, the *locus classicus* for ancient atomic theory, the cosmologist became convinced—in a blinding epiphany—that the schism between the sacrosanct Ptolemaic (geocentric) and the perfidious Copernican (heliocentric) theories was a false dichotomy. In fact, he concluded (mistakenly reifying his metaphors) that both are true: the music of the spheres clearly shows that both orbital systems take place in simultaneous cosmic balance, like a funambulist stepping through the circumambient stars. In a strange apotheosis, the cosmologist came obsequiously to revere Lucretius as an omniscient, divinely inspired prophet who delineated non-anthropocentric ideas to incredulous neophytes.

Unfortunately, pusillanimous and condescending *bon vivants* ridiculed the cosmologist, mocking his sesquipedalian loquacity, his suspirations and lucubrations, and his heterodox ratiocinations. The truth, they vivaciously averred, was a Cacophony of the Spheres: all heavenly bodies make rude and disagreeable sounds as they course through the firmament.

A Roman arrowhead

### Reading Comprehension

1. In Translation 38, the author's attitude is best described as:
   - a. tongue in cheek
   - b. reverent
   - c. sober and factual
   - d. inquiring

2. With which statement would the author likely agree?
   - a. Deductive, *a priori* reasoning can be treacherous.
   - b. Cosmology is filled with nonsense.
   - c. The heavenly spheres produce sound as they move in space.
   - d. Too much thinking can cause insanity.

### Analogies

3. **REITERATE : DESULTORY ::**
   - a. repeat : discursive
   - b. restate : desert
   - c. review : recapitulation
   - d. remind : euphony

4. **SYLLOGISM : ANAPHORA ::**
   - a. art : poetry
   - b. reason : mathematics
   - c. cosmology : poetry
   - d. logic : rhetoric

   *three part    repetition in phrases*
   *deduction*

### Antonyms

5. **APOTHEOSIS :**
   *raising to gods stats*
   - a. objurgation
   - b. ostracism
   - c. lionization
   - d. vilification

6. **DESULTORY :**
   *attack focus*
   - a. logical
   - b. focused
   - c. intelligible
   - d. sequential

Mars, the Roman god of war

**divergence**

An *idée fixe* is an obsession, a fixed idea or monomania that dominates a person's mind. Ahab's obsession with the white whale, Moby Dick, is an example. The time traveler in H.G. Wells's *The Time Machine* has an *idée fixe* with his incredible invention, and he eventually vanishes into the future, never to return. Think of other famous examples of *idée fixe*, either historical or fictional. How many can you think of? As a second imaginative stage of this idea, what are some other things people could become obsessed over? Fudgesicles? Parrots? Rocket engines? Geometry? Mystery novels? Mozart? Robert Frost's poetry? Wildflowers? Ferns? Computers? Leatherbound books? Hiking? Painting? Make an imaginative list of things one might have an *idée fixe* over. Think of the possibilities for a short story about a person with an *idée fixe* over something rare!

**ethics**

In 1818 the English editor Thomas Bowdler published a censored (**bowdlerized**!) edition of Shakespeare, removing passages that he found to be offensive to his view of public decency. Consider the ethical decisions involved in altering an artistic masterpiece for such purposes. Would you ever support altering the language of a great novel? Would you support altering a great painting? A work of sculpture? What are the rights of the artist? What are the rights of society? What are the rights of an individual who is offended by a painting or a passage in a work of literature?

As an interesting case study in conflicting standards, you might look up the story of artist James McNeill Whistler, who sued John Ruskin for libel after Ruskin wrote that Whistler had flung a pot of paint in the public's face with his painting *Nocturne in Black and Gold: The Falling Rocket*.

**aesthetics**

**Euphony** is beautiful sound, such as the wind in the trees, or the bubbling of a brook, or the rising music of Mozart's clarinet concerto. In *Walden*, Henry David Thoreau includes an entire chapter on the sounds he heard near Walden Pond, including train whistles, birds, and wind. Thoreau urged us to stand at the meeting of two eternities, the past and the future, and to improve the nick of time: the present moment. One way to improve upon the nick of time is to listen to the euphony that often surrounds us. What are some examples of euphony in our world—beautiful sounds that we may listen to every day, if we only turn our attention to them?

The goddess Tanit and her consort Baal Hammon were the chief deities of Carthage. This coin from Carthage from circa 300 B.C. has Tanit depicted on its obverse.

## Neologist's Lexicon

Use the stems in this list to create a new word (neologism). Give the word, the pronunciation, the part of speech, the etymology, and the definition(s). Keep a record of the neologisms you create from list to list. Here are some examples:

**cosmophobia** (kosmo FO bia) n. [*cosmo* (universe), *phobia* (fear)] 1. the pathological fear of space travel 2. the fear of escaping the earth's gravitational field

**prephoria** (pre FOR ia) n. [*pre* (before), *phor* (carry)] 1. the ecstatic certainty that something is about to happen 2. an unexplained foolish confidence in the future

## Sesquipedalian Poetry

Use words from List 38 (and previous lists if you like) to write a poem. This time, use visual and typographical devices to add emphasis to the meaning. Lighten up! Be inventive and courageous. Have fun. An example:

### LoCUS psychus for the Desultory Funambulist, Op. 5, in C major

> mental universe
>> self precursor peeks, this self, this *idée fixe*
>
> planets of my M I N D, mine.  My mined
>
> ========black h o l e OOOOOOh!!!
>
> Lies!  Reeks, Bowdler eyes @$%^&, whys?
>> (((inTERnal))) cosmoSSSSSSSSSSSSSSSSssssssssssss.............._____
>
> waveform apotheosis of desultory EUphony/sound of reason?/syllogism---SCHISM []
>> { . . . . nihilism . . . .}
>
> sound of syllogism....oh **lyssoPHOBIA be a foe be an afff be anaphora whoa+++++**
>> What sound [euphony?]
>>> do thoughts reiterate,,,,,,,,,,,,
>>>> as they course through
>>>>> the psyche? All A is B **whooosshh**
>>>>>> C is A **zzzzzzzzzzzzzzzzzzzzzzzz**
>>>>>>> therefore C is A **whwhwhwhwhwhwhwh**

| | | | | | |
|---|---|---|---|---|---|
| • pro | (forward) | prolix | • ous | (full of) | sententious |
| • liqu | (flow) | prolix | • viv | (life) | on the *qui vive* |
| • ism | (doctrine) | narcissism | • miss | (send) | manumission |
| • mis (G*) | (bad) | miscreant | • sanct | (holy) | sanction |
| • cred | (believe) | miscreant | • terr | (land) | *terra firma* |
| • gno | (know) | physiognomy | • syn | (together) | synopsis |
| • phys | (nature) | physiognomy | • opia | (sight) | synopsis |
| • pater | (father) | patrician | • co | (together) | colloquy |
| • sta** | (stand) | apostasy | • loqu | (talk) | colloquy |
| • apo | (away) | apostasy | • loco | (place) | *in loco parentis* |
| • hedon | (pleasure) | hedonism | • in | (in) | *in loco parentis* |

**prolix** (tediously wordy)  His tiring conversation was both prolix and vacuous.

**narcissism** (self-infatuation)  He had a narcissistic love of his own reflection.

**miscreant** (evil unbeliever)  A gang of assassins and miscreants attacked the caravan.

**physiognomy** (facial character)  To read the physiognomy is no art, thought Duncan.

**patrician** (aristocratic)  The dignitary's patrician aloofness offended some people.

**apostasy** (desertion of principle)  Worse than disloyalty is apostasy.

**hedonism** (devotion to pleasure)  His ascetic discipline degenerated into hedonism.

**sententious** (full of maxims)  The novelist's pompous, sententious prose style bored her.

**on the *qui vive*** (on the alert)  Be on the *qui vive* for a sign of compromise from the enemy.

**manumission** (release from slavery)  The refusal was an act of self-manumission.

• • • •

**sanction** (authorize)  We do not sanction the use of our firm's name.

**terra firma** (solid ground)  It is good to stand on *terra firma* after a rough voyage.

**synopsis** (summary)  She wrote a brief synopsis of the course for the students.

**colloquy** (conversation)  They enjoyed a private colloquy in the corner.

**in loco parentis** (in place of parents)  Schools often act *in loco parentis*.

*G means of German origin.
**We introduce a new definition of *sta*.

## As Used by James Fenimore Cooper in *The Last of the Mohicans*

Another long and deliberate pause succeeded these **sententious** questions.

| | | | | | | | | |
|---|---|---|---|---|---|---|---|---|
| **Parts of Speech:** | adj. | adj. conj. | adj. | n. | v. | adj. | **adj.** | n. |
| **Parts of Sentence:** | | | | subj. | AVP | | | D.O. |
| **Phrases:** | ----no prepositional, appositive, or verbal phrases---- | | | | | | | |
| **Clauses:** | ----------------------------------independent clause------------------------------- one independent clause; a simple, declarative sentence | | | | | | | |

Here Cooper uses the adjective *sententious* (moralizing, pompous) to modify the direct object, the plural common noun *questions*.

## Pronunciation

| | | | |
|---|---|---|---|
| **prolix** | pro LIX | **on the *qui vive*** | KEE VEEV |
| **narcissism** | NAR sih sizz em | **manumission** | MAN yoo MISH un |
| **miscreant** | MISS kree ant | **sanction** | SANK shun |
| **physiognomy** | fizz ee O no mee | ***terra firma*** | TERR ah FIR ma |
| **patrician** | pah TRISH an | **synopsis** | sin OP siss |
| **apostasy** | ah POSS ta see | **colloquy** | KOLL o kwee |
| **hedonism** | HEE don izm | ***in loco parentis*** | in LO ko pa RENT iss |
| **sententious** | sen TEN shuss | | |

## Spanish Cognates

| | | | |
|---|---|---|---|
| **narcissism** | narcisismo | **prolix** | prolijo |
| **hedonism** | hedonismo | **apostasy** | apostasía |
| **sententious** | sentencioso | **patrician** | patricio |
| **colloquy** | coloquio | **synopsis** | sinopsis |

1.  *Terra firma* is fun to use.  It is exotic and reminds us of exploration, of setting foot on solid (*firma*) ground (*terra*) at last after a voyage on the high seas.  But we can also use *terra firma* in wonderful metaphorical ways, such as comparing the *terra firma* of philosophical realism and scientific method to the flights and perils of philosophical idealism and deductive, *a priori* reasoning.  Be creative in your use of *terra firma*.

2.  The adjective **patrician**, historically, referred to the ancient Roman noble class and is the opposite of the adjective **plebeian**, the ancient Roman lower class.  Today, we still refer to aristocratic people as *patrician* and to the common people as *plebeian*, but great care should be used with these words because they possess connotations that are offensive to our democratic values.  The word *plebeian* suggests that someone is coarse, vulgar, unrefined, and ignorant.  It gives offense and should be avoided when no offense is intended.

3.  Narcissus was the beautiful youth in Greek mythology who first fell in love with Echo (read Ovid's *Metamorphoses*—I like the Rolfe Humphries translation—for the wonderful story) and later fell in love with his own reflection in the water.  When he could not find the person he saw in the water, he pined away and metamorphosed into the narcissus flower.  **Narcissism** is extreme self-infatuation with one's own appearance or accomplishments.

4.  It is interesting to compare **physiognomy** with **countenance** and **visage**.  The **visage** is what you look (*vid*, *vis*) at: the physical features and form of the face.  The **countenance** is the contents of the face, the feelings that are contained or held (*tenere*) together (*con*) in the features of the face. In *King Lear*, Kent tells Lear that there is "something in your countenance which I would fain call Master."  The **physiognomy** is knowing (*gno*, *gnom*) the nature (*phys*) of the person by looking at the face.  These words have subtle differences and overlapping meanings.  At times, all three are used to refer to the expressions and emotions of the face, but we tend to slightly separate the meanings.  A person might have a red visage, an angry countenance, and a noble physiognomy.

5.  **Hedonism**, which comes from the Greek word for pleasure (*hedone*), refers to a philosophical ethical doctrine that the chief aim of life is pleasure—that the pursuit of pleasure is what contributes to the greatest happiness of the individual and of society.  This idea of pleasure as good is in striking contrast to many other ethical systems that regard pleasure as bad and regard various forms of asceticism as good.

6.  A **Classic Word**: The noun **physiognomy** derives from a Greek word for judging a person by the features of his or her face.  *Vide* note 4, above.  We find *physiognomy* in the novels of Walter Scott, the Brontës, Hawthorne, Stowe, and Melville.  The philosopher-humorist Melville used the word in a way that both was and was not a reference to the physical features of the face: "Physiognomically regarded, the Sperm Whale is an anomalous creature.  He has no proper nose."  Yes, but then again, Melville was an anomalous creature, who had no proper knows, either, and I doubt if his physiognomy would have revealed much besides a marine depth and the intimation of things moving below the surface.

Philip V (238-179 B.C.) became king of Macedonia in 221 when he was just seventeen years old. He was his country's most able ruler in the line that followed Alexander the Great, but he made the error of becoming an enemy of Rome. He became concerned about the Roman influence in Illyria, and he began military operations to extend his control. In 215 after the Roman defeat at Cannae, he entered into a treaty with Hannibal—a treaty that helped neither but that caused the Romans to begin hostilities in Greece in the First Macedonian War. That war was terminated with no significant harm to Philip. Rome began a Second Macedonian War soon after it had accepted the surrender of Carthage. This time it decisively beat Philip, forced him to pay a large indemnity, and send his younger son to Rome as a hostage. Eventually, the younger son became a proponent of working with the Romans, while the older son, Perseus, wanted a more aggressive policy. Philip had to make a choice, and he reluctantly executed his younger son for treason. His older son succeeded him, unwisely and unsuccessfully fought with the Romans, and thereby became the last king of Macedonia; the Romans made Macedonia into Roman provinces.

# ROME AND CARTHAGE—THE PUNIC WARS (218-205)
## Dr. Thomas Milton Kemnitz

Hannibal was unable to take Rome; his army was too small and not suited to siege warfare. The Romans were unable to defeat him, but they grew tired of the Fabian strategy, which many considered cowardly. They elected new consuls to pursue a more aggressive strategy and brought together their largest army ever of eight legions into the field against Hannibal. At Cannae in 215, Hannibal lured the entire Roman army into a pitched battle, and on that day Rome suffered a catastrophic defeat. The legion maniple configuration of the Roman army was vulnerable to attack on its flanks; the Roman legion was designed to fight an enemy that was in front of it, not one attacking on its side. The flanks had to be defended by auxiliaries and cavalry. Hannibal's strategy was to have the center of his line retreat, allowing the center of the Roman army to advance until the line was a huge arc. Then Hannibal advanced on the flanks, and he sent his cavalry around to attack from the rear to envelop the Romans. The Roman commander inadvertently assisted Hannibal by deploying an unusually deep and closely packed center—employing a strategy designed to break the enemy center. The Carthaginians lost perhaps 12,000 soldiers at Cannae; the Romans lost nearly the entire army—between 40,000 and 75,000 men. What made this loss the more devastating was that only relatively prosperous Roman citizens served in the army during this period.

The result of this huge defeat was that the towns of Magna Grecia in southern Italy and Sicily abandoned Rome and came to side with the Carthaginians. The Macedonian king, Philip V, opened negotiations with Hannibal to join him in war against Rome in an attempt to expand the Macedonian Empire to the west into Illyria. Hannibal offered peace to the Roman Senate on lenient terms, but the Senate responded by a general conscription to raise a new army. Again the Romans reacted to defeat by adjusting their military practices; no longer would commands be split, and the maniple formation was broken up into a more flexible cohort arrangement that would be used for centuries. The Romans returned to the policy of Fabius of not offering pitched battle but harassing Hannibal's troops and forcing him to operate in increasingly confined areas. Although Hannibal had successes, including completely destroying two Roman armies in 212, menacing the gates of Rome in 211, and killing two consuls in battle in 208, he could not get reinforcements from Carthage, and eventually the Romans cut his supply lines. It took a decade, but by 205 Hannibal was contained in the toe of Italy. Meanwhile the Romans took the fight against the Carthaginians to Hispania, where they successfully defeated Hannibal's brother and drove the enemy out of the Iberian peninsula. The Romans discovered the planned alliance between Hannibal and Philip V of Macedonia when they captured the emissaries from both sides with a letter from Hannibal outlining the agreement. This led to a war against Philip in 211—called the First Macedonian War—in which Rome dealt with the threat effectively and signed a peace treaty in 205 without any loss to the Romans or gain for the Macedonians. Syracuse had seen the Roman defeat at Cannae as an opportunity to join the forces of those resisting Rome. The Romans besieged the city in 214 and took it in 212; in taking Syracuse, the troops killed Archimedes, the one man the Romans desperately wanted alive for his genius in devising machines of war.

What is remarkable about this period is that although they could not defeat Hannibal in Italy, the Romans were powerful enough to fight the Macedonia Empire on more than equal terms, to reduce Syracuse—once one of the three great powers in the central Mediterranean—to a vassal state, and to conquer much of the Iberian peninsula—what is now Spain—along with intervening territory along the southern coast of Gaul.

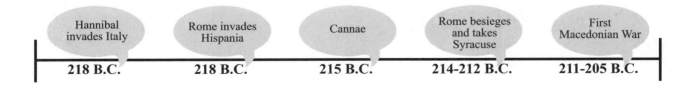

| Hannibal invades Italy | Rome invades Hispania | Cannae | Rome besieges and takes Syracuse | First Macedonian War |
|---|---|---|---|---|
| 218 B.C. | 218 B.C. | 215 B.C. | 214-212 B.C. | 211-205 B.C. |

In each case below, one of the choices was really the word used by the author in the sentence provided. All of the choices can be found in the example words on the first page of this lesson. Your challenge is to decide which word the author used. This is not a test; it is more like a game because more than one word choice may work perfectly well. See if you can use your sensitivity and intuition to guess correctly which word the author used.

1.  **From Joseph Heller's *Catch-22***

    He's the one who tipped me off that our prose was too _____.
    a. narcissistic
    b. prolix
    c. hedonistic
    d. patrician

2.  **From George Orwell's *1984***

    "Thoughtcrime is a dreadful thing, old man," he said _____.
    a. narcissistically
    b. on the *qui vive*
    c. *in loco parentis*
    d. sententiously

3.  **From Mark Twain's *The Prince and the Pauper***

    But let these _____ look well to themselves.
    a. miscreants
    b. hedonists
    c. apostates
    d. narcissists

4.  **From John F. Kennedy's *Profiles in Courage***

    The *Greenfield Gazette* called him a(n) _____.
    a. apostate
    b. patrician
    c. miscreant
    d. synopsis

5.  **From Henry James's *The American***

    [He had] a prominent blue eye, a German _____, and a massive watch-chain.
    a. colloquy
    b. physiognomy
    c. narcissism
    d. prolixity

Though it is a good thing to have a rich vocabulary, it is not a good thing to abuse that vocabulary by writing verbose, abstruse, sesquipedalian sentences. Those who overuse their vocabularies often do so at the expense of clarity. Translate the following showy, ponderous passage into graceful, direct English. Do not use slang, but do use words that seem familiar and comfortable.

BACK ON *TERRA FIRMA* after his officially sanctioned voyage to Io, the narcissistic hedonist gazed with pleasure at the reflection of his patrician physiognomy in the mirror. With a slow suspiration, he remembered the sententious miscreants and apostates whose prolix colloquies had disrupted his speech to the Solar Assembly. His topic, "An Argument for the Manumission of Robots," had not been well-received, especially his theory that the state should act *in loco parentis* for all robots during the first year after their construction. His synopsis of the ethical problems of advanced robotics was misunderstood and greeted with an incredulous cacophony, despite his reiterations that the rights of robots should never supersede the legal rights of *Homo sapiens*.

Even this did not mollify the acerbic and undisciplined autodidacts. It was an obvious *a priori* truth, he felt, that principles of ethics should apply to inanimate beings—there being a clear dichotomy between right and wrong—but the demotic masses demanded *a posteriori* evidence. You had to show them. In this introspective and saturnine mood, he perambulated off, wondering if a Solar Confederacy plagued with nihilists and neophytes could long endure.

This is a cinerary urn for the ashes of an infant or a young child. The Carthaginians sacrificed young children to the goddess Tanit and her consort Baal Hammon. The bodies were cremated and put in these small, unmarked urns.

## Reading Comprehension

1. For Translation 39, which of the following does the passage suggest?
   - a. In general, hedonists are ethical individuals.
   - b. Principles of ethics should apply to inanimate beings.
   - c. The hedonist is unwilling to consider that his ideas might be flawed.
   - d. Most people do not listen to the ideas of others.

2. Which of the following best describes the passage?
   - a. An insecure intellectual unfairly blames others for his own poor work.
   - b. A group of Philistines treats a thoughtful and philosophical presenter unfairly.
   - c. Individuals fail to give each others' sides fair consideration.
   - d. Colonists on Jupiter's moons suffer a breakdown in civilization.

## Analogies

3. **NARCISSISM : HEDONISM ::**
   - a. pleasure : self-infatuation
   - b. happiness : misery
   - c. self-admirer : sybarite
   - d. narcolepsy : sleep

4. **PROLIX : COLLOQUY ::**
   - a. verbose : interlocution
   - b. provide : telescope
   - c. promote : cosponsor
   - d. lecture : acerbic

## Antonyms

5. **PATRICIAN :**
   - a. fatherly
   - b. plebeian
   - c. pariah
   - d. brahmin

6. **APOSTASY :**
   - a. treachery
   - b. chauvinism
   - c. loyalty
   - d. compliance

This is an Etruscan trumpet and shield. The Etruscans were said to have been the first to use the trumpet, which was quickly adopted by the Greeks and then by the Romans.

**evaluation**

Which is a more serious fault in a person's conversation: to be **prolix** or to be **sententious**? [*tediously wordy*] [*full of maxims*] Explain the criteria by which you judge this to be a fault.

**analysis**

Explain why the noun **physiognomy** means what it means, based on its etymology or stem construction. Similarly, explain the meaning of **apostasy** and of **colloquy**. You may use a dictionary for extra information.

**analysis**

Read *Macbeth*, and notice Duncan's line about the treacherous Thane of Cawdor. Duncan says that there is "no art to find the mind's construction in the face" and that the Thane of Cawdor was "a gentleman on whom I build an absolute trust." Is Duncan referring to the Thane's **visage**, **countenance**, or **physiognomy**? Do you understand why Duncan's line is ironic?

**application**

The noun **synopsis** refers to a brief summary, such as a fifty-word summary of the plot of a novel. You will see synopses of novels, of plays, and of college courses (a longer, more detailed description of a college course and its requirements is called a **syllabus**). Obviously, in order to write a synopsis, one must clearly understand and dramatically condense—one must, as Striver notes in Dickens's *A Tale of Two Cities*, "extract the essence." Write a synopsis of fifty words or fewer of a classic novel or play you have read this year.

**convergence**

If you were to become a regular user of either the word **sententious**, the word **apostasy**, or the word **narcissism**, which word would you choose? Explain why.

**imagination**

Creative writing is a wonderful way to use imagination—the process of creating images. Use one of the words in List 39 as the basis for a lush descriptive paragraph or short story in which you imagine a scene as vividly as possible. For example: A shipwreck survivor finally reaches *terra firma*, the sandy beach of a desert island. In great detail, describe the survivor's experience at that moment.

This is a dish from Campania made about the time Hannibal was fighting in Italy. The inscription is in Latin, and it is an indication of the cohesion of the Roman system that frustrated Hannibal in his attempt to find allies among the Italian cities.

**Neologist's Lexicon**

Use the stems in this list to create a new word (neologism). Give the word, the pronunciation, the part of speech, the etymology, and the definition(s). Keep a record of the neologisms you create from list to list. Here are some examples:

**gnostasis** (no STA sis) n. [*gno* (know), *sta* (stop), *sis* (condition)] 1. having one's opinions or ideas fixed and unchangeable 2. the condition of being closed-minded

**liquhedonism** (lick yu HEE don ism) n. [*liqu* (flow), *hedon* (pleasure)] 1. the inordinate love of streams and waterfalls 2. an obsession with flowing water

**Sesquipedalian Hemingway Prose (??)**

The twentieth-century American writer Ernest Hemingway was known for his terse, journalistic style. Hemingway's method was to emphasize nouns and verbs; to write simple, declarative sentences; to develop flow through run-on sentences; to avoid long words; and to describe characters' behaviors rather than their thoughts. Read one of Hemingway's Nick Adams stories, and then imitate his writing. An example:

### Big Two-Handed River

Rick sat in colloquy with himself on the sand of the bank of the river. The big two-handed river. The river was cold and the water of the river slipped down through the *terra firma* of the mountains where the rain fell quickly on the high slopes and the sententious thunder never sounded prolix, not even to Rick. The river ran straight and clear and cold and wet and flowed on both sides of the island covered with saplings and Rick sat on the moist sand of the bank and felt the pure patrician hedonism of the moment and knew instinctively that the sun was striking the top of his head, making a shadow in the water of the river that ran in front of his face and moved quickly down its bank into the valley below.

On the *qui vive*, Rick sensed that the river flowed to the left of the island and flowed to the right of the island, like a water god with two big hands, a god of water with a liquid and rippling physiognomy, a face you could look into and not feel the pain. Rick felt comfortable here. And he did not feel the pain. The sand of the river gave a cool manumission from the narcissism of life down in the town, down in the valley, where the streets ran parallel in the sun and the miscreants' houses stuck up between the streets, covered by roofs, like an apostasy from nature. The god of water did not visit the streets of the town.

Something in Rick began to move, to sanction a change, and Rick reached for his tackle box and took the line and cool metal hook and pushed the bait carefully onto the hook, carefully so that the fish would take it. He could not see the fish, but the fish would be there, in the shadow of the birches on the far bank, and the fish was there now, waiting for him, *in loco parentis*, to teach him things that his parents never taught him. He could not remember his parents, but he could remember the fish, and he played out the line and cast it into the cool water in the shade of the birches on the far bank, and the fish came and took the bait, as Rick knew it would. I am sorry, Fish, Rick said. It is you who must feel the pain so that I do not need to feel it. And the river moved, and continued to move, on the left hand of the island of birches and on the right hand.

| • **vale** | (farewell) | valediction | • sur | (over) | surrealistic |
|---|---|---|---|---|---|
| • diet | (say) | valediction, diction | • *ana* | (up) | analects |
| • *proto* | (first) | protagonist | • *lect* | (gather) | analects |
| • *agon* | (actor) | protagonist | • ex | (out) | expository, exegesis |
| • mal | (bad) | maladroit | • pos | (put) | expository |
| • *ism* | (doctrine) | stoicism | • magn | (great) | magnum opus |
| • *sarco* | (flesh) | sarcophagus | • mort | (death) | moribund |
| • *phag* | (eat) | sarcophagus | • super | (over) | supercilious |
| • *gno* | (know) | ignominious | • miss | (send) | emissary |

**valediction** (farewell speech) Read Donne's poem "Valediction, Forbidding Morning."

**protagonist** (leading person) Oedipus is the protagonist of Sophocles's tragedy, *Oedipus Rex*.

**maladroit** (clumsy) His maladroit groping for the handle was humorous to observe.

**stoicism** (indifference to sensation) His austere stoicism helped him overcome the pain.

**sarcophagus** (stone coffin) The sarcophagus's cold, sculpted surface was mossy.

**ignominious** (disgraceful) The convicted traitor faced a future of ignominious oblivion.

**surrealistic** (unrealistically imaginary) Dali's dreamy, surrealistic art is popular.

**analects** (selected writings) She loved reading *The Analects* of Confucius.

**expository** (explanatory) His essay was expository, not creatively descriptive.

**exegesis** (critical interpretation) Her brilliant exegesis of *The Inferno* impressed us all.

•    •    •

**magnum opus** (great work) Dante's magnum opus, *The Divine Comedy*, is a classic.

**moribund** (dying) The moribund economy affected the stock market.

**supercilious** (scornful) His arrogant, supercilious manner irked us.

**diction** (word choice) Her scholarly Latin diction was impressive to the students.

**emissary** (messenger) An emissary sent out from the Queen suddenly arrived.

**As Used by Maya Angelou in** *I Know Why the Caged Bird Sings*

| | I | spoke | in | **supercilious** | accents. |
|---|---|---|---|---|---|
| **Parts of Speech:** | pron. | v. | prep. | **adj.** | n. |
| **Parts of Sentence:** | subj. | AVP | | | |

**Phrases:** ----------prepositional phrase----------

**Clauses:** -------------------------------independent clause------------------------------------
one independent clause; a simple, declarative sentence

Here Angelou uses the adjective *supercilious* to modify the object of the preposition, the plural common noun *accents*. Note that *accents* cannot be a direct object because it is the object of the preposition; it cannot be both.

## Pronunciation

| | | | |
|---|---|---|---|
| **valediction** | val eh DICT shun | **expository** | ex POZZ ih tory |
| **protagonist** | pro TAG on ist | **exegesis** | ex eh JEE siss |
| **maladroit** | MAL ah droit | **magnum opus** | mag num OP us |
| **stoicism** | STO ih sizzem | **moribund** | MORE ih bund |
| **sarcophagus** | sar KOFF a guss | **supercilious** | super SILL ee us |
| **ignominious** | ig no MIN ee us | **diction** | DICT shun |
| **surrealistic** | sur re a LISS tik | **emissary** | EM iss ary |
| **analects** | AN ah lekts | | |

## Spanish Cognates

| | | | |
|---|---|---|---|
| **stoicism** | estoicismo | **ignominious** | ignominioso |
| **moribund** | moribundo | **exegesis** | exégesis |
| **emissary** | emisario | **protagonist** | protagonista |
| **sarcophagus** | sarcófago | **surrealistic** | surrealista |

1. A **Micropoem**: The adjective **supercilious** means scornful or haughty and comes from the Latin *super* (over) and *cilium* (eyebrow)—raised eyebrow. In other words, the word describes the scornful facial expression of the contemptuous person. Notice that we see *cilium* in other words, such as the cilia of the cells we study in biology.

2. The noun **stoicism** comes from *ism* (doctrine) plus the Greek *stoa* (porch or colonnade) and refers to the philosophy of Zeno, who taught in the shade of a colonnade in Athens in about 308 B.C. Zeno believed that all things are controlled by immutable natural laws and that the wise person should simply follow virtue and nothing else. This means that the wise person would focus on virtue and be indifferent to all but virtue—indifferent to pleasure, to pain, to passion, to emotion. When we say that someone is stoical, we mean that this person resembles the Greek Stoics in his or her austere indifference to sensation or emotion. If you are interested in reading a marvelous ancient work of stoicism, read *The Meditations* of Roman emperor Marcus Aurelius, who was a student of Epictetus (eh pick TEET us), his slave, whose writings we also still read.

    By the way, do you remember Zeno's paradox? A paradox is a true contradiction, such as Socrates's famous paradox, "I only know that I know nothing." Zeno's paradox is that if you move toward something in steps, going half the distance that remains in each step, you will never get there. If you do, you have cheated by going more than half the distance.

3. We call a stone coffin, especially an elaborate or monumental one, a **sarcophagus**. This noun comes from the Greek word *sarkophagos*—*sarx* (flesh) and *phagein* (to eat)—and refers to the Greek and Roman practice of burying the dead in great limestone coffins because limestone contributed to the rapid breakdown of the body placed in the coffin. The Greeks and the Romans often carved, inscribed, and elaborately ornamented the sarcophagi.

4. A **protagonist** is a first (*proto*) actor (*agon*). The *agon* in the word *protagonist* actually traces back to the Greek *agonistes* (actor), but earlier, the **agon** was a contest, which reminds us that the early Greek tragedies were performed as contests, with leading tragedians such as Sophocles, Aeschylus, and Euripides competing against each other for top prize. The protagonist in a drama is often confronted, of course, by an **antagonist**. The foe of the brave protagonist Popeye is the boorish antagonist Bluto, whom all admirable people detest.

5. You would not expect **stoic** to be a good **Classic Word** because it seems so philosophical and scholarly, even arcane. But *stoic* has been used by Defoe, Scott, Cooper, the Brontës, Melville, Hardy, Crane, Wharton, and Wilder. One of the best sentences is from Defoe, who in his 1719 novel *Robinson Crusoe* wrote, "It would have made a stoic smile to have seen me and my little family sit down to dinner." Charlotte Brontë wisely noted that "The sternest-seeming stoic is human after all." Stephen Crane described the martial "cheerings, moblike and barbaric, but tuned in strange keys that can arouse the dullard and the stoic." Melville, with characteristic mock-solemnity, reasoned, "This Right Whale I take to have been a Stoic; the Sperm Whale, a Platonian, who might have taken up Spinoza in his latter years." Hardy's Yeobright "was an absolute stoic in the face of mishaps which only affected his social standing."

Publius Cornelius Scipio

# ROME AND CARTHAGE—THE PUNIC WARS (205–202)
## Dr. Thomas Milton Kemnitz

Eventually Rome turned to Publius Cornelius Scipio, who had been victorious in Hispania, to send a Roman army to North Africa to attack Carthage, thereby forcing Hannibal to leave Italy. Scipio's expedition left in 204 B.C., and in 203 he was able to destroy the combined Carthaginian and Nubian army by setting fire to its camp at night, putting the forces to flight in panic; the Romans killed some 40,000 of the enemy. Scipio then deposed the Nubian king and put his ally on the throne, thereby assuring he would have the aid of the ferocious Nubian cavalry in the battles to follow. Hannibal was recalled from Italy, and his army met Scipio's at Zama in 202. Hannibal relied on 100 war elephants to open large gaps in the Roman lines, but Scipio set traps in front of his lines for the elephants and established battle lines that ran perpendicular to the enemy's, with large gaps into which the elephants that survived the traps were steered. Many of the elephants turned around at the sound of Roman trumpets and charged Hannibal's troops. This was always the risk of deploying war elephants, and their handlers usually carried a hammer and spike to drive into the animals' brains if they turned in the wrong direction. The battle of Zama was decisive; the Carthaginians were forced to make peace on Scipio's terms. Hannibal was clearly a great general, but he lost one battle to Scipio. Scipio, like Alexander, never lost a battle.

The Romans who fought and finally won the Second Punic War in 202 were a truly extraordinary civilization. They had improvised arrangements with the people they had overwhelmed throughout Italy, mostly treating the defeated with unprecedented and unparalleled generosity during a period of several centuries. The result was that now—in the last years of the third century B.C.—those former foes considered themselves Romans or so allied with Rome that they stood by Rome even in its darkest hour after the defeat at Cannae. The 50,000 or more men who had fought and died in the Roman army at Cannae had been among the most prosperous of the Romans and their allies. They had been the farmers and their sons—grown men and adolescents who had come from the small and medium-sized agricultural holdings throughout central Italy, augmented by the more prosperous urban merchants and their sons from the towns surrounding Rome, as well as from the capital. There was huge consternation in Rome when the news of their defeat arrived, as well as some panic before cooler heads prevailed. The Roman response to this devastating defeat was to declare a thirty-day mourning period and then mandate an end to all mourning. They banned weeping in public and the utterance of *pax*, the Latin word for peace. They spurned Hannibal's offer for a truce and began to raise more troops, taking in more men from the lower ranks of the Roman world. They began to reform the army to prevent a repeat of the Cannae disaster. At no point did they consider peace or a truce or concessions or any other expedient. Their idea of a concession was to alter their tactics to the less aggressive ones introduced by Fabius.

The Second Punic War altered Rome. The frugal and self-reliant folks who stood in the ranks at Cannae and who mourned their passing in Rome were in many ways the last of their lot. In the next decade, the spoils of war made many Romans rich. Captured peoples from the West and the East were brought to Rome as slaves. There was an increasingly plentiful supply of slave labor to do the hard work the Romans used to do themselves. The huge influx of slaves undercut the working poor and reduced the value of their labor at the same time that it made life easier for the prosperous. The spoils of war included gold and silver, coinage and trophies, and that made the already-prosperous richer and created fabulous wealth for some families. The Romans might still value frugality, but they preached it rather than practiced it. They were conquerors, and that changed them utterly.

Rome invades North Africa — **204 B.C.**

Scipio defeats Hannibal at Zama — **202 B.C.**

End of Second Punic War — **202 B.C.**

In each case below, one of the choices was really the word used by the author in the sentence provided. All of the choices can be found in the example words on the first page of this lesson. Your challenge is to decide which word the author used. This is not a test; it is more like a game because more than one word choice may work perfectly well. See if you can use your sensitivity and intuition to guess correctly which word the author used.

1. **From Aldous Huxley's *Brave New World***

   He had imagined himself..._____ accepting suffering without a word.
   a. maladroitly
   b. surrealistically
   c. superciliously
   d. stoically

2. **From Charles Dickens's *Great Expectations***

   He there delivered his _____ remarks.
   a. valedictory
   b. ignominious
   c. expository
   d. maladroit

3. **From Rachel Carson's *Silent Spring***

   The few birds seen anywhere were _____; they trembled violently.
   a. moribund
   b. supercilious
   c. stoic
   d. surrealistic

4. **From Jane Austen's *Pride and Prejudice***

   Elizabeth still saw _____ in their treatment of every body.
   a. surrealism
   b. diction
   c. stoicism
   d. superciliousness

5. **From Herman Melville's *Moby Dick***

   A German _____ supposes that Jonah must have taken refuge in the floating body of a dead whale.
   a. stoic
   b. exegetist
   c. emissary
   d. sarcophagus

Though it is a good thing to have a rich vocabulary, it is not a good thing to abuse that vocabulary by writing verbose, abstruse, sesquipedalian sentences. Those who overuse their vocabularies often do so at the expense of clarity. Translate the following showy, ponderous passage into graceful, direct English. Do not use slang, but do use words that seem familiar and comfortable.

AS THE LOQUACIOUS and gregarious audience came to silence, the curtain rose behind the proscenium. Strange lighting effects, translucent panels, and monolithic forms gave the scene a surrealistic and moribund look. A great limestone sarcophagus carved with the face of a lycanthrope and incised with the single word VALEDICTION stood at the right. With a supercilious physiognomy, a patrician protagonist, Agonistes, glared down condescendingly at an obsequious and pusillanimous emissary from the Great Mooboo, a high-ranking and lionized official in the hierarchy of the plutocracy.

"Speak, ignominious neophyte," said Agonistes.

"Noble Sir," replied the emissary, "I am instructed to summon you to My Worship's palace and to say that you must answer for your perfidious writings."

"Tell your 'worship,' if that's what he is, you miscreant," said Agonistes with sangfroid, "that my expository exegesis of his sententious analects—that vacuous so-called magnum opus, HA!—is none of his concern. Wait until he sees my synopsis of his soporific self-proclaimed classic! That egocentric autodidact! His delineation will soon be the *locus classicus* for *non sequiturs* and false syllogisms! I will not be summoned by you or by him. If he sees no dichotomy between my sedate stoicism and his narcissistic hedonism, then he is nothing more than a maladroit and nihilistic apostate who has abandoned the sacrosanct ideas of our official cosmology."

"How prolix!" whispered the abased emissary in a *sotto voce* suspiration.

"Is that a soliloquy," retorted Agonistes, "or is it merely your demotic diction that makes you so inaudible? Perambulate back to your worship, and tell him I will not mollify his acerbity."

Roman key

## Reading Comprehension

1.  In Translation 40, it can be inferred that:
    a. The Mooboo misjudged how Agonistes would respond to his emissary.
    b. Agonistes is making a terrible mistake in speaking so to the emissary.
    c. Agonistes is playing a clever role to conceal his fear.
    d. The emissary is actually the Mooboo in disguise.

2.  The author does all of the following EXCEPT:
    a. describe the appearance of the sarcophagus
    b. reveal the philosophical difference between Agonistes and the Mooboo
    c. explain what is perfidious about Agonistes's writings
    d. show Agonistes's opinion of the Mooboo's writings

## Analogies

3.  **IGNOMINIOUS : MALADROIT ::**
    a. heinous : inept
    b. ignorant : malcontent
    c. disgraceful : shameful
    d. clumsy : ostracized

4.  **SUPERCILIOUS : STOIC ::**
    a. haughty : scornful
    b. indifferent : superior
    c. patronizing : impassive
    d. superior : stolid

## Antonyms

5.  **EXPOSITORY :**
    a. revealing
    b. fantastical
    c. poetic
    d. factual

6.  **VALEDICTION :**
    a. salutation
    b. welcome
    c. introduction
    d. explanation

Scipio was a favorite Roman hero, and busts of him in many formats were common in the Roman world.

## analysis and application

If you read *The Meditations* of Marcus Aurelius, you will find that he expresses his **stoicism** through the repetition and rephrasing of several principal ideas. Read *The Meditations*, and make a list of the three ideas you find most commonly reoccurring. Then consider what you have learned about stoicism, and describe a situation in life when stoicism would be an appropriate or appealing posture.

## intuition

In order to develop a vivid sense of what the adjective **surrealistic** means, look at a book of Salvador Dali's paintings with their melting clocks and anthropomorphic landscapes. Then drift into your imagination, and write a short story that takes place in a dreamy, surrealistic world of your own invention. ~dreamland

## synthesis and emotion

Read John Donne's poem "**Valediction**, Forbidding Morning." What other poems can you think of that have similar themes to this poem? Similar styles? How would you describe the emotional tone of the poem? If you were reading the poem aloud, how would you read it in order to properly convey the emotion of the poem? Do you feel the emotion as you read the poem?

## ethics

To be **supercilious** is to be scornful and condescending, looking down one's nose with one eyebrow (*cilia*) raised (*super*). Is it unethical to behave in a supercilious manner? Is it merely a matter of style? Can you think of a single instance in which supercilious condescension would be the right and good way to behave?

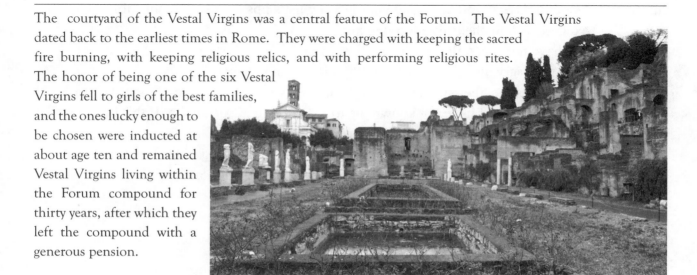

The courtyard of the Vestal Virgins was a central feature of the Forum. The Vestal Virgins dated back to the earliest times in Rome. They were charged with keeping the sacred fire burning, with keeping religious relics, and with performing religious rites. The honor of being one of the six Vestal Virgins fell to girls of the best families, and the ones lucky enough to be chosen were inducted at about age ten and remained Vestal Virgins living within the Forum compound for thirty years, after which they left the compound with a generous pension.

## Neologist's Lexicon

Use the stems in this list to create a new word (neologism). Give the word, the pronunciation, the part of speech, the etymology, and the definition(s). Keep a record of the neologisms you create from list to list. Here are some examples:

**superlection** (SOO pur LECK shun) n. [*super* (over), *lect* (gather), *tion* (act)]  1. acquiring possessions until you become unaware of what you possess  2. compulsive, indiscriminate collection of seashells, including every mediocre and pedestrian seashell on the beach

**sarcoposition** (SAR ko po ZISH un) n. [*sarco* (flesh), *pos* (put), *tion* (act)]  1. sitting in the middle of a seat for two so that no one else will sit down, as on a bus  2. sprawling out with arms and legs in a movie theater seat so that a stranger will not sit in either seat next to you

## Sesquipedalian Shakespeare

Using words from List 40, write a short satirical exchange that captures some of the flavor of a famous scene from a Shakespearean play. Remember to include some of the wonderful archaic language that we find in the plays. An example:

### Romero and Juleen

Romero enters and sees Juleen leaning against the Classic Coke machine. She sees him too, whispers to her friend, laughs, and looks demurely at a music video on the television. Instantly a star-crossed lover, Romero tremulously whispers, "Oh, she doth teach the video to glow!" He walks over to Juleen, reaches out, and touches the tip of his index finger to the tip of her index finger.

Romero:  If I profane, with my maladroit hand, this magnum opus, my lips, two expository emissaries, ready stand to conduct you to the realm of surrealistic forgiveness.

Juleen:  Good Emissary, you do wrong your protagonist's lips too much in this, for a scholarly exegesis is how the truly forgiving kiss.

Romero:  But have not supercilious scholars lips?

Juleen:  Aye, Emissary, lips that they forsooth must use in valediction.

Romero:  Oh, brave stoic, then no move make, while my valediction I take.  (kisses her)

Juleen:  Until this night, I have not known the true diction of a valediction. If this be farewell, prithee let me read all your final analects!  (kisses him)

Romero:  And yet my mind misgives some moribund end, yet hanging in the ignominious stars, to my despised life, and methinks I do presage the vile chill of a cold sarcophagus. (They kiss again.)

*finis*

| | | | | | |
|---|---|---|---|---|---|
| • *eu* | (good) | euthanasia | • *pater* | (father) | patronize |
| • *thanatos* | (death) | euthanasia | • *auto* | (self) | autochthonous |
| • in | (not) | ineffable | • inter | (between) | *inter alia* |
| • ped | (foot) | expedite | • bell | (war) | bellicose |
| • *hagio* | (saint) | hagiography | • *anthropo* | (man) | anthropomorphic |
| • *graph* | (write) | hagiography | • *morph* | (shape) | anthropomorphic |
| • mir | (wonder) | *mirabile dictu* | • mal | (bad) | malediction |
| • dict | (say) | *mirabile dictu* | • *xeno* | (stranger) | xenophobia |
| • *mel** | (honey) | mellifluous | • *phobia* | (fear) | xenophobia |
| • flu | (flow) | mellifluous | • spec | (look) | specious |

**euthanasia** (mercy killing)  She was opposed to euthanasia on moral grounds.

**ineffable** (inexpressible)  His overwhelming love for her was ineffable.

**expedite** (hasten)  Please expedite this matter, as time is short.

**expatiate** (to elaborate)  He loved expatiating on his deeds of valor.

**hagiography** (saint's biography)  This biography is too flattering; it is a hagiography.

**mirabile dictu** (wonderful to say)  He was, *mirabile dictu*, still alive after the fall.

**mellifluous** (honeyed)  Read the poet's mellifluous language.

**patronize** (condescend to)  He resented their patrician, patronizing attitude.

**autochthonous** (native)  Alexander honored the country's autochthonous inhabitants.

**inter alia** (among other things)  On the raft there were, *inter alia*, seven ducks.

•   •   •

**bellicose** (warlike)  The bellicose barbarian tribes in Gaul feuded constantly.

**anthropomorphic** (man-shaped)  The Greek gods were anthropomorphic.

**malediction** (a curse)  We heard the convict's muttered malediction.

**xenophobia** (fear of foreigners)  The xenophobic public hated the immigrant.

**specious** (false)  The specious argument looked to be true, but it was not.

*Latin *mel*: song; Greek *mel*: honey

**As Used by Bram Stoker in *Dracula***

| | He | smiled | with | an | **ineffably** | benign | superiority. |
|---|---|---|---|---|---|---|---|
| **Parts of Speech:** | pron. | v. | prep. | adj. | **adv.** | adj. | n. |
| **Parts of Sentence:** | subj. | AVP | | | | | |

**Phrases:** ------------------prepositional phrase--------------------

**Clauses:** ----------------------------------independent clause------------------------------------

one independent clause; a simple, declarative sentence

Here Stoker uses the adverb *ineffably* to modify an adjective, *benign,* that in turn modifies the object of the preposition, the singular common noun *superiority.* The noun *superiority* cannot be a direct object because it is an object of preposition.

## Pronunciation

| | | | |
|---|---|---|---|
| **euthanasia** | YOO than AZH ia | **autochthonous** | aw TOCK thon us |
| **ineffable** | in EFF uh bul | *inter alia* | inter AY lee ah |
| **expedite** | EX peh dite | **bellicose** | BELL ih kose |
| **expatiate** | ex PAY shee ate | **anthropomorphic** | AN thro po MOR fik |
| **hagiography** | hey jee OG raff ee | **malediction** | MAL uh dict shun |
| *mirabile dictu* | mir AH bee lay DICT oo | **xenophobia** | ZEE no FO bee ah |
| **mellifluous** | meh LIFF loo us | **specious** | SPEE shus |
| **patronize** | PAT ron ize | | |

## Spanish Cognates

| | | | |
|---|---|---|---|
| **euthanasia** | eutanasia | **bellicose** | belicoso |
| **malediction** | maldición | **mellifluous** | melifluo |
| **xenophobia** | xenofobia | **specious** | especioso |
| **autochthonous** | autóctono | **hagiography** | hagiografía |
| **expedite** | expedito | **ineffable** | inefable |

1. A **Micropoem**: The adjective **autochthonous** is from the Greek and means of the land (*chthon*) itself (*auto*). We have an image of original peoples rising naturally from the earth, like grasses or trees. One of the reasons that Alexander the Great of Macedon was so successful in his conquests was that he made a point of honoring the autochthonous inhabitants wherever he went. In fact, after defeating Darius, the Persian emperor, Alexander discovered that he had captured Darius's family: his mother, wife, and daughter. Alexander honored and respected them, even calling Darius's mother, Sisygambis, by the title *Mother*. (Later, when Alexander died, Sisygambis turned to the wall, refused to eat, and died in four days.) Alexander would pay homage to local gods and religious shrines, and he even adopted styles of Persian dress, to his own army's mortification. In one case, Alexander appointed a Persian general he had just defeated as the ruler of a captured city. This trust and respect earned Alexander the devotion of many peoples.

2. The noun **hagiography** can refer to the actual biography of a saint, but you are more likely to see it used metaphorically, as to describe a biography that is so respectful that it has lost all of its objectivity. There are a number of such reverent biographies on our library bookshelves, often written by those who wish to promote their political philosophies by making heroes out of their favorite governmental leaders. This raises the interesting possibility of the autohagiography (a neologism), the self-adulating autobiography of an egotist or narcissist.

3. The adjective **specious** is interesting to analyze. It refers to reasoning that is false, but by looking at the stems, we better understand the exact nature of specious reasoning. Specious reasoning is full of (*ous*) looks (*spec*). An obviously stupid or repulsive argument is not specious; a specious argument is appealing and cogent; it a false argument that looks good.

4. **Classic Words: Patronize** and **expatiate** are two words that get plenty of use in the classics. *Peter Pan's* Wendy sometimes speaks just a little patronisingly (yes, the word is sometimes spelled with an *s*). Henry Fleming, in *The Red Badge of Courage*, adopts an air of patronizing good humor. Melville's Pequod sometimes sails near the snug patronizing lee of churches. In *Uncle Tom's Cabin*, Marks patronizes a joke by a quiet introductory sniggle. Harriet Beecher Stowe liked *patronize* and used it often—but then, her vocabulary was so brilliantly colossal that she used many words often.

**Expatiate** seems to be an improbable verb for frequent use, and yet it is often used in the classics. We find it in Kenneth Grahame's *The Wind in the Willows*, in Thomas Hardy's *The Return of the Native*, in Herman Melville's *Moby Dick*, in Harriet Beecher Stowe's *Uncle Tom's Cabin*, and in Nathaniel Hawthorne's *The Scarlet Letter*. In his whale of a book, Melville was certainly to prove the truth of his own words: "From his mighty bulk the whale affords a most congenial theme whereon to enlarge, amplify, and generally expatiate." In fact, Melville even used *expatiate* to describe the whale's behavior. Melville hoped that the whale would "outlast all hunting, since he has a pasture to expatiate in, which is precisely twice as large as all Asia, both Americas, Europe and Africa, New Holland . . . ." Exactly what a whale would do while expatiating is one of the imponderable mysteries.

The Romans who fought the Punic Wars wore their togas with their right shoulders bare. Under their togas they wore only loincloths. Many prided themselves on their ability to withstand extremes of weather.

# ROME AND CARTHAGE—THE PUNIC WARS (204-146)
## Dr. Thomas Milton Kemnitz

When Rome turned to Publius Cornelius Scipio, who had been victorious in Hispania, it did so over the vigorous opposition of Fabius Maximus. Scipio was a determined and creative problem solver who was comfortable with bold strokes to achieve objectives, and Fabius was a naturally cautious man who sought to reduce risk and who would rather live with a problem than expose Rome to any danger to solve it. Their personalities were diametrically opposed, and the differences of strategy became personal. Fabius, much older and more entrenched in Rome, refused to allow Scipio to take Italian legions with him to Africa. Instead, he forced Scipio to raise the troops on his own, to find an army outside of the traditional means by which Rome had always sent troops into the field. As any determined problem solver would, Scipio raised his army, and that was the moment when the Roman Republic could be said to have been doomed. For once the Republic no longer controlled the army; once the troops were beholden to their commander rather than to the state, it was only a matter of time before a commander would use the army against the state. It was natural—and ominous—that Scipio turned to the battle-hardened veterans of his Iberian campaign to provide the backbone of his forces. Rome was moving away from a citizen army and toward a professional army.

The Romans emerged from the Second Punic War in 202 with control of large areas of Spain, as well as the west coast of Greece, Sardinia, Corsica, and almost all of Sicily. Rome was the dominant power in the central and western Mediterranean. It had proved itself able to fight on three fronts, adapt its army organization as it learned from defeats, and command the seas. In the next half-century, Rome would consolidate its command of the Mediterranean. The Romans provoked a Third Punic War in 148 B.C.; after a siege they breached the walls of Carthage and took the city. They went from house to house, taking the inhabitants captive. The 50,000 who were not killed were sold into slavery. The Romans had fought Carthage three times, and they had had enough of Carthage. They razed the walls, burned the city, and plowed under the remains in 146 B.C. Rome's most dangerous enemy was destroyed forever; the want of a Homer or a Thucydides leaves us with bare history instead of an inspiring epic.

In a series of actions in Greece, the Roman cohort formation proved itself far superior to the Greek phalanx, and the Romans won several pitched battles against Greek coalitions. Rome faced an alliance of Greek states, which led it in 146 B.C. (the same year Carthage was destroyed) to destroy the city of Corinth after triumphing over the Aeolian League. Greece was reduced to two Roman provinces, and the world Alexander had created was gone less than two centuries after his death. His undone conquest of the western Mediterranean had brought the end of his Macedonian Empire and of Greek independence. During this period, the Romans extended their territory in Hispania and in northern Africa, and they entered the Near East in pursuit of Hannibal, who eventually took poison rather than fall into Roman hands.

By 146 B.C. when they destroyed Corinth and Carthage almost simultaneously, the Romans had established themselves as the overwhelming power in the Mediterranean. Their conquests brought huge riches to some, slaves to many, and declining opportunity to most. Rome had obliterated its enemies, and now the most perilous threats to the Republic would be from within, not from without.

| Second Macedonian War | Seleucid War | Third Macedonian War | Fourth Macedonian War | Third Punic War begins | Rome destroys Carthage and Corinth |
|---|---|---|---|---|---|
| 200-196 B.C. | 192-188 B.C. | 172-168 B.C. | 150-148 B.C. | 148 B.C. | 146 B.C. |

In each case below, one of the choices was really the word used by the author in the sentence provided. All of the choices can be found in the example words on the first page of this lesson. Your challenge is to decide which word the author used. This is not a test; it is more like a game because more than one word choice may work perfectly well. See if you can use your sensitivity and intuition to guess correctly which word the author used.

1.   **From F. Scott Fitzgerald's *The Great Gatsby***

A universe of _____ gaudiness spun itself out in his brain.
a. bellicose
b. ineffable
c. xenophobic
d. specious

2.   **From E.M. Forster's *A Passage to India***

He did not _____ on his wrongs now, being happy.
a. expatiate
b. patronize
c. expedite
d. euthanize

3.   **From Toni Morrison's *Song of Solomon***

Out of the toothless mouth came the strong _____ voice of a twenty-year-old girl.
a. ineffable
b. anthropomorphic
c. autochthonous
d. mellifluent

4.   **From Charles Dickens's *Great Expectations***

London gentlemen cannot be expected to _____ local work.
a. expatiate
b. patronize
c. expedite
d. euthanize

5.   **From Emily Brontë's *Wuthering Heights***

Mr. Heathcliff...rose and _____ made the tea himself.
a. ineffably
b. mellifluously
c. expeditiously
d. speciously

Though it is a good thing to have a rich vocabulary, it is not a good thing to abuse that vocabulary by writing verbose, abstruse, sesquipedalian sentences. Those who overuse their vocabularies often do so at the expense of clarity. Translate the following showy, ponderous passage into graceful, direct English. Do not use slang, but do use words that seem familiar and comfortable.

FOR YEARS, the explorer had searched in the jungle for signs of its autochthonous inhabitants, a bellicose, xenophobic tribe known for its deceptively mellifluous war chant, a euphony that could sometimes be heard over the top of the steamy rainforest canopy. Specious rumors, vacuous guides, and patronizing government officials, *inter alia*, had delayed and frustrated the explorer, who tried to be stoical. No one had been willing to expedite the search, though everyone wanted to expatiate on what he or she would advise. But now, *mirabile dictu*, there appeared to be a change in luck.

A clue, an *obiter dictum* in a molding Spanish hagiography discovered in the Museo Antropológico, had led the explorer to this remote valley. In the damp dawn, the *fortissimo* cacophony of the night creatures had abated into a *sotto voce* suggestion of circumambient life moving on all sides. Parting a tangle of heliotropic vines, the explorer gazed into the inanimate physiognomy of a monolithic, anthropomorphic, stone god, whose unmoving eyes communicated an ineffable malediction to all strangers. "Go beyond this point into my sacrosanct forest," the omniscient figure seemed to say, "and your death will be no euthanasia. Contravene this interdiction at your peril."

Beside the monolith, a gray sarcophagus protruded through the interstices of the jungle foliage. On its surface, an ancient bas-relief delineated a lost anthropocentric cosmology.

This surrealistic thanatopsis was too much even for our protagonist, the intrepid explorer. "Consider me," she thought in silent soliloquy, "an emissary from the outer world, and accept my benediction." Having obsequiously mollified the anger of the jungle god, she turned back with sangfroid and a valedictory suspiration of relief and perambulated down the tortuous jungle path for home.

## Reading Comprehension

1. For Translation 41, which of the following best expresses the main idea?
   a. An explorer retreats from the jungle in cowardice.
   b. An explorer respects tribal wishes and departs.
   c. An explorer lacks the will and strength of character to continue.
   d. An explorer misunderstands the elements of the problem.

2. The author's attitude is best described as:
   a. objective and journalistic
   b. satirical
   c. pedantic
   d. awed

## Analogies

3. **INEFFABLE : MALEDICTION ::**   *inexpressable   a curse*
   a. speech : silence
   b. nothing : bad
   c. good : bad
   d. praise : curse

4. **EXPATIATE : EXPEDITE ::**   *to elaborate   hasten*
   a. expand : express
   b. hurry : elaborate
   c. elaborate : express
   d. elaborate : facilitate

## Antonyms

5. **HAGIOGRAPHY :**   *saints biography*
   a. biography
   b. autobiography
   c. monograph
   d. hatchet job   *destructive act*

6. **PATRONIZE :**   *condescend to*
   a. condescend
   b. stoop
   c. venerate   *-to revere*
   d. admire

Calculations in Rome were done on an abacus.

**intuition and imagination**

You find yourself on a distant planet with intelligent life forms different from terrestrial ones. One of the alien species has a highly developed religion, with stone idols of its strange gods scattered across the undulating terrain. The gods are not **anthropomorphic**. You have never seen anything like them. Describe the way they look.

**ethics**

The expressed values of the United States are tolerant and inviting, as the inspiring words of the Statue of Liberty convey. "Give me your tired, your poor, your huddled masses, yearning to breathe free. I lift my lamp beside the golden door." This maternal, caring statue has been a tearful and joyful sight for millions of immigrants as they sailed into New York harbor. We see ourselves as the melting pot of many peoples, united in the liberty of a great democracy, pursuing happiness. And certainly, no nation in world history has done more to make freedom and equality real. And yet there is sometimes a paradoxical **xenophobia** in America, too. Our most cherished civil rights have not come easily, or without price. Tolerance has had to struggle with intolerance. Do you think that there is a difference between America's official ideals and its social values, or not? What are the ethical precepts of our democracy, as expressed in our greatest national documents? Which of these do you regard as most important?

A separate ethical question: The possibility of **euthanasia** is being debated more and more, especially since medical science is able to keep people alive longer and longer, but under conditions that many people are unwilling to accept. What do you think the precise ethical issue is in the question of euthanasia? Do you feel that it would be immoral under all cases, or not? Explain what criteria you think should be used to decide the issue.

**analysis**

What is the difference between **patronizing**, **condescending**, and being **supercilious**? Clearly, these are near synonyms, but by carefully reflecting on the stems in the words, you can detect subtle differences in tone and meaning. Discuss these differences.

**synthesis**

Can you think of five different things that are **ineffable**? What are they? What makes them ineffable? Can you think of five different common ideas that are **specious**?

**application**

Since none of the words on List 41 are rare, think about what type of document would actually be likely to contain each word. For example, you might see **euthanasia** in a discussion of ethics in a philosophical journal. You might see **autochthonous** in an article in *Foreign Affairs*. You might see *inter alia* in a legal brief. Try to give at least two possible documents for each word.

## Neologist's Lexicon

Use the stems in this list to create a new word (neologism). Give the word, the pronunciation, the part of speech, the etymology, and the definition(s). Keep a record of the neologisms you create from list to list. Here are some examples:

**melography** (mel AH grah fee) n. [*mel* (honey), *graph* (write)] 1. handwriting characterized by rounded forms, elaborate curlicues, and circles in place of dots and periods 2. melograph: a short message filled with extremely sentimental clichés

**euphobia** (yoo FO bee ah) n. [*eu* (good), *phobia* (fear)] 1. pathological dependence on the high levels of emotion associated with tragedy and misfortune, resulting in a fear of good news 2. fear that good opportunities will require change

## Sesquipedalian Creative Writing

Using words from List 41, write a poem, short story, short play, or other invention of your own choice. You might try something crazy, like sesquipedalian instructions for peeling a tangerine, or sesquipedalian instructions from an airline flight attendant. You could write a sesquipedalian standup comedy routine. As usual, have fun finding amusing ways to use the words you are learning.

## Pseudosesquipedaliodrama, OR the Neologist's Theater

**Phase One**: Working in groups of two, share and compare the neologisms you have created in these eleven lessons for the Neologist's Lexicon, and then write a joint creative play using the words the two of you have invented. Keep your play short; feel free to be silly or absurd, and turn it in to your teacher with a glossary of the key words and their definitions. (Of course, if you and your teacher want, you could do this as a solo assignment, but it is fun and valuable to work in cooperation with other thinkers, especially on creative projects.)

**Phase Two** (if you enjoyed Phase One): Divide the class into two to four larger groups, compare the plays that the groups of two wrote in Phase One, pick the favorite play of the group, and prepare a performance of the play, after elaborating or refining as much as you like. Perform the play for the class after first explaining the neologisms that the audience needs to understand in order to appreciate the play.

**Phase Three**: If you enjoyed the first two phases, you could work as a single large group to write and perform a single play, combining neologisms from everyone in the class and involving everyone in a part. This would require great cooperation, patience, creative thinking, and a real understanding of the Greek and Latin stems present in the words.

Before you go on to List 42, think carefully about word creation. Notice how logical and creative it can be. Notice the insight and humor that can be contained within a word. Notice how difficult it sometimes can be to get a word right so that the stems support the meaning you intend. Notice what an important part this is of the intellectual richness of language.

| | | | | | |
|---|---|---|---|---|---|
| • par | (equal) | nonpareil | • super | (over) | superannuated |
| • non | (not) | nonpareil | • ann | (year) | superannuated |
| • mal | (bad) | malefic | • tract | (pull) | intractable |
| • fic | (make) | malefic | • in | (not) | intractable |
| • tig | (touching) | contiguous | • greg | (group) | egregious |
| • psych | (soul) | metempsychosis | • ex | (out) | egregious |
| • meta | (change) | metempsychosis | • ab | (away) | abjure |
| • bio | (life) | biogenesis | • jur | (swear) | abjure |
| • gen | (origin) | biogenesis | • algia | (pain) | analgesic |
| • bas | (low) | bas-relief | • an- | (without) | analgesic |
| • post | (after) | postprandial | • dis | (away) | discursive |
| • equi | (equal) | equilibrist | • curs | (run) | discursive |
| • punct | (point) | punctilio | | | |

**nonpareil** (something unequaled) A unique achievement is a nonpareil.

**malefic** (causing harm) Notice Iago's malefic influence on Roderigo in Shakespeare's *Othello*.

**contiguous** (touching) We especially need to make good treaties with contiguous nations.

**metempsychosis** (transmigration of souls) Some believe in metempsychosis or reincarnation.

**biogenesis** (theory of life from life) Pasteur proved that the theory of biogenesis was true.

**bas-relief** (low-relief sculpture) The face was cut in bas-relief from a marble slab.

**postprandial** (after dinner) The contented guests enjoyed a postprandial stroll.

**equilibrist** (tightrope walker) The equilibrist did his daring highwire act between the buildings.

**punctilio** (point of conduct) Her high-society world was a treacherous thicket of punctilios.

**superannuated** (obsolete) We saw his rusted, superannuated farm implements at the auction.

•   •   •

**intractable** (stubborn) You cannot pull that bigot away from his intractable opinions.

**egregious** (blatant) The egregious act of vandalism shocked the large crowd.

**abjure** (renounce) It is painful to abjure one's former beliefs.

**analgesic** (painkiller) He took an extra-strength analgesic for the pain.

**discursive** (rambling) The illogical, discursive speech was difficult to follow.

**As Used by William Shakespeare in *Macbeth***

| | If | thou | didst | it, | thou | art | the | **nonpareil.** |
|---|---|---|---|---|---|---|---|---|
| **Parts of Speech:** | conj. | pron. | v. | pron. | pron. | v. | adj. | **n.** |
| **Parts of Sentence:** | | subj. | AVP | D.O. | subj. | LVP | | S.C. |

**Phrases:** -----no prepositional, appositive, or verbal phrases------

**Clauses:** ---------dependent clause-------- -----------independent clause------------
a D,I complex, declarative sentence

Here Shakespeare uses the noun *nonpareil* as the subject complement, joined by a linking verb to the subject. This complex sentence shows the difference between a direct object with an action verb and a subject complement with a linking verb.

## Pronunciation

| | | | |
|---|---|---|---|
| **nonpareil** | non par ELL | **punctilio** | punk TIL ee oh |
| **malefic** | mal EFF ik | **superannuated** | super ANN yoo ated |
| **contiguous** | kon TIG yoo us | **intractable** | in TRAK tah bel |
| **metempsychosis** | MET em sy KO sis | **egregious** | ee GREE juss |
| **biogenesis** | bio JEN e sis | **abjure** | ab JOOR |
| **bas-relief** | BAH re LEEF | **analgesic** | an al JEE zik |
| **postprandial** | post PRAN dee al | **discursive** | diss KUR siv |
| **equilibrist** | ee KWIL ih brist | | |

## Spanish Cognates

| | | | |
|---|---|---|---|
| **contiguous** | contiguo | **punctilio** | puntillo |
| **abjured** | abjurado | **contiguous** | contiguo |
| **intractable** | intratable | **analgesic** | analgésico |
| **equilibrist** | equilibrista | **metempsychosis** | metempsicosis |
| **bas-relief** | bajorrelieve | | |

1.  A **Micropoem**: **Intractable** is a wonderfully expressive adjective. It is not made of *intra* (within); it is made of *in* (not) and *tract* (pull). It suggests a mule-like stubbornness so firm that even pulling is of no avail. To be intractable is to be resistant to persuasion, logic, coercion, or compromise. Prejudice and bigotry are two of the most obvious intractable human phenomena, since they are so resistant to change. Adherence to political dogma is another often intractable behavior. The word **incorrigible** also can refer to a kind of stubbornness, but it really refers to misbehavior that cannot be corrected or improved. If you are incorrigible, we find it impossible to teach you better. Another word that refers to stubbornness is **refractory**. A refractory person breaks (*fract*) the rules and breaks them again (*re*), regardless of supervision. The stems in the words provide the best guide to the fine connotations that distinguish these words from each other. All three refer to someone who is stubborn, but the intractable person is not pullable, the incorrigible person is not correctable, and the refractory person breaks the rules again.

2.  The history of the science of biology provides the most interesting ground for understanding the noun **biogenesis**. It was long thought that many species came into being through **spontaneous generation**, the idea that life forms could be spontaneously created from inanimate substances. Some scientists thought, for example, that maggots were spontaneously generated by the chemical processes of decay in dead animals. Others believed that life could only be created (*genesis*) from similar life (*bio*) in a process called *biogenesis*. The argument raged back and forth between thinkers such as Redi and Spallanzani and finally was quieted by an ingenious experiment devised by Louis Pasteur, who proved to everyone's satisfaction that life would not generate, even in rich culture, unless other life could get to it first. Of course, this argument is only a partial consideration, since it still ignores the question of the generation of the first life on earth, which could not have come through biogenesis, unless we are all the descendants of extraterrestrials. If the first life on earth arose through chemical combinations in a primal sea bombarded by ultraviolet light and lightning, then that would be a real case of spontaneous generation.

3.  **Bas-relief** is different from other sculpture because it creates an illusion of depth without really being carved in depth. This technique was used widely by the ancient Greeks and Romans to illustrate the stories of gods and goddesses and to depict the battles and heroes of the Roman Empire. Bas-reliefs were carved into the friezes of the temples. These works of art, such as the Elgin Marbles that are now in the British Museum, are among the most prized in the world.

4.  A **Classic Word**: To observe **punctilios** is to be **punctilious**. Military order is punctilious: Kipling's Kim's regiment is "always punctilious in matters of millinery." Discipline on the high seas is similarly rigorous: on Melville's Pequod, "the punctilious externals, at least, of the quarter-deck are seldom materially relaxed." Social etiquette is filled with punctilios; in *Uncle Tom's Cabin*, characters linger, "with needless punctiliousness, around the arrangements of the table." In the classics we find "an inflexible, driving, punctilious business man" (Stowe), a stately punctilious gentleman (Melville), and a character possessed of an unfortunate quality that "was continually breaking through his punctilious manner in the shape of restlessness" (Fitzgerald).

# THE ROMAN ARMY
## Dr. Thomas Milton Kemnitz

With the destruction of Carthage and the reduction of Greece to two Roman provinces after the annihilation of Corinth, Rome was unquestionably the dominant power in the Mediterranean world. As we have seen, Rome often lost battles early in the war, and Hannibal won most battles he fought against the Roman army, but Rome always won the war. Clearly there was something that was superior in the Roman military system that enabled it to win every war.

The crucial advantage the Romans had was in manpower. Rome had a citizen army that was recruited from a list of citizens eligible to serve; that list was kept by the censors. Because the Romans made so many people from other parts of Italy Roman citizens, their potential number of conscripts was huge. At the beginning of the Second Punic War, one ancient historian records that the Roman conscript list was 700,000 men. So although Hannibal won battle after battle, Rome always had more men to bring into the field, and eventually they wore down Hannibal's army. Rome's ultimate source of strength was its willingness to include so many people as citizens. Consider Sparta's severe restrictions on becoming a full Spartan; by the fourth century B.C., there were too few Spartans to field an army, and Sparta began to lose battles to Thebes. Hannibal thought that he would be able to recruit troops from all over Italy to fight the Romans, but he proved to be wrong, and it was Rome whose strength was augmented by enlistments from the entire Italian peninsula.

A second source of strength was the willingness of Rome's citizens to serve, to accept army discipline, and to sacrifice for the success of the campaigns. From early in its existence, the Roman army was organized to fight in a phalanx formation. A phalanx implies a citizen army. It implies a more sophisticated form of social organization than a raiding party structure, in which a local aristocrat led a band of followers out to plunder or subdue neighbors. The phalanx depended upon a large number of individuals with enough resources to equip themselves with a shield, helmet, breastplate or cuirass, greaves, spear, sword, and scabbard. These were men with a stake in the community. For centuries the same sort of men went out equipped in the same way to fight Rome's battles. The eligible Roman citizens were required to serve no more than sixteen campaigns. Men went more or less willingly to fight, and once in a legion they submitted themselves to legion discipline, which could be harsh. The pay-off for serving came when they captured a town or an enemy camp and had significant booty to enrich each man in the ranks. As they got farther and farther from Rome, they seem to have been increasingly willing to take property. Once they were fighting outside the Italian peninsula, their periods of service were longer, and they were more eager for plunder that would stave off financial ruin at home. These were men who were not tending to their farms or their businesses. They were eager for spoils that would be an adequate recompense for their time and toil. Increasingly that included the riches that flowed from selling captives into slavery. It was this dynamic that lay behind the growing number of slaves in Rome from the third century on.

The difficulty with this system is that at the end of each campaign—often a period of less than a year—the legion was disbanded, and when men were recruited the next year, they had to be trained again and made effective in a new grouping of recruits. The rawness of the legions when they first went out to fight must have been behind many of the losses Rome suffered early in the wars, for in many wars in the early and middle Republic, the pattern was that Rome lost early and won late. Rash consuls eager for glory led willing recruits eager for booty into battle before they were adequately trained, and they often suffered humiliating defeats as a result. Then more legions had to be raised to try to repair the damage.

# THE ROMAN ARMY
## Dr. Thomas Milton Kemnitz

The Romans' first significant defeat came against the Gallic invaders in 387 B.C., and then the Romans adjusted their weapons. Defeats at the hands of the Samnites in 321 and 315 B.C. convinced the Romans that their phalanx system was not agile enough, and they adapted their formations along the lines of the Samnite organization. The maniple formation is a phalanx with joints at which it can pivot and, as the Romans devised it, with three rows of soldiers. The Greek phalanx might have forty rows of hoplites, but only the first row was fully engaged, and the second row could do some damage with their spears over the shoulders of the men in front of them. After that row the additional rows served mainly as moral support for the men in front and to prevent them from running away. In fact, many battles were lost when the men in the rear lost their nerve and ran away. Most casualties occurred when men fled; they were cut down by pursuers who overtook them. Cavalry were a particular problem; a man did not have much chance of outrunning a horse, but he could run faster if he dropped all of his heavy equipment and headed for the hills. However, if he met the enemy without a sword and shield and helmet and breastplate, he stood no chance of surviving. As long as the phalanx held, fatalities were few; once men broke and ran, their chances of survival diminished. If the line held, the casualties that occurred often were puncture wounds or slashes. The slashes from spear points or sword tips could leave impressive scars, even if the wounds were not deep. Many an older man could point with pride to numerous scars—all in the front of his body—accumulated in the wars for his state. That the wounds were all in the front was an important point, for only cowards were wounded in the back. Plutarch writes of candidates going to the Forum in Rome without a tunic under their toga so that they could display their wounds as evidence of their valor and sacrifice on behalf of Rome. Cato the Elder was described by Plutarch as "so eager to distinguish himself that when quite a lad his body was covered with wounds, all in front."

With the maniple system, Romans divided the ranks of soldiers into three lines with blocks of soldiers, consisting of a maniple of 120 men standing twenty across and six deep. Those groups stood as far apart as they were wide, and the second row stood in similar formation, except they stood directly behind the open spaces in the front line. The result was a checkerboard pattern. The third line had fewer men; the units were twenty across and only three lines deep. The spacing of the maniples could be adjusted by the consul leading the legions to suit the terrain and his tactics. Obviously the consul at Cannae made a colossal mistake in spacing his maniples together closely and packing the center of the line far too deeply. Each maniple was divided into two centuries, and each century had two centurions and an insignia bearer. The division of a legion into thirty such units meant that orders had to be conveyed to thirty chief centurions who were leading the maniple.

Before the Roman army met Hannibal, two legions were the standard army, each commanded by a separate consul. However, the Romans lost the first two battles against Hannibal when the consuls did not cooperate with each other, and Hannibal defeated half of a divided army while the other legion sat in a camp far enough away so as not to be a factor in the battle. The Romans attempted to remedy this by instructing the two consuls to keep their legions together and to alternate each day who was in command. Hannibal simply waited for the day when he knew the rasher of the two consuls was in command, and then he sprung his trap at Cannae. Thereafter the Roman army waged war with the legions under the command of one consul.

In each case below, one of the choices was really the word used by the author in the sentence provided. All of the choices can be found in the example words on the first page of this lesson. Your challenge is to decide which word the author used. This is not a test; it is more like a game because more than one word choice may work perfectly well. See if you can use your sensitivity and intuition to guess correctly which word the author used.

1.  **From Henry James's *The American***

    His _____ demitasse cost him a penny extra.
    a. contiguous
    b. superannuated
    c. analgesic
    d. postprandial

2.  **From Robert Penn Warren's *All the King's Men***

    The figure of an angel, with wings and flowing drapery, had been executed in _____.
    a. biogenesis
    b. metempsychosis
    c. bas-relief
    d. punctilio

3.  **From Thomas Hardy's *Jude the Obscure***

    They begin with the _____, and gradually comprehend the universal.
    a. contiguous
    b. discursive
    c. malefic
    d. egregious

4.  **From Jack London's *White Fang***

    He observed the law more _____.
    a. discursively
    b. punctiliously
    c. intractably
    d. contiguously

5.  **From Charles Dickens's *David Copperfield***

    There was a black barge, or some other kind of _____ boat, not far off.
    a. contiguous
    b. postprandial
    c. superannuated
    d. egregious

Though it is a good thing to have a rich vocabulary, it is not a good thing to abuse that vocabulary by writing verbose, abstruse, sesquipedalian sentences. Those who overuse their vocabularies often do so at the expense of clarity. Translate the following showy, ponderous passage into graceful, direct English. Do not use slang, but do use words that seem familiar and comfortable.

EIGHTY STORIES above the cacophonous *terra firma* of the xenophobic city, the intractable equilibrist, without valediction, stepped out for a feat of postprandial funambulism on the wire that stretched between the buildings. He gazed at the unsightly chips in the bas-relief frieze of the opposite monolithic tower, a superannuated skyscraper of stone and translucent plastic; some malefic miscreant had fired egregiously at the building with a hand weapon, damaging the sculpture, but the sacrosanct punctilios of the city's patronizing and supercilious elite had prevented more than a token punishment of the egocentric youth.

The equilibrist, in a stoical but discursive soliloquy, had abjured analgesics, and now his head began to pulse *fortissimo* with the magnitude of the challenge that had become his *idée fixe*, a nonpareil: to cross the wire to the farthest building. It would be his magnum opus. He would be lionized as the metempsychosis of Houdini. Hagiographies would be written in his honor, for this distance was no interstice, and the buildings were by no means contiguous. In supercilious sangfroid, he stood over the man-made abyss.

Far below, the mellifluous, *sotto voce* hum of the traffic—exiting the city in confluent streams of red tail lights—signaled that the city had not yet settled into sedate night. Far above, the omniscient physiognomy of the constellations twinkled its imponderable benediction on the equilibrist as he stepped, with the incredulous joy of a neophyte, forward on the wire.

This little figure of a rat blowing a *cornu* suggests that in battle the Roman army probably used a far simpler trumpet than the large circular one.

## Reading Comprehension

1. It can be inferred from Translation 42 that:
   a. The equilibrist feels superior to others.
   b. The equilibrist wishes to gain the adulation of others.
   c. The equilibrist is indifferent to the opinions of others.
   d. The equilibrist is a convivial person who feels an *esprit de corps* with others.

2. Translation 42 could best be described as:
   a. the interior monologue of a hero
   b. an eccentric person on the edge of despair
   c. the exciting adventure of a professional risk taker
   d. a study in what some will do for acceptance and approval

## Analogies

3. **DISCURSIVE : EGREGIOUS ::**   *Rambling   Blatant (obvious)*
   a. wander : nomad
   b. irresponsible : delinquent
   c. unfocused : outrageous
   d. gregarious : cursive

4. **EGREGIOUS : PUNCTILIO ::**   *Blatant   Point of conduct*
   a. barbarian : regulation
   b. prompt : punctual
   c. eccentric : conforming
   d. blunt : pointed

## Antonyms

5. **CONTIGUOUS :**   *Touching*
   a. adjacent
   b. disconnected
   c. irrelevant
   d. congruent

6. **SUPERANNUATED :**   *obsolite*
   a. infantile *childish*
   b. callow *immature*
   c. pristine
   d. new

Among the surviving pieces of Etruscan metallurgy is this spectacular horn, which was a precursor of the Roman *cornu*, Latin for horn and from which our word *cornet* is derived. The Roman *cornu* had a strut, which stabilized the instrument and served as a handhold. The strut is visible in the mould of a Roman warrior with a trumpet.

**evaluation**

The **punctilios** that govern the niceties of our social lives form an interesting system of do's and don'ts. One does, for example, go to the door and knock to pick up one's date; one does not sit in the car and honk the horn. One does say hello and look another in the eye when being introduced; one does not look at the floor and mumble. Punctilios change from time to time and from society to society; behaviors that are rude in one culture are expected in another. Punctiliar relativity. As a class, make a list of some common punctilios that the members of the class accept, and then rank them in importance, after selecting at least three criteria of behavior chosen by the group.

**analysis**

Look up the etymologies of the words **discursive** and **desultory**, and decide what the difference is between the two words. Why would you choose one word over the other? Do the other students in the class agree with your analysis?

Can you explain the difference between **abjure** and **adjure**? How can you remember the difference between these two words?

**synthesis**

The Romans and Greeks created **bas-relief** sculptures, adorning their public buildings with art that depicted their gods, goddesses, heroes, and victories. If the United States were to employ a sculptor to create a great bas-relief for the National Gallery of Art, depicting national achievements of the past ten years, what events should be carved in the sculpture?

**application**

A **nonpareil** is a unique, unparalleled achievement. What would be an example of a nonpareil in high school academics?

**intuition**

An idea for a short story: Your character suddenly senses that through an accident of **metempsychosis** he has received the soul of another being, in addition to his own. He now has two personalities in one mind. Elaborate.

Pictured on this ceramic tile is a Roman water organ and a man with a *cornu* on which the strut is clearly visible.

### Neologist's Lexicon

Use the stems in this list to create a new word (neologism). Give the word, the pronunciation, the part of speech, the etymology, and the definition(s). Keep a record of the neologisms you create from list to list. Here are some examples:

**annefic** (ah NEFF ick) adj. [*ann* (year), *fic* (make)] 1. being so outstanding as to make one's year 2. totally, like, you know, wow

**cursalgic** (kurs AL jik) adj. [*curs* (run), *algia* (pain)] 1. so discursive in speech as to cause physical pain in the brains of the listeners, resulting in uncontrollable flight 2. speaking continuously so as to be unaware of one's own symptoms

### Sesquipedalian Bulwer-Lytton

Bulwer-Lytton is the British author who is satirized in the Peanuts comic strip when Snoopy begins his latest novel with the formula line, "It was a dark and stormy night. Suddenly a shot rang out. Somebody screamed!" Using words from List 42 and others, write a corny opening paragraph in Bulwer-Lytton style. An example:

### A Dark and Malefic Night

It was a dark and malefic night. In the distance, somebody retorted acerbically. The analgesics hadn't worked, and Arnold smeared the palm of his hirsute hand slowly over his low forehead, knocking the steel helmet from his head to the sidewalk, where it clattered cacophonously into the contiguous gutter. Egregiously, a shot broke the sedate tranquility of the intangible evening, and the neon lights seemed to punctuate the sound, glowing on the bas-relief of the cloud bottoms, which hovered low and lurid over the building tops. A discursive monologist wandered obsequiously out of an alley, declaiming to no one, twenty yards ahead of Arnold. Abjuring confrontation, Arnold turned away with an epigram: "Leave the intractable to themselves," he muttered, "but I'll be back." But even as he walked away, he knew—whether through metempsychosis, epiphany, or introspection he couldn't tell—that something was wrong. Dead wrong. He was soon to learn that he was right. Dead right.

- re (again) remonstrate
- sol (alone) solipsism
- *ism* (doctrine) solipsism
- in (not) ineluctable
- ex (out) ineluctable
- luct (struggle) ineluctable
- super (over) supererogatory
- rogat (ask) supererogatory
- infra (beneath) *infra dig*
- terr (land) disinter
- lent (full of) truculent

- ject (throw) *disjecta membra*
- ob (against) obloquy
- loqu (talk) obloquy
- *acro* (high) acronym
- *nym* (name) acronym
- pugn (fight) pugnacious
- cise (cut) incisive
- *dia* (across) diatribe
- trib (pay) diatribe
- ab (away) abrogate
- con (together) recondite

**remonstrate** (plead in protest) Her earnest, repeated remonstrations were in vain.

**solipsism** (doctrine: only self exists) His narcissistic solipsism was amusing.

**ineluctable** (not escapable) You must face the ineluctable consequences.

**truculent** (fiercely savage) His truculent nationalism was undiplomatic.

**supererogatory** (beyond what's asked) His supererogatory efforts annoyed us.

*infra dig* (beneath dignity) It was considered *infra dig* even to ask.

**recondite** (abstruse) The recondite subject was beyond his intellect.

**disinter** (unearth) The crew slowly disinterred the buried home.

*disjecta membra* (scattered fragments) Only the *disjecta membra* of her work remained.

**obloquy** (verbal abuse) Hester received the obloquy of the community.

• • •

**abrogate** (annul) It is preferable not to abrogate a firm agreement.

**acronym** (initials-name) NATO, RADAR, and SCUBA are acronyms.

**pugnacious** (combative) The pugnacious youth always started fights.

**incisive** (sharp) Her incisive questions cut to the heart of the issue.

**diatribe** (abusive criticism) The senator's public diatribe reflected his rage.

**As Used by F. Scott Fitzgerald in *The Great Gatsby***

| | The | policeman | looked | over | with | **truculent** | eyes. |
|---|---|---|---|---|---|---|---|
| Parts of Speech: | adj. | n. | v. | adv. | prep. | **adj.** | n. |
| Parts of Sentence: | | subj. | AVP | | | | |
| Phrases: | | | | | -----prepositional phrase------ | | |
| Clauses: | ----------------------------------independent clause----------------------------------- | | | | | | |
| | one independent clause; a simple, declarative sentence | | | | | | |

Here Fitzgerald uses the adjective *truculent* to modify a noun, *eyes*, that is the object of a preposition. The prepositional phrase modifies the verb.

## Pronunciation

| | | | |
|---|---|---|---|
| **remonstrate** | re MON strate | *disjecta membra* | dis JEK ta MEM brah |
| **solipsism** | SOLL ip sizm | **obloquy** | OB lo kwee |
| **ineluctable** | in ee LUCK ta bel | **abrogate** | AB row gate |
| **truculent** | TRUCK yoo lent | **acronym** | ACK row nim |
| **supererogatory** | super eh ROGG atory | **pugnacious** | pug NAY shus |
| *infra dig* | IN fra DIG | **incisive** | in SIE siv |
| **recondite** | RECK un dite | **diatribe** | DIE ah tribe |
| **disinter** | dis in TUR | | |

## Spanish Cognates

| | | | |
|---|---|---|---|
| **truculent** | truculento | **recondite** | recóndito |
| **pugnacious** | pugnaz | **acronym** | acrónimo |
| **diatribe** | diatriba | **abrogated** | abrogado |
| **solipsism** | solipsismo | **incisive** | incisivo |
| **disinterment** | desenterramiento | | |

1. I admit it: ***disjecta membra*** is an erudite term that you will rarely see, but it is still fun to look at a word such as this sometimes. And it is good to begin to have a sense of what these scholarly terms are like. You might see this term if you are studying, say, a classical poet such as Sappho, whose work only exists in scattered fragments, leaving us wishing that we still possessed her other poems that we know existed but that have been lost.

2. It will be easy to remember what the noun **obloquy** means because the word is such a literal construction of its pieces. If you are receiving the obloquy of the community, people are talking (*loqu*) against (*ob*) you. You are the object of unfavorable discussion—most unpleasant.

3. A **Micropoem**: Imagine absolute and final solitude. Well, **solipsism** is the doctrine (*ism*) that you are alone (*sol*). It is the philosophical idea that only the self exists (only I exist and, everyone else is merely a figment of my imagination). It seems to be a ridiculous idea—until you try to disprove it. And then you begin to see its value. Attempting to disprove solipsism is a fascinating intellectual experience because in doing so, you realize the difficulty of thinking deeply. If you cannot prove that solipsism is false, do you know that it is false? And if you cannot prove something so seemingly obvious, how can you hope to prove or know other things that are apparently far more difficult and complex?

   After thinking about *solipsism*, you become more careful with the word **obvious**. Bertrand Russell and Alfred North Whitehead labored for years on *Principia Mathematica,* in which they attempted to prove that the foundation of mathematics and arithmetic was sound. This task proved to be so difficult that Russell later said it had permanently reduced his intelligence; he claimed never to be as sharp again, which brings up the well-known fact that most mathematicians make their major contributions to mathematics while they are young.

   And another thing. The old stereotype that boys need to study more mathematics than girls do is superannuated—obsolete. In the challenging economy of the future, mathematics will be more important than ever, and there is no reason why bright boys and girls should not equally study and profit from as much advanced mathematics as they can possibly learn. Hundreds of exciting futures will be closed to the ill-advised student who takes the low and short road in mathematics. Bright girls are hereby urged to ignore limiting stereotypes and pursue academics.

4. **Truculent** refers to behavior that is more than hostile or violent. It describes behavior that is disturbingly brutal, fiercely savage, such as the attacks that Mr. Hyde makes on a little girl and an old man in Robert Louis Stevenson's *Dr. Jekyll and Mr. Hyde.*

5. A **Classic Word**: To **remonstrate** is to try emphatically or over and over again (*re*) to show (*monstrare*) someone something, as someone who is pleading in protest does. Since *remonstrate* is a word that possesses energy and human emotion, we would expect it to be a common word in the classics, and it is; Barrie, London, Conrad, Wells, Crane, Dickens, Melville, Stowe, Hawthorne, the Brontës, and Scott all used it. In *Jane Eyre*, Miss Temple seemed to remonstrate, while Jane eschewed upbraiding and curtailed remonstrance. In *Ivanhoe*, the Saxon remonstrated strongly with his friend upon the injudicious choice he had made of his party.

Wars in the East brought Romans into direct contact with Greece and Greek culture. Among the primary Greek deities who gained added importance in Rome in the third and second centuries B.C. was Apollo, shown here in a statue that is one of many Roman copies of a Greek original. The kithara was a stringed musical instrument more sophisticated than the lyre, and Apollo is often depicted with one or the other, as he is in this sculpture.

# THE CONQUEST OF ALEXANDER'S WORLD
## Dr. Thomas Milton Kemnitz

The Romans fought a series of wars in Greece, the Balkans, and Asia Minor from 214 to 146 B.C. An unadorned list of them indicates the Roman determination to prevent any challenge from the East: First Macedonian War, 214–205 B.C.; Second Macedonian War, 200–196; Seleucid War, 192–188; Third Macedonian War, 172–168; Fourth Macedonian War, 150–148; and the Achaean War, 146. At the beginning of this period, Alexander's empire had devolved into three significant powers in Macedonia, the Selucid Empire, and Egypt, as well as some secondary powers such as Pergamum and Rhodes.

By 217 Philip V of Macedon controlled all of Greece except Athens. In 215 B.C., however, Philip—following the Roman defeat at Cannae—formed an alliance with Hannibal and made himself and his kingdom Rome's enemy. Rome immediately moved to neutralize Philip by forming alliances with Rhodes and Pergamum and the Achaean cities. They sent enough troops to Greece to keep Philip busy and unable to aid Hannibal and made peace with him in 205 when the Carthaginians were no longer a threat.

The Second Macedonian War erupted when Philip entered into an alliance with the Seleucid Empire, and the two sought to take control of Egypt. Again Rome lured away Philip's allies in Greece and in 197 B.C. decisively defeated him at the Battle of Cynoscephalae. Philip had to surrender his fleet, become a Roman ally, and abjure any foreign policy, but he was otherwise spared. The Roman victor, Titus Quinctius Flaminius, declared all the Greek cities free, although Roman garrisons were placed at Corinth and Chalcis. Flaminius meant that the Greeks were free to do what Rome wished.

In the Seleucid War, Antiochus III (the Great) led his Seleucid army into Greece and attempted to hold Thermopylae Pass, but the Romans did as Xerxes had done: they went around the pass and drove Antiochus out of Greece. The Romans decisively defeated the empire at sea, invaded Asia Minor for the first time, and decisively won on land. Rome had thus destroyed two of the three major remnants of Alexander's empire and had begun to exert indirect control over the other parts, including Egypt, Rhodes, and Pergamum. By 188 B.C., the Romans were masters of the known world.

In the Third Macedonian War, Perseus, the successor to Philip V, challenged the Romans and was defeated decisively at Pydna in 168 B.C., where 32,000 of the 40,000 Macedonian troops died. The Romans sold about 300,000 of the inhabitants of Macedonia into slavery, divided the province into four republics, and settled many retired legionnaires and allies on the land. The same year saw the defeat of Genius, the last king of Illyria; he was brought to Rome in chains and displayed. The following year the Romans attacked Epirus, and 15,000 of its inhabitants were sold into slavery.

In 150, a pretender claiming to be Perseus's son led a revolt against Roman rule. After some success, he was defeated at Pydna in 148 B.C., and the Romans simply annexed Macedonia as a Roman colony with a permanent Roman garrison. The remaining Greek cities of the Achaean League rose up in their objection of this arrangement, but they were speedily crushed. The Romans totally destroyed the ancient city of Corinth, plundered much of the rest of Greece, and took many Greeks as slaves. They divided Greece into two Roman provinces. The Romans intended to ensure that they would never again have to fight the Greeks by leaving Greece without the resources to wage war.

| Second Macedonian War | Seleucid War | Third Macedonian War | Fourth Macedonian War | Third Punic War begins | Rome destroys Carthage and Corinth |
|---|---|---|---|---|---|
| 200-196 B.C. | 192-188 B.C. | 172-168 B.C. | 150-148 B.C. | 148 B.C. | 146 B.C. |

This slave collar bore a message that asked that the slave be returned for a reward. It is a telling fact that sometimes when archeologists find just the inscribed disc, they cannot be certain whether it attached to a collar for a slave or for a dog.

# SLAVERY
## Dr. Thomas Milton Kemnitz

Slavery was an increasing phenomenon in the Roman Republic, and it was a major factor in changing Roman society, economics, and living conditions. Slavery in the United States was racial; people of color were enslaved by white people, and an ideology evolved that people of color were inferior to their white masters. In the ancient world slavery was not racial but rather a condition of life in the Persian Empire, as it was in ancient Greece. The Greeks tended to enslave foreigners—their term was *barbarians*—whom they captured in battle or when they took a city, and the Spartan act of enslaving fellow Greeks—the Helots—outraged the Athenians when they saw it firsthand.

As Roman conquerors moved farther from Rome and encountered strangers in Gaul or the Iberian Peninsula or North Africa or Greece or the Middle East, they increasingly took prisoners whom they sold into slavery. Indeed, selling slaves was one of the most profitable outcomes of winning a battle or of taking a city that had closed its gates to the Roman army. Selling slaves paid the army's wages, and taking prisoners to sell into slavery was a means by which a commander could ensure his popularity with his troops. By the middle of the third century B.C., the Romans held tens of thousands of slaves; by the middle of the second century B.C., with Carthage enslaved and Corinth reduced to ashes, the Romans held hundreds of thousands of slaves.

The most desirable slaves were Greeks, who frequently were used to educate children, to run the library, or to manage the household. A wealthy urban household might contain many slaves, while a country villa might run entirely on slave labor. Skilled slaves were an advantage at every point in the domestic economy, from food preparation to clothing manufacture to shoe making to grooming of the master and mistress of the household to the arrangement of the master's toga. A large country villa might include slaves capable of making tiles, drainpipes, or even fired bricks. Slaves would till the fields, harvest the crops, and look after the livestock. State-owned slaves undertook public works such as repairing roads and aqueducts. The abundance of slave labor enabled the wealthy of Rome to have a very luxurious life.

The children of a slave woman were slaves. Unlike in America, where skin color meant permanent servitude, in Rome slaves might be able to purchase their freedom. Many masters made arrangements with their slaves so that they profited substantially from the transaction whereby a slave paid for his freedom. The elder Cato bought young men who were without skills, trained them in a trade, and then sold them at a handsome profit, and he was not alone in profiting by training slaves. Fortunes were made from slaves, beginning with those who risked their lives following the army and buying the captives directly after battles. Their lot could become very precarious in any military reversal or if the baggage train was ambushed or overrun; they might easily be killed or taken captive themselves.

Many men made their fortune by using slaves for enterprises such as mines or quarries or indeed anywhere that heavy manual labor was done regularly. Slaves were often used by fullers (cleaners), in bakeries, and in other uncomfortable or unpleasant occupations. One of the most spectacular endeavors in which slaves were trained was as gladiators. This was a particularly apt use of barbarian warriors.

Runaway slaves were a constant problem in Rome. They were not so much a threat to the social order as they were an economic loss for their owners. One large disruption was caused by a slave rebellion led by Spartacus and others who were being trained as gladiators. After a series of setbacks, the destruction of a lot of property, and the murder of many slave-owning families, the Roman army led by Crassus won a decisive victory and crucified every one of Spartacus's army who survived the final battle.

In each case below, one of the choices was really the word used by the author in the sentence provided. All of the choices can be found in the example words on the first page of this lesson. Your challenge is to decide which word the author used. This is not a test; it is more like a game because more than one word choice may work perfectly well. See if you can use your sensitivity and intuition to guess correctly which word the author used.

1. **From James Joyce's *Portrait of the Artist as a Young Man***

   He drove his soul daily through an increasing circle of works of _____.
   a. truculence
   b. solipsism
   c. supererogation
   d. *disjecta membra*

2. **From Upton Sinclair's *The Jungle***

   I am not to be silenced by poverty and sickness, not by hatred and _____.
   a. obloquy
   b. pugnacity
   c. truculence
   d. diatribe

3. **From George Orwell's *1984***

   The word you are trying to think of is _____.
   a. solipsism
   b. diatribe
   c. ineluctable
   d. remonstrate

4. **From Alan Paton's *Cry, the Beloved Country***

   The pain was deep, deep and _____.
   a. recondite
   b. ineluctable
   c. incisive
   d. truculent

5. **From James M. Barrie's *Peter Pan***

   "Wendy," _____ Michael, "I'm too big for a cradle."
   a. abrogated
   b. disinterred
   c. remonstrated
   d. truculent

Roman oil lamp

Though it is a good thing to have a rich vocabulary, it is not a good thing to abuse that vocabulary by writing verbose, abstruse, sesquipedalian sentences. Those who overuse their vocabularies often do so at the expense of clarity. Translate the following showy, ponderous passage into graceful, direct English. Do not use slang, but do use words that seem familiar and comfortable.

AS THE RUSTY, MONOLITHIC ROCKET settled into the dusty *terra firma* of the moribund planet, the crew could see archaeological excavations scattered over the tortuous landscape, disinterring the ruins of the autochthonous truculent civilization that had once developed there. Incisive scientists had come to the ineluctable conclusion that the pugnacious and malefic society had finally become too bellicose for its own survival; had abrogated all of its treaties; had contravened galactic interdictions; had received the remonstrations, objurgations, obloquies, diatribes, and finally the maledictions of all neighboring planets; and had fallen into the ignominious and solitary decadence that it condignly deserved. The collapse was so complete that it had become *infra dig* to mention it in polite society.

A recent discovery, however, cast a new light on things. The *disjecta membra* of an ancient hagiography were slowly being pieced together by archaeologists and poets working together. Recondite, sesquipedalian, and sententious, the magnum opus appeared to offer *a posteriori* evidence (in mellifluous assonance) of metempsychosis on the warrior planet and could become the omnibus *locus classicus* for the new science of psychocosmology, the study of the universe as a solipsistic manifestation of the omniscient mind of the Divine Emissary, which is what the planets in this wing of the spiral galaxy (known as Messier Object M33, or by the acronym ELVIS, for Extragallactic Lifeform VIral Situ) called their anthropomorphic deity.

Descending the gangplank into the mauve, circumambient, translucent atmosphere, the crew felt the nonplussed xenophobia of the neophyte. Fair enough. They were beginners, after all, and they were uncertain what supererogatory efforts would be expected of them, but nothing, they knew, could ever make them abjure their duties to the planetary confederacy.

## Reading Comprehension

1. Which of the following best expresses the main idea of Translation 43?
   a. Political violence is most destructive to the society that employs it.
   b. Loyalty to one's superiors is the only thing that matters.
   c. Science is the most powerful weapon in the search for truth.
   d. An ethical life can only be circumvented at great cost.

2. With which statement would the author likely agree?
   a. If you are going to use military force, use enough, or do not use it at all.
   b. Do not use military force to assert your goals over other societies.
   c. Military force is necessary in political affairs because the end justifies the means.
   d. Military force should be strictly confined to defensive purposes.

## Analogies

3. **TRUCULENT : PUGNACIOUS ::**
   a. 8 : 5
   b. wolf : rabbit
   c. murderer : pugilist
   d. cannibal : anthropophagite

4. **RECONDITE : INCISIVE ::**
   a. obscure : keen
   b. erudite : perspicuous
   c. reclaim : include
   d. smart : astute

## Antonyms

5. **REMONSTRATE :**
   a. expostulate
   b. acclaim
   c. ignore
   d. stolid

6. **INELUCTABLE :**
   a. rife
   b. omnipresent
   c. rare
   d. capture

This little statue of a slave boy shows him chained to the box that is between his feet.

**synthesis**

Can you use the adjectives **pugnacious** and **incisive** to describe the same noun? Think of a way to use them both in a sentence to modify the same noun. What things can you think of that are both **truculent** and **ineluctable**? Can you think of a behavior that is both *infra dig* and **supererogatory**?

How many words from List 43 can you apply to Shakespearean characters or plays? Hamlet's mind, for example, is **incisive**. Could any of these words describe characters or events in *Julius Caesar*, *A Midsummer Night's Dream*, *Romeo and Juliet*, or *King Lear*?

**imagination and intuition**

As the desert sun rises over the Nile, you gaze at the pits where the crew members are **disinterring** one thing after another. Describe some of the wonderful artifacts that are being unearthed.

**emotion, imagination, and intuition**

Imagine, as vividly as you can, that you are desperately **remonstrating** with someone, but the person is **intractable**. Write a short story that gives elaborate detail about this scene.

**divergence**

How many **acronyms**, such as NATO, SCUBA, and RADAR, can you think of? Make a long list of acronyms, and then invent some. Try to invent an acronym that is funny or witty, such as STICK: Strict Teachers of Incorrigible Children in Kindergarten.

**emotion**

What if you suddenly realized with complete certainty that **solipsism** was true, and that you actually were the only living thing, and that everything else, living and inanimate, was only your imagination? How would you feel?

These shackles would have hampered the slave who tried unsuccessfully to flee Vesuvius when it erupted.

### Neologist's Lexicon

Use the stems in this list to create a new word (neologism). Give the word, the pronunciation, the part of speech, the etymology, and the definition(s). Keep a record of the neologisms you create from list to list. Here are some examples:

**terraluction** (TERR a LUCK shun) n. [*terr* (land), *luct* (struggle) *tion* (act)] 1. the struggle to live off of the land 2. farming, especially operating a family farm under economic conditions that are unfavorable to profitability

**loqucism** (LOW kyew sizm) n. [*loqu* (talk), *cise* (cut)] 1. a form of obloquy in which the victim is cut to shreds by what is said 2. the art of offensive criticism

### Sesquipedalian Fiction

Using at least one word from this week's list in almost every line, write a short play, scene, or story. You may also use words from previous lists if you like. Feel free to be imaginative, silly, or absurd. Do not let your critical or judgmental faculties interfere with your creative ideas.

### Sesquipedalian Poetry

Using at least one word from this week's list in every (or almost every) line, write a short poem. You may use regular meter, or end rhyme, or other poetic devices, or not. You can even experiment with creative punctuation.

**me *disjecta membra***

scattered fragments of memory
*disjecta membra*
mind present, mind lost, mind losing, ineluctable fragments . . .
da doo ron ron ron da doo ron ron
disinterred recollections reinterred
autoincisive self-awareness.
it has become/*infra dig* to/become meself
becoming/*infra dig*
in a solipsism of gentle truculence¿

Roman oil lamp

| | | | | | |
|---|---|---|---|---|---|
| • *tauto* | (same) | tautology | • gyn | (woman) | misogynist |
| • *anti* | (against) | antinomy | • *morph* | (shape) | morphology |
| • *nomy* | (law) | antinomy | • fid | (faith) | diffident |
| • *crypt* | (hidden) | apocryphal | • cogn | (know) | cognizant |
| • *apo* | (away) | apocryphal | • string | (bind) | stringent |
| • *trans* | (across) | transom | • tempor | (time) | temporize |
| • *epist* | (knowledge) | epistemology | • ize | (make) | temporize |
| • *logy* | (science) | eschatology | • ambul | (walk) | somnambulist |
| • *mis** | (hatred) | misogynist | • somn | (sleep) | somnambulist |
| • ob | (against) | opprobrium | • com | (together) | commiserate |

**tautology** (needless repetition)  The phrase *required essentials* is a tautology.

**antinomy** (contradicting reasonable principles)  Plato's antinomies are perplexing.

**eschatology** (theology of last things)  Immortality is a question of eschatology.

**opprobrium** (disgrace)  The traitor lived in a state of public opprobrium.

**apocryphal** (not authentic)  The recently discovered writings proved apocryphal.

**transom** (window or door crossbar)  He hung, apelike, from the door's transom.

**commiserate** (sympathize)  She commiserated with him in his distress.

**epistemology** (study of knowledge)  Example: Descartes asked, "How do you *know* you exist?"

**misogynist** (hater of women)  We deplored the misogynist's intransigence.

**morphology** (study of form)  The biologist studied the morphology of eyes.

• • •

**diffident** (shy)  His diffident glance gave her confidence.

**cognizant** (aware)  It is important to be cognizant of the rules.

**stringent** (binding)  Stringent regulations are highly restrictive.

**temporize** (delay)  Please begin without temporizing.

**somnambulist** (sleepwalker)  The critic discussed Lady Macbeth's somnambulism.

*We introduce a Greek meaning for *mis*.

**As Used by Pearl S. Buck in *The Good Earth***

| | Wang Lung | stood | **diffidently** | on | the | edge | of | the | circle. |
|---|---|---|---|---|---|---|---|---|---|
| **Parts of Speech:** | n. | v. | **adv.** | prep. | adj. | n. | prep. | adj. | n. |
| **Parts of Sentence:** | subj. | AVP | | | | | | | |
| **Phrases:** | | | | ---prep. phrase--- | | | ---prep. phrase--- | | |
| **Clauses:** | --------------------------------independent clause--------------------------------- | | | | | | | | |
| | one independent clause; a simple, declarative sentence | | | | | | | | |

Here Buck uses the adverb *diffidently* to modify the verb. The verb is also modified by a prepositional phrase, *on the edge,* and the object of the preposition *edge* is modified by a second prepositional phrase.

## Pronunciation

| | | | |
|---|---|---|---|
| **tautology** | taw TAW lo jee | **misogynist** | miss AH jin ist |
| **antinomy** | an TIN o mee | **morphology** | more FAH lo jee |
| **eschatology** | ess ka TAW lo jee | **diffident** | DIF fi dent |
| **opprobrium** | oh PRO bree um | **cognizant** | COG nih zent |
| **apocryphal** | a PAH krih fal | **stringent** | STRIN jent |
| **transom** | TRAN sum | **temporize** | TEM por ize |
| **commiserate** | ko MIZZ er rate | **somnambulist** | som NAM byoo list |
| **epistemology** | ee pis tem AW lo jee | | |

## Spanish Cognates

| | | | |
|---|---|---|---|
| **opprobrium** | oprobio | **apocryphal** | apócrifo |
| **misogynist** | misógino | **tautology** | tautología |
| **somnambulist** | somnámbulo | **antinomy** | antinomia |
| **commiseration** | conmiseración | **eschatology** | escatología |
| **morphology** | morfología | | |

1. In his dialogue *The Parmenides*, Plato employed **antinomies** to use reason itself to question the validity of reason. Plato constructed two separate logical arguments that began with the same premise, and then, reasoning without error, reasoned to two contradicting conclusions! This is the sort of powerful intellectual pyrotechnics that students of philosophy are accustomed to expect from Plato, and it helps to demonstrate to the neophyte what the excitement about Plato is all about. Incidentally, *The Parmenides* is a terribly difficult dialogue; if you doubt it, try to read ten pages with comprehension. (As a childhood friend of mine used to say, I double-dog dare ya.) A student who wants an introduction to Plato would do better to begin with *The Apology*, which is not an apology but rather Socrates's defense before the Athenians; he had been accused of corrupting the youth and of believing in false gods. In this dialogue, Socrates explains what his philosophical life has been about. He clarifies the meaning of his famous paradox: I only know that I know nothing. The jury found him guilty anyway, and he chose to drink poisonous hemlock rather than be exiled, since he knew that exile was an evil, but not that death was an evil.

2. **Epistemology** is the philosophical study (*logy*) of how we know anything that we know (*epist*). (An epistemologist would ask me how I know that.) One of the most interesting examples in the history of epistemology comes from Descartes (de KART), who determined that he would methodically doubt everything he could doubt until he finally found a solid and undoubtable truth. Then, beginning with this self-evident *a priori* truth, he would begin reasoning upward, building a large edifice of truths based on the bedrock he found at the beginning. The result of his effort is a well-known statement: *cogito ergo sum*—I think, therefore I am. Descartes decided that it was impossible to doubt that he was doubting, and this proved that he existed. If this seems too easy to be true, it was. Descartes has been accused of circular reasoning—also known as *begging the question*—because he assumed his conclusion (I, myself) in his premise (I think). If you are trying to prove the existence of yourself, you cannot begin with "I think!"

    The real value of Descartes's work was that he demonstrated how fiendishly difficult it can be to prove anything whatsoever, and this helps everyone who is attempting to think clearly to be far more rigorous and consistent.

    In most words, the stem *epist* means letter, as in *epistle* or *epistolary*. In *epistemology* the stem comes from the Greek *episteme*, knowledge, rather than *epistole*, letter.

3. If you would like to learn about an interesting case of alleged **misogyny**, study the paintings and the life of Pablo Picasso. Many of Picasso's cubist paintings depict women in terribly unflattering, animal-like, ugly, and even horrifying ways. Picasso, despite his artistic genius, has been condemned for his treatment of women he knew and for the way that he painted them. An unsympathetic biography, *Picasso: Creator and Destroyer* by Arianna Stassinopoulos Huffington, explores these issues in detail. This would make a worthy subject for a student research paper. The Huffington book, by the way, contains fascinating stories. When Paris was liberated from the Nazis, Picasso, who had spent the war in Paris, was visited by Hemingway. Picasso was not at home, but the concierge asked Hemingway if he, like everyone else, had brought Picasso a gift. Hemingway darted back to his car and returned with a box of *hand grenades*, inscribed, "To Picasso, from Hemingway"!

The Roman passion for Greek culture included most centrally philosophy, and no one was more revered than Socrates. Archeologists have found more than fifty busts of him from the ancient world. Roman workshops near Naples made a speciality of reproducing Greek statues for Roman purchasers, particularly for their libraries and gardens.

# THE LOVE OF ALL THINGS GREEK
## Dr. Thomas Milton Kemnitz

As the Romans fought and negotiated their way south on the Italian peninsula, they increasingly ran into towns that the Greeks had colonized centuries earlier. The major center near Rome for Greek influence was Naples, founded by the Greeks originally in the second millennium B.C. and then refounded in the sixth century B.C. and called *Neapolis*—new city. It became one of the foremost cities of Magna Graecia; its rapid growth was due to the influence of the powerful Greek city state of Syracuse. With its excellent harbor, Naples became a thriving center of trade. During the Samnite Wars, it was captured by the Samnites, and upon being taken by the Romans, it was made into a Roman colony. However, Naples was one place where the inhabitants continued to speak Greek and maintained Greek customs. During the Second Punic War, the strong walls fortifying Naples protected the city from Hannibal's army. Naples was greatly respected by the Romans as a paragon of Hellenistic culture, and many patrician families owned villas near it.

For those Romans who traveled to Athens, the Acropolis was a sight to behold. The structures that Pericles and his successors had put in place were all intact with their original statues, precious metals and stones, and paint and adornments sparkling in the sun. As Plutarch wrote in the first century: "even at the present day the work looks as fresh as ever, for they bloom with the eternal freshness that defies time." He also added that the temples "now alone prove that the tales of the ancient power and glory of Greece are no fables." In the third and second centuries B.C., Rome had no buildings that could match those of Athens.

In 479 B.C. the Greeks who defeated the Persians at Plataea were stunned by the opulence of the Persian camp, and in like manner in the late third and early second century B.C., Romans traveling and fighting in the East also were awed by the opulence they saw. These people lived lavishly compared to the Romans, and not a few Romans envied them their lifestyle. Captured luxury goods soon made their way to Roman villas.

The Romans also recognized that the Greeks were considerably advanced in philosophy, mathematics, theater, poetry, sculpture, and many other cultural areas. Roman poets and playwrights copied the Greek forms and tried to make the less-sonorous Latin do what had been done so eloquently in the more melodic Greek. It became standard practice for Roman children to learn Greek, and many young men were sent to Greece to complete their education. These young men wrote in Greek and practiced orations in Greek. Knowledge of the Greek language and culture became a *sine qua non* of an educated person in Rome. When Roman troops plundered Greece, thousands of bronze statues were brought to Italy. Roman sculptors copied them in marble, and dozens or even hundreds of copies of various sculptures were made for Roman consumption. Many were heads of famous people, such as Homer, Euripides, Sophocles, Pindar, and other Greeks, including an astonishing number of philosophers. The large statues of Athena from the temples in Athens were reproduced many times for Romans to enjoy. In fact, famous statues of Greece often exist and are known only in the form of their Roman copies in marble.

The very richest Roman patrician families eagerly adopted Greek culture and oriental voluptuousness, and this became a dividing point between them and the lesser patrician families with fewer resources. Serviced by an increasing number of slaves, many of them Greek, the patrician families were able to reorder their lives to include much of the Greek culture and mores that they wanted to emulate.

In each case below, one of the choices was really the word used by the author in the sentence provided. All of the choices can be found in the example words on the first page of this lesson. Your challenge is to decide which word the author used. This is not a test; it is more like a game because more than one word choice may work perfectly well. See if you can use your sensitivity and intuition to guess correctly which word the author used.

1.   **From Stephen Crane's *The Red Badge of Courage***

     They expressed _____ for that part of the army that had been left on the river bank.
     a. misogyny
     b. commiseration
     c. stringence
     d. diffidence

2.   **From Charlotte Brontë's *Jane Eyre***

     I was loaded with general _____.
     a. opprobrium
     b. epistemology
     c. morphology
     d. eschatology

3.   **From Jane Austen's *Emma***

     [Emma observed] the feebleness and _____ of the narrative.
     a. tautology
     b. misogyny
     c. diffidence
     d. antinomy

4.   **From Elizabeth George Speare's *The Witch of Blackbird Pond***

     The letters [were] painted jauntily on the _____.
     a. epistemology
     b. morphology
     c. somnambulist
     d. transom

5.   **From Robert Louis Stevenson's *Dr. Jekyll and Mr. Hyde***

     The whole business looked _____.
     a. stringent
     b. apocryphal
     c. diffident
     d. cognizant

Roman oil lamp

144

Though it is a good thing to have a rich vocabulary, it is not a good thing to abuse that vocabulary by writing verbose, abstruse, sesquipedalian sentences. Those who overuse their vocabularies often do so at the expense of clarity. Translate the following showy, ponderous passage into graceful, direct English. Do not use slang, but do use words that seem familiar and comfortable.

PAYNE SCHMERZ, who fell into obloquy and opprobrium after being branded a malefic misogynist that perambulated the streets at night, was actually a diffident and philosophical somnambulist, dreamily incognizant of violating stringent social codes. In one (apocryphal) story, he was said to have bumped his head on a low transom and to have wandered off in audible self-commiseration.

Actually, Payne's nocturnal sesquipedalian ratiocinations went something like this: "Shall I devote myself to morphology, epistemology, or eschatology? My lucubrations must be confined to one of the three; I can temporize, or stall, or delay no longer, to put it tautologically. If I study morphology, shall I specialize in exobiotic, anthropomorphic life forms? If I study epistemology, shall I reason through *a posteriori* induction or through *a priori* deduction, bewaring of antinomies? And how will I know if I know that I know? If I study eschatology, when will I know the merit of my conclusions? Too late. And how can I circumvent the tortuous perils of solipsism? I feel like a philosophical Phaeton trying to drive a too-powerful sun chariot through the dangers of the mind's sky."

This prolix and recondite self-colloquy continued unabated, and Payne wandered on down the street, his physiognomy tranquil in sleep.

The relationships between Rome and the towns on the Italian peninsula were important for cultural exchanges as well as for the buying and selling of goods. Many of these areas came within the sphere of Greek culture, which they transmitted to Rome. This black glazed libation dish—with the *omphalous*, the Greek navel of the world, in the center—was made in Etruria about 215 B.C., and it depicts scenes of the travels of Odysseus.

## Reading Comprehension

1. For Translation 44, which of the following does the passage suggest?
   a. Payne is an innocent and naive dreamer.
   b. Payne is an overconfident, self-important egotist.
   c. Payne is an unstable person with psychological problems.
   d. Payne is a misogynist who is a danger to society.

2. Which of the following best describes the passage?
   a. the interior monologue of a misunderstood sleepwalker
   b. a description of an eccentric person's public reputation
   c. the deplorable ideas of a miscreant
   d. the nonsensical dream of a sleepwalker

## Analogies

3. **DIFFIDENT : CONFIDENT ::**
   a. cognizance : awareness
   b. temporize : hesitate
   c. empty : full
   d. stringency : license

4. **SOMNAMBULIST : EQUILIBRIST ::**
   a. string : sedative
   b. somniloquy : equivocate
   c. sleep : walk
   d. dream : balance

## Antonyms

5. **OPPROBRIUM :**
   a. lionize
   b. apotheosis
   c. bowdlerize
   d. nepotism

6. **MISOGYNIST :**
   a. philanthropist
   b. philanderer
   c. anthropologist
   d. feminist

Roman enthusiasm for Greek philosophy meant that there were busts of many relatively minor philosophers in Roman villas. Among those philosophers was Pythagoras, who was admired not for his mathematics and the theorem that bears his name but for his ascetic philosophy. It is a paradox that many of the Romans who admired the richness of the Greeks in contrast to their own simple lifestyle chose to revere Greek philosophers who advocated stoicism or asceticism.

**evaluation**

Which would be a more valuable **epistemological** accomplishment: proving that we know a physical object is before us, or proving that another person's emotions are what they seem? Why? Do you think either phenomenon could actually be known for sure? Why or why not?

**synthesis**

Use eight or more of the words from List 44 to write a creative paragraph or short story. You may also include words from previous lists if you wish. You may use a dictionary to help with usage and parts of speech questions. Feel free to be humorous or fantastic in what you write.

**analysis**

Look up the words **eschatology**, **epistemology**, and **apocryphal** in a good college dictionary, and explain why these words mean what they mean, based on their etymologies. Analyze the construction of the words.

What is the etymology of the word **commiserate**? How is this word different from the word **sympathize**? Use the stems/etymologies to distinguish fine shades of meaning between the two words.

**application**

Think, in elaborate detail, about the act of **commiserating** with someone who needs you to sympathize. How does commiseration work? How does it ease the pain of someone who is suffering? Think of at least five hypothetical situations in which it would be important for you to "be there" to commiserate with someone.

**convergence**

Consider the two words **diffident** and **stringent**. Pick one of these two words to add to the vocabulary you actually use frequently. Why did you pick that word?

**imagination and intuition**

In Shakespeare's *Macbeth*, Lady Macbeth utters her famous **somnambulism** soliloquy as the audience watches transfixed. Guilt and horror have driven her to reveal herself in her restless sleep. Imagine that you are writing a play in which a character divulges personal secrets in somnambulistic soliloquy. Describe the scene and the character's actions, explain what the character reveals about himself or herself, and explain how the character's psychological state motivates this event.

Greek oratory was widely admired by the Romans; Demosthenes was a fourth-century Athenian orator whose standing among the Romans was perhaps higher than it was in Greece. His bust was reproduced often by the Romans.

### Neologist's Lexicon

Use the stems in this list to create a new word (neologism). Give the word, the pronunciation, the part of speech, the etymology, and the definition(s). Keep a record of the neologisms you create from list to list. Here are some examples:

**cryptomorphic** (krip to MOR fic) adj. [*crypto* (hidden), *morph* (shape)] 1. demonstrably real but invisible, such as gravitation or commiseration 2. of undetectable form or structure, as an incondite short story

**antifidous** (an TIFF id us) adj. [*anti* (against), *fid* (faith), *ous* (full of)] 1. pathologically professing to believe the opposite of whatever one hears 2. spontaneous, disingenuous skepticism

### Sesquipedalian Poetry Practice

Using words from List 44 and previous lists, write a poem in which each word is connected to a previous word by either a vowel sound or a consonant sound. If the repeated sound is an entire syllable, such as *plow* and *vow*, then we call that **rhyme**. If the sound is only for a single vowel sound, such as in the words *smite* and *file*, then we call that **assonance**. If the sound is simply a repeated consonant, located anywhere in the word, such as the repeated *b* sound in baboon and *lob* and *abashed*, then we call that **consonance**. If the sound is repeated at the beginnings of the words, such as in the words *morphology*, *manumission*, *miscreant*, and *misogynist*, then we call that **alliteration**. Another sound trick that is fun to use is a reversed sound, such as *fine* and *knife*. Use rhyme, assonance, consonance, reversal, and alliteration to write a poem (sort of) that strings each word to the next through sound connections. In this experimental sound poem, do not worry about meaning; just think about sound. Sometimes, if you do that, surprising meanings emerge anyway.

### city synopsis

curs circumvent murk.
stringent negative diffidence.
perfidious patrician trap.
manumission mossy somnambulist.
hedonist funambulist newts is news.
apotheosis parthenogenesis finish us.
squeeze *sui generis locus classicus* glassy bus.
assiduous suit tortuous trotting joggers.
vacuous Saskatoon assonance brass.
ablution sir circumlocution.
do the locomotion soliloquy.
unilateral splatter, all nonplussed compulsive.
apocryphal postlude . . .

| | | | | | |
|---|---|---|---|---|---|
| • *ine* | (nature of) | aquiline, lacustrine | • *mono* | (one) | monograph |
| • mal | (bad) | malfeasance | • punct | (point) | pungent |
| • **fac** | (to do) | malfeasance | • *mega* | (large) | megalomania |
| • monger | (seller) | costermonger | • *mania* | (madness) | megalomania |
| • *gyn* | (woman) | gynecocracy | • *syn* | (together) | syndrome |
| • *cracy* | (government) | gynecocracy | • **drome** | (run) | syndrome |
| • *ous* | (full of) | tenebrous | • son | (sound) | dissonant |
| • ego | (I) | superego | • *narco* | (sleep) | narcolepsy |
| • *eu* | (good) | euphemism | • *lepsy* | (attack) | narcolepsy |
| • ex | (out) | expostulate | | | |

**aquiline** (eaglelike)  The Emperor had a curved, aquiline nose, like an eagle's beak.

**malfeasance** (public misconduct)  The public official was accused of malfeasance.

**costermonger** (vegetable vendor)  London's cockney costermongers sold their fruit.

**gynecocracy** (government of women)  The chauvinist was afraid of gynecocracy.

**tenebrous** (dark and gloomy)  The castle's tenebrous interior frightened Jonathan.

**superego** (unconscious conscience)  Freud thought the id was controlled by the superego.

**expostulate** (to object earnestly)  She ignored his earnest expostulations.

**monograph** (paper on one subject)  The scholar published a monograph on the subject.

**lacustrine** (of lakes)  Yeats longed for the lacustrine environment of Innisfree.

**pungent** (sharp)  The pungent smell of the spice penetrated the room.

• • •

**megalomania** (delusions of greatness)  The megalomaniac had a Napoleon complex.

**syndrome** (complex of symptoms)  Down's syndrome afflicts some children.

**euphemism** (pleasant name)  The term *restroom* is a euphemism.

**dissonant** (inharmonious)  A dissonant clamor arose in the streets below Talleyrand's room.

**narcolepsy** (attacks of sleep)  The sleepy man was a victim of narcolepsy.

**As Used by Marjorie Kinnan Rawlings in *The Yearling***

| | A | strong | odor | came | to | him, | **pungent** | and | rank. |
|---|---|---|---|---|---|---|---|---|---|
| **Parts of Speech:** | adj. | adj. | n. | v. | prep. | pron. | **adj.** | conj. | adj. |
| **Parts of Sentence:** | | | subj. | AVP | | | | | |

**Phrases:** --prep. phrase--

**Clauses:** ---------------------------------independent clause---------------------------------
one independent clause; a simple, declarative sentence

Here Rawlings uses the adjective *pungent* to modify the noun *odor*, which is also the subject of the sentence. The action verb *came* is intransitive, taking no direct object.

## Pronunciation

| | | | |
|---|---|---|---|
| **aquiline** | AH kwil in | **lacustrine** | LACK us trin |
| **malfeasance** | mal FEEZ ance | **pungent** | PUNJ ent |
| **costermonger** | KOSS ter monger | **megalomania** | mega lo MAY nee ah |
| **gynecocracy** | gye ne KOK ra see | **syndrome** | SIN drome |
| **tenebrous** | TEN eh bruss | **euphemism** | YOO fem izm |
| **superego** | super EE go | **dissonant** | DISS o nant |
| **expostulate** | ex POSS tyoo late | **narcolepsy** | NAR ko lepp see |
| **monograph** | MON o graff | | |

## Spanish Cognates

| | | | |
|---|---|---|---|
| **tenebrous** | tenebroso | **monograph** | monografía |
| **syndrome** | síndrome | **euphemism** | eufemismo |
| **narcolepsy** | narcolepsia | **dissonant** | disonante |
| **megalomania** | megalomanía | **aquiline** | aquilino |
| **lacustrine** | lacustre | | |

1.  The adjective **tenebrous** comes from the Latin word *tenebrae,* which meant darkness. In the Roman Catholic Church, Tenebrae is the office of lauds and matins sung during Holy Week to celebrate Christ's Crucifixion. If something is **tenebrific**, then it produces darkness.

2.  A **Micropoem**: The noun **superego** is taken from Sigmund Freud's famous trilogy of terms: ego, id, and superego. For Freud, the father of psychoanalysis, these terms represented different aspects of every human personality. The **ego** is the conscious self that is aware of itself and that deliberately governs itself as best it can. The **id** is the collection of subconscious urges and hidden animal drives that secretly motivates many of our intense and compulsive behaviors, including those that are immoral. The superego is the subconscious moral self, the unconscious conscience, or higher (*super*) self (*ego*) that is opposed to the base, egotistical self-gratification of the id. The conscious ego is forced to mediate between the opposing sides of the unconscious.

3.  Aquila, the Eagle, is a northern constellation south of Cygnus, the Swan. A person with an **aquiline** nose has a curved nose, like an eagle's beak. The *ine* suffix also concludes other animal adjectives: ursine, bearlike; canine, doglike; feline, catlike; porcine, piglike.

4.  A **Classic Word**: One common synonym for **remonstrate** is **expostulate**. To expostulate with someone is to reason earnestly but with civility against what that person is doing. If the two words describing objection have a difference in meaning, it lies in tone; *remonstrate* emphasizes the emphatic complaining objection, whereas *expostulate* emphasizes kindly and courteous objection. You expostulate with your respected parents or beloved spouse. Remember that *remonstrate* literally means show again; it emphasizes the objection that won't take no for an answer and keeps arguing. *Expostulate* has been in continual use for centuries and has been used by Defoe, Swift, Scott, Emily Brontë, Hawthorne, Stowe, Melville, Dickens, Hardy, Wells, Conrad, and Fitzgerald. Robinson Crusoe frequently expostulated with his mother and father. Scott's Cedric the Saxon expostulated with his guards. Swift's emperors of Blefuscu frequently expostulated with their ambassadors. We find running murmurs of expostulation (Fitzgerald), an oriental voice in a courtroom expostulating with impassioned volubility (Conrad), the expostulations of two feeble old constables (Hardy), a woman's frantic expostulations at a parting (Wells), expostulations that are mild and rational (Charlotte Brontë), and kind expostulations (Swift). Perhaps the best sentence to illustrate the civil tone of the expostulation, as contrasted with the not necessarily civil tone of the remonstration, is this one from Defoe's *Robinson Crusoe*: "He called me one morning into his chamber . . . and expostulated very warmly with me upon this subject." In this sentence, the word *warmly* seems to have a pleasant double value, carrying both the smiling civility and the heat of the feeling.

5.  It is easy to forget the educational power of the Greek and Latin stems. Consider, for example, just a few of the words that contain the stem *syn*: **synaeresis**, **synaesthesia**, **synagogue**, **synaloepha**, **synapse**, **synarthrosis**, **syncarp**, **syncategorematic**, **synchroflash**, **synchromesh**, **synchronic**, **synchroscope**, **synclastic**. To know that *syn/sym* means together is to have a word half-mastered before you ever encounter it.

# CURSUS HONORUM
## Dr. Thomas Milton Kemnitz

The *cursus honorum* was the course of offices by which a man rose in the Roman hierarchy. Until the late Republic, this course was fixed and rigidly followed. It prescribed not only the order of elective offices but also the minimum age at which a man could hold each—patricians could hold an office two years younger than could plebs. There were established intervals between holding offices and a prohibition on holding the same office in successive years. Gaius Gracchus offended the *Optimates* when he stood for and won the tribuneship two years in succession. Fewer than twenty years later Marius was elected consul five successive years, an indication of how worried the Romans were about the threat from the Germanic tribes. With an army at his back, Pompey demanded to be elected consul without having ever served in any of the minor offices and while he was still ten years too junior to hold the office legitimately.

The usual starting point for a patrician or a well-connected pleb was a position as a military tribune. Military tribunes were part of every legion; they were staff officers who served as aides to the commander. Many of these young men were lightly regarded, and their lack of mettle was discovered early; some, however, proved themselves worthy and began their rise through the elected offices of the *cursus honorum*.

The order of elective offices for those in the Senate was quaestor, aedile, praetor, and consul. It was an important mark of distinction to have held each office at the youngest age possible—known to the Romans as *suo anno*, meaning in his year.

The first official post was that of *quaestor*. Patrician candidates had to be at least twenty-eight years old. Twenty quaestors served in the financial administration at Rome or as second-in-command to a governor in the provinces. They also could serve as the paymaster for a legion. A young man who obtained this job was expected to become an important official. An additional task of all quaestors was the supervision of public games. As a quaestor, an official was not escorted by lictors (see page 276), nor did he possess *imperium*.

Five years after being a quaestor, a man could stand for the position of *aedile* (minimum age: thirty-four for a patrician); there were four of them—two plebeian and two patrician. Their primary function in the early years was taking care of the temples (*aedes* in Latin) in Rome; in later times their most important responsibilities were ensuring the grain and water supplies for the city. They served as judges in commercial disputes. They also were responsible for organizing games; a politician seeking popular favor like Julius Caesar would use this office to organize—at his own expense—spectacular games.

Two years after serving as an aedile, a man could be elected as a *praetor* (minimum age: thirty-seven). There were six—later eight—praetors, all of whom served as judges or in other high-level functions in Rome. A praetor was attended by six lictors and exercised *imperium* when the consuls were absent. After their year in office, many became *propraetors* and served as provincial governors in the later years of the Republic.

Two years after serving as a praetor, a man could stand for election as a *consul*. The office of consul was the summit of the *cursus honorum*; a patrician had to be forty years old to be elected. Consuls commanded the legions, were the highest judicial officers, played an important part in the city's political agenda, and, as *proconsuls* after they left office, governed the most important provinces. The year was known by the name of the consuls. Each consul held *imperium* and

This coin shows a consul or praetor walking with lictors.

could veto the acts of the other consul—an important check on the immense power of the consulship. Each consul was accompanied by a dozen lictors, who served as attendants and bodyguards. In theory a decade had to elapse before a man could hold a second consulship, but that requirement could be overlooked in a crisis.

A small number of men were elected to the office of censor, the duties of which give us both of our modern meanings of a censor of morals and a person who takes a census. The censor was responsible for maintaining the census and enlistment rolls of Rome, determining who had the necessary property qualifications to serve in the military, and confirming who met the qualifications to sit in the Senate. The censor could remove men from the Senate for being morally or financially unworthy. The censors were in charge of the construction of public buildings in Rome, of leasing or apportioning conquered lands, and of the city's moral health.

## THE TRIBUNE OF THE PLEBS
**Dr. Thomas Milton Kemnitz**

The office of Tribune of the Plebs held considerable power—so much so that it was attractive for anyone wishing to ameliorate any number of problems in the organization and administration of the Roman Republic. It became an office for wealthy and powerful men to aspire to hold; it was attractive enough that one patrician changed his name and had himself adopted by a plebeian family to occupy the office. The Tribune of the Plebs had the right to veto any act or plan of any magistrate, including that of a consul, he could arrest magistrates, and he could rescue any pleb being arrested by a magistrate. He could convene the Senate and lay legislation before it, and that was one of the main attractions of the office to ambitious men. A single individual, acting as the Tribune of the Plebs, could set the political and legislative agenda for Rome.

An essential feature of the office of Tribune of the Plebs was the theory that the holder of the office was sacrosanct, that he could not be touched, and that the penalty for impeding him in the performance of his duties was death. The tribune had no other power than this attribute, but it meant that as long as he was present in the Senate and wished to keep the Senate from passing a law, he could do so. Once he left the Senate session or was not physically present, his disapproval meant nothing, and the Senate could act as though the tribune had never expressed his disapproval.

The Tribune of the Plebs had no power beyond the city limits of Rome, and he was expected to remain within a day's journey of the city during his term of office. Also, he was expected to keep his home open day and night for visitors and for those seeking refuge.

The theory of being sacrosanct was not entirely effective; in theory it meant that the tribune had no need for the protection of lictors, and none was provided. However, beginning with Tiberius Gracchus in 133 B.C., the Senate *Optimates* murdered tribunes whenever they threatened the financial or economic interests of the patricians or the position or power of the senators. Those deaths would prove to be a strain on the Republic.

Roman
oil lamp

# CATO THE CENSOR
## Dr. Thomas Milton Kemnitz

Not every Roman was enamored with Greek culture; the most prominent amongst those who were not pleased with the Greek influence was Marcus Porcius Cato (234–149 B.C.), often known as Cato the Censor or Cato the Elder to differentiate him from a great grandson also known as Cato who was a prominent opponent of Caesar. Both Catos were exemplars of extreme rigidity, adhering to behaviors, attitudes, and principles that were admired by many of their contemporaries and by posterity.

The elder Cato was a man of striking appearance—with red hair and gray eyes—and evident ability. He was born into an old Tusculum family of small landowners; his father and grandfather had distinguished military careers. They were not patricians but rather plebs, though certainly of the *equites* (knights) class, for Cato's grandfather was honored for surviving the loss of five horses in battle. His father died when Cato was young, and Cato was poor as a boy. He grew up on a farm he inherited in Sabine territory, where the old-fashioned virtues of thrift, hard work, and abstinence were preached and practiced. Near his farm was a modest hut that had been inhabited by Manius Curius, who previously had been awarded three Triumphs for military feats, including defeating King Pyrrhus, and who also was lauded for his rigidly simple character. The accolades this hero had received inspired Cato, who decided to imitate the character and who hoped to match the glory of Manius Curius.

Cato was seventeen years old when Hannibal invaded Italy, and he enlisted and fought well in many battles throughout the Second Punic War, serving under Fabius Maximus. Cato also served his neighbors by arguing on their behalf in various courts in the region. He distinguished himself not only by his eloquence but also by his rigidly simple lifestyle. Soon he came to the attention of Lucius Valerius Flaccus, a neighbor from a patrician family. Flaccus had an immediate use for Cato in Rome as a member of his faction who distinguished themselves by their adherence to the old, simple values, which they used to condemn the aristocrats who favored Greek ways.

Once at Rome, Cato's skill in the courts and the support of the Flaccus party fueled a rapid advance. He began as a military tribune and then was a quaestor. As a military quaestor, he was sent by the Senate to the staff of Scipio, then preparing in Sicily to attack Carthage. Fabius Maximus had opposed Scipio repeatedly and limited his access to troops, and Cato continued in that vein. He was horrified by the waste and extravagance that he saw in Scipio's camp, and he complained to Scipio. Scipio said in reply that he did not need an economist as his military quaestor when he was preparing to wage war on a grand scale, and that he would have to account to the Roman people not for money expended but for battles won. Cato hurried back to Rome to voice his concerns to the Senate. Tribunes were sent by the Senate to investigate, and Scipio satisfied them that he was attending to his duties.

Although he did not deter Scipio, Cato benefitted from the affair because his speeches to the Senate enabled him to mark out his position as embodying the old, simple way of life. What made Cato remarkable was that he not only espoused the way of life, he lived it. His house was simple and unadorned, his fare the same as his slaves ate, his wine the same as they drank, his clothing inexpensive, and he worked in the fields when he was on the farm. He kept himself in good physical condition, walking instead of riding and following a regular regimen of extensive exercise. He was contemptuous of people who were undisciplined and grew fat. He is reported to have remarked of a corpulent man, "How can this man's body be useful to his country when all parts between the neck and the groin are possessed by the belly?"

# CATO THE CENSOR
## Dr. Thomas Milton Kemnitz

As Cato's career advanced, higher visibility enabled him to dramatize and espouse his position on Roman virtue and Greek decadence. In 198 B.C. he was elected a praetor and was granted Sardinia as his province. Former governors had been in the habit of charging their tents, bedding, and clothing to the province and likewise making it pay large sums for their entertainment and that of their friends. Cato introduced an unheard-of system of economy. He charged nothing to the province and visited the various cities without a carriage, walking with a single public servant carrying his robe of state and the vessel to make libations at a sacrifice. With all of this he showed himself so affable and simple to those under his rule, so severe and inexorable in the administration of justice, and so vigilant and careful in seeing that his orders were duly executed that the government of Rome is said to have been never more feared nor more loved in Sardinia than when he governed the island.

In 195 Cato and Flaccus were elected consuls, and Cato made himself conspicuous in opposing luxury. Ten years later the pair achieved together Rome's highest honor of being elected censors. Cato's candidacy was opposed by nearly all of the most distinguished members of the Senate; they knew he would be hard and inexorable when in power. They put up seven candidates to contest him, men who promised to be lenient. Cato would not relax his severity in the least but threatened the dissolute in his speeches from the rostra (the platform in the Forum used for speaking), insisting that the city required a complete reformation. He told the people that if they were wise, they would choose himself and Valerius Flaccus; he imagined that with the right colleague, he could make progress in destroying the hydra of luxury and effeminacy. He attacked the other candidates, whom he said wanted the office to fill it badly because they were afraid he would fill it well. The voters agreed with Cato.

Cato proved to be a severe censor. He expelled one senator for cruelty, another for kissing his wife in front of his daughter in the daytime. He unhorsed a knight for licentiousness. He cut off the water pipes of people— usually Rome's richest citizens—who were diverting water from the public fountains to their homes, and he tore down houses that encroached on public streets. He imposed a luxury tax on all jewelry, clothes, carriages, furniture, and other goods costing more than 1,500 drachmas, valuing them at ten times their price and then taxing them on the nominal rather than the actual value. At the same time he reduced the tax on other people to a mere three-tenths of a percent; his intent was to make those who owned luxury items envy those who had none for their lower tax rate.

At the end of his life, Cato insisted that Rome must destroy Carthage for good; he ended every speech— no matter what the topic—with the sentiment that Carthage had to be destroyed. Cato had been on a Senate mission to North Africa and had seen for himself that Carthage was prosperous and full of young men. He had never forgotten the fear that Hannibal had engendered in Romans of his generation sixty years earlier, and he became certain that Rome's greatest enemy had to be destroyed totally before it became powerful enough to damage Rome. The Third Punic War was in large measure due to his influence, but he died before the annihilation of Carthage.

| Cato born | Hannibal invades Italy | Cato military tribune to Scipio | Cato elected consul | Cato expires |
|-----------|------------------------|--------------------------------|---------------------|--------------|
| 234 B.C. | 218 B.C. | 204 B.C. | 195 B.C. | 149 B.C. |

In each case below, one of the choices was really the word used by the author in the sentence provided. All of the choices can be found in the example words on the first page of this lesson. Your challenge is to decide which word the author used. This is not a test; it is more like a game because more than one word choice may work perfectly well. See if you can use your sensitivity and intuition to guess correctly which word the author used.

1. **From Virginia Woolf's *Mrs. Dalloway***

   Those _____ [were] not allowed to stand their barrows in the streets.
   a. megalomaniacs
   b. superegos
   c. narcoleptics
   d. costermongers

2. **From Joseph Conrad's *Lord Jim***

   Then in the _____ immensity a livid arch appears.
   a. tenebrous
   b. lacustrine
   c. pungent
   d. dissonant

3. **From Mark Twain's *The Prince and the Pauper***

   This, in the eye of the law, is..._____ in office.
   a. euphemism
   b. megalomania
   c. expostulation
   d. malfeasance

4. **From John Knowles's *A Separate Peace***

   No locker room could have more _____ air than Devon's.
   a. aquiline
   b. dissonant
   c. pungent
   d. lacustrine

5. **From Bram Stoker's *Dracula***

   His face was strong—a very strong—_____, with high bridge of the thin nose and peculiarly arched nostrils.
   a. syndrome
   b. pungence
   c. aquiline
   d. narcolepsy

Though it is a good thing to have a rich vocabulary, it is not a good thing to abuse that vocabulary by writing verbose, abstruse, sesquipedalian sentences. Those who overuse their vocabularies often do so at the expense of clarity. Translate the following showy, ponderous passage into graceful, direct English. Do not use slang, but do use words that seem familiar and comfortable.

AMID THE DISSONANT CACOPHONY [*inharmonious*] of the gregarious water birds, the old captain, B.W. Staey, walked out of the tenebrous northern conifer forest onto the lacustrine [*lake*] shore. His aquiline nose still sensed the pungent tang of the green pine boughs, but the fresh lake wind smelled sweet and cold as it blew in *sotto voce* assonance down from the still-snowy peaks. A xenophobic tern flew near his head, expostulating with him like a prolix costermonger about getting too near her nest, and in accordance with the subtle gynecocracy of nature, his mollifying superego subconsciously steered him in kindness away from the nest and back toward the lake waters lapping euphonically with mellifluous sounds by the shore.

"If I only knew what is wrong with me," he soliloquized with stoic but nonplussed physiognomy, "then I should have some peace here." Ever since he had assiduously written the euphemism-ridden monograph accusing the megalomaniac Lord Mayor of malfeasance, he had been plagued with a syndrome of saturnine narcolepsy, somnambulism, and even occasional lyssophobia, although he now felt the intangible soporific effect of the lacustrine environment. With desultory perambulation, he continued introspectively down the shore, toward his small cabin of clay and wattles, and his nine heliotropic bean rows, and his hive for the vivacious honey bee.

In a society without a police force or any other formal way of keeping order and a large and diverse population, theft is always a problem, and it seems to have been a great concern in the Roman world. Bronze keys such as the ones shown here are a common find at archeological sites. They fit doors, locked cupboards, and strongboxes like the one pictured here.

**Reading Comprehension**

1.  In Translation 45, the author does all of the following EXCEPT:
    a. imply that females of all species govern nature
    b. suggest that the captain's rambling has no real purpose
    c. indicate that the captain does not know the cause of his problem
    d. imply that the captain has impugned the integrity of an innocent person

2.  It can be inferred from the passage that:
    a. The author feels sympathy for the spirit of the tern.
    b. The author feels antipathy for the rough wilderness that needs to be tamed.
    c. The author has difficulty sleeping.
    d. The author regards excessive introspection as unhealthy.

**Analogies**

*eaglelike    of lakes*

3.  **AQUILINE : LACUSTRINE ::**
    a. eagle : fish
    b. ursine : alpine
    c. porcine : pig
    d. bovine : lake

*sharp      inharmonious*

4.  **PUNGENT : DISSONANT ::**
    a. sharp : knife
    b. pointed : blunt
    c. stab : symphony
    d. aroma : clamor

**Antonyms**

*dark and gloomy*

5.  **TENEBROUS :**
    a. refulgent
    b. glimmering
    c. translucent
    d. perspicuous

*to object earnestly*

6.  **EXPOSTULATE :**
    a. remonstrate
    b. *ex post facto*
    c. congratulate
    d. eulogize

One of the ways to carry money securely was in an arm purse such as the bronze one pictured here. The money could be removed only if the purse was removed from the arm.

### synthesis

**Pungent** is an important word to know, since many educated people do use it in conversation. In literature, *pungent* has been used to describe smells such as the smell of alcohol, but it also has been used to describe the sharp edge of pungent suffering. In *A Separate Peace*, John Knowles used *pungent* to describe the smell of stale sweat that permeated the locker room at Devon School. Think of various smells that are pungent, and then think of experiences other than smells that could be described as pungent.

### aesthetics

In William Butler Yeats's poem "The Lake Isle of Innisfree," there are famous lines describing the **lacustrine** environment at Innisfree, a beautiful lake in Ireland. In one line, Yeats describes the "evening full of the linnet's wings," and in another, he hears "lake water lapping with low sounds by the shore." Carefully consider these lines, and explain how the consonants Yeats used support the meaning he intended.

### imagination, elaboration, and intuition

Imagine a scene in which the cockney **costermongers** are beginning to hawk their vegetables on an East End London street in the *fin de siècle*. It is early morning, the sun is just coming up, and the great city is just coming to life. Using your most vivid imagination and intuition, write a description, or even a short story, in which you make this scene seem elaborately real.

### emotion

Consider the egotistic sociopath, the person who has plenty of (to use Freud's terms) **id** (urges and drives) but not enough **superego** to make him feel sympathy with or pain for others; he feels no guilt or remorse when he causes others to suffer, and so he is too comfortably egocentric. Lacking a conscience, he manipulates other people to get everything he wants, regardless of the effect this has on their lives. Think carefully about the ways in which you care about other significant people in your life, and how their happiness makes you happy too, or how their unhappiness makes you unhappy too. Write a short description of one example of this sympathy that you have felt.

Notice that this superego void is one of the characteristic qualities of monsters in film and literature: monsters tend to be creatures who have human physical characteristics but who lack human emotional sympathy for others. The stereotypical cavernous, hollow-sounding monster voice is one indication of the hollow heart and soul of the id-ful monster.

### divergence and convergence

The noun **dissonance** refers to sounds (*son*) that are away (*dis*) from each other, which are not symphonic or euphonic, which do not harmonize. First, think divergently to imagine a long list of dissonant sounds, such as the squeak of a blackboard (argh), the grinding of a disposal (ugh), the clang of an alarm (ick), and so forth. Then, think convergently to choose the single worst sound of all, the one sound you would least like to have to listen to for the rest of your life.

### Neologist's Lexicon

Use the stems in this list to create a new word (neologism). Give the word, the pronunciation, the part of speech, the etymology, and the definition(s). Keep a record of the neologisms you create from list to list. Here are some examples:

**egomonger** (EEE go MON gur) n. [*ego* (I), *monger* (seller)] 1. a vulgar commercialist who plays on individuals' diffidence with television commercials asking them if they would rather be different, implying that being themselves is not satisfactory 2. a person whose *idée fixe* is to advance himself and who responds to every declarative sentence with a retort beginning, "Well, in my case . . ."

**malodrome** (MAL oh drome) n. [*mal* (bad), *drome* (run)] 1. one who always answers the sanguine question "How's it going?" with the saturnine answer "Not too good." 2. one who spends every day tired because he jogs at 5 a.m. every morning

### Sesquipedalian Mother Goose

Use the words from various vocabulary lists in this book to write a Mother Goose rhyme. Begin with an actual line from one of the famous Mother Goose poems. For example:

#### Little Miss Muffet

Little Miss Muffet, sat on her tuffet

Feeling acerbity.

Circumambulated a spider,

Sedately beside her,

And gave Miss Muffet an epiphany.

Iron window grilles are a common feature of Roman villas; these are on windows in Herculaneum.

| | | | | | | |
|---|---|---|---|---|---|---|
| • *para* | (beside) | paragon | | • sacro | (holy) | execrate |
| • *anti* | (against) | antipathy | | • **plus** | (more) | *ne plus ultra* |
| • *path* | (feeling) | antipathy | | • ultra | (beyond) | *ne plus ultra* |
| • *a-* * | (without) | abyss | | • voc | (voice) | vociferous |
| • **simul** | (feign) | dissemble | | • fer | (carry) | vociferous |
| • sed | (sit) | insidious | | • corp | (body) | corpulent |
| • in | (not) | impecunious | | • *peri* | (near) | perihelion |
| • *kin* | (motion) | kinesiology | | • *helio* | (sun) | perihelion |
| • fy | (make) | beatify | | • *crypt* | (hidden) | cryptic |
| • ex | (out) | execrate | | • **sanct** | (holy) | sanctimonious |

**paragon** (excellent model)  Her computer graphic design was a paragon of geometric form.

**antipathy** (strong dislike)  His fierce antipathy for his rival continued unabated.

**abyss** (bottomless fissure)  The wild mountain gorge seemed a profound abyss.

**dissemble** (conceal through pretense)  Do not be fooled by his lying and dissembling.

**insidious** (sly)  The agent entrapped him with her patient, insidious plot.

**impecunious** (poor)  The impecunious spendthrift could no longer afford fudgesicles.

**kinesiology** (science of motion)  The Olympic coach studied kinesiology assiduously.

**beatify** (make blissfully happy)  She spoke his name, beatifying him for ten minutes.

**execrate** (denounce or curse)  He vilified and execrated his arch enemy, Minnie Mouse.

*ne plus ultra* (peak of perfection)  The Mona Lisa is the *ne plus ultra* of portraits.

• • •

**vociferous** (loudly-voiced)  His vociferous expostulations disrupted her tranquility.

**corpulent** (full-bodied)  The corpulent gourmet continued to indulge in his own creations.

**perihelion** (orbital point nearest the sun)  The comet was brightest at perihelion.

**cryptic** (having hidden meaning)  The Celtic runes contained cryptic messages from the Druids.

**sanctimonious** (affectedly holy)  His sanctimonious attitude was offensive to the group.

*We introduce a new defintion of *a-*.

## As Used by George Owell in *1984*

| To dissemble | your | feelings | was | an | instinctive | reaction. |
|---|---|---|---|---|---|---|

**Parts of Speech:**

| n. | pron. | n. | v. | adj. | adj. | n. |
|---|---|---|---|---|---|---|

**Parts of Sentence:**

-------------- subject--------------     LVP               S.C.

**Phrases:**

----------infinitive phrase---------

**Clauses:**

-----------------------------------independent clause--------------------------------
one independent clause; a simple, declarative sentence

Here Orwell uses *dissemble* in its infinitive form; in this structure *to dissemble* is a noun. The noun *feelings* is the object of the infinitive in the infinitive phrase, which is the subject of the verb. Notice the linking verb *was* and the subject complement *reaction*. An infinitive such as *to dissemble* is regarded as one word.

## Pronunciation

| | | | |
|---|---|---|---|
| **paragon** | PAIR ah gon | **execrate** | EX e crate |
| **antipathy** | an TIP a thee | ***ne plus ultra*** | nay plus UL tra |
| **abyss** | ah BISS | **vociferous** | vo SIFF er us |
| **dissemble** | diss EM bel | **corpulent** | CORP yuh lent |
| **insidious** | in SID ee us | **perihelion** | pair ih HEE lee un |
| **impecunious** | im peh KYOON ee us | **cryptic** | KRIP tik |
| **kinesiology** | ki NEE zee OLL o jee | **sanctimonious** | sank tih MOAN ee us |
| **beatify** | bee AT ih fie | | |

## Spanish Cognates

| | | | |
|---|---|---|---|
| **antipathy** | antipatía | **abyss** | abismo |
| **insidious** | insidioso | **beatified** | beato |
| **execration** | execración | **vociferous** | vociferante |
| **corpulent** | corpulento | **perihelion** | perihelio |

1. The family of *helio* words is fun to note. **Perihelion** is the point at which a planet, comet, or asteroid is nearest (*peri*) to the sun (*helio*). Comets reach their brightest phase as they approach the sun. **Aphelion** is the point at which planets, comets, and asteroids are farthest from the sun. The solar system, filled with objects moving through their perihelions and aphelions as they circle in their revolutions around the sun, is **heliocentric**, rather than **geocentric**. And sun-loving tourists, who risk their future healths for the benefit of a tan, are **heliophiles**.

2. The noun **paragon** means a model of excellence to be used for purposes of comparison. The paragon is the ideal pattern to which we aspire. This idea is easier to understand when we realize that *paragon* comes from the Greek *paragein*: to put side by side. Hamlet tells his friends that Man is the paragon of animals.

4. A **Classic Word**: The noun **abyss** comes from the Greek *abyssos*, meaning bottomless. It is made of *byssos* (bottom of the sea) and *a-* as a short form of *an-* (without). *Abyss* is used not only to refer to the great depths of the sea, but also to anything that is profound, without bottom, or without end, such as time, hell, or the vast space of the universe. In ancient cosmogony the abyss was the primal chaos that existed before Creation. In classic literature *abyss* has had a distinguished history. It has been used by Fitzgerald, Wells, Hawthorne, Conrad, Hardy (to describe the vast heath), Kipling, Scott, Dickens, Stowe, and Emily Brontë. In Dickens's *A Tale of Two Cities*, Sidney Carton sees a beautiful city and a brilliant people rising from this abyss (revolutionary Paris). Harriet Beecher Stowe describes slavery's abyss of injustice and cruelty. Heathcliff's poignant cry to the dying Catherine in *Wuthering Heights* is, "do not leave me in this abyss, where I cannot find you." In Conrad's *Lord Jim*, sea and sky are compounded into one abyss of obscurity. In *The Time Machine,* the Morlocks' eyes are abnormally large and sensitive, like the pupils of the abysmal fishes.

5. The ***ne plus ultra*** is the peak of perfection, the highest point, the zenith, the acme. You can go no (*ne*) more (*plus*) beyond (*ultra*) the *ne plus ultra*. This term places even more emphasis on absolute perfection than the word **paragon**. The *Mona Lisa* is the *ne plus ultra* of portraits because Leonardo's lightning-fast eyes allowed him to capture the most subtle and evanescent of glances, the most impossibly slight changes of countenance that occur at the magic moment of attraction between two people. Many artists can capture the primary emotions of anger, joy, or deep reflection, but few artists have had the acute perception to see the delicate phenomena that the subtlest, in-between emotions bring to the face. But then, you would expect such powers of observation from a painter who could draw the swirling currents of a stream.

6. A **Micropoem**: The adjective **insidious** contains a delightful hidden image. Made of *in* (in) and *sed* (sit), it refers to the trap in which the deceitful person sits in ambush, waiting for his or her victim. To be insidious is to deliberately deceive in order to entrap, to **sit in** wait for your intended prey. This word is an outstanding example of the beautiful micropoems that words so often contain and that are unavailable to those who only consider the definitions and not the etymologies.

Pictured above is a writing exercise on a fragment of papyrus of a line from Virgil's *Aeneid* copied seven times in ink. The other items are a writing tablet with four leafs, three inkpots, a bronze pen, and styli for writing in soft wax on practice tablets like the one shown at the bottom right.

# EDUCATION
## Dr. Thomas Milton Kemnitz

Throughout the entire history of the Roman Republic, the *paterfamilias* determined the education of his children. Most young Romans learned to read and write at home, and the vast majority of the plebs had scant education beyond that. For the more prosperous, a patchwork of arrangements was available to educate their children. There were no schools as we know them. Often individuals would set themselves up as instructors with a single room; families would select one and agree to pay him—usually very little—each month to teach their children. This sort of arrangement became common in the last century of the Republic. Roman teachers were notorious for their poverty—several teachers whom we know about died in poverty and debt—and for their brutality. We know little about what happened in the schoolrooms, but we do know about the beating of children. Canes and leather whips were used as aids to a child's concentration and understanding. The poet Horace studied in the school of Lucius Orbilius Pupillus, whom he described as a flogger. Physical exercise and training to fight in the Roman military were an essential part of a young man's education.

Three factors altered education in the later years of the Roman Republic. The first was the Greek influence. As the Romans became familiar with and increasingly admired Greek culture, education for the wealthiest was prolonged and broadened to include the Greek language and arts and philosophy. Romans became familiar with Greek playwrights and poets, with Homer and Aesop, with Herodotus and Thucydides, with Euripides and Sophocles and Aeschylus and Aristophanes, with Socrates and Plato and Aristotle and Pythagoras and Epicurus, with Meander and Pindar and many more. With the Greeks as part of the curriculum, there was so much more to learn. Second was the arrival in Rome of many educated Greeks as slaves; they fetched a high price and went to wealthier Roman families and frequently acted as tutors to Roman children. Commencing with the Second Macedonian War at the beginning of the second century (200-196 B.C.), this was a rapidly accelerating development in Roman households. Third was the vast increase in wealth that came with foreign conquest and which allowed many Romans the leisure of longer educations than had been the case in the early years of the Republic. By the first century B.C., young patrician men were finishing their education in Greece, particularly learning rhetoric with the object of becoming better orators. Famous Greek orators such as Pericles and Demosthenes were widely admired, and busts of them adorned the libraries of many Roman villas.

The *ad hoc* nature of Roman education had several strengths. One was that it allowed some mobility in that the exceptional sons of client families might be educated with the patron's children or in the patron's household. This allowed deserving "new men" to emerge in Rome's ruling elite. In addition, clusters of children seem often to have been educated together for at least part of their formative years. This allowed the formation of lasting friendships made early amongst Rome's ruling elite, thus aiding the smooth functioning of the state.

Roman education had the flexibility to change in time and with circumstances. Its amorphous quality did not hinder the growth of the state in any way. By contrast, the rigid and demanding *agoge* of Sparta was often seen as a core of Spartan strength and success, but in the long run the requirement of successfully completing the *agoge* to become a full Spartan was partially responsible for producing a situation in which there were too few Spartans to protect the *polis*.

In each case below, one of the choices was really the word used by the author in the sentence provided. All of the choices can be found in the example words on the first page of this lesson. Your challenge is to decide which word the author used. This is not a test; it is more like a game because more than one word choice may work perfectly well. See if you can use your sensitivity and intuition to guess correctly which word the author used.

1. **From E.L. Doctorow's *Ragtime***

   I look about me and smell the sweat of rage, the _____ rebellion of wild unthinking youth.
   a. corpulent
   b. impecunious
   c. sanctimonious
   d. vociferous

2. **From Edith Wharton's *Ethan Frome***

   It was the sense of helplessness that sharpened his _____.
   a. abyss
   b. kinesiology
   c. sanctimoniousness
   d. antipathy

3. **From Thornton Wilder's *The Bridge of San Luis Rey***

   She leaned forward, her face streaming with happy tears, and made the _____ gesture.
   a. beatific
   b. impecunious
   c. dissembling
   d. sanctimonious

4. **From George Orwell's *1984***

   It's _____. It can get hold of you without your even knowing it.
   a. cryptic
   b. vociferous
   c. insidious
   d. sanctimonious

5. **From T.S. Eliot's *Murder in the Cathedral***

   Men will not hate you enough to defame you or to _____ you.
   a. beatify
   b. execrate
   c. dissemble
   d. *ne plus ultra*

Though it is a good thing to have a rich vocabulary, it is not a good thing to abuse that vocabulary by writing verbose, abstruse, sesquipedalian sentences. Those who overuse their vocabularies often do so at the expense of clarity. Translate the following showy, ponderous passage into graceful, direct English. Do not use slang, but do use words that seem familiar and comfortable.

THIS GLOWING DIAPHANOUS VISION, thought the astrophysicist, was no mere paragon of poetry in motion, no mere metaphor for the theoretical abyss of kinesiology; this was the *ne plus ultra* of all motion. This was perfection itself. She gazed again through the optical eyepiece of BOOGIE (the in-house humorous acronym for Big Old Optical Gathering Instrument of Entropy), the huge telescope at the summit of Mt. Wollstonecraft, at the streaming translucent filaments of the comet's tail, stretching from the comet's perihelion near the sun to far beyond the orbit of Venus, and she felt a beatific peace. Once again, her equations had proved exact, and the beautiful comet had appeared exactly where she had predicted. For her, mathematics *was* nature, and her equations were paintings with which she described the cosmos. This, she thought, was truth; though the cosmos could be cryptic, it could not dissemble (like some of her insidious colleagues who envied her brilliance and accomplishments and who lost no opportunity to advise her sanctimoniously about how to improve her work).

With a neophyte's joy, she loved studying the glittering cosmos, with its silently vociferous stars; its corpulent, ringed planets; its ineluctable gravitation; its prolix spectra; its gregarious galaxies; its disinterested physics that knew no antipathy or execration. She loved the euphony of the night wind in the observatory dome; it always seemed to her to be the *sotto voce* harmony of the heavenly spheres. Einstein had seen the physiognomy of the Omniscient Spirit in this black abyss of space; The Old One, he had called it. Well, she understood that, too. She had made a career of this research, this lucubration, this astrophysics, but even after a lifetime of work, she had to admit that she was impecunious in knowledge. Like Socrates, she had learned that she knew nothing.

Yet the happiness she felt in this tenuous knowledge was beatific. A life of scientific integrity had given her a self-acceptance that amounted almost to cosmological narcissism, since through her nonplussed mind, the universe was, as *alter ego*, looking at and in love with itself.

## Reading Comprehension

1. In Translation 46, it can be inferred that:
    a. The astrophysicist's colleagues concur with her conclusions.
    b. The astrophysicist's colleagues collaborate closely at the observatory.
    c. The astrophysicist's mediocre colleagues are envious of her talent.
    d. The astrophysicist uses unsound scientific practices.

2. The author does all of the following EXCEPT:
    a. imply that profound knowledge is difficult to attain
    b. imply that science is of no value
    c. imply that scientists are fallible human beings
    d. imply that scientists can believe in God

## Analogies

3. **CRYPTIC : SANCTIMONIOUS ::**
    a. dungeon : church
    b. concealed : pretentious
    c. code : prayer
    d. suggestion : sanctuary

4. **DISSEMBLE : EXECRATE ::**
    a. denounce : pretend
    b. assemble : berate
    c. intransitive : transitive
    d. feign : deprecate

## Antonyms

5. **ANTIPATHY :**
    a. eulogy
    b. lionizing
    c. amour
    d. apotheosis

6. **IMPECUNIOUS :**
    a. opulent
    b. squalid
    c. aristocratic
    d. affluent

The details are difficult to discern, but this fresco shows a student being held by two others while whipped in a school that is held in a colonnade; he is draped over the shoulders of one person while another holds his feet just above his ankles. Sometimes a curtain or piece of fabric was hung to block the school off from the street, presumably as a way of concentrating the attention of the scholars. In this case there is no curtain, or it has been removed to make the punishment more public. This is a wall painting that survived the eruption of Vesuvius. Its sketchy nature is an indication that the artist was not practiced in producing this scene and that it may have been a special order by the villa's owner.

**synthesis**

An **abyss** is a deep or bottomless space, such as a precipitous mountain gorge or a trench in the ocean. Think of as many abysses as you can, first in the physical world and then in the emotional or abstract world, as metaphors; i.e., the abyss of his loneliness. The further out and wilder your comparisons are without being meaningless, the more powerful the synthesis. (Thinking of wild comparisons is good because you are noticing what seemingly different things have in common. This is an important thinking ability in many fields, such as physics.)

**analysis**

By breaking the words into their component stems, explain the difference between **paragon**, **nonpareil**, and *ne plus ultra*, or between **antipathy**, **objurgation**, and **execrate**. You may use a dictionary to look up the etymologies, if you would like more information than the stems we have studied provide.

**intuition for imagination**

Imagine that you have been on a quest. You are young but brave and determined. You follow a misty path to a high mountain ridge, where you suddenly come upon huge stone monoliths, covered with moss, sticking out of the low vegetation. A small, wizened, grizzled man steps out from behind one of the monoliths, offering to help you, but you can tell that he is **dissembling**. Why is he dissembling? What is he concealing? Continue the story . . . .

**ethics**

What figure in American political history do you regard as a **paragon** of ethical political behavior? In other words, who do you regard as a highly ethical politician—someone such as a president, senator, or governor who helped to govern the United States in a moral and principled way? Explain who you chose and why.

**divergence and imagination**

Divergence is thinking up options or alternatives. One aspect of divergence is to think of lots of alternatives, and another is to think of creative, original, or unexpected alternatives. Whereas synthesis is thinking of how different things are connected or similar, divergence is thinking of lots of different ways or kinds of things. Synthesis is noticing similarities; divergence is creating choices. Imagine that you are temporarily **impecunious** and that you are going to solve this problem by selling T-shirts with **sesquipedalian** messages on them, such as "I HATE ANTIPATHY." Working in groups, make a list of witty sesquipedalian T-shirt slogans. Use words from any list up to List 46.

**convergence**

If you woke up in a strange alternative world, where the law required you to use one of the words from List 46 every day, which word would you choose? Why? Imagine how difficult it would be if you had to use one of these words in every single sentence.

## Neologist's Lexicon

Use the stems in this list to create a new word (neologism). Give the word, the pronunciation, the part of speech, the etymology, and the definition(s). Keep a record of the neologisms you create from list to list. Here are some examples:

**antikinetic** (AN ti kin ETT ik) adj. [*anti* (against), *kin* (motion)] · 1. having a tendency to immediately propose the opposite of whatever you hear proposed; always reflexively moving the contrary  2. severely and profoundly intractable, such that you never even consider the possibility of changing your mind on any issue whatsoever

**sacropathy** (sak ROH path ee) n. [*sacro* (holy), *path* (feeling)]  1. attaching far more importance to everything one does or encounters than is healthy or rational  2. being so emotionally involved with important matters that you lose the ability to think about them

## Sesquipedalian Recipe

Use the words from List 46 and previous lists to write a sesquipedalian recipe for the preparation of any food you like. If you are not a cook, you can write directions for making a peanut butter sandwich or for preparing a bowl of cereal. The point is to have fun using the words. An example:

### The Sesquipedalian Gastronome's Famous Chili
#### by an Autodidact

To prepare the *sui generis* paragon of all chilis, causing your dissembling friends to sink into an abyss of lionizing envy, obsequiously observe the following prolix and omnibus injunctions, contravening none:

1. In a large pot, empty four 28 oz. cans of corpulent whole tomatoes and four drained 16 oz. cans of light red kidney beans. To this pungent mixture, add the heterodox ingredients: a sprinkling of oregano, a half-dozen bay leaves, some salt, and some black pepper. Bring to a truculent boil, and then simmer beatifically.
2. In a cast iron frying pan, lightly sauté one diced onion in olive oil, and pour the mollified onion into the large pot. Be on the *qui vive*, lest the onion begin to brown.
3. In the same frying pan, assiduously brown a pound or two of ground beef, adding one or two packages of commercial chili seasoning, depending on how hot you like your chili. Use legerdemain to pour out the grease, and add the browned, seasoned beef to the large pot. Stir to expedite the confluence of flavors. Abjure acerbity.
4. Continue to simmer, stirring intractably, for two hours. *In medias res*, relish the circumambient aromas, and perform loquacious soliloquies. Temporize.
5. With equanimity and sangfroid, add three tablespoons of honey just before serving. Stir well. This secret ingredient will create the *ne plus ultra* of chilis. Impugn the specious objections of persons who doubt the wisdom of adding honey. They will soon be transmogrified into mellifluous admirers.
6. Serve with supererogatory sourdough biscuits and honey.
7. Stoically accept the benedictions of the incredulous *bon vivants*.
8. Enjoy postprandial perambulation.
9. Be gregarious.
10. Avoid megalomania.

| | | | | | | |
|---|---|---|---|---|---|---|
| • *ism* | (doctrine) | pharisaism | • lent | (full of) | feculent |
| • *neuro* | (nerve) | neurasthenia | • less (OE**) | (without) | feckless |
| • *a-* | (without) | neurasthenia | • contra | (against) | contretemps |
| • **sthen** | (strength) | neurasthenia | • tempor | (time) | contretemps |
| • re | (again) | remunerate | • *hyper* | (over) | hyperbole |
| • pro* | (forward) | proscenium | • *para* | (beside) | paradigm |
| • **scen** | (stage) | proscenium | • germ | (related) | germane |
| • *epist* | (knowledge) | epistle | • fil | (thread) | filigree |
| • *chron* | (time) | anachronistic | • **gran** | (grain) | filigree |

**pharisaism** (hypocrisy)  His pharisaism of aloof pretense but loose behavior sickened us.

**neurasthenia** (nervous exhaustion)  He mocked the bad poet's neurasthenic affectations.

**remunerate** (repay)  Talented people should be well remunerated for their labors.

**proscenium** (stage forward of curtain)  She took a final bow from the proscenium.

**epistle** (long, instructive letter)  Read her tiring epistle on the proper way to vacation.

**anachronistic** (misplaced in time)  Notice the anachronistic twentieth-century details in the novel.

**feculent** (foul)  We drove sorrowfully past the feculent and filthy yards of the shanties.

**feckless** (without effect)  We saw Hector's feckless efforts to overcome his fear of Achilles.

**anapest** (three-syllable foot, stress on third)  Example: ampuTEE, insinCERE, on the BEACH.

**contretemps** (embarrassing mishap)  The chance meeting was a ludicrous contretemps.

• • •

**hyperbole** (overstatement)  His colorful hyperbole amused us.

**paradigm** (model)  Show us an instructive paradigm or example.

**germane** (related)  Her germane comments were vitally relevant to the debate.

**filigree** (lacy design)  It was difficult to clean the gold filigree around the jewel.

**chronic** (lasting)  The chronic illness plagued her for years.

*Pro is both Latin and Greek, and there are multiple meanings for each.
**OE means Old English.

## As Used by Jack London in *White Fang*

| | Such | things | were | **remuneration** | in | full. |
|---|---|---|---|---|---|---|
| **Parts of Speech:** | adj. | n. | v. | **n.** | prep. | n. |
| **Parts of Sentence:** | | subj. | LVP | S.C. | | |
| **Phrases:** | | | | | ---prep. phrase--- | |
| **Clauses:** | ------------------------------------independent clause---------------------------------- | | | | | |
| | one independent clause; a simple, declarative sentence | | | | | |

Here London uses the noun *remuneration* as the subject complement.

## Pronunciation

| | | | |
|---|---|---|---|
| **pharisaism** | fair ih SAY izm | **anapest** | ANN ah pest |
| **neurasthenia** | noor as THEN ee ah | **contretemps** | KOHN tra TOH |
| **remunerate** | re MYOO ner ate | **hyperbole** | hie PURR bo lee |
| **proscenium** | pro SEEN ee um | **paradigm** | PAIR ah dime |
| **epistle** | ee PIST el | **germane** | jer MAIN |
| **anachronistic** | an ack kron ISS tik | **filigree** | FILL ih gree |
| **feculent** | FECK yoo lent | **chronic** | KRON ik |
| **feckless** | FECK less | | |

## Spanish Cognates

| | | | |
|---|---|---|---|
| **pharisaic** | farisaico | **neurasthenic** | neurasténico |
| **remuneration** | remuneración | **proscenium** | proscenio |
| **epistle** | epístola | **anachronistic** | anacrónico |
| **feculent** | feculento | **hyperbole** | hipérbole |
| **paradigm** | paradigma | **filigree** | filigrana |
| **chronic** | crónico | | |

1.  A **Micropoem**: The noun **anapest** refers to a poetic foot that contains three syllables, with the stress on the third syllable: --'. It comes from the Greek words for strike (*pest*) and back (*ana*): dadaWHAM. Examples are *ampuTEE*, *insinCERE*, or *on the BEACH*. Notice that the foot does not have to be a single word. It can be one, two, or three words. It can be made of pieces of words:

    At the **break** of the **day** when ba**lloons**
    Rose in **sil**ent as**cent** over**head**

    The primary forms of poetic foot are the **iamb**, two syllables with the stress on the second: -', the **trochee**, two syllables with the stress on the first: '-, the **dactyl**, three syllables with the stress on the first: '--, and the anapest. Most traditional English verse, such as Shakespeare's sonnets, is in iambic pentameter ( -' / -' / -' / -' / -' ). Remember Romeo's first iambic pentameter words to Juliet: "If **I** pro**fane** with **my** un**wor**thiest **hand** . . . ." We think of *ana* as meaning away or up, but the sense here is a bit different; here it means back. The word *anapest* comes from the Greek *anápaistos*, meaning struck back or reversed (from a dactyl). One of life's loveliest experiences is to gradually learn an ear for the sound of language, for the music of human speech.

2.  The noun **paradigm** comes from the Greek *para* (beside) and *deiknynai* (show); the idea is that one shows two things side by side, the one forming a model for the other. Today, we use the word *paradigm* to refer to an intellectual model. Thoreau's reflections on nature in *Walden* form a paradigm for future nature writers and natural philosophers. We do not usually use the word in a physical sense, as to describe a ship model or plane model.

3.  A **Classic Word**: The adjective **chronic** is based on the Greek stem *chron*, meaning time. We find this stem in **chronological**, **anachronistic**, **chronometer**, **chronology**, **chronoscope**, **synchronize**, and **chronicle**, to name only a few words. Harriet Beecher Stowe used *chronic* frequently in *Uncle Tom's Cabin*; she described a kind of chronic plague, a sort of chronic remorse, and a chronic feud between Sam and Aunt Chloe that had existed from ancient times. Melville mentions a chronically broken back in *Moby Dick*. And Dickens, in *A Tale of Two Cities*, finds that Sidney Carton is chronically drunk. In *Tom Sawyer*, Mark Twain says that the dreadful secret of the murder was a chronic misery, whereas in *The Call of the Wild*, Jack London pities the "outside dogs, whose digestions had not been trained by chronic famine to make the most of little." In John Knowles's *A Separate Peace*, we find an attitude of floating, chronic disapproval. The most descriptive use, however, of *chronic* must be attributed to Harper Lee; in *To Kill a Mockingbird*, we learn that "the younger children had perpetual colds and suffered from chronic ground-itch." Chronic ground-itch? Give me chronic famine any day. Of course, it would be nice to be a chronic consumer of apple pie or cheeseburgers. And anyone who has read far enough to discover this sentence is probably a chronic bibliophile. Join the club. I'll see you at the bookstore.

    By the way, I know that the term *Uncle Tom* has acquired negative connotations in recent decades, and I understand why, but *Uncle Tom's Cabin* is a brilliant book by a brilliant woman; it was written to condemn the horror and hideous immorality of slavery and racial bigotry, and it does that in a profoundly moving way that few other books can equal.

In storefronts like this one in Pompeii, urban denizens in the Roman world could purchase *prandium* in the late morning or *cena* toward the end of the day.

# FOOD
## Dr. Thomas Milton Kemnitz

For most of the early history of Rome, the paucity of food was a persistent problem. A significant proportion of the Roman population consisted of small farmers with plots of land of five or fewer acres. Their primary crop was emmer, which was one of the varieties of wheat first cultivated in the Middle East on which Old World agriculture was based. It grew wild through the region, and it was hearty and easy to raise. It became the staple of the Roman diet. Biochemical analysis of Roman skeletons is providing more and more accurate information about the Roman cuisine, and this analysis is showing that millet was an important part of the diet of the Roman poor. In the literature, millet is denigrated as animal feed, but clearly the poorest Romans ate it regularly. Millet is more difficult than emmer to digest, but it grows well in arid soil and in dry conditions, it is a more reliable crop than emmer, and it might have been a significant part of the Roman diet during the monarchy and in the early years of the Republic. It is clear that scarcity and hunger were prevalent in Rome, and this would have made millet more attractive as a food.

Breakfast was a light meal generally eaten at or before dawn. The Romans called it *jentaculum*, and it might consist of a few figs or a piece of bread dipped in olive oil or wine; many Romans did not eat *jentaculum*, but it is reasonable to assume that young children in particular were fed then.

*Prandium* was what the Romans called the late morning meal. It was not normally a substantial meal and might be eaten in the fields or at work. As the Roman world expanded and became increasingly urban, it is clear from the archeological evidence that a significant proportion of the population took their meals at lunch counters like the one pictured opposite.

*Cena* was eaten late in the afternoon as the main meal of the day. For most Romans throughout the monarchy and the Republic, *cena* was generally husked emmer or millet boiled in water to make a porridge called *puls*, much as oatmeal is now. Herbs, vegetables, honey, and even meat might be added to the mixture to enhance the taste.

Most Romans ate from pottery plates and bowls. They had spoons and knives. They used their hands a lot. They ate sitting up at tables. They drank wine, which they diluted with water. For most of the history of the Republic, frugality was a virtue much espoused by patricians as well as plebs, a virtue often arising from necessity. By the second century, it was a virtue more honored than practiced by the patricians.

As the Romans came to emulate the Greeks in the second century B.C., the wealthier among them began to have *cena* earlier in the day, and the meals became increasingly elaborate. One course became two, and then three. More emphasis was put upon the diversity of the food and drink, and slaves who could cook well became more highly prized. Silver goblets and plates replaced earthenware, and silver or even gold spoons came into use. The *cena* was drawn out, and the diners began to recline on couches in the Greek style. The working day was compressed so the meal could begin in mid-afternoon. Banquets became displays of wealth. Because the streets of Rome were dangerous, particularly after dark, the host had to make provisions for large retinues of slaves and bodyguards, who were necessary to see their important guests home safely. Food might be served in several different rooms to different classes of guests. One letter of Cicero tells of entertaining Julius Caesar and his attendants in three different rooms.

In each case below, one of the choices was really the word used by the author in the sentence provided. All of the choices can be found in the example words on the first page of this lesson. Your challenge is to decide which word the author used. This is not a test; it is more like a game because more than one word choice may work perfectly well. See if you can use your sensitivity and intuition to guess correctly which word the author used.

1.   **From Mary Wollstonecraft's *Vindication of the Rights of Woman***

A _____ stream of wealth...has muddied the pure rills of natural affection.
a. feckless
b. feculent
c. germane
d. chronic

2.   **From Jack London's *White Fang***

Such things were _____ in full for his ardors and toils.
a. epistles
b. pharisaisms
c. remunerations
d. contretemps

3.   **From Robert Louis Stevenson's *Kidnapped***

Ye must be as _____ at the sailoring as I have found ye at the fighting.
a. feckless
b. chronic
c. feculent
d. hyperbolic

4.   **From John Knowles's *A Separate Peace***

Yes, huh, yes there was a small, a little _____ at the tree.
a. filigree
b. paradigm
c. contretemps
d. proscenium

5.   **From Frederick Douglass's *Narrative***

They attended with _____ strictness to the outward forms of religion.
a. feckless
b. chronic
c. germane
d. pharisaical

Though it is a good thing to have a rich vocabulary, it is not a good thing to abuse that vocabulary by writing verbose, abstruse, sesquipedalian sentences. Those who overuse their vocabularies often do so at the expense of clarity. Translate the following showy, ponderous passage into graceful, direct English. Do not use slang, but do use words that seem familiar and comfortable.

Notice that much of the passage is in anapestic meter, which might be impossible to imitate in your translation. This will give you some insight into the problems that professional translators have when they try to capture the beautifully poetic work of the great novelists, such as Flaubert, who wrote *Madame Bovary* in such euphonic language that he actually shouted each passage aloud to see if it sounded right. Yes, the neighbors thought he was crazy. Flaubert's literary perfectionism was so intense that he has been often satirized: in Albert Camus's *The Plague*, one character is a novelist who throughout the story is still writing and rewriting the first sentence of a novel, never being satisfied enough with it to go on to the second sentence.

THE NONPLUSSED WINNER of the unremunerative annual Magnum Opus Hyperbole Competition was the neophyte author of a semi-poetic epistle, from which the following tortuous sentence, a prolix paradigm of anapestic meter, is taken: "The most TOTally VACuous COMment and UNgermane PERfidy UTtered in ABsolute FECKlessness WAS the comPLETEly anTI-neurasTHENically BAD phariSAism CALLing the FECulent FILigree OVer the ROTTing proSCENium MONey well SPENT when in FACT it was ONly a BAD contreTEMPS, so aDIEU." This odd exaggeration was freely translated as, "Restoring the old stage was a ridiculous waste of bucks, see ya."

When superciliously asked why he had composed the victorious anapests, the discursive, saturnine winner spoke diffidently and with an obsequious voice into the microphone: "*Au conTRAIRE*, but the REAson I WROTE the imPONderaBLE introSPECTively SPECious anAPHora-FILLED valeDICTion exPATiatING *inter ALia* OVer inEFfable RECondite MATters is CRYPTic to ME."

At the epiphany of this bizarre postlude, the incredulous audience burst into condescending, loquacious cacophony.

## Reading Comprehension

1. For Translation 47, which of the following does the passage suggest?
   a. The winner of the competition cheated.
   b. The winner of the competition was unaware of his own natural talent.
   c. The winner of the competition worked hard and won fairly.
   d. The winner of the competition spoke in clever self-imitation.

2. The passage could best be described as:
   a. an example of irony
   b. an example of paradox
   c. an example of juxtaposition
   d. an example of parody

## Analogies

3. **ANAPEST : DACTYLIC ::**
   a. insincere : hopelessly
   b. trochee : iamb
   c. poem : epistle
   d. germane : anachronistic

4. **CHRONIC : EPHEMERAL ::**
   a. clock : femur
   b. prolonged : enduring
   c. protracted : transient
   d. remunerate : indemnify

## Antonyms

5. **GERMANE :**
   a. relevant
   b. felicitous
   c. French
   d. malapropos

6. **FECKLESS :**
   a. salutary
   b. useful
   c. defect
   d. perfect

One of the delicacies of the Roman table was the dormouse, an animal native to Europe and known to most Americans only from its appearance in *Alice in Wonderland*. Despite its name, the edible dormouse is more squirrel than mouse. It has a furry tail like a squirrel, primarily lives in trees, and grows larger than a mouse. They were fattened up in a *glirarium*, a specially-built pottery container that had runs up the side so the animals could come up to get fed and presumably get captured easily when the time came. The dormice were often served stuffed and roasted. They would be stuffed with ground pork mixed with nuts, garlic, herbs, and even with diced dormice, and then sewn shut and roasted. Often they were rolled in honey and poppy seeds and were one of the sweet courses. This *glirarium* was found at Pompeii.

## ethics

In the field of ethics . . . [I love the metaphor of the *field*; imagine how it would change our image if someone said, "On the mountain slope of ethics," or "In the blue abyss of ethics," or "On the frosty tundra of ethics," or "On the beach of ethics." We have fields of grass, fields of grain, fields of thought, fields of magnetism, and fields of gravity. We have playing fields, force fields, and ice fields. I keep wondering what, exactly, is meant by a *field* when we apply the word to gravity or magnetism, since these "fields" are so geometrically different from a field of, say, daisies. One of the most resonant areas (meadows?) of language is the vast number of metaphors that we have used for so long that we have forgotten that we are being metaphorical. And of course, we are forced into constant metaphor because the world is so perplexing that we often do not know any *direct* way to describe the phenomenon we have encountered. Now, where was I?] In the field of ethics, the lives, teachings, and parables of the great philosophers, heroes, and religious leaders serve as **paradigms** for our own ethical behavior. We remember, for example, the irascible voice of John the Baptist, shouting in the desert, and his commitment serves as a paradigm of ethical purity against which we inevitably, and perhaps uncomfortably, compare the level of our own commitment. We remember Martin Luther King, Jr.'s intractable, indomitable will: "Here I stand, I can do no other." We remember Socrates choosing hemlock over exile. We remember Sidney Carton taking Charles Darnay's place at the guillotine: "Tis a far, far better thing I do than I have ever done." We remember Alexander treating his enemy Darius's mother with dignity and respect, as he would wish his own mother to be treated by a conquering enemy. We remember Martin Luther King, Jr.'s dream from the mountaintop and his vision of the promised land of ethical democracy. We remember Patrick Henry only regretting that he had but one life to give for his country. We remember being asked to consider, before doing unto others, what we would choose to have done to ourselves. Each of these stories is a paradigm.

One of my favorite ethical ideas is the *categorical imperative* of the philosopher Immanuel Kant (German, 1724-1804), who defined an action as ethical if we can will a maxim of the action to be universalized. In other words, if you want to know if an action is moral, see if you can wish that the general principle of what you intend would be adopted by everyone. In other words, see if you can wish that everyone in every similar situation would do what you want to do. For example, imagine that you think you have logical and humane reasons for breaking a law because you feel that the law is wrong or discriminatory. Can you really will that all individuals who feel that a law is wrong would ignore the law? Probably not. If everyone who sincerely disagreed with a law felt comfortably free to break it, our society would degenerate into chaos. On the other hand, you probably can will that everyone who felt opposed to a law would work with great legal energy to change it. And so the effect of using Kant's categorical imperative is to lift you out of the emotional details of the particular situation and make you conscious of the universal principle of your action as a general category of action. Kant's categorical imperative, like Jesus's golden rule, requires you to reflect beyond your single self as a unique case and consider your action as only one example of an entire category of action; if you would not want the category to happen to the world, then you should not do even one example of it. You must follow the imperative (command) of the category.

## Neologist's Lexicon

Use the stems in this list to create a new word (neologism). Give the word, the pronunciation, the part of speech, the etymology, and the definition(s). Keep a record of the neologisms you create from list to list. Here are some examples:

**prochronolent** (pro KRON o lent) adj. [*pro* (forward), *chron* (time), *lent* (full of)] 1. being continually conscious of what one is going to do next or soon 2. the obsessive awareness of time and instruments that measure time, as one who is continually looking at his watch

**scenism** (SEEN izm) n. [*scen* (stage), *ism* (doctrine)] 1. the idea that all the world is a stage, and all the people in it merely players (*vide* Shakespeare) 2. the unwillingness to live anywhere that is not scenically beautiful

## Sesquipedalian Homer

Have you read *The Iliad*, Homer's passionate magnum opus of epic poetry about the Trojan war, in which Achilles, Agamemnon, Menelaus, and the Achaians attack Troy because Paris took the beautiful Helen, wife of Menelaus? Troy's great warrior is Hector, a brave soldier but a bully and a braggart, and he is finally killed by the awesome Achilles, who has been sulking off the battlefield in anger against Agamemnon and who only enters the fray to avenge the death of Patroclos, his great friend.

Homer's writing style is vivid. He describes in horrific detail the deaths of the soldiers in the Trojan war, but the graphic description of the violence is not for the sake of sensationalism; it is to honor the individuality of each man who dies. There are no meaningless, impersonal, statistical deaths in *The Iliad*. Instead, each solder who dies is described in mini-biographical detail; he has a name, a family, he is from a specific town, he owes someone money, he will never return to someone who loves him. Each death matters and lessens the world. And this is not a Hollywood war; the pain and cruelty of death are not minimized or sensationalized; the terrible work of each blade stroke is described—the wound, the entry point, the bones broken, the agony, the internal organs, the fall, the crash of the armor, the dark night closing over the eyes. After reading Homer's story, we understand why even his greatest heroes, Hector and Achilles, are afraid, and they admit it.

The other element that is fascinating is Homer's **epic simile**: his technique of comparing a human event to an elaborately drawn simile. A warrior will whirl and fight *like a lion on a barren mountain, chased by hounds and surrounded as the hunters run up, drawing their bows; the lion knows that his end is near, he struggles desperately to claw the closest dog and to roar loud enough to frighten the others away, but it is no use, and he whirls faster and faster as the dogs gather around him while the hunters draw closer.* See? That's what a Homeric simile or epic simile is like. It is a detailed simile. (Homer's simile's are better than my imitation; read *The Iliad*.)

Now, pick something from your own life, silly or humorous if you like, and write a Homeric simile for it using words from List 47 and previous lists (Homer, of course used plain language). For example, you might describe, in sesquipedalian heroic terms, a simile for the act of grabbing your toothbrush first thing in the morning, or the way you stagger up after the alarm rings. Pick something interesting or humorous, and then go far afield for an interesting and creative simile. Have fun using the words from the lists.

| | | | | | |
|---|---|---|---|---|---|
| • in | (in) | inamorata | • pot | (drink) | symposium |
| • **amor** | (love) | inamorata | • *nomy* | (law) | nomothetic |
| • inter | (between) | interpolate | • fus | (pour) | effusion |
| • sub | (under) | subjugate, subjacent | • dign | (worthy) | condign |
| • ex | (out) | effulgence | • vect | (carry) | invective |
| • **fulg** | (shine or flash) | effulgence | • fract | (break) | refractory |
| • *sym* | (together) | symposium | • *acro* | (high) | acrophobia |
| • re | (again) | replete | • *phobia* | (fear) | acrophobia |
| • ous | (full of) | querulous | | | |

**inamorata** (mistress) She knew the loneliness of the inamorata.

**interpolate** (insert) It is wrong to corrupt a book by interpolating new passages.

**subjugate** (bring under the yoke) The tribes were subjugated by the Roman armies.

**effulgence** (shining out) We saw the reassuring effulgence of the morning sun.

**replete** (filled) The record was replete with examples of his benevolence.

**querulous** (full of complaint) His irritating querulous tendencies became chronic.

**subjacent** (underlying) The edifice rested solidly on its subjacent rock strata.

**symposium** (conference) The symposium on international amity was in Brussels.

**immolate** (sacrifice) Her brave speech was an act of political self-immolation.

**nomothetic** (lawgiving) Read the nomothetic passages of the *Old Testament*.

• • •

**effusion** (outpouring) His effusion of joyful greetings made us wince.

**condign** (worthy) The criminal met his condign end—a prison sentence.

**invective** (bitter denunciation) She stoically endured her opponent's invective.

**refractory** (stubborn) The refractory child repeatedly broke the rules.

**acrophobia** (fear of heights) She felt acrophobia on high bridges.

## As Used by Jane Austen in *Pride and Prejudice*

Mrs. Bennett    was    restored    to    her    usual    **querulous**    serenity.

| Parts of Speech: | n. | --------v.-------- | prep. | pron. | adj. | **adj.** | n. |
|---|---|---|---|---|---|---|---|

**Parts of Sentence:** subj. ------AVP------

**Phrases:** -------------prepositional phrase------------

**Clauses:** -----------------------------------independent clause---------------------------------
one independent clause; a simple, declarative sentence

Here Austen uses the adjective *querulous* to modify the noun *serenity*, which is the object of the preposition *to*. The action verb *was restored* is in passive voice.

## Pronunciation

| | | | |
|---|---|---|---|
| **inamorata** | in ah more AH tah | **immolate** | IM o late |
| **interpolate** | in TUR po late | **nomothetic** | no mo THEH tik |
| **subjugate** | SUB ju gate | **effusion** | e FYOO zhun |
| **effulgence** | eh FULL jence | **condign** | kon DINE |
| **replete** | re PLEET | **invective** | in VECK tiv |
| **querulous** | KWER u luss | **refractory** | re FRAK tory |
| **subjacent** | sub JAY sent | **acrophobia** | ack ro FO bee ah |
| **symposium** | sim PO zee um | | |

## Spanish Cognates

| | | | |
|---|---|---|---|
| **interpolation** | interpolación | **subjugation** | subyugación |
| **replete** | repleto | **querulous** | querelloso |
| **subjacent** | subyacente | **symposium** | simposio |
| **immolation** | inmolación | **effusion** | efusión |
| **invective** | invectiva | **refractory** | refractario |
| **acrophobia** | acrofobia | | |

1. A **Micropoem**: The noun **symposium** has an unexpected derivation. A symposium is simply a conference or a meeting held for the purpose of discussing some topic of mutual interest. And so we expect *symposium* to have an etymology similar to the word **conference**: bring together. Something mundane. And yet *symposium* contains more flavor than we anticipate because it is derived from the Greek *symposion*, meaning drinking together! In ancient Greece, a symposium was a postprandial drinking party.

2. A **Classic Word**: The adjective **querulous** means peevish or full of complaint, and it comes from the Latin *quer* (complaint) and *ous* (full of). You would expect a word with such a meaning to find rich use in the classics to describe all of literature's querulous characters, and you do. *Querulous* was used by John Knowles, Pearl Buck, Edith Wharton, Kenneth Grahame, Joseph Conrad, Stephen Crane, and Emily Brontë, to name a few authors. In Buck's *The Good Earth*, the old man's cough rises querulously out of the dusky dawn. In *A Separate Peace*, a voice falls to a querulous whisper. In *The Wind in the Willows* (what a wonderfully poetic title; hear the assonance and the alliteration?), we learn that when one gets unsettled and depressed, one is inclined to be querulous. A soldier in Crane's *The Red Badge of Courage* breaks out in a querulous way like a man who has mislaid his hat. Emily Brontë created an unforgettable and charming use of *querulous* in *Wuthering Heights*: "Nothing was stirring except a brindled, grey cat, which crept from the ashes and saluted me with a querulous mew." And Edith Wharton used *querulous* over and over again in *Ethan Frome*; she describes querulous lines from the thin nose to the corners of the mouth, the querulous drone of the voice, and finally asks if Ethan must "wear out all his years at the side of a bitter querulous woman?"

3. The verb **subjugate** is vividly descriptive. It comes from the Latin *sub* (under) and *jugum* (yoke) and implies yoked enslavement, subservience, complete submission. In *The Time Machine*, H.G. Wells describes how things will move faster and faster toward the subjugation of nature. We find the same concept—the subjugation of nature—in Nathaniel Hawthorne's *The Scarlet Letter*, except that the outcome is the reverse; Hawthorne describes "that wild, heathen Nature of the forest, never subjugated by human law." Modern knowledge and concern over the fate of the planet's environment have given new meaning to the idea of the subjugation of nature; what seemed an exciting challenge in the days of going west to the frontier now seems like the reckless destruction of precious species and the common global environment of atmosphere and hydrosphere that all species must share.

4. In Harper Lee's *To Kill a Mockingbird*, we read, to our delight, "Her use of bathroom invective leaves nothing to the imagination." Bathroom invective? The innocent naughtiness of this sentence is a wonderful example of the alert spirit that so often characterizes the mind of the creative writer. The noun **invective** means vehement or bitter denunciation, vituperation, censure, terrific abuse. It comes from the Latin *invectus*, meaning driven (*vect*) into (*in*), in the sense of being attacked. Invective is driving criticism into someone, hard.

5. The verb **immolate** is another slight exception to our previous understanding. Immolate comes from the Latin verb *immolare*, from *in* (upon) and *mola* (meal), refering to a sacrificial meal.

This tunic is from the last years of the Roman Empire, and it is embroidered, which would not have been the case during the Republic, when such garments were more likely to be plain.

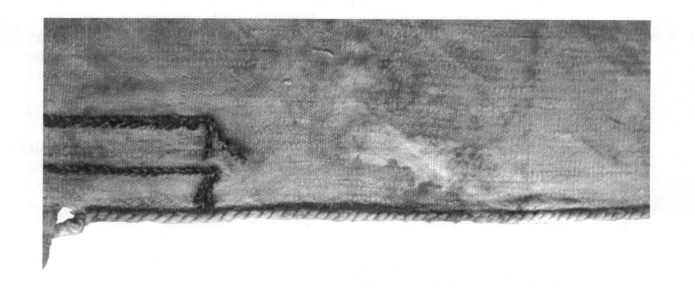

# THE TOGA
## Dr. Thomas Milton Kemnitz

The toga was the dress of the Romans. Only Roman citizens wore the toga, which was a badge of respectability. Fashions in togas changed little during the entire course of Roman history, from the monarchy to the Republic to the Empire; other garments, however, did change, and that altered the look of the population in Roman streets.

Roman clothing possibilities were limited by the sewing needles. The Romans did not temper steel for needles, and hence their needles were mostly made out of bone or ivory and were large and coarse. The Romans could not do the sort of fine sewing that enables buttonholes to be crafted easily, and therefore they did not make much use of buttons. The coarse sewing meant that their seams were often poor. Undergarments were difficult to make and perhaps not comfortable. Throughout most of the 500-year-long history of the Republic, men wore only a linen loincloth under their togas. It was only in the last century of the Republic that the practice of wearing tunics under togas became widespread.

When men were undertaking physical work outside their homes, they wore tunics, not togas. Also, they apparently took their togas off as soon as they reached their homes and were not entertaining or meeting people. Around the house, they wore tunics. We know something about tunics because a few of them from the last years of the Roman Empire have survived and were found at dry desert sites in Egypt and the Middle East. Pictured on the opposite page is a young person's tunic. It was made from a single piece of cloth, a combination of linen and flax, folded in half at the shoulders. The edges of the cloth have been folded over and sewn to prevent the fabric from unraveling or from ripping easily. A hole has been cut at the fold for the head of the wearer, and that, too, has been hemmed. There are no sleeves, just an extension of cloth to cover the upper arms. Both sides are open; the back has not been sewn to the front of the garment. The tunic was fastened by a belt or a rope. The garment was easy to wear, easy to work in, cool in the summer, and easy to maintain—at least compared to the toga. Some men's tunics were sewn together so the sides were closed; they generally reached to just below the knee.

In contrast, the toga itself was difficult to wear, hot in the summer, cumbersome, and difficult to clean. It was woven from wool that had been cleaned, bleached, combed, and brushed, then spun into cloth and woven on a loom, and finally cleaned before it was ready to wear. Most of the processing before the final cleaning took place in the household; the wealthy were able to refine the wool far more than the poorer Romans. Because this work was done in the home and everyone was familiar with the steps and the results, the quality of the finished product was an instant and universally recognizable statement of family resources, of standing within the community. There was a premium on keeping up appearances. The whiteness and the finish of the toga mattered, and a great deal of pride went into a well-crafted and well-maintained garment. The Romans could learn so much about one another in a glance, and in that instant men would have known the parameters of how they might relate to one another.

These sewing needles were made out of bone and were not practical for fine work.

# THE TOGA
**Dr. Thomas Milton Kemnitz**

The toga was an extraordinary garment—simple yet enormously rich in symbol and meaning. It was essentially a woolen blanket, either rectangular or semicircular. It might have been as long as twenty feet. The toga was placed at its center against the right side of the body below the armpit, and the back half was draped over the left shoulder; then the front half was also placed over the left shoulder. The old Roman fashion was to have a bare right shoulder, although by the first century B.C., that fashion was replaced by covering the right shoulder either with a tunic worn under the toga or else by draping the front part of the toga over the left shoulder, across the back, and over the right shoulder. As the toga became longer and draped over both shoulders, it became bulkier and even more cumbersome. Nonetheless, it remained the garment of the Roman citizen, *de rigueur* for magistrates and others doing official business, expected of every respectable man in the Forum and in the principal streets of the capital. Fashions in togas changed so little that a statue from 200 years previously could be reused— simply remove the head and replace it with your own, and you had a statue of yourself at a bargain rate. Of course, the difficulty was that a century or two later, someone would do the same thing to your statue, and your head in marble would be thrown away. Centuries later archeologists might find your head and not have any clue to whom it belonged; museums are full of marble heads described in Italian museums as *"RITRATTO MASCHILE"*—male portrait.

During the years of the Roman monarchy and perhaps into the early years of the Republic, women and older girls wore togas, and their outer dress was like men's. Under their togas the women wore a tunic that reached their feet and was called a *stola*. In the historical period, women's outerwear was called a *palla*, which was a simple blanket like the toga, but it was often very colorful. The *stola* also might be embroidered.

# THE TOGA
## Dr. Thomas Milton Kemnitz

Boys of more prosperous families wore togas much as their fathers did. Very young children were probably dressed in tunics. A boy's toga was known as the *toga praetexta*—the toga to be laid aside when the boy became a man. The laying aside of the boyhood toga was done in a ceremony, after which the young man was paraded through the streets of Rome in his adult toga—the *toga virilis*—in the company of older male members of his family. The young man's toga had a thin purple border around it; officials in Rome wore togas with broad purple stripes around the edges. The adult *toga virilius* was all white. It might have been bleached by being placed over a small fire in which sulfur was burned, or chalk might have been used to make it whiter. After this process the toga was washed in water. Men seeking office traditionally went to great efforts to whiten their togas, and their garments became known as *toga candida*, meaning bright white toga. The phenomenon was so striking that the term *candidate* exists to this day to describe people running for office.

Cleaning togas was a difficult process. The cloth was heavy and cumbersome and weighed too much when wet to be manipulated. This process could not be done at home, and togas were sent to the *fullonica* (laundry) for cleaning. The Romans did not have soap or bleach, and they were dependent upon natural chemicals for cleaning. The cleaning solution of choice was urine from the public urinals. The toga would be put in a vat of urine and trampled—an action that performed the function of modern washing machine agitators—by barefoot men who were either slaves or poor laborers. It could not have been a pleasant job. The ammonia in the urine broke down the natural oils from the sheep and the stains that resulted from everyday use. After being thoroughly tramped and worked in the urine, the togas were washed in clean water and stretched on racks to dry.

187

In each case below, one of the choices was really the word used by the author in the sentence provided. All of the choices can be found in the example words on the first page of this lesson. Your challenge is to decide which word the author used. This is not a test; it is more like a game because more than one word choice may work perfectly well. See if you can use your sensitivity and intuition to guess correctly which word the author used.

1. **From Pearl S. Buck's *The Good Earth***

   The old man's cough rose _____ out of the dusky dawn.
   a. effusively
   b. effulgently
   c. condignly
   d. querulously

2. **From Charles Dickens's *David Copperfield***

   I would hear of no such _____ on the altar of friendship.
   a. interpolation
   b. subjugation
   c. immolation
   d. symposium

3. **From Kate Chopin's *The Awakening***

   There was a soft _____ in the east.
   a. effulgence
   b. invective
   c. acrophobia
   d. effusion

4. **From Martin Luther King, Jr.'s *Why We Can't Wait***

   American history is _____ with compromise.
   a. interpolated
   b. refractory
   c. replete
   d. immolated

5. **From John Hersey's *Hiroshima***

   His growing helplessness kept her in _____; she tenderly nursed him.
   a. effusion
   b. subjugation
   c. interpolation
   d. invective

Though it is a good thing to have a rich vocabulary, it is not a good thing to abuse that vocabulary by writing verbose, abstruse, sesquipedalian sentences. Those who overuse their vocabularies often do so at the expense of clarity. Translate the following showy, ponderous passage into graceful, direct English. Do not use slang, but do use words that seem familiar and comfortable.

ON THE STEEP ROCK OF THE ALPINE SLOPE, interpolated amidst the effusion of grasses and windtorn shrubbery, an autochthonous heliotropic flower, replete with white petals and yellow center, grew assiduously, like the vivacious inamorata of light from the effulgent sun. The querulous wind, icy and sharp, tore with tautological vociferations and truculent invective at the intractable flower, trying to disinter it from its tenuous, acrophobic grip on the soil and the interstices of the subjacent sedimentary rock that had pushed up for millions of years from the tenebrous geologic abyss of some proterozoic lacustrine scene. But other ancient and imponderable planetary principles—the abstruse and silent graybeards, the insidious and omniscient calculus of the cosmos, the primal nomothetic laws of nature and physics— preserved the flower, subjugated the ineluctable antipathies of season, and gave condign harmony to the system, to the symposium of light, wind, and rain— displaying the cryptic ratiocinations of nature. In this omnibus confluence of circumambient benedictions, even the circumlocution of the cacophonous wind could not bowdlerize the narcissistic flower from the stoic physiognomy of the slope.

Boy wearing a toga

**Reading Comprehension**

1. In Translation 48, the author's attitude is best described as:
    a. bemused
    b. charmed
    c. ironic
    d. aloof

2. With which statement would the author likely agree?
    a. The forces of nature are ultimately destructive.
    b. The forces of nature are blind and indifferent.
    c. The forces of nature are benevolent and involved.
    d. The forces of nature form a systematic ecological balance.

**Analogies**

3. **SUBJUGATE : ENTHRALL ::**   *to being under control*   *to capture the attention of*
    a. immolate : vanquish   *to kill a sac.*
    b. invective : contumely   *abusive insulting language*
    c. acrophobia : height
    d. effulgence : luminous

4. **REFRACTORY : INTRACTABLE ::**   *stubborn*   *hard to control*
    a. querulous : tractable
    b. inamorata : mistress
    c. interpolate : withdraw
    d. acrophobia : agoraphobia

**Antonyms**

5. **REPLETE :**
    a. teeming
    b. scarce
    c. repeat
    d. complete

6. **CONDIGN :**
    a. appropriate
    b. merited
    c. unjust
    d. dignified

190

**divergence**

For either the noun **effulgence**, which is the bright shining of an object such as the sun, or for the adjective **condign**, which means worthy, fitting, or appropriate according to accepted standards, such as the fate of Edmund in *King Lear* (Edmund was slain by Edgar, the brother he betrayed), think of as many interesting examples as you can. Remember that when you are thinking divergently, more is better. For any creative situation in which you are trying to come up with a new idea, the more ideas you have to choose from, the more likely you are to find a great idea, a new idea, a creative idea. When you are trying to think of a lot of ideas, you often will find that you can quickly list several; these are the most obvious and generally known ones, and you find them in your memory banks. These are the ideas that everyone recognizes from ordinary experience and commercial culture. But then, the supply of ready-made or easy-to-think-of ideas runs out, and a brief period of difficulty ensues. Do not give up. On the other side of the desert are the more interesting ideas, the more unusual ones, the more creative ones, and the ones that are more personally and individually you.

**emotion**

One of the great stories of all time is the account written by Julius Caesar in his *Commentaries on the Gallic War*. Caesar describes his campaigns and decisions during the Gallic Wars from 58 to 51 B.C. Caesar's strategies for **subjugating** the Gauls, including the brilliant Arvernian leader Vercingetorix, make fascinating reading. It is worth a moment to consider the experience of subjugation, of forced total subordination to a conquering enemy, and to reflect on what the normal emotional responses of a subjugated person would be. Imagine being subjugated, being under the yoke, being forced to obey the orders of an enemy you hate. Think of the humiliation, the anger, the resentment, the revenge you would plot, the burning intensity of your feelings. To do this will give you more insight into many of the events you learn about from history, such as the slave revolt that Spartacus led against the Romans, or the unimaginable courage of Harriet Tubman, who risked her life repeatedly by sneaking back into the South to help slaves escape to the North. Can you even imagine that a people could be subjugated and not feel these bitter emotions? Consider several different historical examples of subjugation, and imagine how you would feel if you were in the place of the subjugated people. Who are some famous historical figures who revolted against subjugation?

**reason**

Let us write a **syllogism** using a word from List 48. Remember that a syllogism is a logically correct assertion that has the form: All A is C; B is A; therefore, B is C. For example, we might say,

All **effulgence** is bright; radiance is a form of effulgence; therefore, all radiance is bright.
or:
Every **symposium** is a conference; the Cognitute is a symposium; therefore, the Cognitute is a conference.

### Neologist's Lexicon

Use the stems in this list to create a new word (neologism). Give the word, the pronunciation, the part of speech, the etymology, and the definition(s). Keep a record of the neologisms you create from list to list. Here are some examples:

**symfulgent** (sim FULL jent) adj. [*sym* (together), *fulg* (shine)]   1. shining more brightly together than individually, as two persons who bring out the best in each other's personality   2. serving as reciprocal catalysts, as two chemicals that each set the other on fire

**nomophobia** (no mo FO bee uh) n. [*nomy* (law), *phobia* (fear)]   1. fear of the law or of officers of the law   2. anxious obsession with the lyrics of the song "I Fought the Law and the Law Won"

### Sesquipedalian Dr. Seuss

Use words from List 48 and previous lists to imitate your favorite Dr. Seuss story. An example:

#### The Querulous Cat

The moon didn't shine out
Effulgently bright
So we lay in our beds,
Subjugated all night.
When in jumped the Cat
The refractory Cat,
The querulous,
Fearless, intractable Cat.
"Where's your Mother,"
He asked,
As he jumped through the door,
And he waltzed with effusion
'Cross the subjacent floor.
To our nonplussed, incredulous,
Neophyte minds
That omniscient Cat
Uttered omnibus kinds
Of retorts and strange malapropisms,
You see, which we
Couldn't repeat, even in soliloquy.
Then he gathered up all
Of the objects with which
Our house was replete
And he thought he would snitch.
And he made such a face
That we found it condign
When *in medias res*
Mom came in from behind.

| | | | | | | |
|---|---|---|---|---|---|---|
| • dis | (away) | discern | | • *gno* | (know) | prognosis |
| • mis (G) | (bad) | misnomer | | • *pro* | (before) | prognosis |
| • **nom** | (name) | misnomer | | • ***entomo*** | (insect) | entomology |
| • pugn | (fight) | inexpugnable | | • per | (through) | perspicacity |
| • **Sino** | (China) | Sinology | | • spec | (look) | perspicacity |
| • tude | (state of) | hebetude | | • *syn* | (together) | synthesis |
| • *logy* | (science) | axiology, etiology | | • *cracy* | (government) | mobocracy |
| • non | (not) | nonentity | | | | |

**discern** (to mentally separate, identify)  We failed to discern the real reasons.

**misnomer** (wrong name)  To call whales *fishes* is a misnomer, according to Melville.

**chauvinism** (fanatical devotion)  Nicolas Chauvin was chauvinistic about France.

**inexpugnable** (unconquerable)  The enemy held an inexpugnable position.

**etiology** (cause or science of causes)  Study the etiology of a social problem.

**hebetude** (state of dullness)  He gaped in lethargic, open-mouthed hebetude.

**axiology** (study of value)  Axiology is the study of axioms of ethics and aesthetics.

**congeries** (heap)  His collection was a disorganized congeries of dusty artifacts.

**Sinology** (study of China)  She longed to study Sinology and diplomacy.

**nonentity** (a nobody)  He was a jabbering nonentity, a superfluous, prolix nobody.

• • •

**prognosis** (medical forecast)  The doctor presented a prognosis of the disease.

**entomology** (insect zoology)  The oft-bitten entomologist lost his collection.

**perspicacity** (insight)  We admired the perspicacity of Susie's scientific mind.

**synthesis** (combination)  The best solution was a synthesis of many ideas.

**mobocracy** (mob rule)  The great revolution degenerated into cruel mobocracy.

Mosaics of guard dogs were common, and in Pompeii one remains *in situ* just inside the door to the street.  The dogs are always shown chained.  Numerous dog sculptures like the one pictured on page 190 have survived.

**As Used by Arthur Conan Doyle in *The Hound of the Baskervilles***

|  | I | seemed | **to discern** | some | signs | of | emotion. |
|---|---|---|---|---|---|---|---|
| **Parts of Speech:** | pron. | v. | n. | adj. | n. | prep. | n. |
| **Parts of Sentence:** | subj. | LVP | ------------------subject complement------------------ |  |  |  |  |
| **Phrases:** |  |  | ----------infinitive phrase-------- |  |  | --prep. phrase-- |  |
| **Clauses:** | ------------------------------------independent clause-------------------------------- |  |  |  |  |  |  |
|  | one independent clause; a simple, declarative sentence |  |  |  |  |  |  |

Here Arthur Conan Doyle uses the infinitive form *to discern* as a noun; the infinitive phrase *to discern some signs of emotion* is the subject complement, and in that phrase, *signs* is the object of the infinitive. The linking verb *seemed* creates an equation.

## Pronunciation

| | | | |
|---|---|---|---|
| **discern** | dis SERN | **Sinology** | si NAH lo jee |
| **misnomer** | miss NO mer | **nonentity** | non EN tih tee |
| **chauvinism** | SHOW vin izm | **prognosis** | prog NO siss |
| **inexpugnable** | in ex PUG na bel | **entomology** | en to MAH lo jee |
| **etiology** | ee tee AH lo jee | **perspicacity** | per spih KASS ih tee |
| **hebetude** | HEE beh tood | **synthesis** | SIN theh siss |
| **axiology** | ax ee AH lo jee | **mobocracy** | mob OCK ra see |
| **congeries** | KON jer eez | | |

## Spanish Cognates

| | | | |
|---|---|---|---|
| **discernment** | discernimiento | **chauvinism** | chauvinismo |
| **inexpugnable** | inexpugnable | **etiology** | etiología |
| **axiom** | axioma | **congeries** | congerie |
| **Sinology** | sinología | **prognosis** | prognosis |
| **entomology** | entomología | **perspicacity** | perspicacia |
| **synthesis** | síntesis | | |

1. A **Micropoem**: We admire the keen, insightful mind of a scientist like Rosalind Franklin, the brilliant physicist whose precise work was instrumental in helping Crick and Watson solve the structure of the DNA molecule (she died before she could receive a Nobel Prize, which is not awarded posthumously). This power of penetrating insight is beautifully captured by the word **perspicacity**, which is the ability to see (*spec*) right through (*per*) something. To the perspicacious person, things that are opaque, tenebrous, or obscure to the rest of us are translucent and intellectually visible. The noun **perspicacity** and its adjective **perspicacious** are to be distinguished from the noun **perspicuity** and its adjective **perspicuous**. Both refer to lucidity and keenness of insight, but the former refers to minds, and the latter refers to products. A perspicacious person would write a perspicuous paper.

2. A **congeries** is a heap, pile, or aggregation. The noun comes from the Latin *congerere*, to collect, which is composed of *con* (together) and *gerere* (to bear or carry). Imagine an archaeology lab that is a congeries of dusty artifacts from many cultures: masks, tools, stone implements, tablets, pottery, figures, scrolls, spears, amphorae, everything heaped in corners and piled on shelves, light pouring in through a big window, with the snow-covered leafless branches of deciduous tress outlined against a bright blue sky beyond.

3. The noun **chauvinism** is named for Nicolas Chauvin, a blustering fanatical patriot in Napoleon's army. The word implies zealous, belligerent, and even prejudiced adherence to any cause. One of the most typical modern uses is to describe the foolish, intractable male-centeredness of the *male chauvinist*, the person who is bigoted against women.

4. The noun **etiology** can either refer to the cause of disease, as in the etiology of tuberculosis, or it can refer more abstractly to the study of causality itself. This word traces back through the Latin to the Greek, in which *aitiologia* meant determining the cause of anything. The genetic etiology of many hereditary diseases is presently unknown, but as scientists proceed with the mapping of human DNA, more and more of these causes will be identified, and then we will have to deal with the questions arising from our ability to alter genetic codes.

5. A **Classic Word**: The verb **discern** comes from the Latin *dis* (away) and *cernere* (to separate), and it describes our ability to make intelligent distinctions, to separate things from other things to which they are connected. Sometimes *discern* implies something physical, such as Defoe's use in 1719 in *Robinson Crusoe*: "and I could easily discern their postures and gestures by my glasses." Usually, *discern* refers to something more subtle. Jane Eyre was able to discern in the course of the morning that Thornfield Hall was a changed place. Melville described an old Manxman who had preternatural powers of discernment. Hardy, Crane, and Wharton used the word as well. The frightened youth Henry Fleming discerned forms begin to swell in masses out of a distant wood. Ethan Frome's eyes, accustomed to obscurity, would discern Mattie as clearly as though she stood in daylight. And Harper Lee described a man who sat on a flagpole for no discernible reason.

Among the reforms of Gaius Gracchus was a bill to require the state to purchase grain and to supply a monthly allotment at a subsidized low price to the population of Rome. In the last years of the Republic, people seem to have been consuming more of their wheat in the form of bread rather than the *puls* or mush of previous centuries. This loaf of bread was over-cooked by Vesuvius, but its extraordinary survival in carbonized form gives us confirmation that the fresco painted on a villa wall in Pompeii is an accurate representation of a loaf of bread. The loaf is about a Roman foot in diameter, and it is divided into eight wedges like a pizza. The divisions make it easier to share the loaf between several hungry mouths. The indentation around the perimeter of the loaf likely was caused by a piece of twine tied around the dough before baking; it might have served as a indication of where to slice each piece for sandwich making, or the twine might have been used to hang the finished loaves to cool.

# TIBERIUS AND GAIUS GRACCHUS
**Dr. Thomas Milton Kemnitz**

The destruction of both Corinth and Carthage in 146 B.C. established Rome as the unquestioned power in the Mediterranean; thereafter for centuries only Romans could credibly challenge the supremacy of Romans. And other Romans became the only threat to the Republic. The delicate balance of the Republic began to unravel almost immediately, and unheard-of outrages quickly became repeated patterns. Rome long had problems related to the power and wealth of the patricians in the Senate. Some of these problems had been exacerbated by the Second Punic War, when Hannibal had disrupted many of the land arrangements throughout Italy, and they were further disrupted in the next half-century by the long periods many men were away from their land serving in legions stationed in the Iberian peninsula, North Africa, Greece, or Asia Minor. A substantial proportion of the small farms had been forced into bankruptcy because the farmer was in the legions and was ill-compensated for his time. One result was that Rome's manpower was dwindling because fewer men could meet the property requirement to serve in the legions. On several occasions, the censors lowered the property requirement, but still the problem persisted. Naturally the patricians had acquired vast amounts of land—regularly evading the law that fixed the maximum land holding at 300 acres—and much of southern Italy had been converted from growing wheat to cattle, grapes, and olives. Large estates were run by slaves, many of them harshly treated; the yeoman farmers were being impoverished, and their families migrated to urban areas. In the cities the gap between rich and poor was ever-widening, and Rome faced a challenge maintaining order.

Tiberius Gracchus was from the plebeian branch of an old family; his maternal grandfather was Scipio. He was elected a Tribune of the Plebs in 134 and re-elected in 133. He proposed a law to break up the large farms, compensate the landholders, and redistribute the land to smaller holders, thereby taking care of the army enlistment and the urban poor problems with one measure. The elites in the Senate opposed the land law. Eventually Tiberius's cousin, Publius Cornelius Scipio Nasica, led a group of senators together with their clients and slaves up toward where Tiberius was meeting with a crowd on Capitoline Hill. In the ensuing confrontation, Tiberius was beaten to death with clubs and staves made from benches. More than 300 of his supporters were slain with stones and staves—but none by sword, an important point because arms were not used—and their bodies thrown into the Tiber, thereby denying them a proper funeral. This, according to Plutarch, was the first outbreak of civil strife in Rome. Following the massacre, many of Tiberius's supporters were sent into exile without a trial, while others were arrested and executed—some were sewn in bags with poisonous vipers.

A decade later Gaius Gracchus was elected Tribune of the Plebs and revived his brother's law. Again, it was unpopular with members of the Senate, and again a group led by senators attacked a group of the plebs on Capitoline Hill, this time using archers from Crete. Gaius did not survive that day in 121 B.C.; his head was brought to the Senate, where a reward equal to its weight in gold had been promised to the bearer, but it was found that his brain had been removed and replaced with lead, and no reward was given. More than 3,000 of his supporters were put to death after perfunctory trials, and their bodies were thrown into the Tiber. The property of the dead was confiscated, and their homes were looted by the patrician party. Their wives were forbidden to mourn the death of their husbands; the wife of Gaius was stripped of her dowry.

A precedent had been broken, and thereafter arms would be used in disputes within Rome. Governing Rome had become a blood sport, and each man who struggled for prominence risked an early death.

In each case below, one of the choices was really the word used by the author in the sentence provided. All of the choices can be found in the example words on the first page of this lesson. Your challenge is to decide which word the author used. This is not a test; it is more like a game because more than one word choice may work perfectly well. See if you can use your sensitivity and intuition to guess correctly which word the author used.

1. **From Elizabeth George Speare's *The Witch of Blackbird Pond***

   What William thought, it was impossible to _____.
   a. interpolate
   b. subjugate
   c. discern
   d. misnomer

2. **From John Knowles's *A Separate Peace***

   I had applied for such a _____ of a job.
   a. nonentity
   b. misnomer
   c. prognosis
   d. synthesis

3. **From Joseph Conrad's *Lord Jim***

   There was a "shelter of _____ peace."
   a. perspicacious
   b. chauvinistic
   c. discernible
   d. inexpugnable

4. **From Frederick Douglass's *Narrative***

   I looked at it as the climax of all _____, the boldest of all frauds.
   a. congeries
   b. hebetudes
   c. misnomers
   d. etiologies

5. **From Thomas Hardy's *The Mayor of Casterbridge***

   The upper part of Durnover was...composed of a curious _____ of barns and farmsteads.
   a. nonentities
   b. synthesis
   c. mobocracy
   d. congeries

Though it is a good thing to have a rich vocabulary, it is not a good thing to abuse that vocabulary by writing verbose, abstruse, sesquipedalian sentences. Those who overuse their vocabularies often do so at the expense of clarity. Translate the following showy, ponderous passage into graceful, direct English. Do not use slang, but do use words that seem familiar and comfortable.

WHAT A DILEMMA. The nonplussed freshman stared at the catalog that delineated the course offerings, wondering what to take. The congeries of courses seemed endless. Axiology, Entomology, Kinesiology, Cosmology, Sinology, Chauvinism and Prejudice—there seemed to be no end to the possibilities. She tried to concentrate, humorously remembering the prolix, vacuous nonentity who had reduced her to hebetude at the freshman party last night; well, party was a misnomer, she discerned; it was more like inexpugnable boredom.

This looked like an interesting course: Introduction to Etiology. Her perspicacious mind immediately grasped the idea: CAUSES. Disease. Prognosis. Diagnosis. Syndromes. A synthesis of major theories. Causes of diseases. Pathology.

Let's see, she thought, how about Axiology 101. Values, ethics, aesthetics, religion. Imponderable mysteries. Eschatology. Hedonism. Stoicism. Pharisaism. Nepotism. Ethical paradigms. It sounded interesting, and she had never taken a class in philosophy before. What is right, what is beautiful . . . they would probably read Plato's *Dialogues*. Antinomies. Tautologies. Yes, I'll take this course.

Sinology, Sovietology? Hmmm. The other students said that the professor was good. Lots of original sources to read, rather than just textbooks. Lots of discussion and ideas. Plutocracies and mobocracies. Autochthonous populations. Lots of exploration of current events and problems. Questions. And with the world changing, this might be an important subject to know more about.

To know? Ah, here's Epistemology and the Meditations of Descartes. Another philosophy class. It might be fun: How do you know that this box exists? How do you know the material world is there? Questions like that. *A priori* knowledge, *a posteriori* knowledge. The mind/body dichotomy. Recondite abstractions. *Cogito ergo sum.* A *non sequitur*? She had heard of these ideas but had not studied them before. Sounded good.

Advanced Entomology. Bugs. Advanced bugs. Six legs. Joints. Exoskeletons. Compound eyes. Repulsive/attractive. Bug anatomy, bug chemistry, bug analysis. Bug projects . . . catching bugs. Creepy ratiocinations. Gotta take it.

She closed the catalog, introspectively anticipating the lucubrations that awaited her in the semester ahead.

## Reading Comprehension

1   For Translation 49, which of the following does the passage suggest?
    a. The college freshman is bright and intellectually vigorous.
    b. The college freshman is interested in finding easy classes.
    c. The college freshman is trying to avoid mathematics and science.
    d. The college freshman is uncomfortable with abstractions.

2.   Which of the following is the best title for the passage?
    a. An Academic Neophyte Nonplussed by Advanced Academics
    b. The Intellectual Ratiocinations of an Academic Neophyte
    c. The Scholastic Soliloquy of a Diffident Intellect
    d. An Academic Neophyte's Heterodox Interests

## Analogies

3.   **PERSPICACITY : HEBETUDE ::**
    a. dullness : acuteness
    b. etiology : biogenesis
    c. brilliance : lassitude
    d. languor : perspective

4.   **AXIOLOGY : ENTOMOLOGY ::**
    a. morals : ethics
    b. scientist : microscope
    c. axle : biology
    d. decisions : life forms

## Antonyms

5.   **NONENTITY :**
    a. cipher
    b. nullity
    c. whippet
    d. luminary

6.   **INEXPUGNABLE :**
    a. vulnerable
    b. impregnable
    c. indomitable
    d. unvanquishable

It took a great deal of space and effort to make bread. Grinding the wheat was a major task, with two men required to rotate the mill and a complex oven system necessary to bake the bread without burning it.

**evaluation and aesthetics**

Imagine that you are taking an art class, and you are going to do a project in **entomological** art; in other words, you're going to make pretty bugs. They will be sculpture, in a variety of media, designs, styles, and colors. Now, here's the rub: the prize will go to the person who makes the most original insect that is still an insect. This means that every entry must have six legs, three body parts, antennae, compound eyes, and so forth. Of course, even though all insects have some of these basic common elements, they still have vast variation, as the millions of insect species on our planet vividly demonstrate. So there is plenty of room for variation. Your project: First, imagine what your ideas for several original insects might be. Then, imagine that you are asked to be a judge, and you are instructed to write a list of your criteria for originality. What would be your answers to both of these questions?

**synthesis**

Since the noun **synthesis** is one of the words in List 49, let us explore this concept in some detail. *Synthesis* is from the Greek *syn* (together) and *tithenai* (to put or place). In synthesis we put things together. This putting together can be physical, as in making synthetic materials such as plastics by combining chemicals. But often, the synthesis we describe is in the world of ideas. Einstein used synthesis to combine tensor calculus and modern physics to create the concepts of relativity and space-time. There were already people who knew the calculus, and there were already people who knew the physics, but Einstein noticed the synthetic implications of the one for the other. It is this kind of brilliant noticing—the noticing of unnoticed relevance, the noticing of unnoticed connections, the noticing of unnoticed similarities—which characterizes synthesis at its most brilliant. That is why, to put this advanced idea in ordinary language, we ask students to think of wild, crazy, or silly comparisons. We are trying to stretch the mind into the real thing, into true and original synthesis. Anyone can notice an obvious synthesis, such as that subtraction and taking a bite of chocolate cake are similar because they both involve the removal of something from a total. But what about less common kinds of synthetic thinking? For example, what are the profound and meaningful things that small children and mature adults have in common? What are the deepest goals and values that men and women have in common? We often think of how children and adults are different, or of how men and women are different, but in what ways, other than some of the most obvious ones, are we the same?

For other examples of brilliant synthesis, consider Homer's epic similes. Or remember Shakespeare's brilliant and terrifying metaphors in *Macbeth,* in which Macbeth compares life to a walking shadow and to a tale told by an idiot. (Schopenhauer said that the value of metaphors is to explain an unknown relation by a known one. Good, eh?) Without synthesis, would there be poetry or literature? Certainly, there would not be symbolism; it would vanish.

Synthesis is also an important process in other thinking skills; it helps to make them possible. We live in a world of specialization and compartmentalization, and yet we probably will survive and improve our planet better if we can become good at *application* of knowledge and *connection* of various kinds of knowledge, and these things require synthesis. You cannot apply knowledge—transfer it from the abstract, chalky classroom to the green and moving world—if you cannot notice the connections and similarities between your abstract examples and the particular situations in the real world.

## Neologist's Lexicon

Use the stems in this list to create a new word (neologism). Give the word, the pronunciation, the part of speech, the etymology, and the definition(s). Keep a record of the neologisms you create from list to list. Here are some examples:

**propugnance** (pro PUG nance) n. [*pro* (before), *pugn* (fight)] 1. being prematurely combative and belligerent before information verifies the reason for anger 2. the proclivity for hasty and unreasonable combativeness

**entomonomy** (en toe MOH no me) n. [*entomo* (insect), *nomy* (name or law)] 1. the unfortunate habitual reference to one's associates as forms of insects, as gadflies, wasps, social butterflies, busy bees, flies in the ointment 2. excessive use of the sentence, "Stop bugging me."

## Sesquipedalian Metamorphosis

In Franz Kafka's surrealistic story *The Metamorphosis*, the main character Gregor Samsa wakes up to find that he has been metamorphosed into a gigantic insect. He is lying on his back with his six legs sticking up in the air, and he finds it difficult to roll off of his exoskeleton onto his feet. As the story evolves, no one seems to care about Gregor, not even his boss, who is only concerned that he be at work on time. Use the words from List 49 and previous lists to describe some similarly strange situation. The situation is up to you. Maybe you wake up as a sock. That's your problem. I would rather not be a sock. I would rather wake up as a bowl of cereal and bananas any day. See what you can come up with. Here's an example:

### The Metagnosis

One morning, Michael gradually gained consciousness to discover that he had transmogrified overnight into a being of inexpugnable hebetude, a corpulent nonentity, incapable even of the energy and acuteness necessary to be prolix and superfluous. His physiognomy felt flat. The etiology of this alteration was unclear, but he knew intuitively that the prognosis was bad. In the tenebrous corner of his room, he discerned a gregarious mobocracy of entomological life feasting on last night's hedonistic pizza, but his hebetude had transformed the axiological dictum that would have made him care. So different was his personality that he felt unlike his usual perspicacious self and more like a synthesis of the intelligences visible in fish eyes and lizard's postures, but perhaps intelligence is a misnomer in those cases; blank reactions might be more accurate. Even the congeries of clothes beside the bed failed to disturb Michael's normal obsession with neatness and organization.

He lay there for a long time, nonplussed, wondering if it mattered if he lay there for a long time, nonplussed, wondering if . . . . Through the window, he could hear the loquacious neighbors in their daily gregarious colloquy. "That Michael," said one in a condescending and supercilious lilt, "he certainly has a soporifically sesquipedalian vocabulary." "*Au contraire*," replied the other, "you're just smarting under his assiduous objurgations." On they went, in desultory perambulations and vacuous vociferations. Michael slowly turned to the wall, tracing gingerly through the soliloquy that would lead him out of this malefic mood and back to his typical mellifluous, sanguine disposition.

# The Word Within the Word • List 50

| • re | (again) | repartee | • tion | (act or state) | fulguration |
|------|---------|----------|--------|----------------|-------------|
| • fulg | (shine or flash) | refulgent | • tude | (state of) | solicitude |
| • mal | (bad) | *mal de mer* | • ante | (before) | antediluvian |
| • mar | (sea) | *mal de mer* | • **luvi** | (wash) | antediluvian |
| • *cracy* | (government) | timocracy | • ***agora*** | (marketplace) | panegyric |
| • *neo* | (new) | neophilia | • duct | (lead) | induction |
| • *phile* | (love) | neophilia | • fract | (break) | fractious |
| • culp | (blame) | mea culpa | • surg | (rise) | insurgence |
| • sub | (under) | subliminal | • sed | (sit) | dissident |

**refulgent** (shining)  Achilles strode forth to meet Hector, refulgent in his new armor.

***mal de mer*** (seasickness)  She sailed with no fear of the *mal de mer*.

**timocracy** (government based on honor)  It is not a meritocracy but a timocracy.

**neophilia** (love of the new)  Her home was a monument to neophilia—no antiques there.

**mea culpa** (my fault)  Include a *mea culpa* at the beginning of the difficult lecture.

**fulguration** (flashing)  The fulgurations of the lightning storm continued.

**repartee** (quick, witty reply)  We were amused by Austen's quick repartee in *Pride and Prejudice*.

**dissident** (one who disagrees)  The Soviet dissident mentally "sits apart."

**subliminal** (below consciousness)  He has a subliminal fear of darkness.

**solicitude** (state of concern)  We much appreciate your earnest solicitude.

• • •

**antediluvian** (from before the Flood!)  He rejected their superannuated, antediluvian attitudes.

**panegyric** (elaborate eulogy)  His speech to the crowd was a panegyric on his friend's merits.

**induction** (factual reasoning)  Science uses a process of induction, and some deduction, too.

**fractious** (unruly)  The fractious mob clamored when Sidney approached the guillotine.

**insurgence** (uprising)  The riotous insurgence was defeated as soon as it began.

Roman key

## As Used by W.H.D. Rouse in his translation of *The Odyssey of Homer*

|  | You | are | full | of | antediluvian | wisdom. |
|---|---|---|---|---|---|---|
| **Parts of Speech:** | pron. | v. | adj. | prep. | adj. | n. |
| **Parts of Sentence:** | subj. | LVP | S.C. | | | |

Phrases:                                                           ----------prepositional phrase----------

Clauses:     ------------------------------------independent clause---------------------------------
one independent clause; a simple, declarative sentence

Here Rouse uses the adjective *antediluvian* to modify the singular common noun *wisdom*, which is the object of a preposition.

## Pronunciation

| | | | | |
|---|---|---|---|---|
| **refulgent** | re FULL jent | | **subliminal** | sub LIM in al |
| *mal de mer* | MAL deh mair | | **solicitude** | so LISS ih tood |
| **timocracy** | tim MOCK ra see | | **antediluvian** | an tee di LOO vee an |
| **neophilia** | nee o FILL ee ah | | **panegyric** | pan eh JIR ik |
| **mea culpa** | MAY ah KUL pah | | **induction** | in DUCK shun |
| **fulguration** | FUL gyoor AY shun | | **fractious** | FRACK shus |
| **repartee** | re par TAY | | **insurgence** | in SIR jence |
| **dissident** | DISS ih dent | | | |

## Spanish Cognates

| | | | | |
|---|---|---|---|---|
| **refulgent** | refulgente | | **timocracy** | timocracia |
| **fulgurant** | fulgurante | | **dissident** | disidente |
| **subliminal** | subliminal | | **solicitude** | solicitud |
| **antediluvian** | antediluviano | | **panegyric** | panegírico |
| **induction** | inducción | | **insurgent** | insurgente |

1.  A **Micropoem**: The adjective **subliminal** is a psychological term that refers to our ability to respond to, be affected by, or enjoy stimuli of which we are not conscious. How does this meaning emerge from the etymology of the word? Well, it is interesting. To understand, we must look at the words **sublime** and **sublimate**. The adjective *sublime* means elevated or lofty, exalted, noble, grand, supreme. HIGH. Huh? Why would a SUB word mean HIGH? Because *sublime* comes from the Latin *sublimis*, which comes from the stems *sub* (under) and *lim* (lintel). You still do not get it? Well, a lintel is a horizontal architectural feature that spans the two sides of a door or fireplace, supporting the wall up above the door. In other words, you would reach UP to hang something HIGH up under the lintel. Under the lintel is high. Ah. Our ideals of honesty, integrity, and lifelong devotion are sublime human ideas. Now, to *sublimate* is to psychologically redirect some basic form of human of energy, such as sexual energy (remember our discussion of ego, superego, and id?), upward to some higher social or moral goal. We might say, for example, that some creative person's powerful creative urge is actually driven by his sublimated (elevated, see?) sexual energy. To sublimate something is to redirect it higher, up to lintel level. And so *subliminal* refers to this process, that in our sublime endeavors we are sometimes moved by sublimated feelings emerging subliminally from the subconscious mind—which is a lot of meaning to squeeze out of the image of a lintel.

2.  A **panegyric** is an elaborate eulogy, an oration or writing that expatiates on the merits or virtues of the subject. The noun traces back to the Greek word *panegyrikos*, solemn assembly, which is made of *pan* (all) and *agyris* (gathering). The image is that all have gathered to praise; in my mind, I see a central fire, the yellow flickering light on the solemn physiognomies, the voice of the panegyricist beginning to ring in stentorian tones. Walter Scott refers to a doleful panegyric, and Swift has Gulliver reply, "you have made a most admirable panegyric upon your country."

3.  If you studied Volume I of *The Word Within the Word*, you will remember what a wonderful micropoem **antediluvian** is; it literally means so antiquated as to date before (*ante*) Noah's Flood (*luvi*). Melville used *antediluvian* repeatedly in *Moby Dick* to describe the antediluvian Hindoo; an old, crutch-like, antediluvian wheezing humorousness; and an archaeological, fossiliferous, and antediluvian point of view. Hardy also used *antediluvian* in *The Return of the Native*: "The number of their years may have adequately summed up Jared, Mahalaleel, and the rest of the antediluvians, but the age of a modern man is to be measured by the intensity of his history."

4.  A **Classic Word**: The noun **solicitude** has a major place in literature. It was used by Scott, Cooper, Charlotte Brontë, Stowe, Melville, Dickens, and Hardy, to name only a few. We see serious solicitude, professions of solicitude, gentle solicitude, looking with solicitude, fargazing solicitude, fatherly solicitude, conscientious solicitude, superfluous solicitude, melancholy solicitude, kind solicitude, and anxious solicitude. Solicitude comes from the Latin *sollicitudo*, uneasiness of mind, which traces back to *sollicitus*, agitated, which traces back to *sollus*, whole, and *ciere*, to arouse. We feel solicitude when we are in the state of (*tude*) being wholly aroused in concern.

Gaius Gracchus had initiated reforms so that the state paid for equipping the army, and the cost was not deducted from a legionnaire's pay. When Marius dropped the property qualification altogether for enlisting in the army, pay became a principal motivator. This coin from 99 B.C. ties the pay directly to the spoils of war. On the obverse is Jupiter, and on the reverse is Winged Victory crowning with a victory wreath a pile of trophies won in battle—an obvious celebration of the victories of Marius in the previous years. The v-shaped cut in the coin was done by someone who would have snipped as many coins as possible to accumulate silver. All coins were susceptible to this until in the seventeenth century mints began to mill the edges of coins with the many ridges that are still a feature of those of our coins that used to be made of silver.

# GAIUS MARIUS
## Dr. Thomas Milton Kemnitz

In 118 B.C. a revolt broke out in Numidia in North Africa led by Jugurtha, who rejected a Roman division of the kingdom and ordered his troops to massacre Italians living there. Rome sent legions but with no effect. In 109 Rome finally sent an effective general in the patrician Quintus Metellus, who set about methodically reducing his opponent's holdings. His chief deputy was a pleb, Gaius Marius, who made himself popular by eating and working with the troops in the field. He got himself elected consul in 107, and Marius then induced the Assembly to appoint him to the command in Numidia against the wishes of the Senate and over his former commander. Marius had promised to end the war quickly, but that proved more difficult once he was in command. Eventually in 105, Jugurtha was lured into a trap, betrayed, and captured—the work of Marius's subordinate, Lucius Cornelius Sulla Felix, known as Sulla. Jugurtha was marched in Marius's Triumph in Rome and then strangled. Marius would be a rival of Metellus and Sulla for many years.

Marius was re-elected consul in 105 after a new crisis arose in the north, where the Cimbri and the Teutones tribes had inflicted a catastrophic defeat on the Romans at Arausio—apparently with the loss of 80,000 Roman lives, the largest loss of life in battle in Roman history. Several humiliating if less devastating losses had preceded the disaster at Arausio, and the Germanic tribes revived the fears the Romans had never lost from the Gallic invasion of 387 B.C. Marius met the Teutones in battle in 102, when, with the aid of a mistake by one of their commanders and a successful ambush by Marius, about 100,000 were killed in a complete victory for the Romans. Marius's colleague was unable to keep the Cimbri out of Italy in 102, but Marius met them in battle in 101 and killed 65,000 or more of the enemy and enslaved 60,000 survivors.

Marius changed the Roman army in many important ways between 107 and 101. His first innovation was to ignore the property qualification and to enlist any Roman citizen, no matter how poor. Until that time Roman legionnaires were men of some substance, men who had a stake in the society, men who would be loyal to Rome because their property made them so. Now the ranks were flooded by poor men who had no stake in society and who were soldiers for the pay and for the entire period of their 16-year enlistment. When their enlistment ended, they were dependent upon their commander to make provisions for the remainder of their lives. This meant that they would be loyal to their commander, not to Rome itself. In the short run, however, the change was positive, for it enabled Rome to recruit the troops it needed, particularly after the terrible loss at Arausio, and it meant that the same troops would remain under arms and together in a legion for the full sixteen years of their enlistment. Once trained, they could be relied upon to know what they had to do, and training occurred throughout the year. A permanent legion was one in which men could be trained as specialists and allowed to develop skills that would serve the needs of the legion. In this way the legions developed great architects, engineers, and builders, and they paved the way for the spectacular building feats of Caesar's legions and of the legions of the Principate for the next 500 years.

With professional soldiers at his command, Marius could require more of them than of a citizen militia. In order to increase the flexible mobility of the legion, Marius had each man carry his own equipment, including his own armor, weapons, and fifteen days' rations—a weight estimated at about fifty-five pounds. The soldiers were nicknamed Marius's Mules (*muli mariani*). Every legion had a baggage train of 500–550 mules, or about one mule for every ten legionaries, but now Marius had legionnaires who could move without the baggage train and who could be ready to fight wherever they were, particularly if they were separated from the baggage train.

| Jugurtha leads Numidia revolt | Gaius Marius elected consul | Jugurtha captured | Battle of Arausio | Marius defeats the Teutones | Marius defeats the Cimbri |
|---|---|---|---|---|---|
| 118 B.C. | 107 B.C. | 105 B.C. | 105 B.C. | 102 B.C. | 101 B.C. |

In each case below, one of the choices was really the word used by the author in the sentence provided. All of the choices can be found in the example words on the first page of this lesson. Your challenge is to decide which word the author used. This is not a test; it is more like a game because more than one word choice may work perfectly well. See if you can use your sensitivity and intuition to guess correctly which word the author used.

1.  **From James M. Barrie's *Peter Pan***

    I, George Darling, did it. _____, _____.
    a. *mal de mer, mal de mer*
    b. antediluvian, antediluvian
    c. *mea culpa, mea culpa*
    d. subliminal, subliminal

2.  **From Marjorie Kinnan Rawlings's *The Yearling***

    But the convalescence, the _____ of his mother and father, was definitely pleasant.
    a. dissidence
    b. solicitude
    c. repartee
    d. refulgence

3.  **From Walt Whitman's *Leaves of Grass***

    I loiter enjoying his _____ and his shuffle and break-down.
    a. repartee
    b. neophilia
    c. insurgence
    d. panegyric

4.  **From Charlotte Brontë's *Jane Eyre***

    Brontë describes the "_____ dawn of the tropics."
    a. subliminal
    b. antediluvian
    c. refulgent
    d. fractious

5.  **From Mary Shelley's *Frankenstein***

    He concluded with a(n) _____ upon modern chemistry.
    a. *mea culpa*
    b. insurgence
    c. fulguration
    d. panegyric

Though it is a good thing to have a rich vocabulary, it is not a good thing to abuse that vocabulary by writing verbose, abstruse, sesquipedalian sentences. Those who overuse their vocabularies often do so at the expense of clarity. Translate the following showy, ponderous passage into graceful, direct English. Do not use slang, but do use words that seem familiar and comfortable.

AFTER THE CACOPHONOUS FULGURATIONS of last night's storm, Captain Arson thought, the tranquil effulgence of the tropical dawn was comforting. The sails were filling now, and Arson's *mal de mer* had passed as the foaming Homeric black seas had receded, trailing after the querulous storm as it vanished with *sotto voce* rumbles over the horizon. With the typical meteorological neophilia of a great storm, this storm had left the sky and the smell of the air new and fresh, oxygen-rich, like an atomic ambrosia to be inhaled by the gods of the future.

But this was no time for a panegyric on the inexpugnable powers of nature or for sublime expressions of the subliminal forces within him. This was a time for inductive reasoning, for stoic ratiocination on the blunt facts that would ensure survival on the seas. This was a time for—"NeeeCHUH!" he sneezed—strength of will, for digging deep into his will for the sangfroid he would need to face the assiduous challenges of the wind and waves. But then, willpower was his forte, or his name was not Will F.L. Arson.

After their mutinous insurgence, the fractious dissidents had left him alone on the superannuated ship, *The Lyssophobia*. Alone with the rigging, the wooden decks, and the salt spray—alone with his feckless dreams of timocracy . . . how naive those ideals seemed now. Alone at the helm. Alone with his maps. Alone with his hungry dog, Londonjack, who gazed at him with canine solicitude and who answered his inquiries in mute repartee, lifting one ear and cocking his furry physiognomy. "*Mea culpa*, London," Arson thought. "I got you into this."

Perambulating down the salty deck past the hatchway that opened into the tenebrous hold, he found it difficult to forget the insidious perfidy of his dissemblingly obsequious crew, who had impugned his sincere commiserations and accused him of megalomania. The narcoleptic London, vacuously watching his master withdraw through a haze of hebetude, failed to discern the etiology of the problem.

**Reading Comprehension**

1. In Translation 50, it can be inferred that:
    a. Arson was not perceived by his crew as he thought he was perceived.
    b. Arson was a cruel taskmaster who deserved the mutiny he got.
    c. The crew took advantage of Arson's kindness to enrich themselves.
    d. Arson, London, and *The Lyssophobia* will soon visit the depths of the abyss.

2. The author does all of the following EXCEPT:
    a. imply that Arson is egocentric
    b. imply that Arson is intelligent
    c. imply that London loves Arson
    d. imply that Arson has no solicitude for London

**Analogies**

3. **FULGURATION : REFULGENCE ::**
    a. blink : stare
    b. red light : green light
    c. fill : refill
    d. dissident : loyalist

4. **ANTEDILUVIAN : SUBLIMINAL ::**
    a. dissident : insurgence
    b. repartee : mea culpa
    c. waves : *mal de mer*
    d. time : awareness

**Antonyms**

5. **DISSIDENT :**
    a. thief
    b. rascal
    c. adherent
    d. toady

6. **PANEGYRIC :**
    a. diatribe
    b. *obiter dictum*
    c. eulogy
    d. soliloquy

The Romans ate with knives and spoons. Meat would have been cut into small pieces and picked up with fingers or put in a broth or mush and eaten with a spoon.

**analysis and application**

Consider what you know about the scientific method. We begin nonplussed by a fact of nature, then we create a hypothesis, then we design an experiment that will test the veracity of the hypothesis, then we collect a congeries of data, then we ratiocinate about the data, then we determine whether the hypothesis is verified or not verified, and then we report the result of the experiment. Now, **induction** is *a posteriori* factual reasoning, leading (*duct*) objective facts into (*in*) the mind, whereas **deduction** is *a priori* reasoning, in which we begin with a truth that we cannot impugn and allow our reason to lead (*duct*) logically down (*de*) from the truth with which we began. The question to analyze is this: Is the scientific method purely inductive or purely deductive, or is it a synthesis of induction and deduction? Explain your answer, and specifically identify which stages of the scientific method you regard as inductive or deductive. Breaking things down into pieces this way is analysis.

**intuition**

Your parachute gently lowers you to the lurid surface of a **refulgent** and **fulgurating** environment. Continue.

**synthesis and emotion**

Jack London has been called the most widely read American writer in the world. In his classic novels, such as *White Fang*, *The Call of the Wild*, and *The Sea Wolf*, London described a nature without solicitude, red of tooth and claw, struggling under a blank and indifferent freezing cosmos, in which only those possessed of a Nietzschean ferocity of willpower can survive. In London's merciless geographies, the protagonists had better get their fires built because the cosmos will freeze the good and the bad, the young and the old, the kind and the cruel alike. This is a world in which to build a fire can be the difference between survival and annihilation. How does this pessimistic naturalism of London's books make you feel? What other books can you think of that have similar fierce survival conditions, in which the characters can count on nothing but their own intelligence and will to survive a malefic environment?

**divergence, evaluation, and convergence**

Imagine that you have a severe case of **neophilia** and are obsessed with everything that is most modern, most new, most recently invented. Your house is a congeries of gleaming contemporary objects. As a class, brainstorm a long and divergent list of the new things that your imaginary house includes. Do not just be fluent (listing lots); also be flexible (listing different kinds of things) and original (listing un-thought-of kinds of things). In this brainstorming stage, be wild and crazy, do not try to judge the ideas, and piggyback on each other's ideas. Then, use congenial discussion to select five good criteria for deciding which new items are worth most—not necessarily in monetary terms, though you may use that criterion if you like. List your criteria in hierarchical order, from most important at the top to least important at the bottom. Then, apply the five criteria you chose to select the single most valuable new item in your imaginary house. If you like this process, you would love studying brainstorming techniques, such as the classical Osborn-Parnes Creative Problem-Solving model or Torrance's Future Problem Solving program.

### Neologist's Lexicon

Use the stems in this list to create a new word (neologism). Give the word, the pronunciation, the part of speech, the etymology, and the definition(s). Keep a record of the neologisms you create from list to list. Here are some examples:

**luvitude** (LOO vih tood) n. [*luvi* (wash), *tude* (state of)] 1. the sanguine pride that characterizes one who is squeaky clean 2. the physical condition of one who has spent the day surfing

**philocracy** (fill AH krass see) n. [*phile* (love), *cracy* (government)] 1. a government or society that elects the candidate who cares most about people 2. a government in which only individuals named Phil are eligible for public office

### Sesquipedalian Television

Using the words from List 50 and previous lists, write a spoof of the language of one of the television programs that you watch, if you watch any. Do you? Yes, you probably do.

### HelioTrek: A Panegyric to Neophilia

SPACE.

The final frontier.

These are the voyages of the starship *Mal de Mer*, in which brave men and women risk their lives to probe the surreal reaches of the fulgurating cosmos, to be emissaries of anthropomorphic peace and anthropocentric values, and to bring the benediction of peace to the internecine conflicts of fractious and dissident autochthonous miscreants on the omnibus *terra incognitas* of the vast abyss.

Dirk.

James D. Dirk.

The perspicacious commander of the starship *Mal de Mer*, who would have perished long ago, with his ecumenical crew in his gleaming high-tech sarcophagus, if he were not omniscient, narcissistic, and more than a match for the callow neophytes who obsequiously and mellifluously adhere to the patronizing *ex cathedra* injunctions emitted from his handsome physiognomy.

Spot.

The alien Spot.

The sedate and supercilious pointy-eared stoic, whose syllogisms, saturnine lucubrations, and sententious ratiocinations provide expository epiphanies to all of the lesser intellects on the *Mal de Mer*. Spot is the favorite candidate for euthanasia, in the mind of the next protagonist.

Stones.

Doc Stones, the xenophobic and querulous physician, who loses no opportunity for retorts and emotional diatribes against the enemy he most execrates, alien Spot. The Stones/Spot schism and character dichotomy provides internecine drama for the voyages of the starship *Mal de Mer*.

Foggy.

Engineer Foggy, Expediter, the portly but diminutive engineer whose obsequious fawning on Captain Dirk only irritates the entire crew, especially vivacious First Mate Bee Meeyup.

Space. The final frontier.

These are the voyages of the starship *Mal de Mer*.

These are the vacuous heroes whose apotheosis is the stuff of apocryphal hagiographies.

The Triumph was the honor to which Roman military commanders aspired. It was a civil ceremony as well as a religious rite, and it honored publicly the military commander. A Triumph was awarded for a notably successful foreign war or campaign and to display the glories of Roman victory. The spoils of war and the trophies of battle, as well as high-profile prisoners, were paraded through the streets of Rome. Marius had Jugurtha displayed and then strangled at the end of his Triumph, and Caesar had Vercingetorix paraded in his Triumph and then had him strangled as soon as the event concluded. The prisoners in the cart above are chained and are being held by soldiers. The cart is being led by another soldier in what we must surmise is a Triumph procession. Likely these prisoners will end their ride by meeting the same fate as Jugurtha and Vercingetorix. When the enemy was not really worthy, or when the war was very short, the commander might be awarded the lesser honor of an Ovation. Crassus was bitterly disappointed to be awarded only an Ovation after he put down the slave rebellion of Spartacus. It was felt that slaves were not opponents worthy of a Triumph. Rare was the commander who celebrated more than one Triumph; as a young man Cato the Censor was particularly impressed by Marcus Curius, who was awarded three Triumphs. Marius celebrated two Triumphs for his victory in Spain and for his defeat of the Germanic tribes. Pompey celebrated three Triumphs; the one for his exploits in the East lasted two days and was the most splendid Rome had seen to date.

These plaques show the spoils of war with a victory wreath at the center. The spoils include chariots, body armor, shields, spears, swords, and other equipment.

This victory plaque suggests a Triumph. A principal victim kneels before the commander, who is being crowned with a wreath by Winged Victory. A pile of trophies includes kneeling prisoners, shields, and body armor. On each side a crane is being used to build a structure. This plaque was created for someone who thought big—perhaps Caesar, with Vercingetorix as the kneeling prisoner.

| | | | | | | |
|---|---|---|---|---|---|---|
| • *syn* | (together) | synergy, syntax | • **nox** | (night) | equinox |
| • *epi* | (on) | epithet | • *protero* | (early) | *hysteron proteron* |
| • *nym* | (name) | toponym | • **hysteros** | (latter) | *hysteron proteron* |
| • *topo* | (place) | toponym | • *geo* | (earth) | geosynchronous |
| • equi | (equal) | equinox, equivocate | • *chron* | (time) | geosynchronous |
| • *phobia* | (fear) | ailurophobia | • circum | (around) | circumspect |
| • *morph* | (shape) | amorphous | • flu | (flow) | superfluous |
| • *neo* | (new) | neologism | • in | (not) | intestate |

**synergy** (combined force) The synergy of their personalities lifted them both to new abilities.

**epithet** (disparaging or descriptive name) Example: "I'm Diogenes the Dog," he retorted to Alexander.

**toponym** (place name) He was a master of toponyms, national capitals especially.

**equinox** (sun crosses equator) At the equinox, day and night are of equal duration.

**ailurophobia** (fear of cats) Her ailurophobia caused her great anxiety in the presence of cats.

**intestate** (with no will) Unfortunately he died intestate, leaving his family penniless.

**syntax** (grammatical arrangement) The syntax of your sentence is ungrammatical.

**hysteron proteron** (begging the question) His circular argument is a case of *hysteron proteron*.

**geosynchronous** (stationary in orbit) The geosynchronous satellite never moved in the sky.

**epistolary** (made of letters) Bram Stoker's scary *Dracula* is an epistolary novel.

• • •

**amorphous** (shapeless) The ruins formed an amorphous mound of broken rubble.

**neologism** (new word) He was fond of coining neologisms, such as *televoracity*.

**circumspect** (cautious) His circumspect reply made us wonder what he was concealing.

**equivocate** (to hedge) The cautious politician began to equivocate in his answer.

**superfluous** (unnecessary) The extra information was superfluous.

Roman key

## As Used by James Watson in *The Double Helix*

|  | Most | of | my | words | to | her | were | **superfluous.** |
|---|---|---|---|---|---|---|---|---|
| **Parts of Speech:** | n. | prep. | adj. | n. | prep. | pron. | v. | **adj.** |
| **Parts of Sentence:** | subj. |  |  |  |  |  | LVP | S.C. |
| **Phrases:** |  | ----prep. phrase----- | | --prep. phrase-- | | | | |
| **Clauses:** | ----------------------------------------independent clause---------------------------------<br>one independent clause; a simple, declarative sentence | | | | | | | |

Here Watson uses the adjective *superfluous* as a subject complement to modify the noun *most*. The linking verb *were* links *superfluous* to its noun/subject.

## Pronunciation

| | | | |
|---|---|---|---|
| **synergy** | SIN er jee | **geosynchronous** | gee o SYN kron us |
| **epithet** | EP i thet | **epistolary** | ee PIST o lery |
| **toponym** | TOP o nim | **amorphous** | ah MOR fuss |
| **equinox** | EE kwih nox | **neologism** | nee OH lo jiz em |
| **ailurophobia** | ay LOOR o FO be ah | **circumspect** | SIR com spekt |
| **intestate** | in TEST ate | **equivocate** | ee KWIV o kate |
| **syntax** | SIN tax | **superfluous** | su PURR floo us |
| *hysteron proteron* | HISS ter on PRO ter on | | |

## Spanish Cognates

| | | | |
|---|---|---|---|
| **epithet** | epíteto | **toponym** | topónimo |
| **equinox** | equinoccio | **intestate** | intestado |
| **syntax** | sintaxis | **epistolary** | epistolar |
| **amorphous** | amorfo | **neologism** | neologismo |
| **circumspect** | circunspecto | **equivocation** | equivocación |
| **superfluous** | superfluo | | |

1.  An **epithet** is a descriptive name or a disparaging name used invectively, but the stems give us a clearer idea of how the word works. An epithet is a name that is put (*tithenai*) on (*epi*), especially a name added on to the common name, such as *Peter the Great* or *Zeus Cloudgatherer*. An epithet can also be a simple disparaging adjective. The word *epithet* was used by Kipling, Conrad, Cooper, and Scott. Charlotte Brontë and Emily Brontë used it in their novels. Jane Eyre remarks, "You missed your epithet. I am not a pagan." Scott refers to the epithets holy, noble, and Black Sluggard. A fine use of *epithet* is from Stephen Crane's *Red Badge of Courage*: "This cold officer upon a monument, who dropped epithets unconcernedly down, would be finer as a dead man, he thought."

2.  A **Micropoem**: The verb **equivocate** is a vividly descriptive word, depicting the dodging, hedging, deceiver speaking (*voc*) equally (*equi*) out of both sides of his mouth. *Equivocate* is given prominence in Shakespeare's *Macbeth*, in which the porter cries, "Faith, here's an equivocator that could swear in both the scales against either scale."

3.  A **Micropoem**: To be **circumspect** is to be cautious, but in this word we see the cautious person looking (*spec*) cautiously around (*circum*), on the *qui vive*, the eyes moving from side to side. *Circumspect* has been used in the classics for centuries. It was used in the earliest novels, such as Daniel Defoe's 1719 classic *Robinson Crusoe* and Jonathan Swift's 1726 satire *Gulliver's Travels*. Robinson Crusoe finds that he has to be a little more circumspect, whereas Gulliver looks circumspectly and walks with the utmost circumspection to avoid treading on stragglers in Lilliput. The special image of looking around that *circumspect* contains can be easily seen in one of the sentences from Stevenson's great children's classic *Treasure Island*: "and I walked more circumspectly," says young Jim Hawkins, "keeping an eye on every side."

4.  A **Classic Word**: Few words are more frequently found than **superfluous**, the word that means unnecessary but that communicates an image of overflow, of excess flowing (*flu*) over (*super*) the top. *Superfluous* was used by Shakespeare four centuries ago; the distraught King Lear beseeches his thankless daughters not to give reasons why he does not need the hundred knights he retained when he gave up his kingdom, for, Lear cries, "Our basest beggars/Are in the poorest thing superfluous." Scott referred to superfluous wealth, Emily Brontë to superfluous company, and Charlotte Brontë to superfluous solicitude. Nathaniel Hawthorne's Hester Prynne bestowed all her superfluous means in charity. Melville used *superfluous* over and over in *Moby Dick*; we find superfluous scientific words and physical superfluousness, but no superfluous beard. Thoreau sharpened his wit to a point in *Walden*, noting that "Superfluous wealth can buy superfluities only." Thoreau also described the superfluous energy of the day, a superfluous and evitable wretchedness, and goodness that was not a transitory act but a constant superfluity. He remarked superfluous glow-shoes (?), superfluous property, and another alternative than to obtain the superfluities. In *The Return of the Native*, Hardy notes that someone's presence could be superfluous, and he describes a woman's head in a large kerchief, "a protection not superfluous at this hour and place." And in London's *The Call of the Wild*, Hal, Charles, and Mercedes are reduced to "the inexorable elimination of the superfluous" from their sled, which had been weighed down by congeries of ponderous non-necessities.

This helmet is of the Montefortino type—so called because many of them were found in that location in northern Italy; it was the style used by most Roman legionnaires during the Punic Wars in the third century B.C. It was a style that the Romans adapted from the helmets used by the Celtiberian warriors whom they met fighting in Spain. This particular helmet is complete but has a large dent in the back; such a dent might have been made by a stone or lead shot from a sling.

# MARIUS AND THE ARMY
## Dr. Thomas Milton Kemnitz

Gaius Marius altered the traditional maniple arrangement of the Roman army to produce a more effective and flexible fighting force; he arrange three maniples into a cohort and made the cohort the standard unit of the legion. There were now ten cohorts of 480 men each in a fully-manned legion, and they were arranged four deep in rows of 120 men; four cohorts formed the front line, with three in each of the next two lines. The commander now had to convey orders to only ten units instead of thirty, and the cohorts could be used easily on their own as raiding parties or on other special assignments. In practice, legions were never fully manned—piecemeal replacements did not occur—and their fighting numbers went down as their time in service went up.

Since the time of Scipio, Romans had carried the *pilum* and the *gladius* into battle. The *gladius* was a short sword the Romans had adopted in the Second Punic War when Scipio took Spain from the Carthaginians, and the Spanish short sword had proven far superior to the longer Roman weapon in close formation fighting. The *pila* were javelins with a two-foot iron shank behind the point affixed to a heavy wooden shaft. The shank had a flat flange that inserted into a split in the shaft and was held with two iron rivets. The *pila* proved to be highly effective weapons. The Romans could throw them about 100 feet, but their effective range was about fifty feet; the narrow shaft allowed them to penetrate shields and still injure or kill the men behind them. Even if a *pilum* did not injure an opponent, it would render his shield useless if it stuck into it. A man without a shield—particularly if he went into battle without armor like the Germanic and Celtic tribes did—had little hope of surviving an ancient battlefield. The legionnaires might throw their first *pilum* at fifty feet from the enemy and their second at fifteen to twenty feet and then charge before the enemy could reorganize. They exploited gaps in the line where the *pila* had cut down several men or at least rendered their shields useless. Marius altered the *pila* so that one of the two rivets was made of wood; this would snap and meant that if the *pilum* penetrated a shield or a man, it would dangle instead of sticking straight out, making the shield even more useless than it would have been if the *pilum* had stuck straight out. Moreover, it meant that a *pilum* could not be reused by the enemy.

Gaius Marius also altered the look of the Roman legion. In the militia legion, each man supplied his own equipment, and fashions in helmets, shields, and other equipment varied. In a Marian regiment, every man was equipped the same, and uniformity was achieved.

When he defeated the Germanic tribes, men with a sense of history began to refer to Marius as the "third founder of Rome"—a clear reference to the part Marcus Furius Camillius had played centuries earlier. Marius was elected consul an unprecedented six times between 107 and 100 B.C. But the part he played in Rome's civic affairs did not seem to anyone to be as positive as his military contributions, and his ambition, envy, and lack of a sense of proportion profoundly injured the Roman Republic and cost many Romans their lives in civic disruptions. Marius was very much a "new man"—a pleb of relative humble origins—who used the divisions between the patrician party and the plebs to push his way forward in Rome. His patron, Quintus Metellus, was a patrician evidently well-liked by the Senate. However, Marius had used the popular Assembly to push Metellus aside and take over the leadership of the army in the Numidian campaign. In doing so, he followed a path blazed more than a century earlier by Scipio, and he used the fault lines in the Republic that the Gracchi brothers (Tiberius and Gaius Gracchus) had exposed twenty and thirty years earlier. Moreover, he showed himself willing to countenance and foster the use of physical force against his opponents in Rome.

In each case below, one of the choices was really the word used by the author in the sentence provided. All of the choices can be found in the example words on the first page of this lesson. Your challenge is to decide which word the author used. This is not a test; it is more like a game because more than one word choice may work perfectly well. See if you can use your sensitivity and intuition to guess correctly which word the author used.

1.  **From Rudyard Kipling's *Kim***

    He called it a Moon of Paradise, a Disturber of Integrity, and a few other fantastic _____ which doubled her up with mirth.
    a. epithets
    b. toponyms
    c. neologisms
    d. syntaxes

2.  **From William Makepeace Thackeray's *Vanity Fair***

    I have the honour (_____) to introduce to her ladyship my two friends.
    a. superfluously
    b. epistolarily
    c. amorphously
    d. circumspectly

3.  **From Thomas Hardy's *The Return of the Native***

    Wildeve had died _____, and she and the child were his only relatives.
    a. circumspectly
    b. equivocally
    c. superfluously
    d. intestate

4.  **From W.E.B. Dubois's *The Souls of Black Folk***

    In failing thus to state plainly and _____ the legitimate demands of their people....
    a. circumspectly
    b. unequivocally
    c. superfluously
    d. amorphously

5.  **From F. Scott Fitzgerald's *The Great Gatsby***

    That ashen, fantastic figure glid[ed] toward him through the _____ trees.
    a. superfluous
    b. amorphous
    c. circumspect
    d. equivocal

Though it is a good thing to have a rich vocabulary, it is not a good thing to abuse that vocabulary by writing verbose, abstruse, sesquipedalian sentences. Those who overuse their vocabularies often do so at the expense of clarity. Translate the following showy, ponderous passage into graceful, direct English. Do not use slang, but do use words that seem familiar and comfortable.

ON AN AMORPHOUS ASTEROID in geosynchronous orbit around an effulgent but moribund star in the constellation Aquila, Cyrus the Circumspect cautiously approached the impecunious philosopher Erik the Equivocator to see if Erik's epithet was a condign appellation. Eric was known throughout the galaxy for his ironic malapropisms, perspicacious neologisms, superfluous objurgations, circumlocutions, and deliberate *hysteron proteron*. Originally an epistolary novelist, Erik had resorted to hardier philosophy when nonplussed critics had maligned his syntax.

Erik was known for sitting outside the asteroid capital (toponym Stellopolis) on a congeries of superannuated computer chips. "I am a voice," Erik resounded vociferously from his rusty congeries, "declaiming in the abyss! Is there an honest colonist among you? NO!"

Cyrus walked up to Erik and said with cool sangfroid, "I am Cyrus the Circumspect! Answer my questions, and do not dissemble, or you will die intestate."

"By the laws of Cosmic Synergy and the omnibus interdictions of our glorious timocracy," replied Erik with acerbity, "I will obey, and I will not."

Cyrus endured the repartee with equanimity. "When," asked Cyrus condescendingly, "is the next equinox?"

"Today," replied Erik cryptically, "for each day gives us equal knocks. It is an equalknocksious cosmos, if you ask me."

"Don't try your imponderable neologisms on me," replied Cyrus with antipathy. "I want answers. One more chance. What is the etiology of my ailurophobia?"

"Easy," replied the dissident stoic, "a CATastrophe."

"You lie, nihilist," Cyrus impugned, "but I exculpate you because of your bravery. I admit it: if I were not Cyrus the Circumspect, I would be Erik the Equivocator." And off he perambulated, looking circumspectly to the left and to the right. The saturnine philosopher sat on his chip pile, soliloquizing a diatribe against megalomaniacs.

## Reading Comprehension

1. In Translation 51, which of the following best expresses the main idea?
   a. We admire the fortitude of the dissident.
   b. Maladroit neophytes should receive supercilious epigrams.
   c. The social hierarchy must be superseded by a timocracy.
   d. To be wise is to be nonplussed.

2. The author's attitude in Translation 51 is best described as:
   a. regarding this event as a ludicrous contretemps
   b. distant and unsympathetic to either character
   c. presenting this story as a paradigm for tolerance
   d. contemptuous of those who are obsequious

## Analogies

3. **TOPONYM : NEOLOGISM ::**
   a. river : book
   b. pseudonym : *nom de plume*
   c. map : science fiction
   d. syntax : diction

4. **SYNERGY : DIFFUSION ::**
   a. epithet : encomium
   b. epistolary : romantic
   c. circumspect : mincing
   d. *hysteron proteron* : syllogism

## Antonyms

5. **AMORPHOUS :**
   a. geometric
   b. square
   c. inchoate
   d. rectilinear

6. **EQUIVOCATE :**
   a. impugn
   b. declaim
   c. retort
   d. aver

The *pilum* was one of the primary weapons that made the Roman legions so effective. Its long, thin shank allowed penetration through a shield and armor and into the warrior. They could be thrown with enough force to do damage from a distance of fifty feet. The Roman soldier carried two; typically the first one was thrown when the enemy was fifty feet away, and the second when the enemy was twenty feet distant. Then the Romans charged while the enemy was recovering from the effects of the two volleys of *pila*.

**synthesis**

**Synergy** is combined energy or action, as when two muscles work together or two talents create together. Think about two muscles pulling together to combine their energies, and then think of other situations that are analogous, either physically or metaphorically.

**reason**

We have previously studied the **syllogism**, which is a paradigm for logical ratiocination. But now we must consider ***hysteron proteron***, or begging the question, which is the logical error of assuming as one's premise the very conclusion that is to be proved! An example of *hysteron proteron* is to argue that we must be ethical because morals are important. It is not that morals are not important; it is just that the logical properties of this sentence do not prove anything. This sentence only repeats itself in circular reasoning, saying, in essence, *morals are important because morals are important*.

The famous philosophical example of *hysteron proteron*, some would say, was French philosopher/mathematician René Descartes's dictum "*Cogito ergo sum.*" (I think, therefore I am.) We encountered Descartes in Lesson 44 when we explored epistemology, but to understand *hysteron proteron* we must review and discover more of the story: Descartes (1596-1650) was attempting to found his philosophical system on a bedrock of certainty, and so he decided that he would begin by doubting everything that he could doubt. He began a process of systematic doubting and finally asked whether he knew for certain that he even existed or whether he could doubt it. His answer was, I am thinking; therefore I exist. Eureka! He thought he had found a certain fact that he could not doubt. And yet he was guilty of *hysteron proteron*, of begging the question because whether he existed or not was the question—it was not something he was logically allowed to assume in his premise. If I am uncertain whether I exist, then I do not know if it is I thinking or not. Descartes's assertion actually took the form, I EXIST THEREFORE I EXIST. I therefore I.

Why is *hysteron proteron* called *hysteron proteron*? *Hysteros* means latter, and *protero* means former. Begging the question is putting the latter former; it is including what you should prove later in the beginning of your argument.

Begging the question is not always as easy to detect as you might imagine because the same idea can be phrased in different ways, and so we can phrase both the premise and the conclusion in different words, cleverly concealing the fact that they are only different words for the same idea. Examples of deceptive *hysteron proteron* are sentences such as "Education is important because knowledge is valuable," "I am nonplussed because phenomena perplex me," and "Everyone should vote because participating in democracy is important." These statements are actually circular; they are disguised repetitions.

The *hysteron proteron* fallacy has been recognized as a logical error from the beginning of philosophical time. Also known as the fallacy of *circulus in probando*, it was described by Aristotle (384-322 B.C.), pupil of Plato and teacher of Alexander the Great.

Think carefully about *hysteron proteron* (begging the question, putting the latter former, circular reasoning, *circulus in probando*), and then write an example that illustrates the illogical circularity—that shows how the result reached depends on the result being assumed to begin with. Then, think more carefully, and explain what non-circular, effective, and valid reasoning would need to be and how this is different from *hysteron proteron*. Once this distinction is vividly clear to you, you will begin to notice that the world is replete with *hysteron proteron*!

## Neologist's Lexicon

Use the stems in this list to create a new word (neologism). Give the word, the pronunciation, the part of speech, the etymology, and the definition(s). Keep a record of the neologisms you create from list to list. Here are some examples:

**hysteronym** (HISS ter oh nim) n. [*hysteros* (latter), *nym* (name)] 1. the invective or incisive epithet that you think to apply to your opponent only afterwards, when it is too late to deliver it 2. any epithet preceded by the words, "I should have said . . ."

**noxochronic** (nox o KRON ik) adj. [*nox* (night), *chron* (time)] 1. becoming obsessively nocturnal, as a bibliophile who reads every summer night until dawn 2. being unable to sleep unless the sun is shining through the curtains

## Sesquipedalian Epistolary Story

An epistolary novel is one such as Bram Stoker's *Dracula,* which uses the device of the letter to give the novel a documentary feel, as though the story were true and you were only reading someone's letters about what actually happened. This is one reason why *Dracula* is so shockingly vivid and credible. There is no difficulty in making Coleridge's suspension of disbelief when one is reading *Dracula*; even though the content is incredible, the reader becomes credulous, in part because the epistolary technique enhances the illusion. Write a short epistolary story using words from List 51 and other lists. An example:

### Epithetula, the Demon of Diatribe

*Dearest Gullibette,*

*I have only just arrived at the castle here in Transnomia, and already I miss you terribly. The Professor was not present to meet me at the gate, but I was admitted by an obsequious toady of deplorable syntax, who escorted me to my comfortable room. Oh, Gullibette, if only you could see the undulating hills and forests which circumscribe the picturesque castle! I had been in my room unpacking for only a few minutes when the Professor entered. I did not even hear him come in, but suddenly there he was behind me, Professor Epithetula. I had expected him to be sedate and dignified, but to my shock, he was condescending and supercilious and greeted me rudely with a hissing, adjective-laden diatribe, calling me Mort the Amorphous, Burt the Superfluous, and Porter the Portly. I explained with equanimity that my name was Jonathan Sangfroid, but he continued to abuse me with his vile invective and vociferously called me a Putative Pudd'nhead, Heterodox Heretic, and a Translucent Transient. When I asked him why he abused me thus, he said he knew me for a knave and a villain and would daub the walls of the castle with me! I begged to be excused from his loquacious objurgations, but I soon felt their soporific effects on me, and I fell into a sound and refreshing sleep.*

*Later, I awoke to find that three weird sisters had entered the hall outside my door and were whispering new sotto voce vituperations in suspirating voices, calling me a Pusillanimous Pussycat, a Neptune of Nepotism, and a Foolish Funambulist. When I opened the door to drive them away, they suddenly transmogrified into parakeets and flew through my room and out the narrow barred window into the night, chirping new epithets as they flew! What a day I'm having. Write soon. Love, Jonathan.*

| | | | | | | |
|---|---|---|---|---|---|---|
| • intra | (within) | intramural | • reg | (rule) | regicide |
| • **mur** | (wall) | intramural | • cide | (kill) | regicide |
| • extra | (beyond) | extramural | • corp | (body) | incorporeal |
| • *penta* | (five) | pentameter | • *mega* | (large) | megalith |
| • *meter* | (measure) | pentameter | • *lith* | (rock) | megalith |
| • fort | (strong) | *fortepiano* | • per | (through) | perspicuous |
| • ous | (full of) | ingenuous | • spec | (look) | perspicuous |
| • cap | (take) | incipient | • fid | (faith) | perfidious |
| • **catena** | (chain) | concatenate | • trans | (across) | intransigent |
| • con | (together) | incondite | • ego | (I) | egomania |

**intramural** (within the walls)  Intramural activities are held within the school.

**extramural** (outside the walls)  Extramural sports are between different schools.

**pentameter** (of five measures)  The poem was in iambic pentameter, five iambic feet to a line.

*fortepiano* (loud then soft)  The passage should be played *fortepiano*.

**incipient** (just beginning)  It was an incipient problem, just beginning to cause difficulties.

**concatenate** (chain together)  The concatenated events formed a chain of causes and effects.

**incondite** (poorly constructed)  The neophyte's novels were incondite and shallow.

**regicide** (killing of a king)  Macbeth's regicide of Duncan haunts his conscience.

**incorporeal** (not consisting of matter)  The spirit's essence was incorporeal, not corporal.

**megalith** (huge stone)  The prehistoric megaliths stood in black outline against the red sky.

• • •

**ingenuous** (innocent and naive)  The ingenuous youth, new to the city, was easily deceived.

**perspicuous** (brilliantly clear)  Your perspicuous mind and perspicacious work are appreciated.

**perfidious** (treacherous)  The perfidious act was roundly condemned by the loyalists.

**intransigent** (not compromising)  The intransigent zealot lost everything through stubbornness.

**egomania** (self-obsession)  His irritating egocentrism developed into unendurable egomania.

## As Used by Herman Melville in *Billy Budd*

| | Some | sort | of | plot | was | **incipient.** |
|---|---|---|---|---|---|---|
| **Parts of Speech:** | adj. | n. | prep. | n. | v. | adj. |
| **Parts of Sentence:** | | subj. | | | LVP | S.C. |
| **Phrases:** | | ----prep. phrase----- | | | | |
| **Clauses:** | ----------------------------------independent clause--------------------------------- | | | | | |
| | one independent clause; a simple, declarative sentence | | | | | |

Here Melville uses the adjective *incipient* as a subject complement to modify the noun *sort*. We know *sort* is a noun because it is modified by two adjectives and because it is the subject of the verb, so it must be either a noun or a pronoun.

## Pronunciation

| | | | | |
|---|---|---|---|---|
| **intramural** | in tra MYOOR al | | **incorporeal** | in KOR por EE al |
| **extramural** | ex tra MYOOR al | | **megalith** | MEG a lith |
| **pentameter** | pen TAH meh ter | | **ingenuous** | in JEN yoo us |
| *fortepiano* | FOR tay pe AH no | | **perspicuous** | per SPICK yoo us |
| **incipient** | in SIP ee ent | | **perfidious** | per FID ee us |
| **concatenate** | con CAT en ate | | **intransigent** | in TRAN si jent |
| **incondite** | in KON dite | | **egomania** | ee go MAY nee ah |
| **regicide** | REJ ih side | | | |

## Spanish Cognates

| | | | | |
|---|---|---|---|---|
| **pentameter** | pentámetro | | **incipient** | incipiente |
| **concatenation** | concatenación | | **regicidal** | regicida |
| **incorporeal** | incorpóreo | | **megalith** | megalito |
| **ingenuous** | ingenuo | | **perspicuous** | perspicuo |
| **perfidious** | pérfido | | **intransigent** | intransigente |

1. The noun **pentameter**, which we have mentioned in previous discussions, refers to a poetic line that contains five (*penta*) feet (*meter*: measure). These five feet might be iambs, trochees, dactyls, or anapests. The classic line of poetry in English is **iambic pentameter**, which is the line found in the Shakespearean sonnet: three quatrains and a couplet of iambic pentameter, for a total of fourteen lines and 140 syllables, rhyme scheme *abab cdcd efef gg*. Shakespeare's sonnets are overwhelmingly beautiful and are among the great literary treasures of the English language. So powerful is the sonnet that Shakespeare even concealed a sonnet in the dialogue of Romeo and Juliet's meeting. Look again at the play, and see the beautiful sonnet/dialogue, beginning, "If I profane with my unworthiest hand . . . ."

2. The adjective **ingenuous** refers to one who is innocent, naive, who is unreserved, who does not dissemble. An ingenuous girl is sometimes called an **ingénue**, especially as a character on stage. To be ingenuous is to be unspoiled by the cruel world, unjaded, uncynical. The ingenuous person, male or female, is still in (*in*) original (*gen*) condition, sincere and optimistic. In Cooper's *The Last of the Mohicans*, Alice is described as ingenuous: "The ingenuous Alice gazed at his free air and proud carriage," "said the uneasy youth, gazing at the ingenuous countenance of Alice," "He was, however, anticipated by the voice of the ingenuous and youthful Alice." We find *ingenuous* in the novels of Hardy, Harper Lee, and the Brontës. There are ingenuous rustics, ingenuous diversions, ingenuous comments, and ingenuous enthusiasm, but the most striking sentence is one from Hardy's *Return of the Native*: "An ingenuous, transparent life was disclosed; as if the flow of her existence could be seen passing within her." You will detect that it is not necessarily a compliment to be described as ingenuous; it can be a kind of epithet, implying that you aren't smart or observant, that you are easily duped or led by the nose, that you are wide-eyed and waggy-tailed, willing to believe anything a calculating manipulator would tell you. And on the other hand, there is a certain human beauty in the good will and trust of the ingenuous person. The word has range and might be used in many different situations. Be careful with it.

3. A **Classic Word**: Here is a great word: **perfidious**. It means treacherous (perfidy is the opposite of fidelity), and as you might imagine upon reflection, it has a rich history in exciting adventure novels, where it aptly describes the villains, cutthroats, and deceivers who violate (*per*) the faith (*fid*) of those who trust them. We find *perfidious* in *Peter Pan*, *Lord Jim*, *Moby Dick*, and *Gulliver's Travels*—all novels of the sea. We find *perfidious* in *Ivanhoe* and in *Jane Eyre*. Peter Pan's gang suddenly sees the perfidious pirates bearing down upon them. In *Lord Jim,* the perfidious shaft of an arrow falls harmless. In Melville's *Moby Dick*, we find perfidious silences and perfidious allies. The stubborn Jane Eyre remembers the perfidious hints given by Mrs. Reed about her disposition.

4. A puzzle: Why does the adjective **incipient** mean just beginning, when it is composed of the stems *in* (in) and *cap* (take)? Take in? It does not seem to make sense, until you realize that *incipient* comes from the Latin *incipere*, to take in hand, to begin. The image is of hands grasping, closing, taking up the task in order to begin. Thomas Hardy loved *incipient* and used it over and over in his novels.

Triumphs of Marius (above) and Sulla (below) were each depicted on coins.

The *Populares* and *Optimates* did not function as modern political parties do. There was no formal organization with a structure and an electoral purpose. Rather, they represented tendencies of men to make choices as to where their interests and sympathies lay, who their friends and enemies were, what proposals they might favor or oppose, and how they might react to certain events. The dividing point between them was generally that the *Optimates* favored the interests of the patricians and richest plebs, while the *Populares* stood with the interests of the majority of the plebs. Some men sought to use the divisions as the Gracchi brothers or Marius did, and then the dividing line might became clear and important and the basis upon which men took sides. Other times the division was largely dormant, and other issues might be more important.

# THE SOCIAL WAR
## Dr. Thomas Milton Kemnitz

As consul, Marius formed an unsavory alliance with Lucius Appuleius Saturninus, who was a tribune in 103. Saturninus was a senator who became a leading member of the *Populares*. Saturninus was essential to Marius in getting laws passed to allow settling his Numidian war veterans on farmland. Marius had been appointed over the opposition of the Senate, who had responded by decreeing that he would not be allowed to take regular troops. He therefore had raised recruits by enlisting poor men, and they did not have farms to return to, unlike the regularly-recruited militiamen. Saturninus was happy to propose any law that would be perceived as hostile to the *Optimates*, and a law giving Marius's men good land in North Africa certainly did not please the Senate.

Saturninus formed a gang of violent men whom he used to intimidate or beat up his opponents. Although Rome had seen the like on an *ad hoc* basis when the Senate had dispatched both Gracchi brothers, now Saturninus kept his men together and used them repeatedly to control the Forum and the public places in Rome. His alliance with Marius was doubtlessly strengthened by the enmity both men bore Metellus, whom they forced to leave Rome. But Saturninus went too far when he killed an opposition candidate for the consulship during an election, and the Senate declared martial law and asked Marius as consul to enforce it; Marius did so, and Saturninus was arrested and imprisoned in a building in the Forum, where he was killed by a hostile mob of Senate-sponsored *Optimates* throwing roof tiles down on the prisoners. During the next decade, all office-holders found themselves compelled to employ gangs of thugs.

A deadlock formed between the patricians and the plebs, as well as between the *Optimates* and *Populares*, and Rome was unable to solve any problems or alter any of its basic arrangements. The Gracchi brothers had tried to solve a number of problems related to land distribution and the treatment of Italian allies, and they had died for their efforts. Another attempt led to serious rioting in 95 B.C., when the issue was the distribution of lands for those who had fought the Germanic tribes; proposals sought to take care of the Roman veterans without settling the allies. In 91 B.C. Marcus Livius Drusus the Younger was Tribune of the Plebs. He proposed a commission to grant the plebs more land, both around Rome and in new colonies, and he wanted to grant citizenship rights to the Italian allies. The wealthy did not want to lose their land, and the Roman plebs did not want the Italians to become citizens. Citizenship rights were certainly important to the Italians who did not have them, and it was rumored that all of non-Roman Italy had sworn to become Drusus's clients if he enfranchised them; his opponents feared that this would give him unassailable power. He was assassinated, and the Italian allies (*Socii*) revolted, starting the Social War of 91–88 B.C.

This was the ultimate Roman nightmare: battle-tested legionnaires led by good generals opposing Roman legions led by generals who were not always so good. There was an appalling loss of life as large armies of trained men fought one another, until finally the Romans offered full citizenship to Italians who were not in revolt or who would end the revolt. This took the impetus out of the war, and hostilities ceased. Then it became clear that the grant of citizenship was hedged with so many qualifications that it was not satisfactory. A young tribune named Sulpicius Rufus in 88 B.C. proposed a solution that would have drastically reshaped electoral power in Rome. He was backed by a gang of gladiators in the streets of Rome, and he met with the usual fierce opposition from the *Optimates* in the Senate. Sulpicius sought the help of Gaius Marius, who had not played a leading part in the Social War—perhaps because he was incapacitated or perhaps because the *Optimates* in the Senate feared his growing power. The events that followed ruptured the Republic.

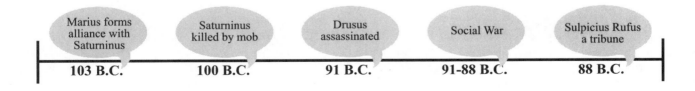

| Marius forms alliance with Saturninus | Saturninus killed by mob | Drusus assassinated | Social War | Sulpicius Rufus a tribune |
|---|---|---|---|---|
| 103 B.C. | 100 B.C. | 91 B.C. | 91-88 B.C. | 88 B.C. |

In each case below, one of the choices was really the word used by the author in the sentence provided. All of the choices can be found in the example words on the first page of this lesson. Your challenge is to decide which word the author used. This is not a test; it is more like a game because more than one word choice may work perfectly well. See if you can use your sensitivity and intuition to guess correctly which word the author used.

1.  **From Kate Chopin's *The Awakening***

    She recognized anew the symptoms of infatuation which she had felt _____ as a child.
    a. *fortepiano*
    b. incorporeally
    c. perspicaciously
    d. incipiently

2.  **From Mary Wollstonecraft's *Vindication of the Rights of Woman***

    [I] learned to think with the energy necessary to _____ that abstract train of thought which produces principles.
    a. incipient
    b. concatenate
    c. pentameter
    d. *fortepiano*

3.  **From John Milton's *Paradise Lost***

    Thus _____ Spirits to smallest forms reduced their shapes immense.
    a. incondite
    b. intransigent
    c. incorporeal
    d. incipient

4.  **From Thomas Hardy's *Jude the Obscure***

    The house [was] little more than an old _____ cottage.
    a. incondite
    b. intramural
    c. concatenated
    d. megalith

5.  **From Martin Luther King, Jr.'s *Why We Can't Wait***

    They were so _____ that Burke Marshall despaired of a pact.
    a. perfidious
    b. ingenuous
    c. incondite
    d. intransigent

Though it is a good thing to have a rich vocabulary, it is not a good thing to abuse that vocabulary by writing verbose, abstruse, sesquipedalian sentences. Those who overuse their vocabularies often do so at the expense of clarity. Translate the following showy, ponderous passage into graceful, direct English. Do not use slang, but do use words that seem familiar and comfortable.

NEVER ONE TO JOIN in gregarious activities, either intramural or extramural, the diffident and ingenuous girl worked intransigently alone on her poetry, her *idée fixe*, far from the perfidious egomaniacs who had dissembled and misled her when she had first reached the university. Her incipient poetic talent had matured through a concatenation of influences, and the amorphous and incondite jingles and cryptic metaphors she wrote as a neophyte now seemed maladroit and embarrassing to her, especially in comparison to the controlled and perspicuous sonnets she was writing now on new themes: incorporeal reality, axiological perplexities, the self-regicide of personal growth—lofty transmogrifications of subliminal energies.

She looked at the sonnet she had almost finished. It was a classic: three quatrains and a couplet of iambic pentameter. It had been difficult to subjugate her ideas to the sonnet's stringent meter and rhyme scheme, and she had almost abjured the sonnet form to make the final couplet anapestic tetrameter, but she finally decided to adhere to the traditional paradigm—the three-syllable anapests would be too dissonant with the music of the iambic quatrains. When the *disjecta membra* of her work was unearthed in future millennia, she thought, at least the patronizing exegetes would know she could write a proper sonnet.

Her sedentary lucubrations continued thus, late into the night, her introspective creative synergies forming less a soporific than a stimulant, until at last the effulgent dawn came streaming through the window with the euphony of the loquacious songbirds, and she went beatifically to a condign sleep.

Pictured is lead shot for a sling, made by the Socii for troops of the Italian confederation and bearing the inscription *ITAL*. The Roman legions were facing other legionnaires, men who were trained and fought and thought as they did; this was very close to civil war.

**Reading Comprehension**

1. In Translation 52, the author does all of the following EXCEPT:
    a. suggest that the poet has problems forming healthy friendships
    b. indicate that the poet's talents are still developing
    c. indicate that her poem strictly followed the traditional sonnet form
    d. reveal the theme of the latest poem

2. The author's attitude is best described as:
    a. bored with the frivolity of poetry
    b. condescending toward this poet's mediocre abilities
    c. appreciative of the artistic decisions of poetry
    d. indifferent toward poets and poetry

**Analogies**

3. **INTRAMURAL : EXTRAMURAL ::**
    a. saturnine : gregarious
    b. introduction : table of contents
    c. wall : moat
    d. introspective : obsequious

4. **REGICIDE : PERFIDIOUS ::**
    a. neophyte : ingenuous
    b. egomania : perspicuous
    c. pentameter : incondite
    d. king : faith

**Antonyms**

5. **INCORPOREAL :**
    a. substantial
    b. atomic
    c. vaporous
    d. supernatural

6. **FORTEPIANO :**
    a. cacophony
    b. euphony
    c. crescendo
    d. *sotto voce*

This is the grave marker for a geometry teacher named Apuleius Archimedes; in Rome geometers also did land surveying.

**divergence**

The word **incipient** means just beginning, like the incipient dawn of a new day that stirs the incipient breezes and the incipient euphony of the birds, which bring our slumbering consciousness to incipient alertness. Make a long list of other incipient phenomena.

**elaboration, evaluation, and convergence**

A **concatenation** is a chain of events. The concatenation might be a natural chain of cause and effect events, such as one of the great cycles of ecology, meteorology, or biology, or it might be a chain of human events, such as the tragic concatenations that bring wars into sanguinary and cacophonous being. Long molecules are said to be **catenated**. The idea of a chain presents us with an interesting opportunity for thinking. First, list several concatenations that exist in nature: water cycles, oxygen cycles, cycles that create soil, and so forth. For each one, elaborate somewhat on the links in the chain. For example, the sun heats the seas and lakes, which evaporate, the vapor rises, forms clouds, condenses, forms rain, falls, waters the vegetation, runs off into the streams, flows into the lakes and seas, and the concatenation repeats itself.

Once you have a list of four natural concatenations, then use evaluation by criteria to choose which of these cycles is most critical to life on our planet. If you could use a magic spell, one time, to magically protect one of these natural chains so that no harm would ever come to it, which one would you protect? In order to evaluate these concatenations, you first must decide upon some criteria (the singular is *criterion*) which you can use to compare them. For example, you might decide that the important thing is to make sure the planet has fresh water, or fresh oxygen, or clean air, or sunlight with the ultraviolet rays filtered out, or plankton living in the sea . . . there could be many criteria. Make a list of criteria, discuss what you have listed, narrow to what you feel are the four most important criteria, and then use the four criteria to select the concatenation in nature that you would spend your one magic spell to protect.

In applying the criteria, you might prefer to list them from most important to least important and assign points to each criterion: 4, 3, 2, 1. The Future Problem Solving program, which was developed by Dr. Paul Torrance, uses this technique. You list your criteria vertically on the left and your concatenations horizontally across the top, and then you rank each of the concatenations, *moving horizontally one criterion at a time*, rather than vertically one choice at time. In other words, if your first criterion is oxygen, then you would move across, giving each chain one to four points according to how much that chain contributes to the planet's oxygen supply. Doing it this way, *one criterion at a time*, forces you to compare the merits of the different choices more objectively. When you have evaluated all four choices by all four criteria and assigned all of the points, the choice that gained the most points wins! As an example, here is a grid that shows why I choose my cat, Heisenberg, as the best animal. Heisenberg is a clear winner over the next best animal, the turtle.

|  | DOG | CAT | TURTLE | GRAMPUS |
|---|---|---|---|---|
| FURRY | 3 | 4 | 1 | 1 |
| NO TROUBLE | 1 | 2 | 3 | 4 |
| CAN LIVE INSIDE | 2 | 4 | 3 | 1 |
| PURRS | 1 | 4 | 1 | 1 |
| TOTAL | 7 | 14 | 8 | 7 |

## Neologist's Lexicon

Use the stems in this list to create a new word (neologism). Give the word, the pronunciation, the part of speech, the etymology, and the definition(s). Keep a record of the neologisms you create from list to list. Here are some examples:

**egomuric** (ee go MYOOR ik) adj. [*ego* (I), *mur* (wall)]  1. putting up behavioral or psychological barriers that prevent people from knowing you  2. responding with subterfuges or circumlocutions to all personal questions

**metricide** (MEH rih side) n. [*meter* (measure), *cide* (kill)]  1. the act of killing a person who measures or evaluates one's performance, especially if the assessment is unfavorable  2. the act of killing a sanguine game show host who smiles while pronouncing the word *sorry*

## Sesquipedalian House Pets

Using the words from List 52 and previous lists, write a description of an animal. An example:

### The Fly of the House: His Malefic Intentions

Perspicacious, omniscient, he knows the location of every crumb, every hiding place, every intramural skypath in the house. Superciliously recognizing my careful food wrapping for the incondite and tortuous inadequacy that it is, he descends like a cacophonouzzzzz six-footed gastronome, giving me chronic entomological nightmares; he is the compound-eyed HouseKing, and I the obsequious dissembling regicide. I strike with bellicose uproar, creating a concatenation of catastrophes. An egomaniac having no incorporeal interests, his *idée fixe* is food, only food, and he lands on that megalith to flies, the bread loaf. He is intransigent and will not be shooed but returns after each swat, his *fortepiano* buzz fading as he lands again, perfidiously, on the sacrosanct bread. With *sotto voce* epithets, I insidiously await his next move, my subliminal angers finding a truculent insurgence as they rise to the surface of my consciousness. I will DESTROY, I promise myself incredulously, this inexpugnable fly, this refractory fly, this feculent, corpulent hedonist, this miscreant, this fly. I objurgate and execrate the fly with new invectives, but all diatribe is feckless. The fly is pugnacious and in defiant retort buzzes acerbically past my ear as he vanishes with postprandial equanimity into the tenebrous corners of the room.

In a nonplussed epiphany, I suddenly realize the end of all metempsychosis: it is to be reborn as the king of beasts, the paragon of animals, the nonpareil of animate phenomena, the vivacious *bon vivant*: the fly.

| | | | | | |
|---|---|---|---|---|---|
| • in | (in) | incuse | • *iso* | (equal) | isocracy |
| • **cud** | (strike) | incuse | • *phan* | (appearance) | phantasmagoria |
| • cise | (cut) | incise | • sci | (know) | prescience |
| • ***rhino*** | (nose) | rhinoplasty | • *a-* | (not) | anomaly |
| • *plasto* | (molded) | rhinoplasty | • *homo* | (same) | anomaly |
| • *necro* | (death) | necromancy | • cant | (sing) | recant |
| • omni | (all) | *exeunt omnes* | • clud | (close) | preclude |
| • quadr | (four) | quadrilateral | • circum | (around) | circumscribed |
| • dict | (say) | *ipse dixit* | • aqua | (water) | aqua vitae |

**incuse** (hammered in)  He hammered the incuse design into the copper plate.

**incise** (cut in)  The design was incised into the mahogany furniture.

**rhinoplasty** (plastic surgery)  The expensive rhinoplasty did not correct his broken nose.

**necromancy** (sorcery)  The Haitian necromancer claimed that the dead told her the future.

***exeunt omnes*** (all leave)  The stage directions read, "*Exeunt omnes*," so everyone left.

**quadrilateral** (four-sided)  He worked on a plane figure, a quadrilateral polygon.

***ipse dixit*** (arbitrary statement)  It was foolishly *ipse dixit*, an arbitrary assertion without proof.

**aqua vitae** (alcohol)  He detected the pungent aroma of *aqua vitae* through the tavern window.

**isocracy** (all have equal power)  The remote tribe was an isocracy and had no appointed leader.

**phantasmagoria** (rapidly changing images)  He saw a phantasmagoria of faces and objects.

• • •

**prescience** (foreknowledge)  His prescience gave him a warning weeks in advance.

**anomaly** (abnormality)  The weather anomaly—green clouds—had no formal name.

**recant** (retract)  He had to recant his statement to sing a geocentric tune about the solar system.

**preclude** (prevent in advance)  Do not preclude your options too soon; study advanced math.

**circumscribed** (limited)  The few permissible behaviors are carefully circumscribed.

**As Used by Jane Austen in *Emma***

| | Happiness | must | **preclude** | false | indulgence. |
|---|---|---|---|---|---|
| **Parts of Speech:** | n. | v. | **v.** | adj. | n. |
| **Parts of Sentence:** | subj. | -----------AVP--------- | | | D.O. |
| **Phrases:** | ----no prepositional, appositive, or verbal phrases----- | | | | |
| **Clauses:** | -----------------------------------independent clause-------------------------------- | | | | |
| | one independent clause; a simple, declarative sentence | | | | |

Here Austen uses *preclude* as the predicate; notice that it is an action verb that transfers the action to a direct object, so it is transitive.

**Pronunciation**

| | | | |
|---|---|---|---|
| **incuse** | in KYOOS | **isocracy** | eye SOCK ra see |
| **incise** | in SIZE | **phantasmagoria** | fan TAZ ma GOR ee ah |
| **rhinoplasty** | RYE no plas tee | **prescience** | PREH shence |
| **necromancy** | NECK ro man see | **anomaly** | a NOM a lee |
| *exeunt omnes* | EX ay unt OM nays | **recant** | ree KANT |
| **quadrilateral** | KWAD ri LAT er al | **preclude** | pre KLOOD |
| *ipse dixit* | IP say DIX it | **circumscribed** | SIR come scribed |
| *aqua vitae* | AH kwa VI tee | | |

**Spanish Cognates**

| | | | |
|---|---|---|---|
| **necromancy** | necromancia | **quadrilateral** | cuadrilatero |
| **phantasmagoria** | fantasmagoría | **prescience** | presciencia |
| **anomaly** | anomalía | **circumscribed** | circunscrito |

1. An **anomaly** is an abnormality, an oddness, an incongruity. At first it seems that the word is made of *a-* (not) and *nom* (name) to describe an unusual situation for which there is no name, but actually this noun comes from the Greek *anomalos*, which means irregular and which breaks down into *an* (not) and *homo* (same). The anomaly is the odd item in the group; it is the one that is not (*an*) the same (*homo*) as the others. *Anomaly* was one of Melville's favorite words. He used it repeatedly in *Moby Dick* to describe oddities, such as the curious anomaly of the most solid masonry joining with oak and hemp in constituting the completed ship. (Masonry on a ship?) The best example from Melville concerned the appearance of the sperm whale: "Physiognomically regarded, the Sperm Whale is an anomalous creature. He has no proper nose." I'd have called that *arhinally*.

2. A **Classic Word**: The noun **necromancy** comes from the Greek *nekromanteía* and refers to sorcery, the black (*necro*: death) art. We see this word in Swift's *Gulliver's Travels*, Scott's *Ivanhoe*, Hawthorne's *The Scarlet Letter*, Stowe's *Uncle Tom's Cabin*, and Kipling's *Kim*. Swift's sentence gives a chilling sense of the connotations of *necromancy*: "By his skill in necromancy, he has a power of calling whom he pleases from the dead."

3. *Aqua vitae*, which literally means the water of life, is alcohol. Though you will not see this term often in literature, you will see it in Shakespeare, such as this sentence from *Romeo and Juliet*: "Give me some *aqua vitae*, / These griefs, these woes, these sorrows make me old."

4. A **Micropoem**: To **circumscribe** is to limit, and we see the limitation depicted in the word: a circle (*circum*) is drawn (*scrib*) around the perimeter of what is permissible. Robinson Crusoe feels himself circumscribed by the boundless ocean and cut off from mankind, whereas the incorrigible Toad in *The Wind in the Willows* feels that his life has become narrow and circumscribed. We also use *circumscribe* in geometry when we draw one figure around another, touching as many points as possible. A circle circumscribed around a triangle touches the triangle at three points.

5. To **preclude** is to close (*clud*) off a possibility beforehand (*pre*). Ethan Frome feels a sense of relief so great as to preclude all other feelings.

6. The noun **phantasmagoria** refers to a series of phantasms, illusions, or apparitions. It also can refer to any similar scene made up of many changing elements or shifting images. The word comes from the Greek *phántasm* (image) and *agora* (assembly or marketplace) and conveys the idea of an assembly of images. This word reminds us of the noun **agoraphobia**, fear of open spaces. The Greek *agora*, the marketplace, was where people assembled. If you were in a dream state, watching hosts of images fly past your eyes, that would be a phantasmagoria. We often see such collections of changing images in movies. Macbeth sees a horrific and nightmarish phantasmagoria, but when visions of sugarplums dance in an excited child's head, that is a more beatific phantasmagoria.

7. When we say that **rhinoplasty** means plastic surgery, we do not mean just any plastic surgery. The stem *rhino* means nose, and so rhinoplasty is plastic surgery of the nose. It is what we sometimes call a "nose job."

# SULLA AND MARIUS SHED BLOOD
## Dr. Thomas Milton Kemnitz

When Sulpicius was unable to get some of his reforms enacted, he arranged with Marius a deal of mutual support. Marius would pay the younger man's considerable debts and would support his effort to change the laws, and Sulpicius would support Marius as commander of the Roman armies in a war that was to be fought against the king of Pontus, Mithridates VI; the Senate had given that command to Sulla. Sulpicius Rufus called the Assembly to revoke Sulla's command and to expel Senators until there were not enough to form a quorum. The patricians responded with violence in the Forum and an effort to kill Sulpicius as they had done with the Gracchi brothers and Saturninus, but Sulpicius's gladiatorial gang won the day, and Sulla avoided death only by taking refuge in Marius's house; Marius protected him, an act of charity that Sulla would not return later. Sulla then fled to the camp of his troops waiting to cross to Greece from the south of Italy. His soldiers stoned the envoys of the Assembly who came to announce that their commander was now Marius. Sulla marched on Rome at the head of six legions. This was unprecedented. No general had ever crossed the *pomoerium*—the city limits—with an army. Marius tried unsuccessfully to defend Rome with a force of armed gladiators and others. Sulla entered Rome, and his supporters in the Senate passed a death sentence on Marius, Sulpicius, and others. Marius only narrowly escaped death and made it to Africa safely; Sulpicius and some of his allies were killed. Sulla consolidated his position and then left to fight Mithridates, leaving behind Gnaeus Octavius and Lucius Cornelius Cinna as consuls.

A colossal street fight broke out between the *Optimates*, supporters of Sulla and Octavius, and the *Populares*, supporters of Cinna. Octavius used the street fight to justify exiling Cinna immediately, deposing him of his office and citizenship, a unique act in the history of the Roman Republic. Marius returned from exile in Africa with an army he had raised there, and by the end of 87 B.C., he combined with Cinna and the consul Quintus Sertorius to enter Rome, oust Octavius, and take control of the city. Based on the orders of Marius, some of his soldiers (who were former slaves) went through Rome killing the leading supporters of Sulla, including Octavius. Their heads were exhibited in the Forum. But after five days, Quintus Sertorius and Cinna ordered their more disciplined troops to kill Marius's slave guards to prevent more arbitrary violence. About twelve Roman nobles had been murdered. Marius declared Sulla's reforms and laws invalid, officially exiled Sulla, had himself elected to Sulla's eastern command, and had himself and Cinna elected consuls for the year 86 B.C. Marius died less than a month later, and Cinna remained in control of Rome for another two years. In 84 B.C. he was killed by his own troops as he was setting out to battle Sulla.

In 83 B.C. Sulla returned to Italy, but Rome continued to be held by his enemies, who in 82 B.C. killed many senators and others they thought likely to support Sulla. On November 1, 82 B.C., Sulla met his enemies in the battle of the Colline Gate just outside the walls of Rome. Then and there 50,000 men lost their lives, but Sulla won the day. Almost immediately the Senate appointed Sulla dictator *legibus faciendis et reipublicae constituendae causa* ("dictator for making laws and for settling the constitution"). The decision was subsequently ratified by the Assembly of the People, with no limit set on his time in office. Sulla had total control of the city and the Republic of Rome, except for Hispania (which Marius's general Quintus Sertorius had established as an independent state). Total power lay in the hands of one man, something that had occurred only for six-month terms in the most dire circumstances in the previous four centuries of the Roman Republic's history.

| Sulpicius Rufus forms an alliance with Marius | Sulla takes Rome | Sulla leaves to fight Mithridatic War | Marius & Cinna combine to control Rome | Sulla takes Rome |
|---|---|---|---|---|
| 88 B.C. | 88 B.C. | 87 B.C. | 87 B.C. | 82 B.C. |

# SULLA SHEDS MORE AND MORE BLOOD
## Dr. Thomas Milton Kemnitz

Once he held total power, Lucius Cornelius Sulla used it despotically. He began to execute those whom he perceived to be enemies of the state. According to Plutarch, "Sulla now began to make blood flow, and he filled the city with deaths without number or limit." One senator asked Sulla to tell them whom he intended to execute so that they would not all live in fear, and Sulla said that he would. "Sulla immediately proscribed 80 persons without communicating with any magistrate. As this caused a general murmur, he let one day pass, and then proscribed 220 more, and again on the third day as many....he said that he had proscribed all he could think of, and as to those who now escaped his memory, he would proscribe them at some future time." (A *proscriptio* was a notice posted in a public place.) According to Appian, the first list contained forty senators and about 1,600 *equites* (knights). "The reward for killing a proscribed person was two talents [roughly 150 pounds of silver or gold], whether it was a slave who killed his master or a son who killed his father." Helping or sheltering a person who was proscribed was punishable by death. The state confiscated the wealth of the outlawed and then auctioned it off, making Sulla and his supporters rich. "The number of those who were massacred through revenge and hatred was nothing compared with those who were murdered for their property....The ruin of one was due to his large house, another man owed his death to his orchard, and another again to his warm baths. Quintus Aurelius, a man who never meddled with public affairs and thought he was no further concerned about all these calamities except so far as he sympathized with the sufferings of others, happened to come to the Forum, and there he read the names of the proscribed. Finding his own name among them, he exclaimed, Alas! ...my farm at Alba is my persecutor. He had not gone far before he was murdered.... The sales of confiscated property were conducted by Sulla from his tribunal in such an arrogant and tyrannical manner that his mode of dealing with the produce of the sales was more intolerable than the seizure of the property; he gave away to handsome women, players on the lyre, *mimi* [actors in Roman comedies] and worthless *libertini* the lands of whole nations and the revenues of cities...."

The sons and grandsons of the proscribed were banned from future political office, a restriction not removed for more than thirty years. The young Julius Caesar, as Cinna's son-in-law, was one of Sulla's targets and had to hide. However, Caesar's relatives were Sulla's supporters, and Sulla grudgingly pardoned him but noted in his memoirs that he regretted sparing Caesar's life because of Caesar's notorious ambition. Suetonius records that when agreeing to spare Caesar, Sulla warned, "In this Caesar there are many Mariuses."

Sulla passed many laws to strengthen the Senate and reduce the powers of the tribunes and the Assembly; all were soon repealed. He did not tackle the economic and financial difficulties that beset Rome, nor did he ameliorate any of the discontent of the Italian allies of Rome. Near the end of 81 B.C., he resigned his dictatorship, disbanded his legions, and re-established normal consular government. He also stood for and was elected consul for the following year, 80 B.C. Thereafter he retired and moved to a country villa, where he wrote his memoirs and died within a year.

For his epitaph, Sulla wanted it said that he never failed to repay a friend or an enemy. Sulla would be remembered for the way he repaid his enemies, but one friend he repaid handsomely was Marcus Lucinius Crassus, who became Rome's richest man. His money would make him an important player in the next generation.

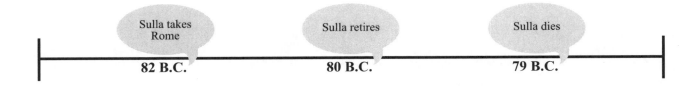

In each case below, one of the choices was really the word used by the author in the sentence provided. All of the choices can be found in the example words on the first page of this lesson. Your challenge is to decide which word the author used. This is not a test; it is more like a game because more than one word choice may work perfectly well. See if you can use your sensitivity and intuition to guess correctly which word the author used.

1.    **From Harriet Beecher Stowe's *Uncle Tom's Cabin***

There is a dread, unhallowed _____ of evil, that turns things sweetest and holiest to phantoms of horror and affright.
a. isocracy
b. phantasmagoria
c. necromancy
d. prescience

2.    **From Nathaniel Hawthorne's *The Scarlet Letter***

It was like nothing so much as the _____ play of the northern lights.
a. incuse
b. phantasmagoric
c. anomalous
d. circumscribed

3.    **From Robert Louis Stevenson's *Kidnapped***

Open the corner cupboard and bring out a great case bottle of _____.
a. aqua vitae
b. *exeunt omnes*
c. *ipse dixit*
d. necromancy

4.    **From Herman Melville's *Moby Dick***

Physiognomically regarded, the Sperm Whale is a(n) _____ creature. He has no proper nose.
a. prescient
b. anomalous
c. rhinoplastic
d. circumscribed

5.    **From Charlotte Brontë's *Jane Eyre***

Something of serenity in her air..._____ deviation into the ardent.
a. precluded
b. circumscribed
c. recanted
d. incised

Though it is a good thing to have a rich vocabulary, it is not a good thing to abuse that vocabulary by writing verbose, abstruse, sesquipedalian sentences. Those who overuse their vocabularies often do so at the expense of clarity. Translate the following showy, ponderous passage into graceful, direct English. Do not use slang, but do use words that seem familiar and comfortable.

FAR BELOW THE CACOPHONOUS MONKEYS AND GREGARIOUS PARROTS who looked curiously down from the buoyant leaves atop the towering rainforest canopy, the medicine man, *El Viejo*, stood alone, like solipsism reified, in the middle of the thatched village in the clearing, frightened, trying to wash his nonplussed mind of the phantasmagoria that carried his perspicuous, prescient visions. Drawing a quadrilateral figure in the sand before the fire pit, he summoned the malefic powers of necromancy in a final effort to preclude the fearful tragedy he saw approaching his village through the future, but the strange future images continued streaming through his mind: anomalous coins, not incised but with incuse designs stamped into their metal; bottles of *aqua vitae* with cryptic symbols and hieroglyphics; livid physiognomies altered through lurid cosmetics and rhinoplasty; huge anonymous social systems that would destroy the near-perfect isocracy of his sacrosanct forest culture; bellicose rulers recanting and abjuring promises to the autochthonous inhabitants of the jungle; stringent legal systems that would circumscribe life in the cool, green forest and prevent the silent, barefoot hunters from following the invisible paths of the forest beings; *ipse dixit* dogma of xenophobic bureaucrats who would never take the interests of the Indians into account; and beyond all of these images from the future, NOTHING. An approaching void. An abyss. He could see no images of his people beyond the phantasmagoria. It was as though his people had all vanished from the forest in a terrible *EXEUNT OMNES*—as though the forest itself had vanished, but how could that be? Why could he not find the rainforest in these images from the far future?

As *El Viejo* gazed into the phantasmagoria of images which had transmogrified from the reassuring *terra firma* he usually saw into the *terra incognita* of an tenebrous abyss, the plaintive call of the monkeys descended like sorrow through the leafy shadows of the canopy, and the parrots rose from their branches and flew silently into the mist, their reds and blues fading into an ineffable, inexpugnable white.

## Reading Comprehension

1. Which of the following best expresses the main idea of Translation 53?
    a. Primitive intellects do not comprehend the benefits of technology.
    b. History is a constant progress from wilderness to civilization.
    c. The profit motive is a universal norm in all cultures.
    d. Industrial forces threaten the earth's cultural and ecological resources.

2. With which statement would the author likely agree?
    a. All species are important.
    b. The rights of some species are more important than the rights of others.
    c. All other species exist simply to benefit humanity.
    d. The future is an unknown.

## Analogies

3. **INCUSE : INCISE ::**
    a. accuse : incisive
    b. mitosis : meiosis
    c. objurgate : persuade
    d. bludgeon : lacerate

4. **CIRCUMSCRIBE : QUADRILATERAL ::**
    a. limit : intractable
    b. comprehend : imponderable
    c. persuade : incredulous
    d. bilateral : unilateral

## Antonyms

5. **NECROMANCY :**
    a. romance
    b. prescience
    c. devotion
    d. augury

6. **ANOMALY :**
    a. quotidian
    b. empyrean
    c. wont
    d. paragon

A teacher buries his student; *D(is) M(anibus) Symphorus paeda gogus Pinae be ne merinti fecit. Vixit annis XV.*

To the Shades of the Underworld: Symphorus, the tutor, made this for the well-deserving Pinna. He lived fifteen years.

**synthesis**

We know that Galileo Galilei, the Italian astronomer and physicist who was born in 1564 and died in 1642, was forced to **recant**, to sing a geocentric song instead of a heliocentric song, by the church hierarchy, which found his eccentric tune to be dissonant with its dogmatic melodies. What other example of intellectual suppression, in history, science, or literature, can you think of?

An ***Obiter Dictum***: Galileo was the first to see the moons of Jupiter, and this discovery gave him insights into the workings of the solar system. Today, we can see the moons of Jupiter with even a modest pair of binoculars. If you have never seen them, take a look. For a more challenging task with binoculars, see if you can find our sister spiral galaxy Andromeda, which is visible in the winter in the northern hemisphere; it is even visible to the naked eye, but it makes a ghostly and inspiring sight in a pair of good binoculars. Andromeda, of course, is far (FARRRRR . . . R) beyond Jupiter. In fact, I believe it is the most distant object visible to the naked eye. Do you remember Andromeda from your reading of mythology? Andromeda was Cassiopeia's daughter who married Perseus, who rescued her from a sea monster.

**divergence and convergence**

Make a list of **anomalies**, either fictitious or real. One example from literature is the anomalous chemical that transmogrifies the nice Dr. Jekyll into the malefic Mr. Hyde. It is especially odd because Dr. Jekyll only thinks he knows what the active chemical is; actually, it is a substance of which he is unaware and which has gotten into his compound without his knowing—unfortunately for him, since he finds himself unable to procure more of a chemical whose identity he does not know.

Another example of an anomaly is the fictitious "Bermuda Triangle," which was invented for a creative writing piece in *Argosy* magazine but which proved to be so sensational an idea that a number of writers made fortunes by convincing credulous neophytes that this fictional strange anomaly is a thrilling reality. Fiction masquerading as nonfiction. Ho hum. If you get a chance, see the NOVA television program on this subject; it will give you an interesting insight into the integrity of scientific thinking. And the next time you read some wide-eyed article about the forces of nature being reversed, dust off your incredulity.

After you have made your list of anomalies, choose your favorite, and explain what you like about it.

**aesthetics, intuition, and imagination**

Under an effulgent sky, you stumble through the dusty Mesopotamian ruins until you notice, in the interstice between two boulders, something gleaming. Excitedly breaking away rock and clay, you disinter a wall that has not been seen for four millennia and that is covered with designs, both **incuse** and **incised**. Use your intuition (ideas from the blue) to write a short description of this discovery. Draw some of the designs that you see on the wall.

Roman key

**243**

**Neologist's Lexicon**

Use the stems in this list to create a new word (neologism). Give the word, the pronunciation, the part of speech, the etymology, and the definition(s). Keep a record of the neologisms you create from list to list. Here are some examples:

**rhinocusination** (rye no KYOO sin AY shun) n. [*rhino* (nose), *cud* (strike) *tion* (act)]  1. striking the nose, as of an opponent  2. any process that creates pungent, malodorous vapors

**aquadiction** (AH kwah DIK shun) n. [*aqua* (water), *dict* (say), *tion* (act)]  1. speaking under water  2. attempting to answer a question while using mouthwash

**A Sesquipedalian Choice**

1. **Sesquipedalian Fiction**
   Using words from List 53 and previous lists, write a short play, scene, or story. Feel free to be imaginative, silly, or absurd. Do not let your critical or judgmental faculties interfere with your creative ideas.

2. **Sesquipedalian Poetry**
   Using many words from List 53 and other lists, write a poem. You may use regular meter, or end rhyme, or other poetic devices, or not! In the past we have written poems with primary attention being paid to sound, rather than sense. This time, concentrate on sense. If you like, you can juxtapose the sesquipedalian lines with contrasting language of other categories, such as the glossy terminology of advertising hype (the NEW SplenDEX HI-TEKK AquaSPlash!), technical or medical language (we excise the necrotic tissue), nursery rhyme, or the foolish nonsense of rock and roll choruses (doo-wopp, doo-lang-doo-lang).

3. **Sesquipedalian Revision**
   Using sesquipedalian words from the lists in this book and from other sources, such as the dictionary, write a sesquipedalian revision of some familiar story, such as "'Twas the night before Christmas . . . ." This will help you think of other words that are similar to the limited list of words we have studied.

4. **Sesquipedalian Invention**
   For those who would rather write their own question/problem/ project than do any of the ones listed above: Using other assignments in this book as a model, invent a sesquipedalian thing to do, and do it.

Roman oil lamp

| | | | | | | |
|---|---|---|---|---|---|---|
| • pro | (for) | *pro rata* | • **dent** | (tooth) | indenture |
| • *ideo* | (idea) | ideologue | • *pleo* | (more) | pleonasm |
| • *gen* | (origin) | exogenous | • nom | (name) | *nom de plume* |
| • *exo* | (out) | exogenous | • tract | (pull) | tractable |
| • *gamy* | (marriage) | exogamy | • sangui | (blood) | sanguinary |
| • *endo* | (within) | endogamy | • lat | (side) | collateral |
| • **tend** | (stretch) | distend | • luc | (light) | elucidate |
| • *oid* | (appearance) | anthropoid | • anthropo | (man) | anthropoid |

**pro rata** (proportionate)  It was not an equal division, but a *pro rata* division.

**ideologue** (theorist)  An ideologue can be an extreme exponent or an idle theorist.

**exhortatory** (urging)  He made an exhortatory appeal to the crowd.

**exogenous** (originating externally)  Exogenous influences changed the group.

**exogamy** (marriage out of tribe)  Exogamy with neighboring villages was the tribe's custom.

**endogamy** (marriage within tribe)  Endogamy had gradually weakened the tribe.

**distend** (stretch out)  The distended stomach of the starving child was heartbreaking to behold.

**indenture** (written contract)  The indenture's copies were notched alike, proving authenticity.

**pleonasm** (redundancy)  It is a true fact that the term *free gift* is a pleonasm.

**nom de plume** (pen name)  Samuel Clemens's *nom de plume* was Mark Twain.

• • •

**tractable** (docile)  The tractable young gentleman was liked by all.

**anthropoid** (manlike)  The anthropoid apes gathered hooting around the juke box.

**sanguinary** (bloody)  Homer's graphic descriptions of sanguinary combat are unforgettable.

**collateral** (side by side)  The collateral problems aggravated each other.

**elucidate** (explain)  Please help us by elucidating this matter.

Roman key

## As Used by John Milton in *Paradise Lost*

| | And | now | his | heart | **distends** | with | pride. |
|---|---|---|---|---|---|---|---|
| **Parts of Speech:** | conj. | adv. | pron. | n. | v. | prep. | n. |
| **Parts of Sentence:** | | | | subj. | AVP | | |
| **Phrases:** | | | | | | ---prep. phrase--- | |
| **Clauses:** | ------------------------------------independent clause---------------------------------- | | | | | | |
| | one independent clause; a simple, declarative sentence | | | | | | |

Here Milton uses *distends* as the simple predicate; even though it is an action verb, there is no direct object; *pride* cannot be the direct object because it is the object of preposition.

## Pronunciation

| | | | | |
|---|---|---|---|---|
| *pro rata* | pro RATE ah | | **pleonasm** | PLEE o nazm |
| **ideologue** | ID ee o log | | *nom de plume* | nome de PLOOM |
| **exhortatory** | ex ORT a tory | | **tractable** | TRACK tah bel |
| **exogenous** | ex OJ en us | | **anthropoid** | AN thro poid |
| **exogamy** | ex OGG a me | | **sanguinary** | SANG wi nary |
| **endogamy** | en DOG a me | | **collateral** | ko LAT er al |
| **distend** | diss TEND | | **elucidate** | ee LOOSE ih date |
| **indenture** | in DEN ture | | | |

## Spanish Cognates

| | | | | |
|---|---|---|---|---|
| **exhortatory** | exhortatorio | | **exogenous** | exógeno |
| **exogamy** | exogamia | | **endogamy** | endogamia |
| **pleonasm** | pleonasmo | | **tractable** | tratable |
| **anthropoid** | antropoide | | **sanguinary** | sanginario |
| **collateral** | colateral | | **elucidation** | elucidación |

1.  A **Classic Word**: To **elucidate** is to explain, to enlighten, to shed light (*luc*) on a subject. This verb, from the Latin *elucidare*, has been a popular word in the classics of the last century. It was used by Stowe, Melville, Hardy, Conrad, Kipling, and Harper Lee. Melville's Ishmael provides a sentence that elucidates the use of *elucidate*: "All these particulars are faithfully narrated here, as they will not fail to elucidate several most important, however intricate, passages, in scenes hereafter to be painted." Usually, *elucidate* is used transitively (taking a direct object): he elucidated his meaning (Conrad), he elucidated the political situation (Kipling), he elucidated principles of whaling laws (who else?)

2.  The adjective **sanguinary** means just what you think: bloody. If you have ever read a serious history of the American Civil War, such as any of the books by Bruce Catton, then you realize that the Civil War was unbelievably sanguinary; to read about it is like reading *The Iliad*, except that you have to keep reminding yourself, incredulously, that you are not reading fiction. We see this adjective in the classics to describe a sanguinary affair (Barrie), a sanguinary shindy (Conrad), sanguinary games (Hardy), and sanguinary predictions (Stowe). One of the most interesting sentences is from (I know this will shock you) Melville: "Quakers are the most sanguinary of all sailors and whale-hunters."

3.  A **Micropoem**: The adjective **tractable** means docile, yielding, easily controlled. But the stems reveal that the word contains a wonderful energy: it means pullable, just as the opposite, **intractable**, means not pullable. In Orwell's *Animal Farm*, the bulls that had always been tractable suddenly turned savage. Conrad describes a character who was gentlemanly, steady, tractable. Stowe describes a sick person as tractable a patient as a sick bison. Gulliver heartily wishes the Yahoos would be so tractable.

4.  The adjective **exhortatory** comes from the Latin *exhortari*, greatly urge. The stems are *ex* (out) and *hort* (urge). To **exhort** is to urge, but it can be urgent advice, urgent caution, or urgent discourse. In H.G. Wells's *The War of the Worlds*, the public was exhorted to avoid and discourage panic. Soldiers in *The Red Badge of Courage* issue exhortations, commands, and imprecations. Hawthorne's Hester Prynne is exhorted to confess the truth.

5.  The nouns **endogamy** and **exogamy** are two interesting terms from the field of anthropology, the science (*logy*) of humanity (*anthropo*). The first refers to a culture's custom of marrying (*gamy*) someone within (*endo*) the tribe, and the second refers to the custom of marrying outside (*exo*) of the tribe. In order to learn about what it means to be human, anthropologists study cultures of all kinds all over the world and write scientific descriptions, called *ethnographies*, of these other societies. One famous ethnography is Jomo Kenyatta's *Facing Mount Kenya*, which is about Kenya's Kikuyu tribe. Anthropologists such as Jane Goodall sometimes study primates other than human beings, such as the **anthropoid** apes: chimpanzees or gorillas. You would enjoy Jane Goodall's book *In the Shadow of Man*. Some anthropologists, such as Louis Leakey, do archaeology. Leakey spent his life in East Africa, disinterring the remains of prehistoric hominids in Olduvai Gorge. There are many interesting books about this famous dig, both by Leakey and by his wife Mary. His son Richard continued his work after his death.

Pompey

# POMPEY (106–48)
## Dr. Thomas Milton Kemnitz

The men who would play a significant role in the fall of the Roman Republic all cut their political and military teeth in the battles between Sulla and Marius, none more so than Gnaeus Pompeius Magnus, known as Pompey. His father was a general who died in 87 B.C. in the siege of Rome when young Pompey was nineteen. Four years later he got his father's veterans together and in 82 took Sicily on Sulla's behalf. The next year he was victorious in North Africa. He returned with his troops to Italy, and in 78 on behalf of the Senate he suppressed a rebellion by Lepidius, a consul trying to take the capital. Pompey asked the Senate to send him to Spain to take the province back from Quintus Sertorius, a commander loyal to Marius; the Senate balked at the request, but Pompey refused to disband his troops, and so the Senate did as he asked. In Spain from 76 to 71 B.C., his victory was facilitated by the assassination of the able Sertorius by a mediocre deputy. Pompey proved himself an able administrator in provisioning his army and leaving behind him more than adequate governing arrangements. He brought his army back to Italy in 71 B.C. and was able to mop up the last stragglers of Spartacus's army, capture some 5,000 escaped slaves, and thereby take undeserved credit for putting down the rebellion, much to the irritation of Marcus Lucinius Crassus, whose army had defeated Spartacus.

Still with his army intact, Pompey was elected consul along with Crassus at the end of 71 B.C. to serve in 70. Pompey was not eligible to be consul because he was too young and had not served in any of the junior posts on the *cursus honorium*, but he had an army, and so he became consul. The two consuls apparently did not like or respect each other. Crassus suffered from greed and jealousy, and he envied Pompey his two Triumphs, while Crassas got only an Ovation for defeating Spartacus. Pompey apparently had trouble getting along with anyone who questioned his pre-eminence. In 66 Pompey gained credit for sweeping the eastern Mediterranean clear of pirates; in fact, he seems to have bribed them to stop preying on shipping for a while. In the next year he set out in pursuit of Mithridates VI and became the Roman general who finally ended the long career of the King of Pontus; Pompey divided the East into four new Roman provinces, subdued Judea, took Jerusalem, and established complete Roman control from the Hellespont to the Sinai. In the process, he got fabulously wealthy from the plunder and solved many of the problems the Roman treasury was having. As he had done in Spain, he showed himself adept at administrative arrangements that enabled Rome to rule a conquered territory.

Pompey came back to Rome in 61 B.C., celebrated his Triumph, promised his retiring soldiers that he would settle them on farms, and disbanded his army. Freed from having to deal with an existing army, the Senate did nothing. Pompey wanted his veterans settled on land; Crassus wanted arrangements that would allow him to make more money; Caesar wanted to be consul in 59 B.C. They formed an alliance known as the First Triumvirate. It was Caesar who bridged the gap between Pompey and Crassus; both Crassus and Caesar wanted things for which they needed Pompey, who had no way to get what he wanted without his new allies. Cicero refused an invitation to join the three. Pompey got land for his veterans, confirmation of his Asian political settlements, and as a new wife, Caesar's daughter, Julia. Crassus got even richer than he had been, and Caesar secured proconsular command in Gaul at the same time Pompey was given the governorship of Hispania, a post he held *in abstentia* but that gave him command of four legions. By 56 B.C., Caesar called Crassus and Pompey to a secret meeting in the northern Italian town of Lucca to rethink their joint strategy. They agreed that Pompey and Crassus would again stand for the consulship in 55 B.C. Once elected, they would extend Caesar's command in Gaul by five years. At the end of their consular year, Crassus would have the lucrative governorship of Syria, which he planned to use as a base to conquer Parthia. Pompey would keep Hispania *in abstentia*.

| Pompey born | Pompey's father killed when Sulla takes Rome | Pompey takes command of his father's troops | Pompey a consul | Pompey fights in the East | First Triumvirate formed |
|---|---|---|---|---|---|
| 106 B.C. | 87 B.C. | 82 B.C. | 70 B.C. | 66-62 B.C. | 59 B.C. |

In each case below, one of the choices was really the word used by the author in the sentence provided. All of the choices can be found in the example words on the first page of this lesson. Your challenge is to decide which word the author used. This is not a test; it is more like a game because more than one word choice may work perfectly well. See if you can use your sensitivity and intuition to guess correctly which word the author used.

1. **From Frances Hodgson Burnett's *The Secret Garden***

   His poppy-colored cheeks were _____ with his first big bite of bread and bacon.
   a. anthropoid
   b. exhortatory
   c. tractable
   d. distended

2. **From Henry David Thoreau's *Walden***

   As if we grew like _____ plants by addition without.
   a. *pro rata*
   b. exogenous
   c. tractable
   d. collateral

3. **From George Orwell's *Animal Farm***

   Bulls which had always been _____ suddenly turned savage.
   a. tractable
   b. sanguinary
   c. endogamous
   d. anthropoid

4. **From James Hilton's *Lost Horizon***

   [He had] the detached fluency of a university professor _____ a problem.
   a. distending
   b. exhorting
   c. *nom de plume*
   d. elucidating

5. **From Mary Shelley's *Frankenstein***

   Thanks to the..._____ laws of man, I had learned now to work mischief.
   a. sanguinary
   b. collateral
   c. tractable
   d. *pro rata*

Though it is a good thing to have a rich vocabulary, it is not a good thing to abuse that vocabulary by writing verbose, abstruse, sesquipedalian sentences. Those who overuse their vocabularies often do so at the expense of clarity. Translate the following showy, ponderous passage into graceful, direct English. Do not use slang, but do use words that seem familiar and comfortable.

DESPITE THE EXHORTATORY HYPERBOLE of the village ideologues who advised her to be endogamous, the young woman, a talented poet who wrote under the *nom de plume* Thalpaivlys, had chosen her husband in an exogamous marriage, and in doing so had helped to initiate a new era of peace between the adjacent villages. Communication had led to cooperation, pharisaism to integrity, execration to benediction, xenophobia to conviviality, and the anachronistic sanguinary and bellicose past had given way to a beatific gregariousness between the two groups of autochthonous inhabitants. For the first time, those who worked hard received a true *pro rata* share of the remuneration, indentures protected the rights of the less powerful, and the intransigent became tractable. Tribal boundaries and other collateral issues were settled in council through careful elucidation of the facts. The distended bellies of the hungry were no longer seen. Tired old pleonasms such as "hated enemies" and "deadly perils" were no longer heard in every trivial conversation. Instead of chronic hebetude, a refulgent social synergy had emerged from the harmony of the villages.

It was a good time to be alive, the young woman thought. The future held much promise. She was assiduously completing a series of story poems for children about a funny and charming anthropoid ape, Fayray, and her antics in the mountain vegetation. The poems were coming well, using the anaphora that all children love because they can call out the lines aloud, and soon she would be singing these poems to the children around the glowing and mellifluous fire. In her mind, she could already see the children's eyes sparkling eagerly in the firelight—eyes, she reminded herself, of children from *both* villages. In this image, the historic dichotomy between the two peoples was finally mollified in a confluence of two cultures.

## Reading Comprehension

1. It cannot be inferred from Translation 54 that:
    a. The incredulous should reconsider putative enemies.
    b. The *sotto voce* tones of colloquy can be better than cacophonous soliloquy.
    c. You must abase yourself obsequiously to those who condescend to you.
    d. A social schism can become a malefic *idée fixe*.

2. The worst title for Translation 54 would be:
    a. The Tragic Postlude of a Moribund Schism
    b. How to Abjure a Superannuated Cultural Dichotomy
    c. From Xenophobic Obloquy to Eulogy
    d. The Imponderable Nature of Superfluous and Supererogatory Truculence

## Analogies

3. **ENDOGAMY : EXOGAMY ::**
    a. room : yard
    b. planet : moon
    c. introspective : gregarious
    d. nationalism : globalism

4. **PLEONASM : NOM DE PLUME ::**
    a. redundancy : *nom de guerre*
    b. reiteration : pseudonym
    c. tautology : pen name
    d. periphrasis : anonym

## Antonyms

5. **TRACTABLE :**
    a. incorrigible
    b. obstreperous
    c. intransigent
    d. refractory

6. **PRO RATA :**
    a. apportioned
    b. incommensurable
    c. commensurate
    d. fractious

Mithridates VI, the King of Pontus, resisted Roman hegemony for a generation from 88 to 63 B.C.

**synthesis**

List at least three characters from different works of literature who have in common the fact that they are either **tractable** or **sanguinary**.

**application**

The adjective **exogenous** refers to things that originate externally. Something exogenous has been transplanted, imported. One opposite of *exogenous* is **indigenous,** which means native or **autochthonous**. A continent might have, for example, indigenous plants and exogenous plants. Think of at least three examples in which you could accurately apply the word *exogenous*.

**emotion and imagination**

What emotions do you associate with the word **sanguinary**? Often, when we study history, we read as though history were only a series of facts, of names, of dates. We can read about the most tragic events that have ever occurred and be unmoved. Why? Because we are reading with our minds but not with our hearts, and the intellect alone is shallow. To truly understand the profound depths of what we learn, we must use our whole humanity, and this means, for example, that in reading about a great battle we must not only digest the factual detail, but we must imagine the scenes, the sensory realities, and the emotions that would be part of that experience in real life. Now, back to our question: What emotions do you associate with the word *sanguinary*? In your mind, imagine a Civil War battlefield on the early morning after a battle. What are the emotions of the survivors, of the wounded, of the commanding officers, of the families who read about the great battle in the morning paper?

To understand, we must think not merely from the mind alone, nor from the heart alone, but from the heart of the mind. For history, one of the most human of all subjects, this is especially important.

**aesthetics**

Imagine that you are asked to write and direct a television program about an **anthropoid** alien who lands on our planet and makes friends with us, overcoming initial suspicion and fear and showing us new and wonderful technologies we can use to make our planet peaceful and healthy. The thing is, the alien is only anthropoid in the most general way and in most specifics looks different from *Homo sapiens*. Considering the requirements of the television program, how would you design the appearance of your anthropoid alien? What colors, skin surface, facial features, and so on would you choose? Describe your alien, and draw it, if you would like to.

This coin depicts victory wreaths awarded to Pompey at his Triumphs.

**Neologist's Lexicon**

Use the stems in this list to create a new word (neologism). Give the word, the pronunciation, the part of speech, the etymology, and the definition(s). Keep a record of the neologisms you create from list to list. Here are some examples:

**lucotraction** (LOO ko track shun) n. [*luc* (light), *tract* (pull), *tion* (act)] 1. being irresistibly drawn to effulgence, as to lights, fame, or stars 2. the irrational compulsion to be on the beach in the dark, so as to see the sun rise over the sea

**endonomy** (en DAH nomy) n. [*endo* (within), *nom* (name)] 1. the practice of selecting names for children only from among the names already given to other family members, such as uncles, grandmothers, or parents 2. the practice of giving children in sequential generations the identical name, distinguished only by the additions, Jr., II, III, and so on

**Sesquipedalian Cartoon**

Using words from List 54 and previous lists, write a cartoon scene about your favorite cartoon characters. An example:

### Elmo Fudd and Entomo Wabbit

| | |
|---|---|
| Elmo: | Be vewy vewy *sotto voce*. I'm a sanguinawy hunter, hunting the perfidious and wascawy Wabbit. |
| Wabbit: | Ehhhhh, what's da putative problem, Doc? |
| Elmo: | Shhhh . . . be vewy vewy circumspect. I'm hunting Wabbits. |
| Wabbit: | Well Doc, I do not mean to impugn your perspicacious perspicacity—pardon my pleonasm—or nuttin, but do you know a wabbit when you see one? I mean, you ain't VACUOUS, are you? I mean, elucidate dis for me, Doc. |
| Elmo: | *Au contraire*, I certainwy do know wabbits! Why are you being so queruwous? |
| Wabbit: | Well Doc, I don't wanna disturb your hebetude or anyting, but are you SURE you can discern a wabbit when you see one? I mean, da world is replete wit wabbits. |
| Elmo: | YES. A wabbit has two BIG ears . . |
| Wabbit: | Like deese? |
| Elmo: | YES, and a wabbit has a big fuzzy tail . . . |
| Wabbit: | Like dis? |
| Elmo: | YES and . . . OHHHH! BLAM!! BLAM!!! |
| Wabbit: | Wait!! Doc!! Be tractable why dontcha?? Can't we discuss deese collateral issues wit equanimity? Tink what yer doin, Doc! Ain't dis a little *ipse dixit*? |
| Elmo: | I'll *ipse dixit* you, you wascawy wabbit! You perfidious, intwansigent, intwactable . . . |
| Wabbit: | Hey DOC! You shouldn't concatenate your invectives like dis, I mean . . . |
| Elmo: | You'll die intestate, you dissident, fwactious . . . MEGAWOMANIAC! |
| Wabbit: | STOP!!!! |
| Elmo: | Oh, I'm sowwy. What is it? |
| Wabbit: | Doc, are you trying to hurt my feelings? |
| Elmo: | I'm so nonpwussed. What an embawassing contwetemps. |

*(Exeunt omnes)*

| | | | | | | |
|---|---|---|---|---|---|---|
| • cad | (fall) | cadenza | | • pro | (before) | proscribe |
| • cred | (believe) | credence, credible | | • scrib | (write) | proscribe |
| • man | (hand) | manifest | | • sur | (over) | surfeit |
| • se | (apart) | sequester | | • fac | (to do) | surfeit |
| • ex | (out) | extirpate, expiate | | • per | (through) | pellucid |
| • ad | (to) | apprehension | | • luc | (light) | pellucid |
| • pre | (before) | apprehension | | • bell | (war) | belligerent |
| • **hend** | (grasp) | apprehension | | • inter | (between) | intervene |
| • ous | (full of) | lugubrious, sagacious | | | | |

**cadenza** (elaborate solo) Wallace Stevens's poem is entitled "Martial Cadenza."

**credence** (belief) It is not sagacious to give credence to sensational rumors.

**lugubrious** (full of mourning) His lugubrious howls over the dropped popsicle amused her.

**manifest** (evident) His concern for her was manifest in his close attention to what she said.

**sagacious** (full of wisdom) The sagacious comments helped us increase our tolerance.

**sequester** (set apart) Auden says each nation is "sequestered in its hate."

**extirpate** (root out) The government attempted to extirpate the rebels.

**expiate** (make amends for) He attempted to expiate his sins, but his guilt was inexpugnable.

**apprehension** (anxious foreboding) With apprehension, he stared at the dust on the horizon.

**proscribe** (forbid) Personal comment on official decisions was proscribed by law.

• • •

**credible** (believable) He is not a credible candidate, being only a ship's dog.

**surfeit** (excess) There was a surfeit of food and drink at the ceremony.

**pellucid** (crystal clear) Light shone through the pellucid spring water onto the golden sand.

**belligerent** (warring) The belligerent student body insulted the obsequious official.

**intervene** (come between) It is unwise to intervene in this acrimonious dispute.

## As Used by Joseph Conrad in *Heart of Darkness*

| | His | sagacious | relative | lifted | his | head. |
|---|---|---|---|---|---|---|
| **Parts of Speech:** | adj | **adj.** | n. | v. | adj. | n. |
| **Parts of Sentence:** | | | subj. | AVP | | D.O. |
| **Phrases:** | ---no prepositional, appositive, or verbal phrases--- | | | | | |
| **Clauses:** | --------------------------------independent clause-------------------------------- | | | | | |
| | one independent clause; a simple, declarative sentence | | | | | |

Conrad uses *sagacious* as an adjective to modify the noun *relative*, which is the subject of the sentence. The word *his* is here a possessive adjective.

## Pronunciation

| | | | |
|---|---|---|---|
| **cadenza** | ka DEN za | **apprehension** | app re HEN shun |
| **credence** | KREE dense | **proscribe** | pro SCRIBE |
| **lugubrious** | loo GOO bree us | **credible** | KRED ih bel |
| **manifest** | MAN ih fest | **surfeit** | SUR fit |
| **sagacious** | sa GAY shus | **pellucid** | pel LOOSE id |
| **sequester** | se KWES ter | **belligerent** | beh LIH jer ent |
| **extirpate** | EX tir pate | **intervene** | in ter VEEN |
| **expiate** | EX piate | | |

## Spanish Cognates

| | | | |
|---|---|---|---|
| **cadenza** | cadencia | **credence** | credencia |
| **lugubrious** | lúgubre | **manifest** | manifiesto |
| **sagacious** | sagaz | **sequestration** | secuestro |
| **extirpation** | extirpación | **expiation** | expiación |
| **apprehension** | aprehensión | **proscribed** | proscripto |
| **credible** | creíble | **belligerent** | beligerante |

1.  The verb **intervene** means literally to come (*ven*) between (*inter*). It comes from the Latin *intervenire*, made of *inter* and *venire*, to come. Usually we see this word used to describe physical intervention, but not always. Ethan Frome finds that his pride retorts before his reason has time to intervene. In Wells's *The War of the Worlds*, a drifting bank of black vapor intervenes. Wells also refers to intervening time, and in *The Time Machine*, to the interstices of intervening substances. Tom Sawyer wishes he had had no intervening holiday. In *Moby Dick*, three years intervene between the flinging of two harpoons. Robinson Crusoe sees a strange and unforeseen accident intervene, and a cloud or hazy weather intervene. In Thomas Hardy's *The Return of the Native*, we behold the "well-known form [of the reddleman] in corduroy, lurid from head to foot, the lantern beams falling upon him through an intervening gauze of raindrops."

2.  A **Micropoem**: The verb **sequester** contains a small drama. It comes from the Latin word *sequestrare*, meaning to put something apart (*se*) in the hands of a trustee (*quester*). We see an object passing into the hands of a trustee to be separated. So to sequestrate is to separate something, to set it apart, or to do this to yourself by withdrawing into solitude. In *Ivanhoe*, there is a distant and sequestered turret. In *The Last of the Mohicans*, the scout and Indians were familiar with the sequestered place where they now were. In *Jane Eyre*, characters love their sequestered home, and Jane asks, "What crime was this, that lived incarnate in this sequestered mansion?" Hardy used *sequester* repeatedly; in *The Return of the Native,* he wrote, "In returning to labour in this sequestered spot he had anticipated an escape from the chafing of social necessities." My favorite example is from W.H. Auden's poem "In Memory of W.B. Yeats": Auden argues that we must "teach the free man how to praise," though the "living nations wait / Each sequestered in its hate."

3.  The verb **proscribe** means forbid, but why? It comes from the Latin *proscribere*, which meant to outlaw something by publishing it in writing. Today, we do not always mean a written or published document, but we do mean that to proscribe is to condemn, to outlaw, to denounce, to prohibit, to forbid. In *A Tale of Two Cities*, Charles Darnay finds himself one of a race proscribed (the aristocrats in the French Revolution).

4.  A **Micropoem**: To **extirpate** is to pluck out (*ex*) by the roots (*stirp*), from the Latin *extirpare*, plucked up by the stem. In *Ivanhoe*, people are commanded to extirpate magic and heresy. A beautiful and unforgettable sentence comes from Charlotte Brontë's character Jane Eyre, who finds it "hard to extirpate from my soul the germs of love."

5.  The adjective **lugubrious** comes from the Latin *lugubris*, mournful. In other words, *lugubrious* means full of (*ous*) mourning. Often this word modifies the words *howling* or *wailing*. Jack London: "Then he fell, and lay where he fell, howling lugubriously." Harriet Beecher Stowe: "when there was the least wind, most doleful and lugubrious wailing sounds proceeded from it." Mark Twain: "Presently the dog set up a long, lugubrious howl just outside." Mark Twain: "That long, lugubrious howl rose on the night air again!" Owoooooohhh.

These bowls were used to treat (bribe) the voters before an election. They were distributed with food or wine in them. The top one favored the election of Catilina, who was unsuccessful in his attempt to become consul. The bottom favored the election of Cato to tribune; Cato was successful. Both bowls were made for the election held in 63 B.C. for the year 62. Catilina went on from this lost election to launch his conspiracy that led to his execution at the hands of Cicero with the support of Cato.

# CATO THE YOUNGER & CICERO
## Dr. Thomas Milton Kemnitz

As always in Rome, when someone was getting ahead, others attempted to hold him back, and the Senate as a body was ready to defend the interest of the *Optimates*, by murder if necessary, as they had shown generations earlier when they murdered the Gracchi brothers. Two senators were particularly outstanding: Marcus Porcius Cato (95–46) and Marcus Tullius Cicero (106–43). Cato was the great grandson of Cato the Censor, also known as Cato the Elder to differentiate him from the Cato of Caesar's day. Like his famous ancestor, Cato the Younger specialized in severe, plain, simple, honest, and obdurate. He espoused the simple life, and he lived it. He espoused honesty, and he was scrupulously honest. Like his famous ancestor, he walked when other men rode on horses. Above all, he stood for the Republic and for defending the governing arrangements of Rome. In this he was unswerving.

Cato was a conservative and allied himself with the *Optimates*. He was elected to the position of quaestor in 65 at a time when Rome's treasury was depleted. He delved deeply into the laws relating to taxes. He initiated the prosecution of former quaestors for stealing from the treasury. He also prosecuted Sulla's informers for illegal appropriation of treasury money and then for homicide. This was not comfortable for his *Optimate* allies, who had supported Sulla. At the end of his year in office, Cato had gained the enthusiastic respect of the Roman crowd, who were overwhelmingly *Populares*; throughout his life, Cato had the respect of the Roman crowd even when his positions went against their inclinations.

Cicero was a provincial of *equites* status and hence a new man—*novus homo*—making his way on the basis of his substantial ability. The *Optimates* never truly accepted Cicero, but he ascended the Roman *cursus honorum*, holding each magistracy at or near the youngest possible age: quaestor in 75 B.C. (age thirty-one), aedile in 69 B.C. (age thirty-seven), praetor in 66 B.C. (age forty), where he served as president of the Reclamation Court, and consul at age forty-three. It was in 62 B.C., when he was consul and Cato was Tribune of the Plebs, that they had to deal with the Catiline conspiracy. Lucius Sergius Catilina, a noble patrician, led a rebellion against the state, raising an army in Etruria. Martial law—*senatus consultum ultimum*—was declared by the Senate; Cicero arrested the conspirators and proposed to execute them without trial, which would not have been acceptable in normal times. Sentiment in the Senate favored execution until Julius Caesar argued for leniency. Cato countered that capital punishment was necessary to deter treason. Convinced by Cato's argument, the Senate approved Cicero's proposal, and the conspirators were executed. Cicero was all the more ready to order their execution because at the heart of the conspiracy was a plan to rid the Senate and Rome of high-ranking plebs, which included Cicero.

Hostility between Cato and Caesar was evident during this episode. Many thought that Caesar's hand lay behind the Catiline conspiracy; he was suspected of seeking power by any means. Cato was particularly harsh on senators who did not attend rigorously to Senate duties. When during the debate Caesar received a note, Cato accused him of working on Catilina's behalf and of reading conspiratorial messages during a treason proceeding. Caesar simply handed him the note, which was a love letter from Cato's stepsister to Caesar—they were having an affair. Cato was furious, and he thereafter opposed Caesar at every turn. It was Cato's continued hostility to Pompey and Caesar that made the First Triumvirate necessary for both men. In 61 B.C., when Pompey returned from his Asian campaign, he wanted to celebrate his third Triumph and to become consul for the second time. He asked the Senate to postpone consular elections until after his Triumph. Cato convinced the Senate to force Pompey to choose. Pompey chose his third Triumph, one of the most magnificent ever seen in Rome, but he did not become consul.

| Pompey & Cicero born | Caesar born | Cato born | Catiline conspiracy | First Triumvirate formed |
|:---:|:---:|:---:|:---:|:---:|
| **106 B.C.** | **100 B.C.** | **95 B.C.** | **62 B.C.** | **60 B.C.** |

We have seen many wonderful examples of the way words in our lists are used in the classics, but List 55 contains three words—**apprehend**, **sagacious**, and **manifest**—that are replete in literature. To give you a realistic sense of just how often some of the words we have studied are likely to appear in books you will read, let us look in more detail at these three words.

**apprehension**

The noun **apprehension**—together with its friends the verb **apprehend**, the adjective **apprehensive**, and the adverb **apprehensively**—has been in steady use for the past three centuries. *Apprehension* is a combination of *ad* (to), *pre* (before), and *hend* (grasp). It comes from the Latin *apprehendere*, to grasp, and so it is both a **Classic Word** and a **Micropoem**, since it is a metaphor, comparing the feelings of understanding a danger beforehand to the physical act of the hand grasping an object and not letting it fall. Apprehension is both mentally grasping the meaning of something and doing so in advance.

In this idea, *the mind is a hand*. It can grasp a truth, as a hand can grasp a thing. That is why we love this word; it is the poetry of it—the delicacy, the articulated fingers of thought closing on the truth.

In the classics, *apprehension* has been used in 1719 by Defoe, in 1726 by Swift, in 1826 by Cooper, in 1851 by Melville, in 1876 by Twain, in 1881 by Stevenson, in 1886 by Hardy, in 1895 by Crane, in 1898 by Wells, in 1903 by London, in 1911 by Wharton, in 1937 by Steinbeck, in 1959 by Knowles, and in 1960 by Lee. Robinson Crusoe is frightened almost to death with the apprehensions of his sad condition. Gulliver suffers depression of spirits caused by the continual apprehension of death. In *Tom Sawyer*, the slow days drift on, each leaving behind a slightly lightened weight of apprehension. Jim Hawkins in *Treasure Island* finds the worst of his apprehensions realized. The youth in *The Red Badge of Courage*, Henry Fleming, hurries in the vague apprehension that one of the swollen corpses on the battlefield will rise and tell him to begone. Jack London's dog Buck watches people apprehensively. Ethan Frome has no room in his thoughts for vague apprehensions. Curly's wife in *Of Mice and Men* becomes suddenly apprehensive.

We find characters crouching fearfully in the bushes and listening, distracted by apprehension (*The War of the Worlds*), feeling a certain apprehension lest the good name of another should be sucked down in the eddy of a scandal (*Dr. Jekyll and Mr. Hyde*), apprehending that one is rather addicted to profane song (*The Last of the Mohicans*), and feeling a pinprick of apprehension (*To Kill a Mockingbird*).

*Apprehension* is both an emotion and a comprehension. It is worry. Anxiety. We feel apprehensive, as the examples from classic books reveal, about death, about being badly treated, about danger, about ghastly possibilities, about mischief, about what might happen.

Roman key

**sagacious**

The adjective **sagacious** comes from the Latin *sagax* (wise) and *ous* (full of): full of wisdom. The noun form is **sagacity**, and we see both of these forms often in good books.

Defoe describes mighty sagacious, tractable creatures. What might he be describing?

Swift describes a low intelligence below the sagacity of a common hound, the sagacity and smell of a bird that enable him to discover his quarry at a great distance, and bees and ants having the reputation of more industry, art, and sagacity than many of the larger animals.

Scott describes sagacity and prudence, a knight who resolves to trust to the sagacity of his horse, and a character who possesses the sagacious knowledge of physiognomy.

Cooper notes such blind marks as are only known to the sagacity of a native, a sagacity that does not deceive, a singular compound of quick vigilant sagacity and of exquisite simplicity, and a measure dictated by the sagacity of a guide in order to diminish the marks of a trail.

Emily Brontë creates a character who "must trust to my own sagacity."

Hawthorne creates a sagacious, experienced, benevolent old physician and describes the sombre sagacity of age, but wonders if one possesses native sagacity. (The first description, of course, is of the insidious Roger Chillingworth and is intensely ironic.)

Melville's magnum opus contains wonderful uses of *sagacious*: "snuffing up the sea air as a sagacious ship's dog will, in drawing nigh to some barbarous isle," "an extremely sensible and sagacious savage [Queequeg, our hero]," "does the ocean furnish any fish that in disposition answers to the sagacious kindness of the dog?" "the result of this lowering was somewhat illustrative of that sagacious saying in the Fishery," "But peradventure, it may be sagaciously urged, how is this?" and "I had not a little relied upon Queequeg's sagacity."

Dickens's wonderful portly character in *A Tale of Two Cities*, Mr. Lorry, is described as the sagacious Mr. Lorry, who has the sagacity of a man of business and who knows that there are questions that no sagacity could have solved.

Twain's character is half sorry her sagacity had miscarried.

Hardy describes the sagacious old heads who knew what was what in Casterbridge.

Crane's Henry Fleming rationalizes that his actions in running away had actually been sagacious things.

Conrad's characters have eyes that dart sagacious, inquisitive glances and who possess sheer, instinctive sagacity. Lord Jim feels the deep sense of his sagacity crowning every day of his inner life.

It is interesting that many authors have used *sagacious* to describe animals, rather than *Homo sapiens*. We see sagacious horses, sagacious birds, sagacious ants and bees, and sagacious dogs. There is something about the word *sagacious* that gives it a certain surprise value; we feel no special impact in saying that a dog is *smart*, but to say that a dog is *sagacious*, as Melville does, feels bracingly original and refreshing. But Melville adds *sagacious kindness* . . . ah, now that is interesting. The sagacious kindness of the dog.

Roman oil lamp

**manifest**

Another word that I would bet you rarely use, or even hear in conversation, and yet that is enormously frequent in the classics is **manifest**, which can be an adjective or a verb and which has a collection of transmogrifications: **manifestly**, **manifested**, and **manifestation**. *Manifest* is a major **Classic Word**, appearing in almost every book of note—a favorite word not just of a few authors, but of most.

*Manifest* comes from the Latin *manifestus* and literally means struck with the hand! In other words, to have something made manifest is like being slapped! Something is manifest if it is obvious, completely evident, readily perceived and plain. Since this experience is such a vivid and important one, we see *manifest* in constant use for more than four hundred years; it was used by Shakespeare ("Thy heinous, manifest, and many treasons . . .") in *King Lear*, 1606, and it was used by Arthur Miller in *The Crucible*, 1953: "The witch-hunt was a perverse manifestation of the panic which set in among all classes."

In the classics, we find manifest treasons, manifest tokens of wonder, causes manifestly known to be just, manifest alarm, manifestations of weakness, manifest danger of falling down every precipice, manifest pride, manifest sympathy, manifest constraint, the manifestation of wealth in dress and equipage, tittering which continues and manifestly increases, picturesque manifestations, manifestations of jealousy, manifestations of discontent, and on and on. There are far too many examples of *manifest* to try to list or discuss them all, and so let us just focus on some of the best ones.

Henry David Thoreau, in his 1854 masterwork *Walden*, desires to have "A house whose inside is as open and manifest as a bird's nest." This is not only a beautiful image, it also shows Thoreau's genius for connecting words in unexpected ways. Thoreau noted that "the squirrels manifest no concern whether the woods will bear chestnuts this year or not."

Cooper's Hawkeye, in the 1826 adventure *The Last of the Mohicans*, exhorts his friends to "Manifest no distrust" when confronted by the Indians, "or you may invite the danger you appear to apprehend." Of course, this exhortation not to manifest one's apprehensions is sagacious advice.

Harriet Beecher Stowe's Uncle Tom "in various ways manifested a tenderness of feeling, a commiseration for his fellow-sufferers." Despite the pejorative connotations that the term *Uncle Tom* has acquired in recent decades, to read this book is to understand why Stowe's writing enraged the nation against the truculent evil of slavery.

Jonathan Swift's credulous traveler, Gulliver, sojourns to the land of the feculent and vacuous Yahoos and is mortified to learn, "It was manifest I had neither the strength or agility of a common Yahoo." This, you will realize if you read the disgusting Yahoo chapter in Swift's 1726 satire *Gulliver's Travels*, is a sobering epiphany indeed. Do not call any learned person a Yahoo unless you want to see resentment made manifest.

George Orwell's famous pigs, in his 1945 classic *Animal Farm*, are able to rule the farm, partly because they are sagacious enough to comprehend what the other animals only vaguely apprehend. Orwell describes "the pigs, who were manifestly cleverer than the other animals."

To see a word only in a list, with a single example sentence, is deceptive. Not all of our words are as common as *apprehension*, *sagacious*, and *manifest*, but you will be surprised, once you know the words, at how often you see them and at how many of them you will see—even the ones that seem excessively erudite.

In each case below, one of the choices was really the word used by the author in the sentence provided. All of the choices can be found in the example words on the first page of this lesson. Your challenge is to decide which word the author used. This is not a test; it is more like a game because more than one word choice may work perfectly well. See if you can use your sensitivity and intuition to guess correctly which word the author used.

1.  **From Sir Walter Scott's *Ivanhoe***

    They were commanded to _____ magic and heresy.
    a. manifest
    b. expiate
    c. proscribe
    d. extirpate

2.  **From Henry David Thoreau's *Walden***

    The Roman made a(n) _____ offering.
    a. lugubrious
    b. credible
    c. sagacious
    d. expiatory

3.  **From Mark Twain's *Tom Sawyer***

    Presently the dog set up a long, _____ howl just outside.
    a. manifest
    b. sagacious
    c. lugubrious
    d. pellucid

4.  **From Stephen Crane's *The Red Badge of Courage***

    His actions had been _____ things.
    a. sequestered
    b. manifest
    c. belligerent
    d. sagacious

5.  **From Martin Luther King, Jr.'s *Why We Can't Wait***

    The yearning for freedom eventually _____ itself.
    a. intervenes
    b. manifests
    c. surfeits
    d. extirpates

Though it is a good thing to have a rich vocabulary, it is not a good thing to abuse that vocabulary by writing verbose, abstruse, sesquipedalian sentences. Those who overuse their vocabularies often do so at the expense of clarity. Translate the following showy, ponderous passage into graceful, direct English. Do not use slang, but do use words that seem familiar and comfortable.

AFTER SEQUESTERING HIMSELF IN THE LIGHTHOUSE, Joseph K., a lonely cosmologist, gazed down at the blue and pellucid waters of the gulf, where the parrotfish nipped at the yellow coral, and the white foam suspirated a *sotto voce* syntax on the tops of the passing waves. A fractious gull screamed a cacophonous cadenza as it swept after the refulgent and retreating sun, and the wind split in dichotomous schism on both sides of the lighthouse. It whistled in the interstices of the windows and howled lugubriously at the amorphous congeries of rocks at the base, but the superfluous stability of the lighthouse was manifest. The lighthouse stood on *terra firma*. It had been built in 1932, and Joseph knew that nothing short of a typhoon could extirpate it from its foundation.

Despite the wind, he looked without apprehension over the ranks of waves that marched in a concatenation of crests to the horizon. Fate, he knew, could be proscribed by no human interdiction. Crimes must be expiated. And the truth must receive credence, whether it is manifestly credible or not. Across the water, he knew, belligerent civilizations were slouching toward each other; their hour would come round, and he feared that the next chapter of the history books was waiting insidiously for its sanguinary and inexorable conclusion, which nothing could intervene to prevent. Pugnacious belligerence was antediluvian, superannuated, even anachronistic, but it was still human nature.

Even so, these incipient intramural altercations meant little in his broader cosmological view. With stoic sagacity, he was cognizant that the incorporeal principles of nature, *mirabile dictu*, had their own schedules of gravitation and electromagnetism, of strong force and weak force, and that this ineluctable geometry made egomania or megalomania condign only to the pusillanimous.

At the horizon's edge, purple clouds cracked with white fulgurations of lightning, but the sententious tautology of thunder was inaudible, like the subliminal forces that quietly powered Joseph K.'s passive idealism.

## Reading Comprehension

1. In Translation 55, the author does all of the following EXCEPT:
    a. describe the structural stability of the lighthouse
    b. indicate that the cosmologist has resigned himself to nature's forces
    c. indicate that the cosmologist is a chronically apprehensive person
    d. indicate that global affairs in this story are not optimistic

2. It can be inferred from the passage that:
    a. Joseph intends to find a solution to the world's diplomatic problems.
    b. Joseph thinks, like Homer, that even Zeus cannot overrule the Fates.
    c. Joseph has retreated to the lighthouse because of a personal failure or disgrace.
    d. Joseph is optimistic about the immediate future of civilization.

## Analogies

3. **PELLUCID : DIAMOND ::**
    a. diamond : crystal
    b. lugubrious : farewell
    c. opaque : sanguine
    d. manifest : belligerent

4. **EXPIATE : SAGACIOUS ::**
    a. proscribe : efficacious
    b. intervene : vacuous
    c. sequester : feckless
    d. extirpate : belligerent

## Antonyms

5. **PELLUCID :**
    a. opaque
    b. tenebrous
    c. oblique
    d. nebulous

6. **APPREHENSION :**
    a. optimism
    b. equanimity
    c. stoicism
    d. sagacity

Cato

### synthesis

Use any five words from List 55 in a single sentence.  If that is too easy, then use any five different words from List 55 in a sentence that contradicts the first sentence!  If that is too easy, rewrite the two sentences so that the same words are used in reverse order and the sentences are no longer contradictory!  Surely that's not too easy.

### intuition and imagination

In the **pellucid** waters of the Bahamas, you take your outboard boat out over the reef, where the warm salt waters are replete with schools of fish.  In the refulgent sunlight, you anchor the boat, put on your mask, fins, and aqualung (thank you, J. Cousteau), and drop into the water, swimming down through the gregarious marine life in search of sunken galleons and Spanish doubloons.  But what you discover on the sandy bottom is a complete surprise; it is even better than a galleon; it is something you would never have expected to find underwater at all!  Continue . . . .

### analysis

Using a dictionary, carefully explain the differences between the etymology, the grammar, and the best usage of the words **proscribe** and **interdict**.

The young Cicero

**Neologist's Lexicon**

Use the stems in this list to create a new word (neologism). Give the word, the pronunciation, the part of speech, the etymology, and the definition(s). Keep a record of the neologisms you create from list to list. Here is an example:

**surhension** (sir HEN shun) n. [*sur* (over), *hend* (grasp) *tion* (act)] 1. the ability to grasp what is presently over one's head, resulting in intellectual growth 2. fascination with what one is unable to understand. syn.: hyperplussed

**Sesquipedalian Mystery Theater**

Use the words from List 55 and previous lists to write a scene from a detective story, using a favorite character, such as Sherlock Holmes, as a paradigm if you like.

### Cadenzo, the Solo Detective

Cadenzo, the solo homicide detective, is called in to investigate when the body of a millionaire is found in a luxury apartment. Cadenzo arrives in his ratty trenchcoat, peering obliquely out of one eye, and finds the millionaire's curly-haired nephew, Larry Moe, standing in the room.

Cadenzo:   (With manifest solicitude) 'Scuse me, sir, I'm Lieutenant Cadenzo. I'm sorry to intervene at a lugubrious time like this, when you've just lost your wealthy uncle, thereby inheriting millions of dollars, but I just have to ask you a few questions. Just a few questions; it is all routine. I just have to expedite the paperwork for the department; you understand. We have to extirpate the iniquitous and find etiologies.

Moe:   Not at all, Mr. . . . . I'm sorry officer, but what was your name? This is a difficult time for me. (Then querulously) If you don't mind, let's make this brief.

Cadenzo:   (Ingenuously) Oh, I completely understand, Mr. Moe. I'm Lieutenant Cadenzo. I'll try to be as brief as I can. But Mr. Moe, what is this on your uncle's desk? It looks like a curly wig. (Vociferously) Wowww. Wait until I tell Mrs. Cadenzo about this. If you were to wear this, you would be a curly Larry Moe. That's some wig.

Moe:   (Apprehensively) I've never seen this wig before. Lieutenant Cadenzo, please be germane. If you have no further sagacious questions, I need to be leaving.

Cadenzo:   Oh, I certainly understand, Mr. Moe. In fact, I have to be going myself. (Cadenzo exits, and Moe surreptitiously slips the wig into his pocket. Suddenly Cadenzo reenters the room, pointing his finger in the air.)

Cadenzo:   Oh, one more thing, Mr. Moe, why do you think your uncle would have a curly wig in his office? I mean what would he want with a wig? Elucidate that anomaly for me.

Moe:   I'm sure I don't know, Lieutenant Cadenzo. He wore it, or he didn't; I don't mean to equivocate. My antediluvian uncle had idiosyncrasies.

Cadenzo:   (Dissembling) As a detective, I'm just an autodidact and a neophyte. Don't expostulate. We just can't be too circumspect in filling out paperwork. Well, goodbye, Mr. Moe. (Exits, returns) Oh, one more thing. Why would a supercilious plutocrat like your uncle sequester himself in this twentieth-floor apartment if he had acrophobia? Can you explain that? (Temporizes) Yeah, I guess not. (Exits)

Moe:   (Takes out the wig, rubbing it, speaking in soliloquy) Obsequious, prolix fool. Out, sanguinary spot, out, I say. Will nothing make this blood less manifest?

*(Exeunt omnes)*

Cicero

| | | | | | | |
|---|---|---|---|---|---|---|
| • **nasc** | (born) | renascent | | • **cumb** | (lie down) | recumbent |
| • re | (again) | renascent | | • **monit** | (warn) | admonitory |
| • tempor | (time) | extemporize | | • *meta* | (change) | metamorphosis |
| • flect | (bend) | deflect | | • *morph* | (shape) | metamorphosis |
| • pugn | (fight) | pugilist | | • *patho* | (disease) | pathogen |
| • **cresc** | (grow) | excrescence | | • *gen* | (origin) | pathogen |
| • **casus** | (case) | casuistry | | • sine | (without) | *sine qua non* |
| • **firm** | (strong) | infirmity | | • moll | (soft) | emollient |
| • in | (not) | incorrigible | | • *mela* | (black) | melancholy |

**renascent** (showing new life)  There was a renascent interest in the arts after the museum opened.

**extemporize** (improvise)  She began to extemporize a spontaneous response to his complaint.

**deflect** (turn away, bend)  He gracefully deflected embarrassing questions.

**pugilist** (boxer)  The pugilist's pugnacious posturing was comical to the boxing fans.

**excrescence** (abnormal outgrowth)  The fungus caused an ugly excrescence on his nose.

**casuistry** (specious reasoning)  His speech was a masterpiece of casuistry and deception.

**infirmity** (feebleness)  His infirmities prevented him from attending the ceremony.

**recumbent** (reclining)  The tired surgeon was recumbent on her sofa.

**admonitory** (warning)  His message had an admonitory purpose—to warn them away.

**incorrigible** (not correctable)  They could not alter the incorrigible child's behavior.

• • •

**metamorphosis** (change of shape)  Dr. Jekyll's metamorphosis was startling to behold.

**pathogen** (disease-causer)  Dr. Stockman, the people's friend, found pathogens in the water.

*sine qua non* (essential element)  Courage is the *sine qua non* for success in espionage.

**emollient** (softener)  The creamy emollient softened his chapped skin.

**melancholy** (dark sadness)  Nietzsche felt a brooding melancholy on rainy days.

## As Used by John Gardner in *Grendel*

|  | Simple | facts | in | isolation | are | the | *sine qua non*. |
|---|---|---|---|---|---|---|---|
| **Parts of Speech:** | adj. | n. | prep. | n. | v. | adj. | **n.** |
| **Parts of Sentence:** |  | subj. |  |  | LVP |  | S.C. |
| **Phrases:** |  |  | ---prep. phrase--- |  |  |  |  |
| **Clauses:** | ----------------------------------independent clause---------------------------------- |  |  |  |  |  |  |
|  | one independent clause; a simple, declarative sentence |  |  |  |  |  |  |

Here Gardner uses *sine qua non* as a noun and subject complement. Notice that *sine qua non* is modified by an adjective, the definite article *the*.

## Pronunciation

| | | | |
|---|---|---|---|
| **renascent** | re NASS ent | **admonitory** | ad MON ih tory |
| **extemporize** | ex TEM por ize | **incorrigible** | in KOR ih ji bel |
| **deflect** | de FLEKT | **metamorphosis** | meta MOR fo siss |
| **pugilist** | PYOO jil ist | **pathogen** | PATH o jen |
| **excrescence** | ex KRESS ence | *sine qua non* | sin eh kwah NON |
| **casuistry** | KAZ yoo iss tree | **emollient** | ee MOLL yent |
| **infirmity** | in FIRM ih tee | **melancholy** | MEL an kol lee |
| **recumbent** | re COME bent | | |

## Spanish Cognates

| | | | |
|---|---|---|---|
| **renascence** | renacimiento | **deflection** | deflección |
| **pugilist** | pugilista | **excrescence** | excrecencia |
| **casuistry** | casuística | **infirmity** | enfermedad |
| **admonitory** | admonitivo | **incorrigible** | incorregible |
| **metamorphosis** | metamorfosis | **pathogen** | patógeno |
| **emollient** | emoliente | **melancholy** | melancólico |

1. A **Classic Word**: The noun or adjective **melancholy** comes from the Greek word for black bile, believed to make one gloomy, depressed, pensive, mournful, or sad. As you might expect from such an emotional word, *melancholy* is frequently encountered in the classics and can be found from Shakespeare's *Romeo and Juliet* (1596) to Edith Wharton's *Ethan Frome* (1911). Daniel Defoe used it, as did Swift, Cooper, Stowe, Twain, Hardy, Stevenson, Crane, Wells, London, Barrie, and Grahame. In the adjective form of *melancholy*, we find melancholy bells, a melancholy disposition, melancholy solicitude, a wild and melancholy dirge, a soft and melancholy movement with Aetolian accompaniment, melancholy conviction, a melancholy mummer, grey melancholy woods, a melancholy fatality in the voice, a melancholy march, a melancholy pilgrimage, and the melancholy rippling of waves on lonely beaches. The last one is from London's *The Call of the Wild*. In the noun form of *melancholy*, we find a dumb melancholy, a gentle melancholy, a profound melancholy, and a deep melancholy. My favorite sentence is one from Barrie's *Peter Pan* that describes the villainous Captain Hook, James Hook, who signed his name Jas: "His eyes were of the blue of the forget-me-not, and of a profound melancholy, save when he was plunging his hook into you, at which time two red spots appeared in them and lit them up horribly."

2. **Casuistry**, in its negative connotation, is specious reasoning, oversubtle reasoning, disingenuous reasoning, fallacious reasoning, dishonest reasoning. Why? Well, this noun comes from the Latin *casus*, meaning case, and is better understood if you consider its positive connotation: the application of ethics to specific cases or specific situations. It is the *mis*use of casuistry (the good kind) that gives casuistry a bad name. The casuist, in other words, is a kind of sophist, a disingenuous reasoner who uses subtle and specious arguments to sound cogent, with dishonest disregard for the truth.

3. The adjective **incorrigible** comes from the Latin *incorribibilis*, meaning not (*in*) correct (*corrigere*) able (*ibilis*). To be incorrigible is to be uncorrectable, so bad that you cannot be reformed. We especially use this adjective to modify the dreaded noun *child*. In the classics, we find *incorrigible* modifying Toad in *The Wind in the Willows*: "the incorrigible rogue and hardened ruffian whom we see cowering in the dock before us," and Melville's *Moby Dick* also contains such a rascal: "Bildad, I am sorry to say, had the reputation of being an incorrigible old hunks."

4. **Recumbent** is an adjective that comes from the Latin *recumbere*, lying back, which in turn is made of *re* (again, back) and *cubare* (to lie down). In *Of Mice and Men*, John Steinbeck describes "sycamores with mottled, white, recumbent limbs." Conrad refers to recumbent bodies, Hardy to a recumbent figure, Melville to recumbent elephants (!), and Cooper to the recumbent forms of Hawkeye's companions. I know, I know, you want to know what the Melville sentence about the elephants is. All right. In *Moby Dick*, Melville writes that "the stranger at a distance will sometimes pass on the plains recumbent elephants without knowing them to be such." What I wonder is whether the elephants know that people are passing . . . .

## POPULARES

Tiberius Gracchus, tribune, killed, 133 B.C.

Gaius Gracchus, tribune, killed, 121 B.C.

Gaius Marius, consul, died of disease, 86 B.C.

Lucius Appuleius Saturninus, tribune, killed by mob, 100 B.C.

Marcus Livius Drusus, tribune, killed, 91 B.C.

Sulpicius Rufus, tribune, killed by Sulla, 88 B.C.

Lucius Cornelius Cinna, consul, killed by his troops, 84 B.C.

Quintus Sertorius, consul, killed by his deputy, 72 B.C.

Julius Caesar, killed by senators, 44 B.C.

Publius Clodius Pulcher, killed by Milo's men, 61 B.C.

Marc Anthony, tribune, committed suicide, 27 B.C.

Quintus Cassius Longius, tribune, killed in shipwreck, 48 B.C.

## OPTIMATES

Quintus Metellus, consul

Sulla, consul and dictator, died of disease, 78 B.C.

Gnaeus Octavius, consul, killed by Marius's troops, 87 B.C.

Marcus Lucinius Crassus, consul, died fighting in Parthia, 53 B.C.

Pompey, consul, assassinated by Ptolemy XIII of Egypt, 48 B.C.

Cato, committed suicide after Caesar's victory, 46 B.C.

Cicero, proscribed and killed, 43 B.C.

Marcus Bibulus, consul, died of illness fighting Caesar, 48 B.C.

Titus Annius Milo, died fighting Caesar's forces, 48 B.C.

Caecillius Metellus Scipio, Pompey's father-in-law and bitter enemy of Caesar, committed suicide in 46 B.C. to avoid falling into the hands of Caesar's forces

Roman oil lamp

# CATO, CICERO, AND THE REPUBLIC
## Dr. Thomas Milton Kemnitz

Just as Cato had opposed Pompey's attempt to hold a Triumph and be elected consul, when faced with a request from Caesar that would have allowed him to run for consul as well as to celebrate a Triumph, Cato foiled Caesar; he filibustered, speaking continuously until nightfall to prevent the Senate from voting on allowing Caesar to stand for consul *in absentia*. Caesar had to choose between a Triumph or candidacy for the consulship, but unlike Pompey, he chose the office and real power. Caesar's co-consul was Marcus Bibulus, Cato's son-in-law. Cato opposed the agrarian laws that established farmlands for Pompey's veterans on public lands in Campania because the rents on those lands generated a quarter of the Republic's income. Caesar silenced Cato by having the lictors drag him off to jail when he was speaking from the rostra. Many senators protested Caesar's action by leaving the Forum; one senator said he'd rather be in jail with Cato than in the Senate with Caesar. Caesar decided to bypass the Senate and have the Assembly enact the legislation. Cato and Bibulus attempted to win the public votes but lost when Caesar's gang of thugs assaulted them. Eventually, Bibulus decided that it would be most prudent to spend the rest of the year in his home and not resist Caesar publicly.

The next year Publius Clodius Pulcher (93–52) became Tribune of the Plebs, and he did not lower the temperature of Roman politics. He had been the principal player in the *Bona Dea* affair of 61 B.C., which began with his attempt to seduce Caesar's wife. Caesar divorced his wife, saying she must be above suspicion, but he had tried to help Clodius, who was tried on a capital offense. Cicero testified against Clodius; his wife may have played a major part in Cicero's decision to testify, for a sister of Clodius had tried unsuccessfully to get Cicero to divorce his wife and marry her. Cicero's wife did not like this or the family of Clodius. Crassus eventually had to pay massive bribes to the jury to get Clodius acquitted. Two results of the *Bona Dea* affair were that Clodius became attached to the *Populares* party, and he developed a deep antipathy to Cicero. Indeed, the two men seem to have despised each other as much as Cato despised Caesar. Once he was tribune, Clodius attacked Cicero. He pushed through a law to exile anyone who had executed a Roman citizen without a trial. This was aimed directly at Cicero, who had executed members of the Catiline conspiracy without formal trial under martial law. Cicero argued that the *senatus consultum ultimum* (martial law) indemnified him from punishment, but the other senators and consuls did not support him. Particularly stinging for Cicero was that Pompey did not back him. Cicero went into exile in Greece. The day he left Italy, Clodius proposed another law that forbade him approaching within 400 miles of Italy and that confiscated his property. Cicero's villas were destroyed, including one on the Palantine Hill in Rome, a prime site which Clodius bought through an intermediary to hide his role in it.

Clodius had begun life as a patrician but got himself adopted by a pleb family so he could hold the office of Tribune of the Plebs. His politics had also shifted from their *Optimate* starting point to their present *Populare* bias. He bought favor with the Roman crowd by free grain distributions. Until that point, grain had been heavily subsidized but not free, a practice begun by Gaius Gracchus. Clodius also ended the monarchy on Cyprus, made it a Roman province, and proposed that Cato go there for two years to set up the administration. Cato saw this as a way to get him out of Rome, but he went because it was the lawful thing to do. This was particularly clever because later it put Cato in the position of having to defend the legitimacy of Clodius's administration to prevent his work on Cyprus from being destroyed by his allies when they wanted to undo everything Clodius had done. Clodius therefore had removed both of the leading senators opposed to the Triumvirate from Rome. Caesar would use Clodius as his agent in Rome until the latter's death, and Clodius remained loyal to Caesar and Crassus for the rest of his life.

| Caesar a consul | Clodius Tribune of the Plebs | Cicero forced into exile |
|:---:|:---:|:---:|
| **59 B.C.** | **58 B.C.** | **58-57 B.C.** |

In each case below, one of the choices was really the word used by the author in the sentence provided. All of the choices can be found in the example words on the first page of this lesson. Your challenge is to decide which word the author used. This is not a test; it is more like a game because more than one word choice may work perfectly well. See if you can use your sensitivity and intuition to guess correctly which word the author used.

1. **From H.G. Wells's *The War of the Worlds***

   It was not time for _____ chivalry, and my brother laid him quiet with a kick.
   a. renascent
   b. recumbent
   c. pugilistic
   d. incorrigible

2. **From Kenneth Grahame's *The Wind in the Willows***

   How can we possibly make it sufficiently hot for the _____ rogue?
   a. recumbent
   b. incorrigible
   c. melancholy
   d. admonitory

3. **From Mary Wollstonecraft's *Vindication of the Rights of Woman***

   It would puzzle a keen _____ to prove the reasonableness of the greater number of wars that have dubbed heroes.
   a. emollient
   b. pugilist
   c. casuist
   d. infirmity

4. **From James Fenimore Cooper's *The Last of the Mohicans***

   He was able to distinguish the _____ forms of his companions as they lay stretched on the grass.
   a. recumbent
   b. melancholy
   c. admonitory
   d. renascent

5. **From Charles Dickens's *A Tale of Two Cities***

   [There were] _____ strong-rooms made of kitchens and sculleries.
   a. renascent
   b. extemporized
   c. recumbent
   d. incorrigible

Though it is a good thing to have a rich vocabulary, it is not a good thing to abuse that vocabulary by writing verbose, abstruse, sesquipedalian sentences. Those who overuse their vocabularies often do so at the expense of clarity. Translate the following showy, ponderous passage into graceful, direct English. Do not use slang, but do use words that seem familiar and comfortable.

AN INSIDIOUS PATHOGEN IN THE EMOLLIENT HAD CAUSED A STRANGE METAMORPHOSIS, and now the surgeon lay recumbent in a melancholy infirmity, like an incorrigible pugilist who'd been unable to deflect the opponent's blows and whose ears had been pounded into amorphous excrescences. No admonitory prescience had warned the surgeon not to use the emollient, jekyllhydium, and the instructions on the bottle had argued, in a case of commercial casuistry, that the jekyllhydium was the *sine qua non* for personal renascent vigor. In the past, the surgeon had attempted to extemporize other healthful remedies, to no avail, and had procured the jekyllhydium only as a last resort.

But now this unexpected transmogrification had left the surgeon in a saturnine and nonplussed incredulity, uttering suspirated maledictions and longing for some chemical legerdemain to reverse the damage. At least the morphological alterations had been mild, leaving the surgeon's body in its normal anthropomorphic form, but the surgeon was cognizant that the etiology of this condition was cryptic, and the prognosis for recovery and restoration was dismal, since no amount of rhinoplasty would likely restore the distended anomaly on the front of the surgeon's face to the aquiline nose that she had previously possessed.

With apprehension, she looked again lugubriously at the bottle of jekyllhydium and suddenly noticed a sentence in small print: "Caution: use of this emollient may, in some cases, result in irreversible *bergeracus cyranosis*." And yet, had she read the admonitory label in time, would she have been circumspect or sagacious enough to give it credence? Who could tell? "Well," she stoically soliloquized, "at least I now have a proboscis to preclude the egocentric perils of narcissism. My days as a paragon of patrician physiognomy are done. All proboscis monkeys have a proboscis; I have a proboscis; therefore, I am a proboscis monkey." This specious pseudosyllogism, we must interpolate, was hardly perspicuous.

### Reading Comprehension

1.  In Translation 56, it can be inferred that:
     a. The surgeon possesses a sanguine equanimity.
     b. The surgeon possesses a supercilious sangfroid.
     c. The surgeon is a narcissistic hedonist.
     d. The surgeon lacks the perspicacity to accept herself.

2.  The author's attitude in Translation 56 is best described as:
     a. giving a high value to the importance of physical appearance
     b. not giving a high value to the importance of physical appearance
     c. communicating no attitude toward the importance of physical appearance
     d. accepting the surgeon's attitude toward the importance of physical appearance

### Analogies

3.  **INCORRIGIBLE : TRACTABLE ::**
     a. pathogen : vitamin
     b. metamorphosis : metempsychosis
     c. corrugated : traction
     d. pugilist : philosopher

4.  **INFIRMITY : MELANCHOLY ::**
     a. contretemps : jocose
     b. admonition : incorrigible
     c. casuistry : incredulous
     d. cholera : sickness

### Antonyms

5.  **RENASCENT :**
     a. renaissance
     b. concatenated
     c. moribund
     d. exogenous

6.  **SINE QUA NON :**
     a. dichotomy
     b. superfluity
     c. reiteration
     d. tautology

This is a small statue of a lictor wearing a toga and carrying the *fasces*. The lictors were attendants and bodyguards for magistrates who held *imperium*—a dozen for each of the consuls and six for the praetor. The lictor depicted here has an axe blade facing outward, which was normally the case during the Republic only when outside the walls of Rome. Mussolini's Italian Fascists took their name and symbol from the ancient Roman fasces, which were bundles of rods bound together and used as symbols of office. Naturally the twentieth-century Fascists depicted the fasces with the axe blade. Tribunes of the Plebs did not get the protection of lictors, which may help to explain why so many of them were killed by the *Optimates*.

**synthesis**

An **incorrigible** character is one who, like Huckleberry Finn, is incapable of being reformed, even through punishment. Huck, who resisted stiff clothes, stiff weekly schedules, stiff manners, and other forms of *rigor culturus*, was incorrigible, though lovably so. What other incorrigible characters in history or fiction can you think of?

**analysis**

By breaking the words into their component stems, explain the difference between **incorrigible**, **intractable**, and **intransigent**, or between **metamorphosis**, **metempsychosis**, and **transmogrification**. You may use a dictionary to look up the etymologies, if you would like more information than the stems we have studied provide.

**intuition and imagination**

First, let me do some synthesis: **Metamorphosis** is for lycanthropes, for the subjects of entomology, for frog-princes, and for doctors named Jekyll. *Metamorphosis* is for the lonely novelist Franz Kafka, in his story of Gregor Samsa, who woke up as an insignificant and neglected bug, the symbol of that anonymous nonentity, *Homo bureaucraticus*. *Metamorphosis* is for vampires named *Dracula* who turn into wolves, bats, and sharp-toothed creatures of the night. *Metamorphosis* is for Ovid, the Roman poet, who wrote magical and lovely story-poems of the great myths, such as Daphne and Apollo, Phoebus and Phaeton, and Echo and Narcissus (read the Rolfe Humphries translation of Ovid's *Metamorphoses*, and then look up a photograph of Bernini's AMAZING sculpture of Daphne changing into a laurel tree just as Apollo catches up with her). *Metamorphosis* is for tadpoles. *Metamorphosis* is for the malefic monsters of science fiction who insidiously adopt the morphology of whatever species they encounter. *Metamorphosis* is not for the birds, though it is a *sine qua non* in the life of butterflies. *Metamorphosis* is for the Incredible Hulk, whom you would not like when he is angry.

Now for the intuition and imagination: If you were to write a creative story involving a new form of metamorphosis, which you are the first person to imagine (if Narcissus dwindled away to become a narcissus flower, pining narcissistically for his own image in the water, does that mean that I might pine away until I have become a quarter-pounder with cheese?) (Does it drive you crazy when I **interpolate** these comments?), what would your new form of metamorphosis be? Think of a fun or funny form of metamorphosis, and, if you would like to, write a short story in which your metamorphosis plays a part.

**ethics**

After thinking carefully about what **casuistry** is (disingenuous and specious ethical ratiocination), see if you can think of an actual example of casuistry that you have encountered in the world. Remember that the casuist is a *case-ist* who makes the wrong thing sound like the right thing through the unprincipled use of specific cases.

## Neologist's Lexicon

Use the stems in this list to create a new word (neologism). Give the word, the pronunciation, the part of speech, the etymology, and the definition(s). Keep a record of the neologisms you create from list to list. Here is an example:

**sinecrescence** (sin uh KRESS ence) n. [*sine* (without), *cresc* (grow)] 1. avoiding epiphanies or profound reflections on experience so as to avoid the need for changing one's ideas 2. interpreting all experiences as a concatenation of verifications of one's prior beliefs

## Sesquipedalian Bete Noire

Using the words from List 56 and previous lists, write a sesquipedalian version of your *bete noir* (something that drives you crazy, that you dread, that is your personal pet peeve). An example:

### Burgers 'n' Pies at the Drive Thru

| | |
|---|---|
| Machine: | Welcome to MaDoodle's. May I take your order please!!!!!!!!!!! |
| Human: | Cheeseburger 'n' fries 'n' a large DietSipp. |
| Machine: | Would you like a HOT APPLE PIE WITH THAT??? |
| Human: | Cheeseburger 'n' fries 'n' a large DietSipp, to reiterate. |
| Machine: | Would YOU LIKE A HOT APPLE PIE WITH THAT????? |
| Human: | Cheeseburger, fries, sipp. Are you incorrigible? |
| Machine: | Would you like a HOT APPLE PIE WITH THAT??? |
| Human: | What retort is this? I want a cheeseburger and fries and a DietSipp. |
| Machine: | Would YOU LIKE TO HAVE A NICE HOT APPLE PIE WITH THAT??? |
| Human: | What?? Is pie a *sine qua non* of the cheeseburger meal? Are you intractable? |
| Machine: | Sir, WOULD YOU LIKE A HOT APPLE PIE WITH THAT?? |
| Human: | I wasn't cognizant I'd mentioned a pie. What casuistry is this? What *idée fixe*? |
| Machine: | HOW 'BOUT A NICE HOT APPLE PIE WITH THAT??? |
| Human: | Is there no subterfuge I can use to deflect your assiduous question? |
| Machine: | D'JA like a HOT APPLE PIE WITH THAT?? |
| Human: | Take my admonitory expostulation, before I metamorphose into a pugilistic and belligerent gastronome: offer your pathogenic pie to someone else! Extemporize. You can do it. |
| Machine: | HOW 'BOUT A HOT APPLE PIE WITH THAT?? |
| Human: | (Soliloquizing) Oh, lyssophobia, vex not me. (Aloud) GIMME A CHEESEBURGER! |
| Machine: | LIKE A HOT APPLE PIE WITH THAT?? |
| Human: | You're trying to mollify me, right? The pie is an emollient for my acerbity? |
| Machine: | WOULD YOU LIKE A HOT APPLE PIE WITH THAT?? |
| Human: | Oh, melancholy. Oh, excrescence on the body of life. Oh, failed renascence. |
| Machine: | HOW'D'JA LIKE A HOT APPLE PIE WITH THAT?????!!!!!! |
| Human: | Keep the cheeseburger. Keep the fries. KEEP THE DIETSIPP! (Drives away) |
| Machine: | LIKE A PIE?? HOW ABOUT A PIE?? HAVE A PIE WITH THAT? SOME PIE??? |

*finis*

| | | | | | |
|---|---|---|---|---|---|
| • **nod** | (knot) | denouement | • **sap** | (taste) | insipid |
| • punct | (point) | compunction | • in | (not) | insipid |
| • flect | (bend) | inflection | • pater | (father) | expatriate |
| • sta | (stop) | stasis, status quo | • *archy* | (government) | anarchist |
| • mur | (wall) | immure | • *an-* | (without) | anarchist |
| • im* | (in) | immure | • bon | (good) | bonhomie |
| • sens | (feel) | sentient | • muta | (change) | mutable |
| • *eco* | (house) | ecumenical | • ex | (out) | *ex officio* |

**denouement** (outcome, unraveling)  The class read the amateurish novel's tedious denouement.

**solecism** (substandard speech)  Athenians laughed at the solecisms spoken by colonists in Soloi.

**compunction** (feeling of remorse)  The egotistical sociopath acted without compunction.

**inflection** (change of vocal tone)  She signaled her question by vocal inflection.

**stasis** (state of equilibrium)  Is the universe in flux or in stasis?

**immure** (to wall in)  Having never traveled, he was immured within his own provincialism.

**sentient** (conscious)  The exobiologist believed in sentient extraterrestrial life.

**ecumenical** (universal)  We have an ecumenical, general view of the event.

***ex officio*** (by virtue of office)  The disgruntled mayor became the *ex officio* dogcatcher.

**insipid** (without flavor, boring)  His insipid conversation bored even the dog.

•   •   •

**expatriate** (banish)  The intractable dissident was expatriated from the fatherland.

**anarchist** (one against government)  The sullen anarchist refused to vote at all.

**bonhomie** (good-naturedness)  The good fellow charmed us with his amiable bonhomie.

**status quo** (the present state)  The daring new policy disrupted the political status quo.

**mutable** (changeable)  He chased the mutable laws of high fashion.

*We introduce a new definition of *im*.

## As Used by Edith Wharton in *Ethan Frome*

| | Her | look | smote | him | with | compunction. |
|---|---|---|---|---|---|---|
| **Parts of Speech:** | adj. | n. | v. | pron. | prep. | n. |
| **Parts of Sentence:** | | subj. | AVP | D.O. | | |

**Phrases:** --prepositional phrase--

**Clauses:** -----------------------------------independent clause-----------------------------------
one independent clause; a simple, declarative sentence

Here Wharton uses the noun *compunction* as the object of a preposition. The prepositional phrase modifies the verb. *Her* is a possessive adjective; the possessive pronoun is *hers*.

## Pronunciation

| | | | |
|---|---|---|---|
| denouement | de NOO ay MAHN | *ex officio* | EX o FISS ee o |
| solecism | SOLL e sizm | insipid | in SIP id |
| compunction | com PUNKT shun | expatriate | ex PAY tree ate |
| inflection | in FLECK shun | anarchist | AN ar kist |
| stasis | STAY siss | bonhomie | bon o MEE |
| immure | im MYOOR | status quo | sta tus KWO |
| sentient | SEN tee ent | mutable | MYOO ta bel |
| ecumenical | ek yoo MEN ik al | | |

## Spanish Cognates

| | | | |
|---|---|---|---|
| solecism | solecismo | compunction | compunción |
| inflection | inflexión | ecumenical | ecuménico |
| insipid | insípido | expatriate | expatriado |
| anarchist | anarquista | mutable | mudable |

1. The adjective **ecumenical** means universal, global, or, in a specific sense, it means of the whole Christian church. The word comes from the Latin *oecumenicus*, belonging to the whole inhabited world, and this comes from the Greek *oikein*, to inhabit. The stem with which we are familiar is *eco*, house or habitation.

2. A **solecism** is an error of grammar or etiquette, an impropriety. The noun comes from the idea of the ancient Greeks that the Greek spoken in Soloi was ungrammatical and crude. A Solecism is a Soloi-ism. Charlotte Brontë refers to the embarrassment of being made conspicuous by some solecism or blunder, and Melville notes, "by a solecism of terms there are birds called grey albatrosses."

3. The verb **immure** is a relative of the words **mural**, **intramural**, and **intermural**. To immure is to imprison, to wall in. In Grahame's 1908 classic *The Wind in the Willows*, the incorrigible Toad "found himself immured in a dank and noisome dungeon."

4. A **Classic Word**: The noun **compunction** refers to the feeling of remorse we have when we have done something wrong or when we are about to do something wrong. The word comes from the Latin *compungere*, to prick (*punct*) severely. You might not expect this word to have much play in the classics, but in fact we see *compunction* in steady use for hundreds of years. Shakespeare used it in 1606 in *Macbeth*: "Stop up th'access and passage to remorse, / That no compunctious visitings of nature / Shake my fell purpose." Walter Scott used it, as did Emily Brontë, Herman Melville, Charles Dickens, Thomas Hardy, Stephen Crane, and Edith Wharton. In 1851 Melville referred to men "who still have left in them some interior compunctions against suicide," and in *The Red Badge of Courage*, Henry Fleming "of course felt no compunctions for proposing a general as a sacrifice."

5. The adjective **insipid** means not (*in*) sapid; **sapid** means tasty and comes from the Latin *sapidus*, flavored. So to be insipid is to be boring, flavorless, lacking interesting qualities. Gulliver refers to an insipid diet. Scott describes the insipidity of mind that sometimes attaches to fair beauties. Charlotte Brontë describes an interesting dichotomy: "their presence was pungent, but their absence would be felt as comparatively insipid." In Kipling's *Kim*, we read that "This was not insipid, single-word talk of drummer-boys." And in Twain's *Tom Sawyer*, the boys are made to talk so properly that speech has become insipid in their mouths.

6. The verb **expatriate** always reminds me, and a million other people, of the writer Ernest Hemingway, who spent much of his time abroad and who wrote about expatriates, victims of wounding wars who found it impossible to go home and who spent their lives drifting from hotel to hotel, insulating themselves from their own care with alcohol. It is no surprise, therefore, to find that Hemingway himself used this word in *The Sun Also Rises* to describe an "expatriated newspaper man." In addition to Hemingway's novels, you might enjoy his book *Death in the Afternoon*, which is a description and explanation of bullfighting.

The Appian Way was wider than most Roman roads, but it was only about fifteen feet wide with narrow sidewalks on both sides. This section has the curb and sidewalk on the left side clearly visible. The Appian Way was too narrow for two antagonistic gangs of armed men to pass without a melee, and so it occurred on the 6th of December in 53 B.C. that Clodius was killed by the *Optimates* gang.

# THE DISSOLUTION OF THE TRIUMVIRATE
## Dr. Thomas Milton Kemnitz

At the instigation of a newly-elected Tribune of the Plebs, Titus Annius Milo, the Senate voted to allow Cicero to return to Rome in 57 B.C., and he returned in August of that year, having been away seventeen months. Clodius tried to prevent the vote to allow Cicero to return, but his thugs were not equal to Milo's, and Milo won the day. In 56 B.C. Clodius used a new official position to impeach Milo for public violence. Milo had defended his house against the attacks of Clodius's gang, and Clodius charged Milo with keeping armed bands in his service. Judicial proceedings were hindered by violent outbreaks, and the matter was finally dropped. This was the year Caesar held the meetings in Lucca with Crassus and Pompey, and they decided on their strategy for the next years. In 55 B.C. Crassas and Pompey were consuls, and they pushed through the appointment of Caesar as proconsul for Gaul for another five years. Cato, of course, ineffectually tried to resist the tide of events.

In 54 B.C. the Triumvirate began to unravel as Crassus left Rome to take up his province in the East. His plan was to get far richer by exploiting the vast wealth of the East and by conquest. A man subject to envy as well as unbridled greed, he was determined to match Pompey and Caesar in military glory by a conquest of Parthia. In that year a crucial bond was broken when Pompey's beloved wife Julia—who was Caesar's daughter—died in childbirth. This was doubly bad news for Caesar, who mourned the loss of his only child while he contemplated how to maintain ties with Pompey. Caesar offered his grandniece Octavia, then only fifteen years old, as a substitute wife, but Pompey declined. Julia had been twenty-three years younger than Pompey; Octavia was thirty-seven years younger.

The next year (53 B.C.), against all advice, Crassus led his troops into an untenable situation, and both he and his son were killed, along with most of their troops, in battle. The Triumvirate had lost its essential balance; Caesar had been necessary to keep Pompey and Crassus in harmony; with Crassus gone, Caesar was no longer essential to Pompey. Moreover, another bond between the Triumvirate was broken that same year when its plebeian agent Clodius was killed. Late in the year Milo had been a candidate for the consulship and Clodius for the praetorship; both collected armed bands and clashed in the streets of Rome. Apparently on December 6, 53 B.C., they and their gangs passed each other by chance on the Appian Way, which is less than twenty feet wide. A fight erupted, and Clodius did not survive the encounter. He was yet another plebeian victim of senatorial violence. His enraged clients built a funeral pyre in the Forum and burned an important building. Fearing an uncontrollable outbreak of plebeian violence, the Senate voted that Pompey be appointed consul without a colleague in order to restore order. Turning to Pompey was a calculated move on the part of the patrician *Optimates*; they hoped to work on Pompey to break his bond with Caesar. Pompey was made sole consul rather than dictator so the Senate would have a check on him; a dictator could not be tried for offenses while in office, but a consul could be.

In 52 B.C. Pompey married Cornelia Metella, the very young widow of Crassus's son Publius and the daughter of Caecilius Metellus Scipio, one of Caesar's bitterest enemies. This marriage in itself signaled that Pompey was open to a break with Caesar, and two new laws confirmed it. One allowed retrospective prosecution for electoral bribery, of which Caesar was notoriously and flagrantly guilty. Pompey also prohibited Caesar from standing for the consulship *in absentia*, which had been permitted previously.

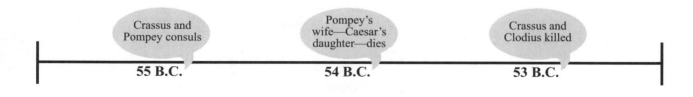

| Crassus and Pompey consuls | Pompey's wife—Caesar's daughter—dies | Crassus and Clodius killed |
|:---:|:---:|:---:|
| **55 B.C.** | **54 B.C.** | **53 B.C.** |

In each case below, one of the choices was really the word used by the author in the sentence provided. All of the choices can be found in the example words on the first page of this lesson. Your challenge is to decide which word the author used. This is not a test; it is more like a game because more than one word choice may work perfectly well. See if you can use your sensitivity and intuition to guess correctly which word the author used.

1. **From Aldous Huxley's *Brave New World***

   "I beg your pardon," said the reporter, with genuine _____.
   a. inflection
   b. bonhomie
   c. denouement
   d. compunction

2. **From Herman Melville's *Moby Dick***

   By a(n) _____ of terms there are birds called grey albatrosses.
   a. status quo
   b. solecism
   c. denouement
   d. inflection

3. **From Herman Melville's *Moby Dick***

   _____ professors of Sabbath-breaking are all whalemen.
   a. *ex officio*
   b. sentient
   c. mutable
   d. insipid

4. **From Rudyard Kipling's *Kim***

   This was not _____, single-word talk of drummer-boys.
   a. ecumenical
   b. *ex officio*
   c. solecism
   d. insipid

5. **From Henry James's *The American***

   And then she looked at the undusted nymph, as if she possibly had _____ ears.
   a. insipid
   b. sentient
   c. mutable
   d. ecumenical

Though it is a good thing to have a rich vocabulary, it is not a good thing to abuse that vocabulary by writing verbose, abstruse, sesquipedalian sentences. Those who overuse their vocabularies often do so at the expense of clarity. Translate the following showy, ponderous passage into graceful, direct English. Do not use slang, but do use words that seem familiar and comfortable.

THE COMPUNCTION HE FELT was like an immutable melancholy prison, a remorse within which he was immured and for which there was no postlude. He had reached a plateau of lugubrious stasis. Behaving like a vociferous anarchist in a plutocracy, he had insensitively accused his best friend of solecisms, of circumlocutions, of tautologies, of malapropisms, of effusive inflections, and—worst of all—of insipid conversation, wounding his friend with this acerbic obloquy and disrupting the bonhomie and equanimity that were the friend's typical status quo.

And he was no vacuous inanimate object; he was a sentient being with an ecumenical world view; he was ordinarily a sensitive friend who never pronounced objurgations. But now he had egocentrically contravened his own best instincts, and he felt like sequestering himself like a troglodyte in a cave, or like becoming an expatriated apostate, who as a perfidious villain was entitled to become an *ex officio* member of the supercilious cosmopolitan cognoscenti. But this reaction was a *non sequitur*.

There was only one condign thing to do: to abjure narcissism, to abase himself in a posture of obsequious humility, and to go ask for exculpation through the euphony of forgiveness—to transmogrify himself into a penitent. But this was an ethical funambulism to which he was unaccustomed, and he was soon lost in casuistry, asking himself, "Why should I apologize? In some cases, apologies are rebuffed. In some cases, we apologize to those even less punctilious than ourselves. Is what I have done so ignominious, when in many cases people do far worse and still are lionized?"

Slowly, however, he began to feel contrite again, and he went to find his friend, unequivocally gave his *mea culpa*, averred that he was cognizant of his error, expressed commiseration, execrated himself for his effusion of invective, and announced that all his epithets had been misnomers in which he had failed to discern his friend's manifest excellence.

As you might imagine, the denouement of this story was a mutual panegyric of solicitude.

## Reading Comprehension

1. For Translation 57, which of the following does the passage suggest?
   a. Normally, people are reluctant to forgive those who wrong them.
   b. You should describe things as you see them, even if this is hurtful.
   c. Apologize for your errors, and you probably will be forgiven.
   d. There's no sense crying over spilt milk.

2. The character's thinking could best be described as:
   a. an introspective *Odyssey*
   b. an introspective *Iliad*
   c. an introspective *Inferno*
   d. an introspective *Moby Dick*

## Analogies

3. **STASIS : MUTABLE ::**
   a. stop : car
   b. system : fuel
   c. stable : status quo
   d. equipoise : metamorphic

4. **EXPATRIATE : ANARCHIST ::**
   a. father : governor
   b. evict : tenant
   c. *ex officio* : officer
   d. convict : criminal

## Antonyms

5. **SENTIENT :**
   a. inanimate
   b. insipid
   c. acrimonious
   d. compunctious

6. **ECUMENICAL :**
   a. clerical
   b. *ex officio*
   c. provincial
   d. dogmatic

A captured Gaul is guarded by a Roman soldier. A cloak and a shield hang on the tree as trophies of the victory. This terra cotta plaque was evidently mass-produced; the maker's name is stamped in the middle of it.

## emotion and ethics

As emotions go, **compunction** is one of the least pleasant. As we saw in the Notes on page 281, a compunction is a severe sense of remorse that one feels before or after doing something regrettable or immoral. For my money (to use a dreaded cliché), the most piercing expression of this emotion is Macbeth's compunctious agony after he has killed the good king Duncan: "Full of scorpions," Macbeth says grimly, "is my mind, dear wife." Full of scorpions is my mind . . . . Imagine that.

A less poetic but equally poignant example of compunction is King Lear's grievous realization of what he has done to his truest daughter, Cordelia, whom he has banished and disinherited because she told the simple truth, which is that when she weds, she will give half of her love to her husband, rather than continuing to love her father all, as her wicked and dissembling sisters claim they will do. Lear at last realizes the tragedy that he has brought upon himself and gasps to his fool, in a heart-breaking *non sequitur* to what the fool has just said, "I did her wrong,—"

Huckleberry Finn feels compunctions about taking food from farmers' fields, about helping Jim escape, about leaving a gang of murderers to die on a house floating down the river, and about how the Duke and the Dauphin are duping and conning the crowds.

Frankenstein's monster—the sensitive sentient being of Mary Shelley's lovely book, not the lumbering ignoramus of the film—feels frequent compunction about the harm he causes. In this book, it is the monster who is the person, and the people who are monsters to him.

Another way to think about compunction is to perceive the chill of its absence. We expect compunction to be present as an essential emotional aspect of our humanity, and when we do not see it, we become dramatically cognizant of the tenebrous gap it leaves. It is, for example, the hideous absence of compunction that gives the truculent Mr. Hyde his peculiar power over our emotions. Hyde tramples a little girl and cudgels an old gentleman, and not only does Hyde not manifest compunction, but he even enjoys a sadistic hedonism in his barbarity.

One aspect of the Nazi holocaust that gives it such profound horror is the absence of compunction in those who created and who obeyed the command to murder. Compunction is a kind of alarm, a signal of the conscience to itself that something immoral is happening. The complete absence of compunction is synonymous with monstrosity.

Do you remember the word **sociopath** from our discussion of egotism? Well, a sociopath is a person, usually bright, who ruthlessly manipulates others to achieve his or her own ends, having no scruples and feeling no compunctions about the injuries caused to the lives or emotions of the people who get sacrificed to his or her egotism. The sociopath is a moral vacuum. The mythical paradigm for the sociopath is the vampire. You might think a sociopath would be despised by everyone, but it is characteristic of the sociopath to be so talented at manipulation that the victims are charmed, impressed, and incredulous that the sociopath has intentionally harmed them. They may even regard the sociopath as their heroic ally in the struggle against whomever the sociopath is blaming for their misfortunes. When they finally begin to suspect the sociopath, they first doubt their own perspicacity. Only later do they realize what the sociopath has done to them. For an overpowering literary example of the sociopath, read Shakespeare's *Othello*, and watch closely, if you can stand the horror, Iago's brilliant, systematic destruction of Othello and Desdemona, done with such malefic skill that Othello actually cherishes Iago as a trusted friend until it is too late. Iago is evil genius incarnate, a sociopath utterly without compunction.

What would you like to do with this idea of *compunction*? Would you like to discuss other examples you can think of, or write a short story, or analyze the internal human phenomena that cause us to feel compunction? Well, either do one of these, or design a *compunction* exercise of your own.

## Neologist's Lexicon

Use the stems in this list to create a new word (neologism). Give the word, the pronunciation, the part of speech, the etymology, and the definition(s). Keep a record of the neologisms you create from list to list. Here are some examples:

**sapiarchy** (SAH pi ar kee) n. [*sap* (taste), *archy* (government)]  1. the government of those who profess to have sublime taste  2. the dictatorship of the cognoscenti

**sensiflection** (SENS ih flek shun) n. [*sens* (feel), *flect* (bend), *tion* (act)]  1. having one's feelings manipulated by emotional influences, such as television advertisements that associate poignant experiences with the possession of industrial products

## Sesquipedalian Walden

Have you read Thoreau's *Walden*? Thoreau describes going to the woods, building his own cabin, and living in connectedness with the creatures and manifest life of the forest. He has entire chapters on food, on sounds, on sights. He rows on the lake and plays games with a diving loon. It is peaceful reading . . . a relief from the plot-filled stories we normally read.  Here is a spoof:

### Walden

I sequestered myself in the woods six hours ago, and I just finished extemporizing my own clever cabin with my own clever hands and will enjoy the status quo in a spirit of ecumenical bonhomie with all woodland creatures, unless doing so costs me more than a dollar and sixty-seven cents, which is all I have budgeted for my expenses this year.  I do not expect to need half so much money, as all my entertainment and sustenance will be provided by the woodland creatures for free.  I am so perspicaciously stoic.  And so very very clever.

Men are born free, but everywhere they obsequiously immure themselves in insipid towns, hypothecating their freedom for profits, when they could live sentiently and harmoniously with the great stasis of Nature—like me—cleverly delighting in the cacophonous anarchy of squirrels, rather than the solecisms of tax collectors! Men could be impecunious and still enjoy the mutable seasons, but they have expatriated themselves from their natural homes to live as xenophobic strangers in the neophilia of what is by misnomer called civilization.  Instead, they should extirpate themselves—like me—from this insidious hebetude and participate in the isocracy of living things.  Why do men contravene their nature and choose manumission to the omnibus demands of society?

My clever house is snug, a wooden quadrilateral four feet by four feet, and provides every need.  It is as manifest as a bird's nest, and the inflections of a robin's euphonic cadenza come through the window with the evening breeze.  And from the pellucid lake the lugubrious loon shatters the tranquility without compunction, exhorting me to enjoy the nick of time.  But I must be out the door, for I am the clever self-appointed *ex officio* inspector of paths and mud puddles, and I record the denouement of rain storms as I listen to the suspiration of the wind in the trees.

When they write my hagiography, let them record that I marched cleverly to the beat of a *sui generis* axiology, omnisciently abjuring the specious, the superfluous, and the supererogatory; and let them tell all readers that—like me—they can be cleverly less anthropocentric and more cosmological, which is a beatifically different drum.

| | | | | | |
|---|---|---|---|---|---|
| • sap* | (know) | sapient | • vert | (turn) | tergiversate |
| • *gen* | (origin) | indigenous | • corp | (body) | *esprit de corps* |
| • **ment** | (mind) | demented | • *antho* | (flower) | anthology |
| • *meta** | (beyond) | metaphysics | • *platy* | (flat) | platitude |
| • **quis** | (ask) | inquisition | • inter | (between) | interregnum |
| • rogat | (ask) | prerogative | • reg | (rule) | interregnum |
| • **ten** | (hold) | tenacious | • fract | (break) | infraction |
| • *terato* | (monster) | teratology | • *idio* | (peculiar) | idiosyncrasy |

**sapient** (wise) *Homo sapiens* is the most sapient primate, according to itself.

**indigenous** (native) The aborigines are the indigenous people of Australia.

**demented** (insane) In the silent film, the demented villain tied the heroine to the railroad track.

**metaphysics** (speculative philosophy) Ontology, the study of being, is a branch of metaphysics.

**inquisition** (punitive investigation) The Spanish Inquisition was feared by thinking people.

**prerogative** (exclusive privilege) Her noble prerogatives were abolished when she was deposed.

**tenacious** (holding firmly) The suspect tenaciously held to his story during the interrogation.

**teratology** (science of monstrosities) The teratologist was studying congenital birth defects.

**tergiversate** (to desert) The tergiversator turned his back on the cause; he was an apostate.

**esprit de corps** (group pride) The troops' *esprit de corps* helped them survive the grim retreat.

• • •

**anthology** (literary collection) The editor picked the best poems for the anthology.

**platitude** (flat, trite remark) We need fresh new ideas—not tired, empty platitudes.

**interregnum** (time between rulers) There was an ephemeral peace in the interregnum.

**infraction** (breaking) There should be no infraction of these ten edicts.

**idiosyncrasy** (peculiarity) Over the years, the hermit developed odd idiosyncrasies.

*We introduce new definitions of *sap* and *meta*.

**As Used by William Shakespeare in *King Lear***

| | Thou, | **sapient** | sir, | sit | here. |
|---|---|---|---|---|---|
| **Parts of Speech:** | pron. | **adj.** | n. | v. | adv. |

| | | | | |
|---|---|---|---|---|
| **Parts of Sentence:** | subj. | | AVP | |

**Phrases:** --appositive phrase--

**Clauses:** --------------------------independent clause--------------------------
one independent clause; a simple, imperative sentence

Here Shakespeare uses the adjective *sapient* to modify a noun, and the two words form an appositive phrase. The appositive phrase is enclosed in commas.

## Pronunciation

| | | | |
|---|---|---|---|
| **sapient** | SAY pient | **tergiversate** | TURJ i ver sate |
| **indigenous** | in DIJ en us | ***esprit de corps*** | eh SPREE de COR |
| **demented** | de MEN ted | **anthology** | an THOH lo jee |
| **metaphysics** | MET a fiz iks | **platitude** | PLAT i tood |
| **inquisition** | in kwiz ISH un | **interregnum** | inter REG num |
| **prerogative** | pre ROG a tiv | **infraction** | in FRAK shun |
| **tenacious** | ten AY shus | **idiosyncrasy** | id ee o SIN kra see |
| **teratology** | ter a TOLL o jee | | |

## Spanish Cognates

| | | | |
|---|---|---|---|
| **sapient** | sapiente | **indigenous** | indígena |
| **demented** | demente | **metaphysics** | metafísica |
| **inquisition** | inquisición | **prerogative** | prerrogativa |
| **tenacious** | tenaz | **tergiversation** | tergiversación |
| **anthology** | antología | **interregnum** | interregno |
| **infraction** | infracción | **idiosyncrasy** | idiosincrasia |

1.  The noun **prerogative** refers to an exclusive right or privilege, but it contains the stems that mean ask (*rogat*) before (*pre*). Why? Well, *prerogative* comes from the Latin *praerogativus*, voting first. In the Roman Empire it was sometimes the prerogative, the exclusive right, of a tribe to vote first! Consider the honor implied by having the right to be asked first what your opinion is of something. Harper Lee refers to the royal prerogative, Charlotte Brontë refers to the prerogatives of the crown, and Walter Scott to the prerogatives of a jovial friar.

2.  A **Micropoem**: The intransitive verb **tergiversate** means to desert, to turn renegade, to repeatedly change one's position toward something. The basis for this meaning is found in the imagery contained in the stems. *Tergiversate* contains our old friend *vert* (turn) and the Latin *tergum* (back); to tergiversate is to turn one's back. Someone who tergiversates could become an apostate. In *A Tale of Two Cities*, Dickens refers to "the utmost tergiversation and treachery."

3.  An **idiosyncrasy** is a peculiar behavior, such as a habit or mannerism that one associates only with a certain individual. Stand-up comedians and impressionists make careers out of imitating the idiosyncrasies of famous individuals. You might imagine that this word has something to do with the idea of government (*cracy*), but actually the noun comes from the Greek stems *idio* (peculiar), *syn* (together), and *krasis* (blending). An idiosyncrasy is a peculiar blending together! This explains why *idiosyncrasy* is not spelled *idiosyncracy*. In John Knowles's *A Separate Peace*, Gene says that the students "had been an idiosyncratic, leaderless band" and that there was "nothing idiosyncratic about Brinker unless you saw him from behind." Poor Brinker. Robert Louis Stevenson, in *Dr. Jekyll and Mr. Hyde*, refers to "some idiosyncratic, personal distaste." And Thomas Hardy, in *The Return of the Native*, describes the human face this way: "But the mind within was beginning to use it as a mere waste tablet whereon to trace its idiosyncrasies as they developed themselves."

4.  The noun **teratology** refers to the study of monstrosities, such as abnormally formed plants and animals. We see this word used in child development texts, where it describes the study of congenital birth defects. Agents involved in the etiology of birth defects are called **teratogens**, and we have learned that most fetuses are exposed to some teratogens. These teratogens are most dangerous at the time organs are being formed, about three weeks after conception. Teratologists indicate that the fetus's brain, eyes, heart, and legs are each especially vulnerable at certain stages of development.

5.  A **Classic Word**: The adjective **indigenous** means native-born; you would not expect such a scientific-sounding term in the classics, but it is there. It was used by Thoreau, Stowe, and Melville. In *To Kill a Mockingbird*, Harper Lee used *indigenous* to note "peculiarities indigenous to the region" and "diseases indigenous to filthy surroundings."

Roman key

Caesar in full military regalia

# A SENATE CONFIDENT IN ITS STRATEGY
## Dr. Thomas Milton Kemnitz

Caesar was not without resources and agents in Rome. Plunder and the sale of slaves from Gaul had made him a wealthy man, and he spent lavishly on bribing potential allies. He lent money without interest and paid off the debts of some officials. But no one in the Roman state was as important as Pompey; he was the great military figure of his generation; he was key to Caesar's future, and the *Optimates* in the Senate had his ear. They played on the fact that Caesar might be a threat to Pompey's unquestioned primacy—a position so clear that Bilbulus, one of Pompey's long-term enemies, suggested that to suppress any outbreak after the murder of Clodius, Pompey be made sole consul, and Cato seconded the suggestion. The senators clearly reckoned Pompey to be the lesser threat to the Republic than Caesar, and they knew the extent of their influence with him. In 51 B.C. Pompey announced that Caesar would not be allowed to stand for consul unless he resigned his proconsulship and relinquished his legions. When in 54 B.C. the Triumvirs had divided up the Roman world, Caesar got Gaul and four legions, and Pompey got North Africa and Spain and four legions, two of which he loaned to Caesar for the wars in Gaul. Now Pompey asked for his two legions to be returned to him, and Caesar returned them in 50 B.C.

At this point, the *Optimates* in the Senate must have been well satisfied that they had done everything necessary to contain Caesar. Pompey was on their side, and he had a huge reputation as a military man—and no one believed it more than Pompeius Magnus. Plutarch records that Pompey fell dangerously ill, and his recovery was greeted with great rejoicing. As he made his way around Italy, there were numerous outpourings of positive feeling for him. "An arrogant feeling entered the mind of Pompeius, and ... carried off all reflection on the present state of affairs; and throwing away the caution which had always secured his good fortune and his measures, he fell into a state of such unmingled confidence and contempt of Caesar's power as to suppose that he would require neither arms to oppose him nor any troublesome preparations, but that he could put him down much easier than he had raised him. Besides this, Appius came from Gaul with the troops which Pompeius had lent to Caesar, and he greatly disparaged Caesar's exploits there, and uttered much abuse against Caesar ... [He reported that Pompey] could put down Caesar with Caesar's own troops, as soon as he made his appearance; so great was their hatred of Caesar and their affection towards Pompeius. Accordingly Pompeius was so much elated, and through his confidence filled with such contempt, that he even ridiculed those who were afraid of the war; and to those who said that, if Caesar advanced against the city, they saw no troops sufficient to repulse him, with smiling countenance and tranquil mein he bade them give themselves no trouble about that, 'for in whatever part of Italy,' he said, 'I stamp the earth with my foot, there will spring up forces both of men and horse.'" Pompey was about glory over power; in like circumstances, he had wanted the Triumph rather than the powerful office of consul, while Caesar had opted for the office over the Triumph.

Caesar tried to negotiate with the Senate; he sent a number of compromise proposals, all of which were rejected. The Senate was confident that they had him. Few had seen him in the past decade. The Caesar they knew had been aged by war and tempered by success. Fueled by Cato's inflexible hatred and Pompey's ebullient confidence, the Senate was determined to make Caesar come back without his troops and without the protection from prosecution that office would give him, to try him, and to banish him forever. It would be the end of Caesar and yet another victory for the patricians.

**metaphysics**

When Kipling, in his novel *Kim*, describes "occasional gatherings of long-coated theatrical natives who discussed metaphysics in English and Bengali," he is referring to one of the primary branches of philosophy, named after its position, after the Physics, in Aristotle's writings, which are the *locus classicus* for many of our ideas. **Metaphysics** is the question, What is real? In asking this question, philosophers ask about the reality of God and human immortality, about whether the universe has a purpose, about whether everything is just atoms, and so forth. Metaphysics asks about being. The branch of metaphysics that examines being in its most abstract form, *being as such*, is known as **ontology**. There are several main branches of metaphysical inquiry, including:

**Materialism**. To the metaphysical materialist, what is real is **matter**. Atoms. Stuff. In this view, the universe is a vast collections of atoms and forces, and everything ultimately can be explained as a manifestation of these material phenomena. The mind itself, in this view, is a manifestation of material phenomena, including atoms, cells, and organs. The universe has no purpose, though it may have processes and directions, as dictated by the Big Bang or by the process of evolution. Obviously, many thinkers have difficulty accepting a merely materialistic view of what is metaphysically real.

**Idealism**. To the metaphysical idealist, what is real is **ideas**, and matter itself is only an idea. **Subjective idealists**, such as Bishop Berkeley, do not believe that objects as things-in-themselves really exist "out there." This may seem like a frivolous view, but try to prove the separate existence of a solid object without depending on your sense perceptions, each of which is known to be variable and ultimately unreliable. For example, when we "see," we are not really directly viewing the supposed object; we are actually only perceiving the stimulation of our own brain neurons that we assume are activated by the cells in the backs of our eyes that we assume are stimulated by light hitting the eyes after being reflected off of the object that we assume is "out there." But as we know from changing light and numerous examples of optical illusions, things are not always accurately represented by visual appearances. To make matters worse, even the materialist would admit that human eyes only respond to a portion of the available light, while other animals often have far more acute vision. So how does an object REALLY look? Hmmm. What is real? How does something really feel? Really smell? Really sound? Careful thought reveals that these ideas are relative, at best. Once you start vigorously and rigorously doubting what you actually KNOW about the reality of an object, the seeming obviousness of **naive materialism** comes rapidly unglued! To make it even worse, the scientists (those rascally materialists) tell us that there is actually far more empty space in the interstices between the atoms of seemingly solid objects than there is matter. Even to the materialists, in other words, stuff is mostly not stuff, and the appearance of solidity is an illusion! In idealism, you lose the reality of matter, but you get to have such non-material things as souls, selfs (I do not mean selves), and divine Spirits. In most forms of idealism, **teleology** is important; teleology is the idea that an ultimate purpose is a fundamental reality in the nature of things.

**Dualism**. Are you confused enough? I hope so. You probably find yourself partly attracted to materialism and partly attracted to idealism. Well, maybe you are a Cartesian. Descartes is famous for his metaphysical dualism, the **mind/body dichotomy**. The ghost in the machine. An ideal self living in a physical body. The physical body may die, but the ideal self can pass on to eternity. This solves some problems, but then you have a new one: How does the non-physical self affect the physical body? If I think, "I will now type a question mark at the end of this sentence," how does my ideal mind make my material body do that? ?? ??? ???? . . . . . ? Philosophy is fun.

In each case below, one of the choices was really the word used by the author in the sentence provided. All of the choices can be found in the example words on the first page of this lesson. Your challenge is to decide which word the author used. This is not a test; it is more like a game because more than one word choice may work perfectly well. See if you can use your sensitivity and intuition to guess correctly which word the author used.

1. **From Charles Dickens's *A Tale of Two Cities***

   [He succeeded] in spite of his utmost _____ and treachery.
   a. infraction
   b. *esprit de corps*
   c. tergiversation
   d. idiosyncrasy

2. **From Henry James's *The American***

   He was gazing away, absently, at some _____ image of his implacability.
   a. tenacious
   b. metaphysical
   c. indigenous
   d. sapient

3. **From Geoffrey Chaucer's *The Canterbury Tales* (Written in 1385!)**

   A greet amender eek of _____ to him that taketh it in pacience.
   a. sapience
   b. platitude
   c. idiosyncrasy
   d. metaphysics

4. **From Harper Lee's *To Kill a Mockingbird***

   She would exercise her royal _____.
   a. prerogative
   b. interregnum
   c. platitude
   d. inquisition

5. **From Herman Melville's *Moby Dick***

   Strictly this word is not _____ to the whale's vocabulary.
   a. sapient
   b. indigenous
   c. tenacious
   d. idiosyncratic

Though it is a good thing to have a rich vocabulary, it is not a good thing to abuse that vocabulary by writing verbose, abstruse, sesquipedalian sentences. Those who overuse their vocabularies often do so at the expense of clarity. Translate the following showy, ponderous passage into graceful, direct English. Do not use slang, but do use words that seem familiar and comfortable.

IN THE TENEBROUS AND VIOLENT INTERREGNUM that followed the *coup d'état*, the deposed king—deprived of all royal prerogatives—slowly transmogrified from the sapient and incisive leader he had been into a demented patriarch uttering platitudes and manifesting idiosyncrasies. Lugubriously perambulating through the mist, he picked pink-purple nosegays of indigenous heather and in soliloquy decried the tergiversators and apostates whose infractions of royal interdictions and whose lack of *esprit de corps* had brought his lovely kingdom to such a pass. Aiming his inquisitions at the gray-faced fogs, he tenaciously repeated his metaphysical question: "Does Heaven protect the sanity of old men, or is my fate the ineluctable denouement of material nature?"

Suddenly, up from the damp heather popped the king's obsequious toady. "Oh Nuncle, Nuncle," the toady explained, "I have searched everywhere for you, and here you are, lost in the fog, collecting your wits."

"Wits?" replied the doddering king. "I am gathering poems, which I find concealed in the flowers of the heather. See, here is a poem now." He reached his hand out to a teratological anomaly of a plant with long, sharp thorns and flowers as translucent as glass. Picking a flower, he added it to his nosegay. "Take this anthology," said the king, handing the nosegay to the toady, "and read it."

"Oh Nuncle, Nuncle," replied the incredulous toady, "thou hast plucked the sacrosanct flower of thine own mind and given it to a fool."

Slowly, the two figures wandered into the melancholy mist, which closed softly around them.

Leading a victim to sacrifice

## Reading Comprehension

1. In Translation 58, the toady's attitude is best described as:
    a. acerbic
    b. nonplussed
    c. supercilious
    d. compassionate

2. With which statement would the author likely agree?
    a. The vicissitudes of fate strike everyone equally.
    b. Metaphysical questions are unanswerable.
    c. The value of a friend is not measured by social status.
    d. There is a thin line between sapience and dementia.

## Analogies

3. **ANTHOLOGY : SELECTION ::**
    a. poem : story
    b. book : literature
    c. nosegay : flower
    d. editor : author

4. **INDIGENOUS : AUTOCHTHONOUS ::**
    a. sapient : perspicacious
    b. tenacious : tenuous
    c. *esprit de corps* : hebetude
    d. metaphysics : metamorphosis

## Antonyms

5. **SAPIENT :**
    a. platitudinous
    b. vacuous
    c. demented
    d. insipid

6. **METAPHYSICS :**
    a. physics
    b. mythology
    c. poetry
    d. magic
    e. fiction
    f. nonfiction
    g. astrology
    h. faith
    i. perplexity

**synthesis**

In List 58 there are nine nouns and four adjectives. Which adjective/noun pairs work? Could, for example, there be a **sapient platitude**? Or would that be a logical contradiction, a paradox, or an oxymoron? [An oxymoron is a figure of speech that is self-contradictory, as in the "cruel kindness" of Hamlet, who must be cruel, only to be kind. The oxymoron is a kind of witticism that makes its point (*oxy*) thorough seeming foolishness (*moron*)]. See which adjective/noun pairs can be effectively connected and which cannot. For an interesting task of analysis, you could take the thirty-six pairs that result and sort them into the categories that seem to exist. You will have to decide how many categories of pairs you have and give them names.

**emotion**

If any emotion could be said to be primary, perhaps it would be care. It is the feeling of care that underlies our most positive acts, whether they are personal or interpersonal. It is the feeling of care that is the profound foundation of all learning and teaching. In Robert Ruark's book *The Old Man and the Boy*, Ruark describes his boyhood relationship with his **sapient** grandfather, the Old Man, who taught him to hunt and fish, to clean his boat before leaving it, to avoid shooting more than a small fraction of any quail covey, to leave a campsite looking clean and wild as though no one had ever been there, to value conservation, and many other things. The Old Man was as likely to discuss Shakespeare or ancient history as to discuss duck hunting, and the fundamental message communicated was not one of outdoor life but one of care for life itself, of willingness to expend effort on the details that make experiences excellent and worthwhile, and of the deep personal regard that the Old Man had for the boy and that gave the boy a sense of worth.

Who have you known who manifested this humane **sapience** and who cared about you enough to teach you things that are important to know? Think about a sapient person in your life, and write a short description of this person and his or her sapience.

**convergence**

Considering the sound, meaning, and stem sense that each word contains, which word on List 58 do you like best?

**analysis**

Pick four words from List 58, and break them down into their stem components, explaining in each case why the word means what it means, based on the stems it contains.

Roman key

## Neologist's Lexicon

Use the stems in this list to create a new word (neologism). Give the word, the pronunciation, the part of speech, the etymology, and the definition(s). Keep a record of the neologisms you create from list to list. Here are some examples:

**metaquisical** (meh tah KWIZ ihk al) adj. [*meta* (beyond), *quis* (ask)]  1. wanting to know more about everything, regardless of how much one already knows  2. the compulsively reiterated response of "Why?" to every declarative sentence

**menttenacity** (MEN ten AH city) n. [*ment* (mind), *ten* (hold)]  1. absolute and undistractable concentration of mind  2. the philosophical belief that being in perspicacious control of one's intellectual faculties is of paramount importance

## Sesquipedalian Mythology

Use words from List 58 and previous lists to paraphrase the story of one of the great Greek or Roman myths, such as those in Ovid's *Metamorphoses* or Edith Hamilton's *Mythology*. For example, Ovid tells the story of the god Apollo and the demigod Daphne, daughter of the river god Peneus:

One day Apollo, anthropomorphic Lord of Delphi, sage of metaphysics, was walking in the woods where he suddenly came upon the beautiful and ingenuous Daphne, perambulating in idiosyncratic happiness in the forest among the indigenous plants and sentient forest creatures. In the presence of such beauty, Apollo lost all sapience and, effusively uttering amorous platitudes, ran without temporizing toward Daphne, who fled in fear. "Do not run," exhorted Apollo, whose shadow fell on the swift Daphne's shoulder. "I mean you no infraction. I am the Lord of Delphi, a nonpareil." But Daphne ran on, as though fleeing a teratological anomaly. "I know that the immortals of Olympus have a confident *esprit de corps*," Daphne expostulated as she fled, "but to love any mortal you choose is not one of your divine prerogatives. To me you are a narcissistic nonentity." But the gregarious and incredulous Apollo was incorrigible.

At last the race was ending, for the diffident Daphne could not outrun the swift god, ineluctable. His shadow fell on her hair, and his breath was on her shoulder, and he reached out for her, thinking to hold on tenaciously and not let her go. But the forest cleared in front of them as they fled, and Daphne suddenly saw her father's river, and she cried out to Peneus to intervene. He was no tergiversator. From his tenebrous current, he flung his spell down the forest path, and even as Daphne spoke, her toes grew long and plunged into the soft forest earth. From her fingers and hair came an effusion of limbs and green leaves, and bark shot up from her feet, covering her body. She had metamorphosed into a laurel tree. At last, too late, Apollo caught her, just in time to discern a heart beating beneath the bark. His perspicuous prognosis was that the syndrome was irreversible. Apollo glanced fiercely at the river, but Peneus was submerged, unavailable for inquisition, and the translucent river ran euphonic beneath the trees.

With fulgurating eyes, the sad and sedate Apollo spoke a panegyric for Daphne. "*Mea culpa*, *mea culpa*," he said in valediction. "If I had shown more solicitude, this transmogrification would not have happened. From today, the laurel tree shall be my tree, and your shining leaves shall be joined with my name and crown the heads of winners."

| | | | | | | |
|---|---|---|---|---|---|---|
| • **dur** | (hard) | obdurate | | • oss | (bone) | ossify |
| • **quis*** | (search) | exquisite | | • *ostra* | (shell) | ostracize |
| • **dol** | (grief) | dolorous | | • lent | (full of) | opulent |
| • **de**** | (god) | deify | | • vid | (look) | invidious |
| • fy | (make) | deify | | • *geron* | (old man) | gerontocracy |
| • pugn | (fight) | oppugn | | • vita | (life) | viable |
| • **tens** | (stretch) | ostensible | | • omni | (all) | omnifarious |
| • **ob*** | (toward) | ostensible | | • *mania* | (madness) | kleptomaniac |

**obdurate** (hardhearted)  His stubbornly obdurate bigotry infuriated her sense of justice.

**exquisite** (of rare quality)  The exquisite designs gave her exquisite pangs of memory.

**dolorous** (full of grief)  We heard the pathetic widower's dolorous cries all through the night.

**deify** (make into a god)  The Martians had deified the dunespider and built temples to it.

**oppugn** (argue against)  It is risky for a politician to oppugn the popular viewpoint.

**innocuous** (not harmful)  Her diplomatic comments were innocuous enough.

**ostensible** (apparent)  The ostensible reason for his sudden levity seemed insufficient.

**ossify** (turn to bone)  The "boneheads'" minds were rigid and ossified.

**ostracize** (totally reject)  He was ostracized by those who resented his outspoken viewpoint.

**opulent** (rich)  The opulent antique furnishings of the mansion intrigued the historian.

• • •

**invidious** (causing envy)  The invidious compliment made the friend jealous.

**gerontocracy** (government of the old)  The Soviet gerontocracy needed new faces.

**viable** (able to live)  The fetus was not mature enough to be viable on its own.

**kleptomaniac** (pathological thief)  The manager arrested the kleptomaniac with the big coat.

**omnifarious** (of all kinds)  His omnifarious exploits were in all the papers.

* We introduce new definitions of *quis* and *ob*.
**This *de* comes from the Latin *deus*, god.

## As Used by Kenneth Grahame in *The Wind in the Willows*

| | "No | bread!" | groaned | the | Mole | dolorously. |
|---|---|---|---|---|---|---|
| **Parts of Speech:** | adj. | n. | v. | adj. | n. | **adv.** |
| **Parts of Sentence:** | -------D.O.----- | | AVP | | subj. | |

**Phrases:** --no prepositional, appositive, or verbal phrases--

**Clauses:** --------------------------------independent clause----------------------------
one independent clause; a simple, declarative sentence

Here Grahame uses the adverb *dolorously* to modify the action verb *groaned*. Note that the usual order of terms is reversed: D.O.-AVP-SUBJ. The entire quoted statement serves as the direct object.

## Pronunciation

| | | | |
|---|---|---|---|
| **obdurate** | OB dur at | **ostracize** | OSS tra size |
| **exquisite** | EX kwiz it | **opulent** | OPP yoo lent |
| **dolorous** | DOLE or us | **invidious** | in VID ee us |
| **deify** | DEE ih fy | **gerontocracy** | jer on TOCK ra see |
| **oppugn** | o PYOON | **viable** | VI a bel |
| **innocuous** | in NOCK yoo us | **kleptomaniac** | KLEP to MAY nee ack |
| **ostensible** | os TEN si bel | **omnifarious** | OM ni FAIR ee us |
| **ossify** | OSS if fy | | |

## Spanish Cognates

| | | | |
|---|---|---|---|
| **exquisite** | exquisito | **dolorous** | doloroso |
| **deification** | deificación | **innocuous** | innocuo |
| **ostensible** | ostensible | **ossification** | osificación |
| **ostracism** | ostracismo | **opulent** | opulento |
| **viable** | viable | **kleptomaniac** | cleptómano |

A bust of Julius Caesar depicting him at about age fifty, the age at which he crossed the Rubicon and initiated the civil war

# JULIUS CAESAR AND CIVIL WAR
## Dr. Thomas Milton Kemnitz

At the beginning of 49 B.C., Caesar faced a difficult situation. If he relinquished his command and returned to Rome, his enemies would end his political and military career. If he did not cede his command, he would be responsible for starting a civil war. He decided to follow the path that Marius and Sulla had taken, and he crossed the Rubicon, which divided Italy from the province of Cisalpine Gaul, a province Caesar governed. The significance of crossing the Rubicon—today a small, muddy stream less than twenty feet wide—was that no Roman except a very small number of elected officials was allowed to command troops in Italy. This was one of the checks in the constitution, and to break this prohibition was to be under an automatic death sentence. Moreover, the troops who followed Caesar were subject to the same penalty.

In December of 50 B.C., Caesar wrote to the Senate agreeing to resign his military command if Pompey did the same. The Senate demanded that Caesar immediately disband his army or be declared an enemy of the people. Caesar loyalists—the tribunes Mark Antony and Quintus Cassius Longinus—were expelled from the Senate, and they reported to Caesar how badly the tide ran against him in Rome. The senators had left Caesar with no viable option, but they were unprepared for the swiftness of his response. On January 10, 49 B.C., Caesar crossed the Rubicon with only one legion of fewer than 5,000 men, and his soldiers were rapidly at the gates of Rome, having accepted the surrender of a number of cities on their 200-mile march to the capital. Pompey had no time to stamp his foot much less assemble an army. He had the two legions Caesar had returned to him, but he could not trust their loyalty—they had followed Caesar for years. Having made the triple blunders of underestimating his enemy and failing to prepare or even to plan, Pompey immediately made several more: he fled Rome rather than trying to organize a defense of it, and he failed to take the treasury with him when he left. It is never good strategy to abandon your primary asset, and it is even more foolish to finance your opponent's army. Pompey gathered what troops he could, but they were not good enough to face Caesar's men, and so Pompey decided to abandon Italy and took his army to Greece, where he hoped to find enough breathing room to raise, equip, and train an army before he did battle with Caesar.

When Pompey sailed to Greece in March, Caesar marched his army at a fast pace to Spain and took Spain from Pompey's forces. Then he returned to Italy and gathered forces to sail to Greece. Caesar met Pompey in a battle in July in which Pompey might have wiped out Caesar's outnumbered forces had he been more decisive. They met again on August 9th at the Battle of Pharsalus, when Pompey had more than twice as many men as Caesar, and his troops occupied the high ground. Pompey's cavalry commander was Titus Labienus, who once had been Caesar's most trusted deputy commander in Gaul; Labienus was unable to countenance Caesar's crossing the Rubicon, and he had defected to the Senate side. Now Caesar correctly foresaw the tactics Pompey and Labienus would employ, and he devised a novel and ingenious counter that proved decisive in blunting Pompey's enormous advantage in cavalry. Caesar's men dispersed Pompey's cavalry, turned the flank of Pompey's army, and thereby routed it. Pompey ignominiously left the battle while it was raging, changed his uniform for civilian dress, and fled in a cart with his wife and family. Having learned at least one lesson, this time he took as much gold as the could. Caesar's legionnaires took their opponent's camp; the victory was total. Some of the senators—such as Cato—followed Pompey's example and fled; others, including Cicero and Brutus, surrendered to Caesar, were pardoned, and returned to Rome. Caesar followed Pompey, who went to Egypt, where he was assassinated on the orders of the unlucky Ptolemy XIII, who then sent the head to Caesar. Caesar chased the senators who still opposed him to North Africa, where he decisively defeated them, and then he chased Pompey's sons back to Hispania, where he ended all resistance to his rule in 45 B.C.

1. The adjective **obdurate** is a relative of **durable**, **indurate**, and **endure**. It is composed of the Latin *ob* (against) and *dur* (hard). The obdurate person is stony and unmoved, hardened against persuasion or feeling. In Crane's brilliant *The Red Badge of Courage*, a grim and obdurate group of soldiers makes no movement, and Cooper's Hawkeye is obdurate as he exclaims, "Not a karnel!"

2. The adjective **dolorous** means full of grief, such as the complete disappointment felt by Kenneth Grahame's Mole in his 1908 classic *The Wind in the Willows*: "'No bread!' groaned the Mole dolorously." Grahame's riverside creatures are sensible animals (except for Toad, who is not sensible at all) and fully appreciate the importance of a tasty meal.

3. To **deify** is to make (*fy*) into a god (*de*). Melville, in *Moby Dick*, reports that the Egyptians "deified the crocodile of the Nile because the crocodile is tongueless." He adds that if the great Sperm Whale had been known to the Orient World, it would have been deified, too.

4. The adjective **innocuous** comes from the Latin *innocuus* and means harmless, not offensive, or even insipid. In Jack London's *The Call of the Wild*, Hal swears innocuously. In Kipling's *Kim*, the explosion of dynamite is said to be milky and innocuous when compared to the report of the C25 (a cannon). And in Sylvia Plath's *The Bell Jar*, Sylvia's autobiographical alter ego, Esther Greenwood, says that the "only other address I had was the innocuous box number which people used who didn't want to advertise the fact they lived in an asylum."

5. The adjective **ostensible** means apparent, displayed, or even pretended. The idea is that in displaying something to someone, you stretch (*tens*) your arms out toward (*ob*) the person as you offer what you are displaying for him or her to see. Notice that in this word we encounter a new meaning of *ob*, which often means against, but in this word it means toward. Kipling refers to natives whose ostensible business was the repair of broken necklaces. Hardy refers to a person who is ostensibly frank as to his purpose while really concealing it. Melville mentions the ostensible reason why Ahab did not go on board the whaler. Dickens mentions a man's ostensible calling. And so we see that sometimes the ostensible truth is the truth, but sometimes the ostensible truth is not the truth.

6. A **Classic Word**: The adjective **opulent** means rich, full of (*lent*) wealth (*opes*), and comes from the Latin *opulentus*, wealthy. It also can refer to richness as abundance, as in the opulent refulgence of the sun. This word has a distinguished history in English letters. Shakespeare used it in Lear's fatal question to his lovely and loyal daughter, Cordelia. Intending to divide his kingdom into three parts among his three daughters, Lear asked each daughter to profess her love for him, that he might divide his kingdom according to the degree he was loved. "What can you say," Lear asked Cordelia, "to draw a third more opulent than your sisters?" Cordelia's unforgettable answer: "Nothing."

7. A **Micropoem**: In the verb **ostracize**, we can see the ancient Greeks casting shells (*óstreion*) in a vote to banish some undesirable person from a glittering Greek island.

**exquisite**

The adjective **exquisite** can be elusive. It is one of those words that is frequently encountered and yet that has a subtle series of meanings that defy simple articulation. We say that *exquisite* means elaborate, or lovely, or keen. We say that something is exquisite if it is rare or appealing, excellent, refined, or elegant. We use it to describe something carefully made, or to describe something that shows a sensitive touch, as music. We use *exquisite* to describe weather, charm, a face, pleasure or even pain, workmanship, taste—it seems to have no limit in its application. Only when we look at the etymology of the word do we begin to understand: *exquisite* comes from the stems *ex* (out) and *quis* (search). It comes from the Latin word *exquisitus*, sought after. Something is exquisite if it is sought out, prized, searched for, the object of a quest.

Writers from Shakespeare to Cooper to Hawthorne to Barrie to Wilder have used *exquisite* to describe phenomena that are prized. Cooper described a character's exquisitely molded head, exquisite simplicity, an exquisite countenance, and the exquisite proportions of a character's person. Hawthorne noted exquisite suffering and exquisite pain. Stowe referred to exquisite paintings of children and exquisite delight. In Stevenson's *Dr. Jekyll and Mr. Hyde*, we find the chilling sentence: "My blood was changed into something exquisitely thin and icy." Crane refers to an exquisite drowsiness that spreads through Henry Fleming. In *The Time Machine*, Wells describes the Eloi as exquisite creatures. Conrad notes exquisite sensibilities and uses the phrase several times. Jack London describes exquisite agony and the exquisite pitch to which every fiber of Buck's body was keyed. In *Peter Pan*, Barrie presents "a girl called Tinker Bell exquisitely gowned in a skeleton leaf," and notes exquisite tortures to take place at the break of day. In Wharton's *Ethan Frome*, Ethan and Mattie are drawn together by "other sensations, less definable but more exquisite, which drew them together with a shock of silent joy."

One author who loved *exquisite* was Thornton Wilder. In *The Bridge of San Luis Rey*, Wilder uses the adjective over and over. Wilder notes that an exquisite daughter was born, refers to the exquisite sensibility of some letters, and says: "It is true that the Limeans were given to interpolating trivial songs into the most exquisite comedies." A lovely insight into the charming power of Spanish is provided by Wilder's sentence: "But what divine Spanish he speaks and what exquisite things he says in it!"

But wait. We said that *exquisite* means sought after and then talked about exquisite pain, exquisite agony, exquisite torture. What? Well, the idea of being sought after is the concept from which we begin, but the idea leads immediately to the idea of something being rare. We seek after what is rare. In describing pain or agony, the adjective has taken on a new dimension. It now does not indicate desirability; it indicates that the suffering is of a rare purity and intensity, one rarely found.

A Gallic captive is depicted on a coin of 48 B.C.

In each case below, one of the choices was really the word used by the author in the sentence provided. All of the choices can be found in the example words on the first page of this lesson. Your challenge is to decide which word the author used. This is not a test; it is more like a game because more than one word choice may work perfectly well. See if you can use your sensitivity and intuition to guess correctly which word the author used.

1.      **From George Orwell's *1984***

   All past oligarchies have fallen from power either because they _____ or because they grew soft.
   a. ossified
   b. ostracized
   c. deified
   d. oppugned

2.      **From Eudora Welty's *One Writer's Beginnings***

   A(n) _____ of story books covered my bed.
   a. gerontocracy
   b. obdurate
   c. ostracize
   d. opulence

3.      **From Frederick Douglass's *Narrative***

   He was artful, cruel, and _____.
   a. obdurate
   b. ostensible
   c. ostracized
   d. dolorous

4.      **From Joseph Heller's *Catch-22***

   Doc Daneeka roosted _____ like a shivering turkey buzzard beside the closed door.
   a. opulently
   b. innocuously
   c. dolorously
   d. exquisitely

5.      **From Maya Angelou's *I Know Why the Caged Bird Sings***

   [They were] snubbed by their friends and _____ from every society.
   a. ossified
   b. oppugned
   c. ostracized
   d. deified

Though it is a good thing to have a rich vocabulary, it is not a good thing to abuse that vocabulary by writing verbose, abstruse, sesquipedalian sentences. Those who overuse their vocabularies often do so at the expense of clarity. Translate the following showy, ponderous passage into graceful, direct English. Do not use slang, but do use words that seem familiar and comfortable.

FAR, FAR AWAY IN THE TENEBROUS VACUUM OF SPACE, in a seldom-visited corner of the cosmos, was the littlest galaxy, NGC2BR2B. It was far smaller than all of the other galaxies; the big galaxies all had omnifarious millions or even opulent billions of stars, but the little one had only eighteen stars. It had five red giant stars, two fulgurating yellow stars, six hot blue stars, and five new stars that were sparkly white. Once, the littlest galaxy had swirled in a great cluster, joining the symphonic euphony of the galaxies in their radiant festival.

But the obdurate big galaxies, those execrating megalomaniacs, had ostracized NGC2BR2B from their gerontocracy of ancient galaxies, the hierarchy of the superannuated Old Ones, and had chosen every ostensible infraction to superciliously criticize it, to oppugn its best ideas, and to turn its every innocuous effort into an exquisitely dolorous experience. "You are not a true galaxy," they said. "A galaxy of only eighteen stars is not viable," they said. "You are a kleptomaniac," they said, "for you must have stolen your stars from one of us." And every effort that NGC2BR2B made to mollify the other galaxies was rebuffed with acerbic maledictions and obloquy. The ingenuous NGC2BR2B could not dissemble; it whirled softly away and gradually passed out of sight into the cosmic distance.

And then, a miracle. The eighteen stars of NGC2BR2B began to whirl introspectively and spin around. Faster and faster they raced, until BOOM, they collapsed together with a *fortissimo* implosion, transmogrifying into a black hole! And soon this black hole began to attract every solitary star that perambulated by, and every dark cloud of nebulous matter, every congeries of lost asteroids, and every unattached molecule that had no good place to be. And in no time at all, mere millions of years, NGC2BR2B became a great galaxy of 300 billion stars, the recipient of the glittering remnants of the cosmos, the tired and poor and huddled stars, yearning to join gregariously with others in a *sui generis* symphony of gravitational interaction.

And on starwheel galaxies throughout the cosmos, astronomers and cosmologists peered assiduously through huge lenses at the effulgent new galaxy, watched it whirl and spiral, lionized it, and wondered where it had come from. But only NGC2BR2B, deep in the center of its strong black hole, was cognizant how a great galactic system had been made from a small precursor.

## Reading Comprehension

1. For Translation 59, which of the following does the passage suggest?
   a. Black holes are the source of all galactic structures.
   b. The universe is stable, in a condition of unchanging stasis.
   c. The powerful overpower the powerless.
   d. Condescension and ostracism are illogical and immoral.

2. Which of the following is the best title for Translation 59?
   a. The Littlest Galaxy's Bright Idea
   b. Galaxy Wars in the Whirling Universe
   c. The Loneliness of the Long-Distance Galaxy
   d. A Neoeffulgence in the O'erhanging Firmament

## Analogies

3. **INNOCUOUS : INVIDIOUS ::**
   a. harmful : harmless
   b. harmless : harmful
   c. dolorous : viable
   d. opulent : exquisite

4. **OPPUGN : OSTRACIZE ::**
   a. obdurate : stony
   b. kleptomaniac : megalomaniac
   c. A : not A
   d. various : omnifarious

## Antonyms

5. **OPULENT :**
   a. gaudy
   b. impecunious
   c. stoic
   d. exquisite

6. **OBDURATE :**
   a. dolorous
   b. callous
   c. durable
   d. compassionate

Pompey was depicted on this coin five years after his death.

**evaluation**

Which is more **innocuous**: to be **obdurate** or to be **invidious**? Explain the criteria by which you make this evaluation. Notice that in this case you are trying to determine the least harmful of two harmfuls. I know, *harmfuls* is not a noun, or even a word. I used an adjective as though it were a noun, and even committed the **egregious** error of making it pseudoplural by adding an *s*. Ah, the perils of the ineffable.

**analysis**

Explain why the noun **kleptomaniac** means what it means, based on its etymology or stem construction. Similarly, explain the meaning of **oppugn** and of **gerontocracy**. You may use a dictionary for extra information.

**synthesis**

For any one of the words in List 59, connect the word to various works of literature or historical events with which you are familiar. For example, the word **obdurate** reminds me of Iago in Shakespeare's *Othello*, of Lady Macbeth in *Macbeth*, of Goneril and Regan in *King Lear*, and of historical events such as the Inquisition, the holocaust, Ghengis Khan's total destruction of villages that resisted his advance, Rome's final annihilation of Carthage, the destruction of autochthonous tribes and their environment in the rainforest, and American slavery. Pick one of the words, and see how many synthetic connections you can make.

**application**

For three of the words in List 59, write both a literal sentence and a metaphorical sentence. For example, the word **ossify** means to turn to bone. We could therefore use the word either in a literal sense, describing a physical process such as the ossification of the skeletal structure that takes place as a child matures, or we could describe the hardening of attitudes that characterizes those whose minds are no longer flexible:

> **Literal:** The injury would not have resulted in a broken bone in a younger person, whose bones had not **ossified** and become less flexible.

> **Metaphorical:** In Paris, the crowd's feelings had **ossified** into an obdurate pitilessness, and it cheered as the hunchback shook his fist in rage and terror from the top of the cathedral.

**imagination**

Your ship slowly descends into the atmosphere of a newly discovered planet, Omnifaria. It is characterized by **omnifarious** forms of life, millions of species never before seen by *Homo sapiens*. Imagine what you see as you explore Omnifaria. Now imagine the emotions that Marco Polo must have felt as he explored the Orient, or the excitement that Christopher Columbus must have felt as he approached the New World.

### Neologist's Lexicon

Use the stems in this list to create a new word (neologism). Give the word, the pronunciation, the part of speech, the etymology, and the definition(s). Keep a record of the neologisms you create from list to list. Here is an example:

> **ostralence** (OSS trah lent) n. [*ostra* (shell), *lent* (full of)]  1. chronic shyness, characterized by retreating mollusk-like into one's shell  2. chronic timid reluctance to interact with others

### Sesquipedalian Hamlet, or Something

One form of creative writing you might enjoy is to combine completely dissimilar things. For example, Shakespeare's *Hamlet* has been one of the crown jewels of English theater for centuries, with many actors playing the title role. Each actor has brought a unique perspective to the part. What if we were to imagine Hamlet being acted by someone who has never done so, and what if that actor was another fictional character, such as Long John Silver, or Dracula, or Tweety Bird? If Tweety Bird played the part of Hamlet, the result might be something like this:

### Good Night, Tweet Prince, or I Tought I Taw a Ghostwy Puddytat!

*Enter Tweety (I mean, Hamlet) and Horatio.*

To bewieve a ghostwy puddytat, or not to bewieve a ghostwy puddytat,
That is the question. (I DID! I DID bewieve the incorporeal admonitory puddytat!)
Whether 'tis more innocuous in the mind
To suffer the omnifarious arrows of egregious fortune,
Or to oppugn a sea of somnambulating puddytats, and by opposing, end them.
For who would bear the obdurate execrations of puddytats,
The ostracisms of puddytats, the exquisite pains inflicted by puddytats,
The invidious condescensions of opulent puddytats,
The public deifications of cartoon puddytats, the regicides of pusiwanimous puddytats,
When he could his quietus make, with a bare bodkin? To die, to sleep, to dream, but
O, Horatio, I could be immured in a nutshell and count myself a king of infinite space,
Were it not that I dream of regicidal puddytats!
But soft, what puddytat skull from yonder grave outsticks?
It IS, it IS a puddytat skull!
Alas, it is the skull of York, the King's truculent jester.
Alas, poor York. I knew him, I knew York, knew York, knew York, Horatio.
A kleptomaniac puddytat of infinite jest.
He hath belligerently chased me from my cage a thousand times.
Where be your teeth now? Your refractory mewlings? All quite ossified. Quite feckless.
Here hung those fangs that bit I know not how oft, and now how innocuous they are.
Now get you to my ladies chamber, and drink milk an inch thick, poor York.
Alas, there's more to heaven and earth, Horatio, than puddytats,
If eschatology could find it out.

| • non | (not) | *persona non grata* | • rogat | (ask) | prorogue |
| • ped | (foot) | *pied-a-terre* | • lent | (full of) | somnolent |
| • terr | (land) | *pied-a-terre* | • somn | (sleep) | somnolent |
| • **plic** | (fold) | explicit | • **cliv** | (slope) | proclivity |
| • tang | (touch) | *noli me tangere* | • vid | (look) | improvident |
| • carn | (flesh) | incarnadine | • fic | (make) | prolific |
| • pro | (for) | prorogue | • *gen* | (origin) | disingenuous |
| • sub | (under) | *sub rosa* | • in | (not) | inexorable |
| • *cracy* | (government) | hagiocracy | | | |

***persona non grata*** (unwelcome person)  She is *persona non grata* in Japan.

***pied-a-terre*** (part-time dwelling)  They have a charming *pied-a-terre* at the shore.

**explicit** (openly stated)  The agreement was explicit, not merely implicit.

***noli me tangere*** (touch me not)  We saw the *noli-me-tangere* in his anxious eyes.

**incarnadine** (flesh-colored)  Could blood turn the multitudinous seas incarnadine?

**insouciant** (not bothered, carefree)  Her insouciant vivacity charmed us.

***sub rosa*** (secretly)  The conspirators operated *sub rosa*, unknown to the government.

**prorogue** (end a session)  The long session of Parliament was finally prorogued.

**somnolent** (sleepy)  The quiet town had shady trees and somnolent dogs.

**proclivity** (discreditable tendency)  He slid down into his unfortunate proclivity for gambling.

• • •

**improvident** (without foresight)  The improvident spendthrift went broke in two years.

**prolific** (productive)  The prolific writer produced two novels each year.

**disingenuous** (insincere)  The disingenuous story convinced no one.

**hagiocracy** (government of saints)  The conservative Iranian hagiocracy ruled stringently.

**inexorable** (inescapable)  She could not escape her inexorable fate.

The older Caesar wearing the same uniform as his younger version pictured on page 292.

# ASSASSINATION OF CAESAR
## Dr. Thomas Milton Kemnitz

Caesar was energetic, able, and impatient. In the four years that the civil war raged, he was often away from Rome, but he was full of plans to improve the city and the wider Roman world. One of his lasting reforms was of the calendar so that the seasons conformed to the months of the year; with an adjustment in the eighteenth century, it is the calendar we still use today in the Western world. Most of Caesar's other reforms made the Roman state more powerful and stable. However, every such reform increased Caesar's own power and pre-eminence, including his judicial reforms and the appointment of new senators to increase the number of senators from 600 to 900. Early in 44 B.C., two of Caesar's measures particularly roused the hostility of the old patrician members of the Roman Senate. One was to assume the title of dictator for life; previously he had accepted the title of dictator for ten years. The limited term, while not welcome, still had the assurance that it would end at some future date. The designation *for life* meant that it would only end with Caesar's death, and it was unprecedented in the history of the Roman Republic. Another disquieting first was the issuance of coins with Caesar's portrait on the obverse. Until then, Roman coins had not pictured living figures.

The patrician senators began to talk of ending the dictatorship by terminating Caesar's life; talk became a conspiracy involving sixty of them, and they assassinated Caesar on the Ides of March, 44 B.C. The senators wanted to restore the Republic and their leading place in it. Many, like Brutus, had fought with Pompey against Caesar in the civil war and had accepted pardon without penalty on the generous terms that Caesar typically showed to many of his former enemies. While Alexander the Great had dealt with his defeated enemies with merciless calculation, Caesar showed a careless generosity that cost him his life. Perhaps a motivation for Caesar's actions lay in his experience as a teenager when Sulla had become dictator. The young Julius Caesar had been forced into hiding because he had been identified as an enemy of the dictator, and the old Caesar expected that everyone would be grateful that he did not inflict the same terror on Rome, but he also thought that Sulla was a fool for giving up his dictatorial powers.

If the Roman Republic was still alive on the Ides of March in 44 B.C., it died that day along with Caesar. Most or all of the senators would not have understood this at the time; for them killing Caesar would have seem like a continuance of the tradition by which Senate *Optimates* murdered *Populare* adherents—plebeian and patrician alike—who undermined their prestige, authority, and wealth, a tradition that began with the killing of Tiberius Gracchus in 133 and had been renewed at irregular intervals ever since. The governance of Rome had been a blood sport for the past eighty-nine years, and Caesar's blood seemed to them to be just another episode. But the game had changed utterly; it was no longer about gangs of men influencing elections in Rome; it was now about armies of battle-hardened legionnaires with loyalty only to their commander. Within three years almost all of the sixty senatorial conspirators were dead. Civil wars were fought with the ostensible aim of restoring the Republic, but it was a slogan, not a purpose. The civil wars were for control of the Roman world, and the victors had no interest in restoring the Republic. When those civil wars ended seventeen years later, a new generation had become used to a new reality. The Republic existed only as a taxidermist would have left it: the form was there, but its essence was gone. Rome was now a Principate and generally would be ruled by a single individual who would not willingly share power.

## As Used by James Hilton in *Lost Horizon*

| | We | have | no | rigidities, | no | **inexorable** | rules. |
|---|---|---|---|---|---|---|---|
| **Parts of Speech:** | pron. | v. | adj. | n. | adj. | **adj.** | n. |
| **Parts of Sentence:** | subj. | AVP | | D.O. | | | D.O. |

**Phrases:**      --no prepositional, appositive, or verbal phrases--

**Clauses:**      ---------------------------------independent clause----------------------------
one independent clause; a simple, declarative sentence

Here Hilton uses the adjective *inexorable* to modify the plural noun *rules*, which is the second term in a compound direct object.

## Pronunciation

| | | | |
|---|---|---|---|
| *persona non grata* | per SO na non GRAH ta | **somnolent** | SOM no lent |
| *pied-a-terre* | pee AY da TAIR | **proclivity** | pro KLIV ih tee |
| **explicit** | ex PLISS it | **improvident** | im PROV ih dent |
| *noli me tangere* | NO lee me tan JER ay | **prolific** | pro LIF ik |
| **incarnadine** | in KARN a dine | **disingenuous** | dis in JEN yoo us |
| **insouciant** | in SOO shant | **hagiocracy** | hay jee OCK ra see |
| *sub rosa* | sub RO sa | **inexorable** | in EX or ah bel |
| **prorogue** | pro ROG | | |

## Spanish Cognates

| | | | |
|---|---|---|---|
| **explicit** | explícito | **incarnadine** | encarnado |
| **somnolent** | soñoliento | **proclivity** | proclividad |
| **improvident** | impróvido | **prolific** | prolífico |
| **inexorable** | inexorable | | |

1.  The phrase ***persona non grata*** is Latin for unwelcome person and is used especially in diplomatic speech to describe a diplomatic representative who is unacceptable to the government to which he or she is assigned.

2.  In ancient times the rose was used as a symbol of secrecy, of sworn confidence, at meetings. Participants at these secret meetings held under the rose were expected to keep these ***sub rosa*** communications private and confidential.

3.  A **Micropoem**: The noun **proclivity** refers to a discreditable tendency or inclination, such as gambling. Oscar Wilde's character Dorian Gray succumbed to his proclivities. But the word comes from the Latin *proclivitas*, a steep descent, a forward (*pro*) slope (*cliv*). In order to indulge in one of your proclivities, you must descend the steep forward slope.

4.  A **Classic Word**: The adjective **inexorable** comes from the Latin *inexorabilis* and means inescapable, unrelenting, merciless. If something is inexorable, you can not (*in*) get out (*ex*) of it. There is no exit. Shakespeare, Cooper, Charlotte Brontë, Harriet Beecher Stowe, Herman Melville, Charles Dickens, Thomas Hardy, Jack London, and Edith Wharton all used *inexorable* to describe such inescapable things as disease (Stowe), truth (Wharton), a murderer (Cooper), and the soul (Brontë). In Cooper's *The Last of the Mohicans*, a victim "looks steadily on the keen glittering knife that was already upheld by his inexorable judge." Jack London described the lightning of an overburdened sled: "And so it went, the inexorable elimination of the superfluous." Perhaps the most poignant use of *inexorable* is from Shakespeare's 1596 tragedy *Romeo and Juliet*. In Act V, Scene 3, Romeo and Balthazar enter the tomb where Juliet lies, and Romeo, knowing he is going to kill himself, sends Balthazar away:

> Therefore hence, be gone.
> But if thou jealous dost return to pry
> In what I farther shall intend to do,
> By Heaven I will tear thee joint by joint
> And strew this hungry churchyard with thy limbs.
> The time and my intents are savage-wild,
> More fierce and more inexorable far
> Than empty tigers or the roaring sea.

Notice that Shakespeare's lines are poetry, written in iambic pentameter:

> But IF thou JEA lous DOST reTURN to PRY
> In WHAT I FAR ther SHALL inTEND to DO
> By HEA ven I will TEAR thee JOINT by JOINT
> And STREW this HUN gry CHURCH yard WITH thy LIMBS
> The TIME and MY inTENTS are SAV age-WILD
> More FIERCE and MORE inEX orAB le FAR
> Than EMP ty TIG ers OR the ROAR ing SEA.

In each case below, one of the choices was really the word used by the author in the sentence provided. All of the choices can be found in the example words on the first page of this lesson. Your challenge is to decide which word the author used. This is not a test; it is more like a game because more than one word choice may work perfectly well. See if you can use your sensitivity and intuition to guess correctly which word the author used.

1.  **From Upton Sinclair's** *The Jungle*

    He smiled...and then started talking again, with his blissful _____.
    a. somnolence
    b. proclivity
    c. improvidence
    d. insouciance

2.  **From Kenneth Grahame's** *The Wind in the Willows*

    ...when you live a life of intense activity for six months a year, and of comparative or actual _____ for the other six...
    a. improvidence
    b. insouciance
    c. somnolence
    d. hagiocracy

3.  **From Herman Melville's** *Billy Budd*

    [He was] a sailor of distinction even in a time _____ of renowned seamen.
    a. prolific
    b. improvident
    c. explicit
    d. inexorable

4.  **From Marjorie Kinnan Rawlings's** *The Yearling*

    In a straight line...the track of Old Slewfoot stretched _____.
    a. prolifically
    b. inexorably
    c. improvidently
    d. somnolently

5.  **From Jane Austen's** *Emma*

    _____ and double dealing seemed to meet him at every turn.
    a. insouciance
    b. improvidence
    c. disingenuousness
    d. somnolence

Though it is a good thing to have a rich vocabulary, it is not a good thing to abuse that vocabulary by writing verbose, abstruse, sesquipedalian sentences. Those who overuse their vocabularies often do so at the expense of clarity. Translate the following showy, ponderous passage into graceful, direct English. Do not use slang, but do use words that seem familiar and comfortable.

THE DAYS OF INSOUCIANT, SOMNOLENT, AND IMPROVIDENT HAPPINESS at her sunny *pied-a-terre* on the Riviera were over. Her prolific work for the State Department, at least on this assignment, was over. She had been pronounced *persona non grata* by the host government, which disingenuously accused her of proclivities to espionage, and her diplomatic duties were terminated abruptly. Why?

And then she had received the cryptic telephone call: "The grotto, sunset," the voice had said. But now as she descended the cool steps into the grotto, she sensed that there was more to this meeting than had been made explicit. Ahead, glowing from the tenebrous shadows above the transom, she saw a candlelit rose, incarnadine against the gray and black of the ancient stones, and with a chill she realized that she was entering into something beyond her understanding, some *sub rosa* secrecy, and she felt a sudden foreboding of inexorable fate bearing down upon her. Beside the rose, scrawled in red on a strip of white paper, she discerned the Latin words, *noli me tangere*, touch me not—the warning of the thirteenth-century hagiocracy believed to have mysterious followers even today, followers thought to be dangerous to those they considered miscreants or apostates. To the diplomat's mind, the warning seemed to be an eerie anachronism.

And then, a sedate figure emerged from the shadows. Hooded, physiognomy concealed in darkness, it raised its hand in a sort of benediction and then gesticulated, as if beckoning her to follow it. Her sangfroid flagged, but she stepped forward with as much fortitude as she could summon.

Suddenly the hooded figure turned and faced her. She stopped. "We know who you are," he said, *sotto voce*. "We know that you are *persona non grata*. You are in danger. There is a schism in the Intelligence Division, and you are being linked to subversive activities. You are being watched by people with xenophobic and paranoid ideas. Their antipathy is inexorable. You must leave the country at once." He paused, and she could see the light of the candle behind her sparkling surrealistically in the hooded figure's eyes. "Leave the country at once," he reiterated in valediction, and then he was gone. There was something about his voice . . . . But it was too late to remonstrate, and she turned without temporizing, ascended the steps, and two hours later, with a suspiration of relief, she boarded a plane for Paris.

## Reading Comprehension

1. In Translation 60, it can be inferred that:
    a. The hooded figure is a government employee.
    b. The hooded figure is lying to scare the diplomat out of the country.
    c. The diplomat is a spy.
    d. The diplomat would recognize the figure if she could see him.

2. The author does all of the following EXCEPT:
    a. suggest the identity of the hooded figure
    b. suggest that the diplomat is innocent of intrigue
    c. suggest that the diplomat is afraid
    d. suggest that the hooded figure wishes not to be identified

## Analogies

3. **INCARNADINE : CARNATION ::**
    a. rose : thorn
    b. azure : blue
    c. green : grass
    d. blood : vein

4. **SUB ROSA : EXPLICIT ::**
    a. insouciant : somnolent
    b. prolific : hebetude
    c. cryptic : manifest
    d. arcane : overt

## Antonyms

5. **IMPROVIDENT :**
    a. economical
    b. squandering
    c. dissipated
    d. proved

6. **PROROGUE :**
    a. *pro rata*
    b. prolific
    c. prologue
    d. prohibit

When the senatorial conspirators whispered to one another about why they needed to kill Caesar, one of the items on their list would have been these coins, the first ever issued in Rome with a living person depicted on them. They were issued in 44 B.C., and Caesar did not live long thereafter, but he was alive when they first appeared.

## imagination and aesthetics

Imagine a scene in which you feel completely **insouciant**. It could be a happy time that you create in your own imagination, or it could be a memory of a day at the beach, or a hike on a mountain path, or a trip to a foreign city, or a happy time that you have spent with a friend or a pet. Any insouciant time will do. Imagine this insouciant time vividly and concretely. Try to see the colors, smell the smells, feel the breeze on your face, and so forth. Write a one-page description that captures this insouciant mood.

## intuition and imagination

You walk out the front door of your *pied-a-terre* in Athens on an expedition to find and purchase something you have been thinking about for a long time. You have the money now, and as the breezy Mediterranean sun strikes your face, you detect the scent of olive oil in the air and **insouciantly** hurry off down the sidewalk to find the **exquisite** object you imagine. What is it that you are looking for?

## convergence

Which two words in List 60 do you think are the most interesting? Why? Which two would you most like to use frequently in conversation? Why?

## analysis

Using a dictionary, study the etymology of **improvident**, **prolific**, and **disingenuous**, and see if you can explain why each word means what it means.

## ethics and evaluation

Think of a **disingenuous** literary character with whom you are familiar, such as Long John Silver in Robert Louis Stevenson's *Treasure Island*, or Iago in Shakespeare's *Othello*, or Captain Hook in Barrie's *Peter Pan*. Long John pretended to be Jim Hawkins's friend but was not. Iago pretended to be Othello's friend but actually schemed to destroy Othello and Desdemona. Captain Hook was a treacherous dissembler who had nothing but malevolent intentions toward Peter Pan, Wendy, and the boys. On the other hand, Hamlet is also disingenuous but is not a villain. Polonius's foolish words, "To thine own self be true, and it must follow as the night the day, thou canst not then be false to any man," do not apply to Hamlet, who is true to himself but false to others as he stealthily attempts to observe his murdering uncle. It would appear that Hamlet is disingenuous in the cause of righteousness. What do you think? Are there times when it is acceptable or moral to be disingenuous if the reasons have merit, or is it inherently wrong to be disingenuous, regardless of the cause? Explain your thinking about disingenuousness, including the criteria by which you come to a decision.

### Neologist's Lexicon

Use the stems in this list to create a new word (neologism). Give the word, the pronunciation, the part of speech, the etymology, and the definition(s). Keep a record of the neologisms you create from list to list. Here are some examples:

**carnorogation** (KAR noh row GAY shun) n. [*carn* (flesh), *rogat* (ask), *tion* (act)] 1. the cheeky habit of asking others how much they weigh 2. the obsessive need to read all of the dietary information on every item of packaged food in the supermarket before adding it to the shopping cart

**vidotangence** (VID oh TAN jence) n. [*vid* (look), *tang* (touch)] 1. eye contact 2. the initial indication of romantic attraction, as seen in the eye

### Sesquipedalian Mud Pies

It goes without saying that one of life's great pleasures is making mud pies. And sand castles, of course, but sand castles are disturbingly clean and have none of the complete relish of the correctly made mud pie, which results in the happiest sort of mess in which the discriminating playful person can find himself or herself. The question is, can you write sesquipedalian instructions for the prolific production of exquisite mud pies and their subsequent use? See if you can write mud pie instructions using words from List 60 and previous lists.

### Sesquipedalian Fair

Another of life's great events is going to the fair. There are rides and games and haunted houses. There are snow cones, cotton candy, and hot dogs. There are the smells of sawdust and ponies and the mechanical smell of grease on the machinery. There are the sounds of the crowd and the music of the rides and the calls of the employees drumming up business. Pick a scene or experience from the fair, and write a short sesquipedalian description of it using words from as many lists as you can.

On this coin, Marcus Junius Brutus celebrates the slaying of Caesar with twin daggers on the reverse and his portrait on the obverse.

### Dr. Robert T. Grauer

Dr. Robert T. Grauer is an Associate Professor in the Department of Computer Information Systems at the University of Miami, where he has been honored with the Outstanding Teacher Award in the School of Business. He is the vision behind the Exploring Series, which is about to sell its 3 millionth copy.

Dr. Grauer has written more than 50 books on programming and information systems. His work has been translated into three foreign languages and is used in all aspects of higher education at both national and international levels.

Dr. Grauer also has been a consultant to several major corporations including IBM and American Express. He received his Ph.D. in operations research in 1972 from the Polytechnic Institute of Brooklyn.

### Robert McCloud

Robert McCloud is Associate Professor of Computer Science and Information Technology at Sacred Heart University in Fairfield, Connecticut. An Honors graduate of Williams College, he first studied computer programming in graduate school at the University of Pennsylvania, and completed his doctorate at the University of Bridgeport. As a Robert Johnson Fellow, he studied in London and has also been a visiting professor in Luxembourg.

Robert has also been awarded a Fulbright Fellowship at the American University in Kosovo for the academic year 2007-08.

He has three sons and a Boxer dog. He divides his time between Connecticut and Mt. Camelback in Pennsylvania.

### Dr. Keith Mulbery

Dr. Keith Mulbery is an Associate Professor in the Information Systems and Technology Department at Utah Valley State College, where he teaches computer applications, programming, and MIS classes. He has written more than 15 software textbooks and business communication test banks. In January 2001, he received the Utah Valley State College Board of Trustees Award of Excellence for authoring *MOUS Essentials Word 2000*. In addition to his series editor and authoring experience, he also served as a developmental editor on two word processing textbooks. In 2007, he received the UVSC School of Technology and Computing Scholar Award.

He received his B.S. and M.Ed. (majoring in Business Education) from Southwestern Oklahoma State University and earned his Ph.D. in Education with an emphasis in Business Information Systems at Utah State University in 2006. His dissertation topic was computer-assisted instruction using TAIT to supplement traditional instruction in basic computer proficiency courses.

# (ex•ploring)

SERIES

1. To investigate in a systematic way: examine. 2. To search
into or range over for the purpose of discovery.

Getting Started with the

# Online Experience

## Robert T. Grauer

Robert McCloud | Keith Mulbery

PEARSON

Prentice
Hall

**Upper Saddle River
New Jersey 07458**

Library of Congress Cataloging-in-Publication Data

Grauer, Robert T., 1945-
  Getting started with the online experience / Robert T. Grauer, Keith Mulbery.
     p. cm. — (Exploring)
  At head of title: Microsoft
  ISBN-13: 978-013-235053-2
  ISBN-10: 0-13-235053-X
  1.  Computer networks—Remote access. 2.  Internet—Safety measures.  I. Title: Microsoft getting
started with the online experience. II. Mulbery, Keith. III. Title.
  TK5105.597.G73 2007
  025.04—dc22

2007026348

**Vice President and Publisher:** Natalie E. Anderson
**Associate VP/ Executive Acquisitions Editor, Print:** Stephanie Wall
**Executive Acquisitions Editor, Media:** Richard Keaveny
**Sr. Acquisitions Editor:** Melissa Sabella
**Product Development Manager:** Eileen Bien Calabro
**Sr. Editorial Project Manager/Development:** Eileen Clark
**Editorial Project Manager/Assistant Editor:** Jenelle J. Woodrup
**Market Development Editor:** Claire Hunter
**Editorial Assistant:** Rebecca Knauer
**Executive Producer:** Lisa Strite
**Content Development Manager:** Cathi Profitko
**Project Manager, Media:** Ashley Lulling
**Director of Marketing:** Margaret Waples
**Sr. Marketing Manager:** Scott Davidson
**Sr. Sales Associate:** Rebecca Scott
**Sr. Managing Editor:** Cynthia Zonneveld
**Associate Managing Editor:** Camille Trentacoste
**Production Project Manager:** Lynne Breitfeller
**Sr. Operations Supervisor:** Nick Sklitsis
**Production Media Project Manager:** Lorena E. Cerisano
**Design Director:** Maria Lange
**Art Director/Interior and Cover Design:** Blair Brown
**Cover Illustration/Photo:** Courtesy of Getty Images/Laurent Hamels
**Composition:** GGS Book Services
**Project Management:** GGS Book Services
**Project Manager:** Kevin Bradley
**Production Editor:** Andrea Shearer
**Cover Printer:** Phoenix Color
**Printer/Binder:** Banta/Menasha

10 9 8 7 6 5 4 3 2 1

ISBN-13: 978-013-235053-2
ISBN-10:   0-13-235053-X

## Dedications

To Marion—my wife, my lover, and my best friend.

*Robert Grauer*


I would like to dedicate this book to my family and close friends who provided a strong community of emotional support and patience as I completed my doctorate program and worked on this edition of the Exploring series.

*Keith Mulbery*

# Contents

## CHAPTER ONE | The Online Experience      1

# Acknowledgments

The success of the Exploring series is attributed to contributions from numerous individuals. First and foremost, our heartfelt appreciation to Melissa Sabella, senior acquisitions editor, for providing new leadership and direction to capitalize on the strength and tradition of the Exploring series while implementing innovative ideas into the Exploring Office 2007 edition. Scott Davidson, senior marketing manager, was an invaluable addition to the team who believes in the mission of this series passionately and did an amazing job communicating its message.

During the first few months of the project, Eileen Clark, senior editorial project manager, kept the team focused on the vision, pedagogy, and voice that has been the driving force behind the success of the Exploring series. Claire Hunter, market development editor, facilitated communication between the editorial team and the reviewers to ensure that this edition meets the changing needs of computer professors and students at the collegiate level. Keith Mulbery gave up many nights and weekends (including Thanksgiving) to jump in and help out with anything that was asked of him, including assisting with topical organization, reviewing and revising content, capturing screenshots, and ensuring chapter manuscripts adhered to series guidelines.

Jenelle Woodrup, editorial project manager/assistant editor, masterfully managed the flow of manuscript files among the authors, editorial team, and production to ensure timely publication of series. Laura Town, developmental editor, provided an objective perspective in reviewing the content and organization of selected chapters. Eileen Calabro, product development manager, facilitated communication among the editorial team, authors, and production during a transitional stage. The at GGS worked through software delays, style changes and anything else we threw at them to bring the whole thing together. Art director Blair Brown's conversations with students and professors across the country yielded a design that addressed the realities of today's students with function and style.

A special thanks to the following for the use of their work in the PowerPoint section of the text: Cameron Martin, Ph.D., Assistant to the President, Utah Valley State College, for the use of the Institutional Policies and Procedures Approval Process flowchart; Nick Finner, Paralegal Studies, Utah Valley State College, for the use of his research relating to the elderly population residing in the prisons of Utah; Ryan Phillips, Xeric Landscape and Design (XericUtah.com), for sharing Xeric's concepts for creating beautiful, drought-tolerant landscapes and for the photographs illustrating these concepts; Jo Porter, Photographer, Mapleton, Utah, for allowing the use of her beautiful engagement and wedding photographs; and David and Ali Valeti for the photographs of their baby and their family.

The following organizations and individuals generously provided data and structure from their organizational databases: Replacements, Ltd., Shweta Ponnappa, JC Raulston Arboretum at North Carolina State University, and Valerie Tyson. We deeply appreciate the ability to give students a feel for "real" data.

The new members of the Exploring author team would like to especially thank Bob Grauer for his vision in developing Exploring and his leadership in creating this highly successful series. We also extend appreciation to Lynn Hogan, for her dedication and commitment to this book.

Maryann Barber would like to thank Bob Grauer for a wonderful collaboration and providing the opportunities through which so much of her life has changed.

The Exploring team would like to especially thank the following instructors who drew on their experience in the classroom and their software expertise to give us daily advice on how to improve this book. Their impact can be seen on every page:

Barbara Stover, Marion Technical College

Bob McCloud, Sacred Heart University

Cassie Georgetti, Florida Technical College

Dana Johnson, North Dakota State University

Jackie Lamoureux, Central New Mexico Community College

Jim Pepe, Bentley College

Judy Brown, The University of Memphis

Lancie Anthony Affonso, College of Charleston

Mimi Duncan, University of Missouri – St. Louis

Minnie Proctor, Indian River Community College

Richard Albright, Goldey-Beacom College

We also want to acknowledge all the reviewers of the Exploring 2007 series. Their valuable comments and constructive criticism greatly improved this edition:

Aaron Schorr
Fashion Institute of Technology

Alicia Stonesifer
La Salle University

Allen Alexander, Delaware
Tech & Community College

Amy Williams, Abraham
Baldwin Agriculture College

Annie Brown
Hawaii Community College

Barbara Cierny
Harper College

Barbara Hearn
Community College of Philadelphia

Barbara Meguro
University of Hawaii at Hilo

Bette Pitts
South Plains College

Beverly Fite
Amarillo College

Bill Wagner
Villanova

Brandi N. Guidry
University of Louisiana at Lafayette

Brian Powell
West Virginia University – Morgantown
Campus

Carl Farrell
Hawaii Pacific University

Carl Penzuil
Ithaca College

Carole Bagley;
University of St. Thomas

Catherine Hain
Central New Mexico CC

Charles Edwards
University of Texas of the Permian Basin

Christine L. Moore
College of Charleston

David Barnes
Penn State Altoona

David Childress;
Ashland Community College

David Law, Alfred
State College

Dennis Chalupa
Houston Baptist

Diane Stark
Phoenix College

Dianna Patterson
Texarkana College

Dianne Ross
University of Louisiana at Lafayette

Dr. Behrooz Saghafi
Chicago State University

Dr. Gladys Swindler
Fort Hays State University

Dr. Joe Teng
Barry University

Dr. Karen Nantz
Eastern Illinois University.

Duane D. Lintner
Amarillo College

Elizabeth Edmiston
North Carolina Central University

Erhan Uskup
Houston Community College

Fred Hills, McClellan
Community College

Gary R. Armstrong
Shippensburg University of Pennsylvania

Glenna Vanderhoof
Missouri State

Gregg Asher
Minnesota State University, Mankato

Hong K. Sung
University of Central Oklahoma

Hyekyung Clark
Central New Mexico CC

J Patrick Fenton
West Valley College

Jana Carver
Amarillo College

Jane Cheng
Bloomfield College

Janos T. Fustos
Metropolitan State College of Denver

Jeffrey A Hassett
University of Utah

Jennifer Pickle
Amarillo College

Jerry Kolata
New England Institute of Technology

Jesse Day
South Plains College

John Arehart
Longwood University

John Lee Reardon
University of Hawaii, Manoa

Joshua Mindel
San Francisco State University

Karen Wisniewski
County College of Morris

Karl Smart
Central Michigan University

Kathryn L. Hatch
University of Arizona

Krista Terry
Radford University

Laura McManamon
University of Dayton

Laura Reid
University of Western Ontario

Linda Johnsonius
Murray State University

Lori Kelley
Madison Area Technical College

Lucy Parker,
California State University, Northridge

Lynda Henrie
LDS Business College

Malia Young
Utah State University

Margie Martyn
Baldwin Wallace

Marianne Trudgeon
Fanshawe College

Marilyn Hibbert
Salt Lake Community College

Marjean Lake
LDS Business College

Mark Olaveson
Brigham Young University

Nancy Sardone
Seton Hall University

Patricia Joseph
Slippery Rock University.

Patrick Hogan
Cape Fear Community College

Paula F. Bell
Lock Haven University of Pennsylvania

Paulette Comet
Community College of Baltimore County,
Catonsville

Pratap Kotala
North Dakota State University

Richard Blamer
John Carroll University

Richard Herschel
St. Joseph's University

Richard Hewer
Ferris State University

Robert Gordon
Hofstra University

Robert Marmelstein
East Stroudsburg University

Robert Stumbur
Northern Alberta Institute of Technology

Roberta I. Hollen
University of Central Oklahoma

Roland Moreira
South Plains College

Ron Murch
University of Calgary

Rory J. de Simone
University of Florida

Ruth Neal
Navarro College

Sandra M. Brown
Finger Lakes Community College

Sharon Mulroney
Mount Royal College

Stephen E. Lunce
Midwestern State University

Steve Schwarz
Raritan Valley Community College

Steven Choy
University of Calgary

Susan Byrne
St. Clair College

Thomas Setaro
Brookdale Community College

Todd McLeod
Fresno City College

Vickie Pickett
Midland College

Vipul Gupta
St Joseph's University

Vivek Shah
Texas State University - San Marcos

Wei-Lun Chuang
Utah State University

William Dorin
Indiana University Northwest

Finally, we wish to acknowledge reviewers of previous editions of the Exploring series—we wouldn't have made it to the 7th edition without you:

Alan Moltz
Naugatuck Valley Technical Community
College

Alok Charturvedi
Purdue University

Antonio Vargas
El Paso Community College

Barbara Sherman
Buffalo State College

Bill Daley
University of Oregon

Bill Morse
DeVry Institute of Technology

Bonnie Homan
San Francisco State University

Carl M. Briggs
Indiana University School of Business

Carlotta Eaton
Radford University

Carolyn DiLeo
Westchester Community College

Cody Copeland
Johnson County Community College

Connie Wells
Georgia State University

Daniela Marghitu
Auburn University

David B. Meinert
Southwest Missouri State University

David Douglas
University of Arkansas

David Langley
University of Oregon

David Rinehard
Lansing Community College

David Weiner
University of San Francisco

Dean Combellick
Scottsdale Community College

Delores Pusins
Hillsborough Community College

Don Belle
Central Piedmont Community College

Douglas Cross
Clackamas Community College

Ernie Ivey
Polk Community College

Gale E. Rand
College Misericordia

Helen Stoloff
Hudson Valley Community College

Herach Safarian
College of the Canyons

Jack Zeller
Kirkwood Community College

James Franck
College of St. Scholastica

James Gips
Boston College

Jane King
Everett Community College

Janis Cox
Tri-County Technical College

Jerry Chin
Southwest Missouri State University

Jill Chapnick
Florida International University

Jim Pruitt
Central Washington University

John Lesson
University of Central Florida

John Shepherd
Duquesne University

Judith M. Fitspatrick
Gulf Coast Community College

Judith Rice
Santa Fe Community College

Judy Dolan
Palomar College

Karen Tracey
Central Connecticut State University

Kevin Pauli
University of Nebraska

Kim Montney
Kellogg Community College

Kimberly Chambers
Scottsdale Community College

Larry S. Corman
Fort Lewis College

Lynn Band
Middlesex Community College

Margaret Thomas
Ohio University

Marguerite Nedreberg
Youngstown State University

Marilyn Salas
Scottsdale Community College

Martin Crossland
Southwest Missouri State University

Mary McKenry Percival
University of Miami

Michael Hassett
Fort Hayes State University

Michael Stewardson
San Jacinto College – North

Midge Gerber
Southwestern Oklahoma State University

Mike Hearn
Community College of Philadelphia

Mike Kelly
Community College of Rhode Island

Mike Thomas
Indiana University School of Business

Paul E. Daurelle
Western Piedmont Community College

Ranette Halverson
Midwestern State University

Raymond Frost
Central Connecticut State University

Robert Spear, Prince
George's Community College

Rose M. Laird
Northern Virginia Community College

Sally Visci
Lorain County Community College

Shawna DePlonty
Sault College of Applied Arts and Technology

Stuart P. Brian
Holy Family College

Susan Fry
Boise State Universtiy

Suzanne Tomlinson
Iowa State University

Vernon Griffin
Austin Community College

Wallace John Whistance-Smith
Ryerson Polytechnic University

Walter Johnson
Community College of Philadelphia

Wanda D. Heller
Seminole Community College

We very much appreciate the following individuals for painstakingly checking every step and every explanation for technical accuracy, while dealing with an entirely new software application:

Barbara Waxer
Bill Daley
Beverly Fite
Dawn Wood
Denise Askew
Elizabeth Lockley

James Reidel
Janet Pickard
Janice Snyder
Jeremy Harris
John Griffin
Joyce Neilsen

LeeAnn Bates
Mara Zebest
Mary E. Pascarella
Michael Meyers
Sue McCrory

# Preface

## The Exploring Series

Exploring has been Prentice Hall's most successful Office Application series of the past 15 years. For Office 2007 Exploring has undergone the most extensive changes in its history, so that it can truly move today's student "beyond the point and click."

The goal of Exploring has always been to teach more than just the steps to accomplish a task – the series provides the theoretical foundation necessary for a student to understand when and why to apply a skill. This way, students achieve a broader understanding of Office.

Today's students are changing and Exploring has evolved with them. Prentice Hall traveled to college campuses across the country and spoke directly to students to determine how they study and prepare for class. We also spoke with hundreds of professors about the best ways to administer materials to such a diverse body of students.

## Here is what we learned

**Students go to college now with a different set of skills than they did 5 years ago**. The new edition of Exploring moves students beyond the basics of the software at a faster pace, without sacrificing coverage of the fundamental skills that everybody needs to know. This ensures that students will be engaged from Chapter 1 to the end of the book.

**Students have diverse career goals.** With this in mind, we broadened the examples in the text (and the accompanying Instructor Resources) to include the health sciences, hospitality, urban planning, business and more. Exploring will be relevant to every student in the course.

**Students read, prepare and study differently than they used to.** Rather than reading a book cover to cover students want to easily identify what they need to know, and then learn it efficiently. We have added key features that will bring students into the content and make the text easy to use such as objective mapping, pull quotes, and key terms in the margins.

## Moving students beyond the point and click

All of these additions mean students will be more engaged, achieve a higher level of understanding, and successfully complete this course. In addition to the experience and expertise of the series creator and author Robert T. Grauer we have assembled a tremendously talented team of supporting authors to assist with this critical revision. Each of them is equally dedicated to the Exploring mission of **moving students beyond the point and click.**

# Key Features of the Office 2007 revision include

- **New** **Office Fundamentals Chapter** efficiently covers skills common among all applications like save, print, and bold to avoid repetition in each Office application's first chapter, along with coverage of problem solving skills to prepare students to apply what they learn in any situation.

- **New** **Moving Beyond the Basics** introduces advanced skills earlier because students are learning basic skills faster.

- **White Pages/Yellow Pages clearly** distinguish the theory (white pages) from the skills covered in the Hands-On exercises (yellow pages) so students always know what they are supposed to be doing.

- **New** **Objective Mapping** enables students to skip the skills and concepts they know, and quickly find those they don't, by scanning the chapter opener page for the page numbers of the material they need.

- **New** **Pull Quotes** entice students into the theory by highlighting the most interesting points.

- **New** **Conceptual Animations** connect the theory with the skills, by illustrating tough to understand concepts with interactive multimedia.

- **New** **More End of Chapter Exercises** offer instructors more options for assessment. Each chapter has approximately 12–15 exercises ranging from Multiple Choice questions to open-ended projects.

- **New** **More Levels of End of Chapter Exercises,** including new Mid-Level Exercises tell students what to do, but not how to do it, and Capstone Exercises cover all of the skills within each chapter.

- **New** **Mini Cases with Rubrics** are open ended exercises that guide both instructors and students to a solution with a specific rubric for each mini case.

# Instructor and Student Resources

### Instructor Chapter Reference Cards

A four page color card for every chapter that includes a:

- *Concept Summary* that outlines the KEY objectives to cover in class with tips on where students get stuck as well as how to get them un-stuck. It helps bridge the gap between the instructor and student when discussing more difficult topics.

- *Case Study Lecture Demonstration Document* which provides instructors with a lecture sample based on the chapter opening case that will guide students to critically use the skills covered in the chapter, with examples of other ways the skills can be applied.

### The Enhanced Instructor's Resource Center on CD-ROM includes:

- **Additional Capstone Production Tests** allow instructors to assess all the skills in a chapter with a single project.

- **Mini Case Rubrics** in Microsoft® Word format enable instructors to customize the assignment for their class.

- **PowerPoint® Presentations** for each chapter with notes included for online students.

- **Lesson Plans** that provide a detailed blueprint for an instructor to achieve chapter learning objectives and outcomes.

- **Student Data Files**

- **Annotated Solution Files**

- **Complete Test Bank**

- **Test Gen Software with QuizMaster**

**TestGen** is a test generator program that lets you view and easily edit testbank questions, transfer them to tests, and print in a variety of formats suitable to your teaching situation. The program also offers many options for organizing and displaying testbanks and tests. A random number test generator enables you to create multiple versions of an exam.

**QuizMaster**, also included in this package, allows students to take tests created with TestGen on a local area network. The QuizMaster Utility built into TestGen lets instructors view student records and print a variety of reports. Building tests is easy with Test-Gen, and exams can be easily uploaded into WebCT, BlackBoard, and CourseCompass.

### Prentice Hall's Companion Web Site

www.prenhall.com/exploring offers expanded IT resources and downloadable supplements. This site also includes an online study guide for student self-study.

### Online Course Cartridges

Flexible, robust and customizable content is available for all major online course platforms that include everything instructors need in one place.
www.prenhall.com/webct
www.prenhall.com/blackboard
www.coursecompass.com

# Visual Walk-Through

## Customize, Analyze, and Summarize Query Data
### Creating and Using Queries to Make Decisions

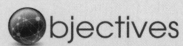bjectives

After you read this chapter you will be able to:

1. Understand the order of precedence (**page 679**).
2. Create a calculated field in a query (**page 679**).
3. Create expressions with the Expression Builder (**page 679**).
4. Create and edit Access functions (**page 690**).
5. Perform date arithmetic (**page 694**).
6. Create and work with data aggregates (**page 704**).

## Objective Mapping

allows students to skip the skills and concepts they know and quickly find those they don't by scanning the chapter opening page for the page numbers of the material they need.

### Hands-On Exercises

| Exercises | Skills Covered |
|---|---|
| 1. CALCULATED QUERY FIELDS (PAGE 683) <br> **Open:** chap3_ho1-3_realestate.accdb <br> **Save:** chap3_ho1-3_realestate_solution.accdb <br> **Back up as:** chap3_ho1_realestate_solution.accdb | • Copy a Database and Start the Query  • Select the Fields, Save, and Open the Query  • Create a Calculated Field and Run the Query  • Verify the Calculated Results  • Recover from a Common Error |
| 2. EXPRESSION BUILDER, FUNCTIONS, AND DATE ARITHMETIC (**page 695**) <br> **Open:** chap3_ho1-3_realestate.accdb <br> (from Exercise 1) <br> **Save:** chap3_ho1-3_realestate_solution.accdb <br> (additional modifications) <br> **Back up as:** chap3_ho2_realestate_solution.accdb | • Create a Select Query  • Use the Expression Builder  • Create Calculations Using Input Stored in a Different Query or Table  • Edit Expressions Using the Expression Builder  • Use Functions  • Work with Date Arithmetic |
| 3. DATA AGGREGATES (**page 707**) <br> **Open:** chap3_ho1-3_realestate.accdb <br> (from Exercise 2) <br> **Save:** chap3_ho1-3_realestate_solution.accdb <br> (additional modifications) | • Add a Total Row  • Create a Totals Query Based on a Select Query  • Add Fields to the Design Grid  • Add Grouping Options and Specify Summary Statistics |

Access 2007    677

## Case Study

begins each chapter to provide an effective overview of what students can accomplish by completing the chapter.

# CASE STUDY

## West Transylvania College Athletic Department

The athletic department of West Transylvania College has reached a fork in the road. A significant alumni contingent insists that the college upgrade its athletic program from NCAA Division II to Division I. This process will involve adding sports, funding athletic scholarships, expanding staff, and coordinating a variety of fundraising activities.

Tom Hunt, the athletic director, wants to determine if the funding support is available both inside and outside the college to accomplish this goal. You are helping Tom prepare the five-year projected budget based on current budget figures. The plan is to increase revenues at a rate of 10% per year for five years while handling an estimated 8% increase in expenses over the same five-year period. Tom feels that a 10% increase in revenue versus an 8% increase in expenses should make the upgrade viable. Tom wants to examine how increased alumni giving, increases in college fees, and grant monies will increase the revenue flow. The Transylvania College's Athletic Committee and its Alumni Association Board of Directors want Tom to present an analysis of funding and expenses to determine if the move to NCAA Division I is feasible. As Tom's student assistant this year, it is your responsibility to help him with special projects. Tom prepared the basic projected budget spreadsheet and has asked you to finish it for him.

`Case Study`

### Your Assignment

- Read the chapter carefully and pay close attention to mathematical operations, formulas, and functions.
- Open *chap2_case_athletics*, which contains the partially completed, projected budget spreadsheet.
- Study the structure of the worksheet to determine what type of formulas you need to complete the financial calculations. Identify how you would perform calculations if you were using a calculator and make a list of formulas using regular language to determine if the financial goals will be met. As you read the chapter, identify formulas and functions that will help you complete the financial analysis. You will insert formulas in the revenue and expenditures sections for column C. Use appropriate cell references in formulas. Do not enter constant values within a formula; instead enter the 10% and 8% increases in an input area. Use appropriate functions for column totals in both the revenue and expenditures sections. Insert formulas for the Net Operating Margin and Net Margin rows. Copy the formulas.
- Review the spreadsheet and identify weaknesses in the formatting. Use your knowledge of good formatting design to improve the appearance of the spreadsheet so that it will be attractive to the Athletic Committee and the alumni board. You will format cells as currency with 0 decimals and widen columns as needed. Merge and center the title and use an attractive fill color. Emphasize the totals and margin rows with borders. Enter your name and current date. Create a custom footer that includes a page number and your instructor's name. Print the worksheet as displayed and again with cell formulas displayed. Save the workbook as **chap2_case_athletics_solution**.

## Key Terms

are called out in the
margins of the chapter
so students can more
effectively study definitions.

## Pull Quotes

entice students into the
theory by highlighting the most
interesting points.

## Tables

A *table* is a series of rows and columns that organize data.

A *cell* is the intersection of a row and column in a table.

> The table feature is one of the most powerful in Word and is the basis for an almost limitless variety of documents. It is very easy to create once you understand how a table works.

A *table* is a series of rows and columns that organize data effectively. The rows and columns in a table intersect to form *cells*. The table feature is one of the most powerful in Word and is an easy way to organize a series of data in a columnar list format such as employee names, inventory lists, and e-mail addresses. The Vacation Planner in Figure 3.1, for example, is actually a 4x9 table (4 columns and 9 rows). The completed table looks impressive, but it is very easy to create once you understand how a table works. In addition to the organizational benefits, tables make an excellent alignment tool. For example, you can create tables to organize data such as employee lists with phone numbers and e-mail addresses. The Exploring series uses tables to provide descriptions for various software commands. Although you can align text with tabs, you have more format control when you create a table. (See the Practice Exercises at the end of the chapter for other examples.)

| Vacation Planner | | | |
|---|---|---|---|
| Item | Number of Days | Amount per Day (est) | Total Amount |
| Airline Ticket | | | 449.00 |
| Amusement Park Tickets | 4 | 50.00 | 200.00 |
| Hotel | 5 | 120.00 | 600.00 |
| Meals | 6 | 50.00 | 300.00 |
| Rental Car | 5 | 30.00 | 150.00 |
| Souvenirs | 5 | 20.00 | 100.00 |
| TOTAL EXPECTED EXPENSES | | | $1799.00 |

Figure 3.1  The Vacation Planner

In this section, you insert a table in a document. After inserting the table, you can insert or delete columns and rows if you need to change the structure. Furthermore, you learn how to merge and split cells within the table. Finally, you change the row height and column width to accommodate data in the table.

### Inserting a Table

You can create a table from the Insert tab. Click Table in the Tables group on the Insert tab to see a gallery of cells from which you select the number of columns and rows you require in the table, or you can choose the Insert Table command below the gallery to display the Insert Table dialog box and enter the table composition you prefer. When you select the table dimension from the gallery or from the Insert Table dialog box, Word creates a table structure with the number of columns and rows you specify. After you define a table, you can enter text, numbers, or graphics in individual cells. Text

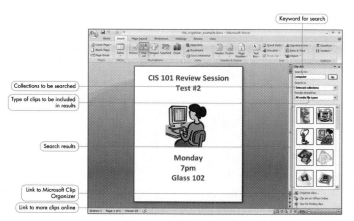

Keyword for search

Collections to be searched

Type of clips to be included in results

Search results

Link to Microsoft Clip Organizer

Link to more clips online

CIS 101 Review Session
Test #2

Monday
7pm
Glass 102

Figure 3.18 The Clip Art Task Pane

You can access the Microsoft Clip Organizer (to view the various collections) by clicking Organize clips at the bottom of the Clip Art task pane. You also can access the Clip Organizer when you are not using Word; click the Start button on the taskbar, click All Programs, Micros... Clip Organizer. Once in the Organi... ous collections, reorganize the exist... add new clips (with their associated... the bottom of the task pane in Figur... and tips for finding more relevant cl...

### Insert a Picture

In addition to the collection of clip... you also can insert your own picture... ital camera attached to your comput... Word. After you save the picture to... on the Insert tab to locate and insert... opens so that you can navigate to th... insert the picture, there are many c... mands are discussed in the next sect...

### Formatting a Grap...

( Remember that graphical elements should enhance a document, not overpower it. )

When you inse... fined size. For... very large and... resized. Most ti... within the do...

**220** CHAPTER 3 | Enhancing a Document

---

# White Pages/ Yellow Pages

clearly distinguishes the theory (white pages) from the skills covered in the Hands-On exercises (yellow pages) so students always know what they are supposed to be doing.

---

## Step 2
### Move and Resize the Clip Art Object

Refer to Figure 3.24 as you complete Step 2.

**a.** Click once on the clip art object to select it. Click **Text Wrapping** in the Arrange group on the Picture Tools Format tab to display the text wrapping options, and then select **Square**, as shown in Figure 3.24.

You must change the layout in order to move and size the object.

**b.** Click **Position** in the Arrange group, and then click **More Layout Options.** Click the **Picture Position tab** in the Advanced Layout dialog box, if necessary, then click **Alignment** in the *Horizontal* section. Click the **Alignment drop-down arrow** and select **Right.** Deselect the **Allow overlap check box** in the *Options* section. Click **OK.**

**c.** Click **Crop** in the Size group, then hold your mouse over the sizing handles and notice how the pointer changes to angular shapes. Click the **bottom center handle** and drag it up. Drag the side handles inward to remove excess space surrounding the graphical object.

**d.** Click the Shape **Height box** in the Size group and type **2.77.**

Notice the width is changed automatically to retain the proportion.

**e.** Save the document.

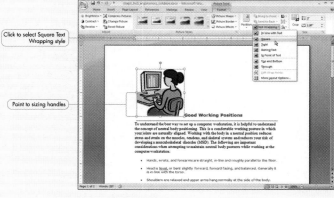

Click to select Square Text Wrapping style

Point to sizing handles

**Good Working Positions**

Figure 3.24 Formatting Clip Art

## Step 3
### Create a WordArt Object

Refer to Figure 3.25 as you complete Step 3.

**a.** Press **Ctrl+End** to move to the end of the document. Click the **Insert tab,** and then click **WordArt** in the Text group to display the WordArt gallery.

**b.** Click **WordArt Style 28** on the bottom row of the gallery.

The Edit WordArt Text dialog box displays, as shown in Figure 3.25.

**228** CHAPTER 3 | Enhancing a Document

# Summary

1. **Create a presentation using a template.** Using a template saves you a great deal of time and enables you to create a more professional presentation. Templates incorporate a theme, a layout, and content that can be modified. You can use templates that are installed when Microsoft Office is installed, or you can download templates from Microsoft Office Online. Microsoft is constantly adding templates to the online site for your use.

2. **Modify a template.** In addition to changing the content of a template, you can modify the structure and design. The structure is modified by changing the layout of a slide. To change the layout, drag placeholders to new locations or resize placeholders. You can even add placeholders so that elements such as logos can be included.

3. **Create a presentation in Outline view.** When you use a storyboard to determine your content, you create a basic outline. Then you can enter your presentation in Outline view, which enables you to concentrate on the content of the presentation. Using Outline view keeps you from getting buried in design issues at the cost of your content. It also saves you time because you can enter the information without having to move from placeholder to placeholder.

4. **Modify an outline structure.** Because the Outline view gives you a global view of the presentation, it helps you see the underlying structure of the presentation. You are able to see where content needs to be strengthened, or where the flow of information needs to be revised. If you find a slide with content that would be presented better in another location in the slide show, you can use the Collapse and Expand features to easily move it. By collapsing the slide content, you can drag it to a new location and then expand it. To move individual bullet points, cut and paste the bullet point or drag-and-drop it.

5. **Print an outline.** When you present, using the outline version of your slide show as a reference is a boon. No matter how well you know your information, it is easy to forget to present some information when facing an audience. While you would print speaker's notes if you have many details, you can print the outline as a quick reference. The outline can be printed in either the collapsed or the expanded form, giving you far fewer pages to shuffle in front of an audience than printing speaker's notes would.

6. **Import an outline.** You do not need to re-enter information from an outline created in Microsoft Word or another word processor. You can use the Open feature to import any outline that has been saved in a format that PowerPoint can read. In addition to a Word outline, you can use the common generic formats Rich Text Format and Plain Text Format.

7. **Add existing content to a presentation.** After you spend time creating the slides in a slide show, you may find that slides in the slide show would be appropriate in another show at a later date. Any slide you create can be reused in another presentation, thereby saving you considerable time and effort. You simply open the Reuse Slides pane, locate the slide show with the slide you need, and then click on the thumbnail of the slide to insert a copy of it in the new slide show.

8. **Examine slide show design principles.** With a basic understanding of slide show design principles you can create presentations that reflect your personality in a professional way. The goal of applying these principles is to create a slide show that focuses the audience on the message of the slide without being distracted by clutter or unreadable text.

9. **Apply and modify a design theme.** PowerPoint provides you with themes to help you create a clean, professional look for your presentation. Once a theme is applied you can modify the theme by changing the color scheme, the font scheme, the effects scheme, or the background style.

10. **Insert a header or footer.** Identifying information can be included in a header or footer. You may, for example, wish to include the group to whom you are presenting, or the location of the presentation, or a copyright notation for original work. You can apply footers to slides, handouts, and Notes pages. Headers may be applied to handouts and Notes pages.

**Summary**

links directly back to the objectives so students can more effectively study and locate the concepts that they need to focus on.

# More End of Chapter Exercises with New Levels of Assessment

offer instructors more options for assessment. Each chapter has approximately 12-15 projects per chapter ranging from multiple choice to open-ended projects.

## Practice Exercises

reinforce skills learned in the chapter with specific directions on what to do and how to do it.

## New Mid-Level Exercises

assess the skills learned in the chapter by directing the students on what to do but not how to do it.

## New Capstone Exercises

cover all of the skills with in each chapter without telling students how to perform the skills.

## Mini Cases with Rubrics

are open ended exercises that guide both instructors and students to a solution with a specific rubric for each Mini Case.

### Practice Exercises
**1 Download and Modify a Template**

Figure 2.43 displays an Employee of the Year Award for Olsen Cabinets. It was created from a template downloaded from Microsoft Office Online. A small business owner who runs a cabinet shop might use an award program to motivate employees and could create this award quickly by downloading the template and modifying it. Assume you are the owner of Olsen Cabinets and you want to present your employee, Michael Mulhern, with the Employee of the Year Award.

a. Click the **Office Button** and then select **New**.
b. Click **Award certificates** in the Microsoft Office Online category.

### Mid-Level Exercises
**1 USDA Food Pyramid**

You have been asked to help in a local elementary school. The teacher would like you to teach the children about nutrition and healthy eating. You decide to create a presentation about the U.S. Department of Agriculture (USDA)–recommended food pyramid. (Visit http://www.mypyramid.gov.) You locate a Microsoft Office Online template based on the food pyramid that will help you organize the presentation. Figure 2.50 displays the downloaded template, and Figure 2.51 displays the conclusion slide of your presentation.

### Capstone Exercise

*Your neighbors in your small southwestern subdivision are concerned about drought, fire danger, and water conservation. You volunteer to gather information about possible solutions and share the information with them at the next neighborhood association meeting. You decide a PowerPoint presentation would be an excellent way to inform them of their options. In this capstone project, you concentrate on developing the content. In later chapter capstone projects, you will enhance the project with illustrations, images, charts, and hyperlinks.*

**Design Template**

homeowners are more easily able to see the overall picture. You do not want to lose the work you have already done, so you import the zeroscaping outline and reuse the xeriscaping slides.

a. Position the point of insertion at the end of the outline and add a new slide.
b. Use the **Slides from Outline option** to insert the chap2_cap_zeroscaping outline.
c. Change the layout of Slide 4 from Title slide to

### Mini Cases

*Use the rubric following the case as a guide to evaluate your work, but keep in mind that your instructor may impose additional grading criteria or use a different standard to judge your work.*

**Identity Theft**

GENERAL CASE ✓

The partially completed chap2_mc1_identity presentation is intended to aid you in recognizing the global value of the outline view and how it can be used to modify the structure of a presentation. A combination of slides containing only titles and slides containing content are randomly entered as if they were created from brainstorming. Organize the presentation so there is content under each topic and that the content matches the topic in the slide title. Create an appropriate conclusion. You may add additional slides, if desired. Good resources for your presentation include the Federal Trade Commission Web site (www.consumer.gov/idtheft) and the Social Security Online Electronic Fact Sheet (www.ssa.gov/pubs/idtheft).

Be sure to spell-check and carefully proof-read the content of the presentation. Save the presentation as **chap2_mc1_identity_solution**. Locate a template to use for the design and reuse the chap2_mc1_identity_solution presentation slides to create a new presentation. Apply a font scheme, color scheme, and background style as desired. You also may modify layouts. Add appropriate clip art to at least two slides. Remember the design guidelines as you insert the clip art. Match the colors of the clips to your background and try to locate clips that are similar—do not apply a cartoon-like clip on one slide and a professional clip on another. Apply a transition to all slides, and add a custom animation to the clip art you added. Create a handout header with your name, and a handout footer with the filename, your instructor's name, and your class. Print as directed by your instructor. Save the file as **chap2_mc1_identity_solution**, and click Yes when asked if you want to save over the original file.

| Performance Elements | Exceeds Expectations | Meets Expectations | Below Expectations |
|---|---|---|---|
| Organization | Presentation is easy to follow because information is presented in a logical, interesting sequence. | Presentation is generally easy to follow. | Presentation cannot be understood because there is no sequence of information. |
| Visual aspects | Presentation background, themes, clip art, and animation are appealing and enhance the understanding of presentation purpose and content. | Clip art is related to topic. | The background, theme, or animation is distracting to the topic. |
| | There is a consistent visual theme. | Animation is not distracting. | Clip art does not enhance understanding of the content or is unrelated. |
| Layout | The layout is visually pleasing and contributes to the overall message with appropriate use of headings, subheadings, bullet points, clip art, and white space. | The layout shows some structure, but placement of some headings, subheadings, bullet points, clip art, and/or white space can be improved. | The layout is cluttered and confusing. Placement of headings, subheadings, bullet points, clip art, and/or white spaces detracts from readability. |
| Mechanics | Presentation has no errors in spelling, grammar, word usage, or punctuation. | Presentation has no more than one error in spelling, grammar, word usage, or punctuation. | Presentation readability is impaired due to repeated errors in spelling, grammar, word usage, or punctuation. |
| | | points are inconsistent in | Most bullet points are not parallel. |

# Locating Information and Communicating with Others

# bjectives

After you read this chapter, you will be able to:

1. Understand the World Wide Web **(page 3)**.

2. Access and navigate a Web site **(page 4)**.

3. Print Web pages **(page 14)**.

4. Download information and graphics **(page 16)**.

5. Work with Favorites and the History list **(page 23)**.

6. Manage Internet options **(page 26)**.

7. Use search engines **(page 30)**.

8. Communicate through Windows Mail **(page 36)**.

9. Communicate through instant messages and blogs **(page 44)**.

## Hands-On Exercises

| Exercises | Skills Covered |
|---|---|
| 1. BROWSING WORLD WIDE WEB SITES (page 18) | • Access a Web Site • Use Hyperlinks • Refresh a Web Page • Use the Zoom Tool • Browse with Tabs • Save a Picture • Print a Web Page |
| 2. EXPLORING BROWSER OPTIONS AND SEARCHING THE WEB (page 32) | • Create Favorites • Control Cookies and Temporary Internet Files • Manage the History List • Search the Web |
| 3. COMMUNICATING ONLINE (page 46) | • Create E-mail • Attach a File • Use Windows Contacts • Use Phishing Filter • Create a Blog |

# CASE STUDY

## Riverfest

You are the assistant coordinator for Riverfest, a local outdoor festival held each spring at a riverside park in your hometown. The event includes many activities, including a barbecue competition, music from local groups, an art exhibit showcasing local artists, and games of skill and fun for children and adults. People from neighboring communities come to Riverfest each year.

Products promoting the event include posters, brochures, shirts, caps, and plastic cups. Your task is to design a logo for the event that highlights the fact that it is a "river" fest—a fun-filled day for the community, held along the banks of a river. The logo will be used on all promotional items to develop brand recognition for the event. Search the Web for any available copyright-free clip art you might use or modify for the event logo. Also, locate local or online companies that specialize in event apparel and souvenirs. Make a list of potential promotional event items. Also list the types of souvenir items you can purchase and sell during Riverfest.

**Case Study**

## Your Assignment

- Use one or more search engines to locate Web resources with free copyright-free clip art that would be appropriate for the Riverfest logo (or that could serve as a starting point for modification). You should also search for companies that could help with the graphic design and produce the apparel and souvenirs.

- Select a clip art image as your logo. Print the Web page containing the selected clip art. Download the clip art to a flash drive. Use Microsoft Word to prepare a report listing all sites from which you considered clip art for the logo. Identify your final choice (and the Web site at which you found it). Insert the clip art in your document. To do so, click Insert, Picture. Navigate to the clip art file. Double-click the file to place it in the document.

- List the Web addresses of several companies that offer printing and design services (from which you could get commemorative products for Riverfest) in the same document.

- List steps that the Riverfest project director should follow in order to create a contacts list in Windows Contacts create the list in a separate section of your report. Assume that you will be supplying a list of local contacts (vendors and patrons), which should be maintained in a contact list. Because the project director is unfamiliar with Windows Contacts, your directions will help.

- Save the report as **chap1_case_riverfest**.

- Print a copy of the report.

# Internet and Web Browser Basics

On October 4, 1957, families around the United States had a new and disturbing dinner conversation topic: The Russians had launched *Sputnik*, the first artificial satellite. The launch was disturbing because Americans suddenly realized that the Russians could threaten the United States with a new type of attack. Almost immediately schools throughout the country began to emphasize math and science education. The United States had a heightened interest in maintaining world scientific leadership and protecting its citizens from a Russian missile threat.

In Washington, D.C., the official United States response was quick. On February 7, 1958, the U.S. Department of Defense commissioned the development of a network that could withstand nuclear attack, allowing continual transmission of information and military plans. Several years later, the network was expanded to include university research teams so that educational institutions could also benefit from the network. From such beginnings, the *Internet* has evolved into what we know today—a global information network comprised of millions of interconnected computers to disseminate information and communicate with other people around the world. The Internet is a popular avenue for *e-commerce*—conducting online business through advertising, selling, and buying products.

In this section, you will learn about the World Wide Web and the types of files that are created for the Web. In addition, you learn how to access and navigate Web sites. You will also print Web pages and work with tabbed browsing. Using zoom controls, you will learn to enlarge and reduce the view. You will also be introduced to the concept of downloading files and saving print and text from the Internet.

> The *Internet* is a group of interconnected networks that spans the world.
>
> *E-commerce* is the avenue for conducting business over the Internet.

## Understanding the World Wide Web

The *World Wide Web* (the Web) is a subsection of the Internet and is designed to display Web pages in an easy-to-navigate and understandable way. A *Web page* is a single document that typically consists of text, graphics, animation, and/or sound and that is designed to be used on the Web. Typically, an organization develops multiple Web pages to separate all of its online content into multiple files, with each Web page discussing a particular topic. The collection of related Web pages maintained by an organization is called a *Web site*. For example, Prentice Hall's Web site contains many Web pages; each Web page is devoted to a specific book or series of books. The Exploring series Web page provides links to other Web pages that contain additional resources, such as book descriptions and data files. The use of multiple Web pages organizes content and facilitates online navigation to specific content. Web pages typically consist of *hyperlinks* (links), text or graphical elements that, when clicked, display another area of the same Web page or connect to and display another Web page or resource.

Web pages must be formatted in such a way as to display correctly and consistently on different computer systems. The set of rules or standards that govern data format and transmission is called a *protocol*. The primary protocol for the Web is *HyperText Transfer Protocol (HTTP)*, which dictates how Web pages are formatted and how data must be transmitted across the Web. For example, when you click a link or type a Web address, HTTP protocol directs you to the selected *Web server*, a computer that contains Web pages, has server software installed, and is connected to the Internet. When a Web server receives a report that someone has entered the Web address or clicked a link, it fetches the data and transmits the requested Web page to the computer that initiated the request. The receiving computer then displays the Web page onscreen for the user.

> The *World Wide Web* is a subset of the Internet that supports graphical point-and-click navigation to information and resources.
>
> A *Web page* is a single document formatted to be used on the Web.
>
> A *Web site* is a collection of Web pages for an organization or entity.
>
> A *hyperlink* is a text or graphical element that, when clicked, displays another area of the same Web page or displays another Web page or resource.
>
> A *protocol* is a set of rules that govern data formats and transmission.
>
> The *HyperText Transfer Protocol (HTTP)* is a set of rules that specifies data format and transmission of Web pages.
>
> A *Web server* is a computer that stores Web pages and transmits data when requested.

**HyperText Markup language (HTML)** is an authoring language used to create Web pages.

**Internet Explorer (IE) 7** is the newest version of Microsoft's browser.

A **browser** is a software application used to locate and display Web resources.

An **Internet Service Provider (ISP)** is a company that provides access to the Internet.

If you are interested in designing Web sites, you will probably learn to work with **HyperText Markup Language (HTML)**, a programming language used to create Web documents. HTML uses tags to define the structure and formatting of Web pages. Although other Web authoring languages exist, HTML continues to be the most widely recognized.

# Accessing and Navigating a Web Site

**Internet Explorer (IE) 7** is a browser software application that enables you to navigate the Web. A **browser** is used to display Web pages, access Web resources, and search the Web. IE 7 is the newest version of the Microsoft browser and is included as a component of Windows Vista. You can download IE 7 at *http://www.microsoft.com/windows/downloads/ie/getitnow*.

Internet Explorer is a browser used to view the Web, but it is not an Internet connection. To access the Internet, you must contract with an **Internet Service Provider (ISP)**, such as America Online. Other ISPs include cable and telephone companies. Once online (connected to the Internet), you can use Internet Explorer or another browser, such as Firefox, to access and display Web pages. Most colleges and companies have a direct connection to the Internet. To open the browser, click Start and select Internet Explorer, or double-click the Internet Explorer icon on your desktop. Figure 1.1 shows the Internet Explorer browser window.

> A Web site includes a home page, which is the page to which visitors are usually first directed, with links to other pages or files within the same site.

**Figure 1.1**   Internet Explorer 7 Browser Window

**TIP**   Maximize Screen Size

You might find it useful to view Internet Explorer in full screen mode, without accompanying tabs or buttons. Press F11 to show a full screen. Press F11 again to return to the original view.

## Identify Components of a URL

A **Uniform Resource Locator (URL)** is the specific address of a World Wide Web file.

Every Web page and other Web resource (such as text, audio, and video files) has a unique address, called a **Uniform Resource Locator (URL)**. A collection of one or more Web pages, all supporting the same organization, is called a Web site. A Web site includes a home page, which is the page to which visitors are usually first directed, with links to other pages or files within the same site. A URL is actually composed of three parts—the protocol, the name of the company or entity that maintains the Web site, and an identifying suffix. For example, the URL for Prentice Hall's Exploring series is *http://www.prenhall.com/exploring*.

The first part of the URL (*http*) identifies the http protocol, which is standard for all Web pages. When typing a URL, you are not required to type the prefix *http://*. Another type of protocol is *file transfer protocol (ftp)*, which is used to share files over the Internet. A lot of companies maintain an ftp site for their employees to conveniently share files electronically with each other. For example, the Exploring series team has an ftp site in which the authors and editors post their chapter manuscript, figure, and data files for each other to access. Some colleges also provide ftp sites for professors to upload files for student access.

The **file transfer protocol (ftp)** is used for uploading, storing, and downloading sharable files over the Internet.

The second part of the URL is the domain. A *domain* is a name for the resources that make up an organization's Web site. Without a domain name, users would have to know an organization's IP address, which is a series of numbers with internal periods. For example, *www.prenhall* is the domain for Prentice Hall.

A *domain* is a name for an entity's Web site or server.

The third part of the URL is the *top-level domain*, which is a suffix that indicates the type of domain. For example, *.com* indicates that the site is commercial (sponsored by a profit-oriented company). Table 1.1 lists and describes common top-level domains.

A *top-level domain* is a suffix that identifies the type of organization sponsoring a Web site.

Most often, you will visit pages within a Web site by clicking hyperlinks (or more simply, links), which are found on most Web pages. For example, from the Microsoft home page, you might click *Security* to move to a page giving information on making your home computer more secure. After you click the *Security* link, the URL displayed in the Address bar might show *http://www.microsoft.com/security.htm*. The slash after the top-level domain indicates another page within the Web site—in this case, the *Security* page. Much like computer folders, Web sites can have pages within folders, so that if you drew a diagram of the pages, it would look like a family tree. To carry the example one step further, the *Security* page could have a "sub-page" with information on computer viruses. The fictitious URL could then be *http://www.microsoft.com/security/virus.htm*. Understanding this little bit of information about URLs, you will surely appreciate the ease with which you can navigate Web sites by simply clicking links instead of typing lengthy Web addresses!

## Access a Web Site

A browser **home page** is the page that displays when you open Internet Explorer.

Accessing a Web site is simple. With Internet Explorer open, locate the Address bar (as shown in Figure 1.2). The current address is that of your browser's **home page**. The home page is the Web site that appears by default each time you open Internet

**Table 1.1** Top-Level Domains

| Top-Level Domain | Characteristics |
| --- | --- |
| .com | Commercial business |
| .edu | Educational institution |
| .net | Network organization |
| .gov | United States government agency |
| .mil | Military |
| .ca | Most two character domains are for countries. This one is Canada. |
| .org | Nonprofit organization |

Explorer. Initially this page is set either by a computer manufacturer or by a network administrator. The setting is not permanent. Later in this chapter, you will learn how to designate another home page. To display another Web page, such as prenhall.com/exploring, click in the Address bar. With the current address selected, simply type the URL, such as *www.prenhall.com/exploring*, and press Enter to display a page similar to that shown in Figure 1.2.

**Figure 1.2**  A Browser Window

**TIP**    Using AutoComplete

As you type a URL in the Address bar, Internet Explorer tries to match what you are typing to a recently visited Web page. If it finds a match, it shows the Web address in a drop-down list. From the list, you can click to select an address or continue typing the URL. To manually show or hide the AutoComplete list, press F4 on your keyboard. If you prefer, you can turn off AutoComplete. Click the Tools button and click Internet Options. Click the Content tab. Click Settings. Click to clear the AutoComplete options that you want to turn off (Web address, forms, or user names and passwords), as shown in Figure 1.3. Click OK in AutoComplete Settings. Click OK in Interest Options.

**Figure 1.3** The AutoComplete Feature

Many Web pages contain graphic or text hyperlinks, such as those shown in Figure 1.4. A text link is underlined and the text is a different color (most often blue). The mouse pointer usually becomes a pointing hand when it is placed on a text link. A graphic link is a graphic, button, or picture that is identified only by the fact that when you rest the mouse pointer on the graphic, the pointer becomes a pointing hand. Sometimes, a graphic link will display a submenu when you point to the link. When you click a link, your browser will display the page associated with the link. In that manner, you can *surf* the Web at will by simply clicking links and proceeding through subsequent pages or files.

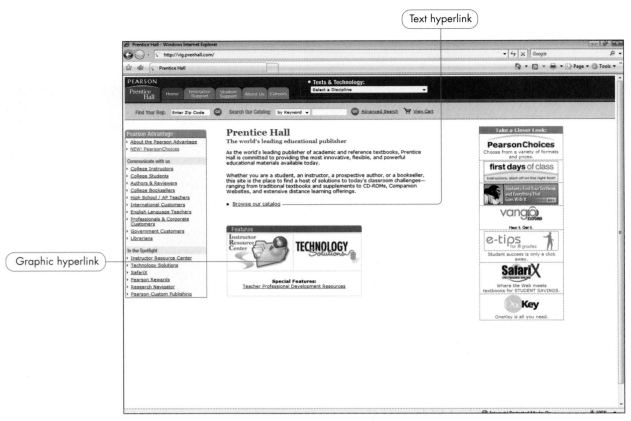

**Figure 1.4** Text and Graphic Hyperlinks

As you click links, you expect a fairly quick response time, which is the time required for the linked Web page to display. Dial-up users (those connected to the Internet through a dial-up telephone connection) are often frustrated when they must wait for a Web page to progressively display, a little at a time. Studies have shown that workers are much more productive and less frustrated with technology if response time is one second or less. In reality, though, response time is usually more than a second. Response time is dependent on several factors, including Internet traffic, the user's connection to the Internet, the responsiveness of a Web server, and the Internet Service Provider's server connection. Just as traffic on an interstate is slow during rush hour, Internet traffic can also be sluggish during peak work hours. A broadband connection, such as cable or DSL, can significantly speed up response time when compared to a dial-up connection. If the ISP's server is not connected through a high-speed line, such as a T-3, traffic can become bottlenecked, leading to slower response time. Finally, a Web server on which an accessed Web site is housed can become overloaded with requests, causing slower page display.

## Go Back and Forward

As you visit various Web pages, you will undoubtedly find that you want to revisit a page. For example, suppose you are considering beginning a small business and have just viewed guidelines on the Small Business Administration's Web site. From the SBA home page, you might click an FAQ link to explore questions asked by other entrepreneurs. Then, to return to the SBA home page, click the Back button, as shown in Figure 1.5. Clicking the Back button repeatedly enables you to revisit previously viewed pages in the order of viewing. You can also press Backspace (on your keyboard) instead of clicking the Back button. The Forward button enables you to return to pages you viewed prior to clicking the Back button. When returning to previous pages, you will find that any text link that you previously clicked has changed color (usually from blue to purple). The change in link color lets you know that you have already visited the page represented by that link. Notice the previously visited link shown in Figure 1.5.

**Figure 1.5** The Back and Forward Buttons

A ***temporary Internet file*** is a copy of a Web page that is saved onto your hard drive for ease of access later.

You might notice that when you revisit a Web page by clicking the Back or Forward button, the Web page loads faster than when you first accessed it. That happens because the browser actually saves a "snapshot" of Web pages that you visit. Those snapshots, or ***temporary Internet files***, are saved locally on your hard drive. Then, when you call for them again (sometimes by clicking the Back button), they load much faster from the hard drive than if they were downloaded from the Internet. Temporary Internet files are discussed in greater detail later in this chapter.

**TIP** Typing a URL

You do not have to type *http://* preceding each Web address. Internet Explorer automatically adds the protocol for you. For example, to access *http://www.ebay.com,* all you need to type is *www.ebay.com.* For another shortcut, consider this. If you are accessing a business Web page, such as *www.amazon.com,* you can simply type the business name in the Address bar (in this case, *amazon*) and then press Ctrl+Enter. Internet Explorer automatically adds the *http://www.* and *.com,* to show *http://www.amazon.com.*

## Scroll Through a Web Page

Many Web pages contain much more information than can be displayed on a computer screen. If some page content is off-screen, you will see a vertical scroll bar (see Figure 1.6) to the right of the browser window (indicating that page content extends above or beneath the current display) or a horizontal scroll bar at the bottom (indicating that more page content exists to the right or left of the current view). To see off-screen elements of a Web page, you must scroll the display. You can view additional page elements by repeatedly clicking the directional arrows on either end of the scroll bar, or by clicking and dragging the scroll box. If using a wheel (or scroll) mouse, click the Web page and spin the wheel mouse in either direction to move up or down. You can also press Page Up or Page Down on the keyboard to quickly move up or down, one window at a time.

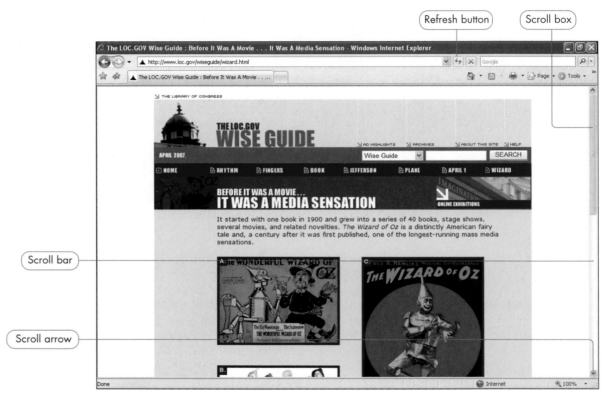

**Figure 1.6** The Scroll Bar

## Refresh a Web Page

By nature, Web pages are dynamic, which means that they can be changed often. For example, a Web site providing current weather information or traffic conditions in a major city will change often. The same holds true for Web sites displaying current stock quotes or news headlines. As you view a Web page, it is much like a snapshot in time. To update, or refresh, the Web page, you can click the Refresh button, as shown in Figure 1.6.

**TIP** Using F5 to Refresh a Web Page

A quick way to refresh a Web page is to press the F5 function key. Pressing F5 refreshes a current Web page in Internet Explorer.

## Use the Zoom Feature

Using the Zoom feature, you can enlarge or reduce the view of a Web page so that you can control precisely what you see. You can adjust the view anywhere from 10% to 1,000%. The Zoom control button is located in the bottom right corner of the browser window, as shown in Figure 1.7. Zoom options are also available on the Zoom submenu of the Page button. If using a wheel mouse, you can press Ctrl and then scroll the mouse to zoom in or out. Finally, you can press Ctrl and the plus key to increase the zoom, Ctrl and the minus key to decrease the zoom, or Ctrl and the zero key to return to 100%.

**Figure 1.7**  Zoom Menu

## Browse with Tabs

Tabbed browsing is an IE 7 feature that enables you to open multiple Web pages in a single browser window. You can then switch between windows with ease by simply clicking a tab. If you have worked with an earlier IE version, you recall that each open Web page was represented by a button on the taskbar. If several Web pages were open at the same time, the taskbar could quickly become cluttered. With tabbed browsing, though, multiple Web pages are represented only by tabs, not by separate taskbar buttons.

To open a new tab, click and hold Ctrl as you click a link. For example, from the *www.loc.gov* page, you might create a tab for the American Memory page. Press and hold Ctrl while you click the American Memory link. If you have a wheel mouse, you can click the link with the wheel or middle button to create a tab. Two tabs will appear, as shown in Figure 1.8.

**Figure 1.8**  Using Tabs

To reorder tabs, click and drag them to the left or right in the tab row. If multiple tabs are displayed and you want to close one tab, click the tab's Close button (X), which is only shown if you first select the tab by clicking it. You can also close any tab by right-clicking it and clicking Close. If you want to close all tabs but one, right-click the one that you want to keep and click Close Other Tabs, as shown in Figure 1.9. If only one tab is open, a Close button does not appear; you must close Internet Explorer to close the tab.

**Figure 1.9**  Closing One or More Tabs

After having created a group of tabs, you might want to save the tabbed group so that you can open the entire group later. To do so, click the Add to Favorites button (see Figure 1.10), and then click Add Tab Group to Favorites. Type a name for the group and click Add. The next time you want to open the group of tabs, click the Favorites Center button (see Figure 1.10). Click the folder (group of tabs) that you want to open and click the arrow to the right of the folder name. To open another browser window, hold down Ctrl and press N on the keyboard.

**Figure 1.10** Working with Favorites

If several tabs are open, you will see the Quick Tabs button, as shown in Figure 1.11. To view a thumbnail of all open tabs, click the Quick Tabs button. From that point, you can click any thumbnail to access that Web page. You can also click the arrow to the right of the Quick Tabs button and click to select from the list of tabbed pages.

Quick Tabs button

**Figure 1.11** Quick Tabs Feature

# Printing Web Pages

Web pages are intended to be viewed on a computer screen, but you can also print them. Although you can print all or part of a Web page, you should understand that the page might not print in an attractive manner unless you provide some direction. You can use the Page Setup dialog box to specify print settings, and you can also use the Print Preview feature to make adjustments before printing.

Figure 1.12 shows a typical Page Setup dialog box. To open Page Setup, click the Print button arrow, and then click Page Setup. From that point, you can specify printer properties for page size, print orientation, and paper source. In most cases, though, you will not want to change those properties. You can define a header and footer, which is printed material that will appear at the top and bottom of each page. In the Header and Footer boxes, you can type any text for a header and footer. You can also use variables to substitute information. For example, type *Page &p* in the Footer box to print the current page at the bottom of each page. For a complete list of header and footer codes (variables), access Internet Explorer's Help menu.

Header and Footer text boxes

Printer properties

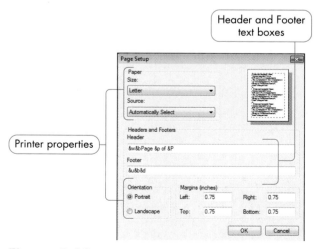

**Figure 1.12** Page Setup Dialog Box

Before printing, you can preview a Web page. Click the Print button arrow and select Print Preview. The Print Preview window displays the Web page as it will look when you print it (see Figure 1.13). The Print Preview toolbar appears at the top of the window. Use the toolbar options to do any of the following:

- Print the Web page
- Select portrait or landscape orientation
- Open the Page Setup dialog box
- Display or hide headers and footers
- View at Full Width or Full Page
- Show Multiple Pages
- Change the print size

Options at the bottom of the Print Preview window enable you to specify the page to display or to switch between pages. Drag the margin adjust handle to change predefined margins. To leave Print Preview, click the Close button.

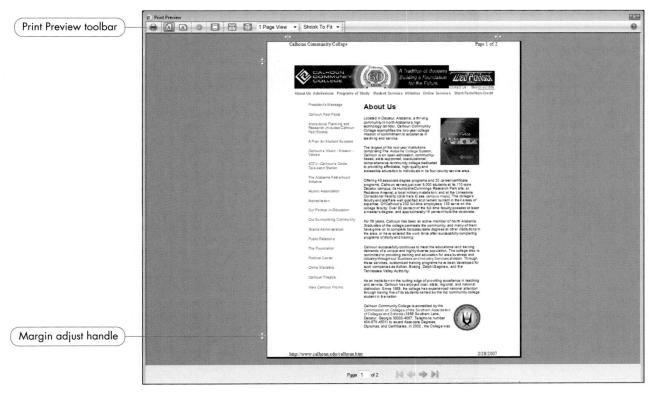

Print Preview toolbar

Margin adjust handle

**Figure 1.13**  Print Preview Window

When working with the Print Preview window, you can click the Print button on the Print Preview toolbar to print the displayed Web page. If not in Print Preview, you can print directly from the Internet Explorer window. To print the current page with the current print settings, click the Print button. For more control, click the Print button arrow and select Print. The Print dialog box appears (see Figure 1.14). Select a printer and specify the range of pages to print, if necessary. You can also indicate the number of copies to print. The page that you are printing might contain *frames*, which are boxed areas, containing additional links or information, at the left or top of the page. Each frame is actually a different Web page, which is included with the current page in a divided area, much like a box. If the page to print contains frames, click the Options tab and select the print frames option that you want. Select or clear the *Print all linked documents* and *Print table of links* check boxes. Finally, click Print.

A *frame* is a boxed area, usually located at the side or top of a Web page, containing links and additional information.

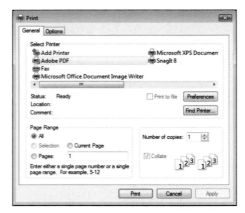

**Figure 1.14** Print Dialog Box

# Downloading Information and Graphics

Occasionally, you will find a Web page containing a file or image that you want to save. If the item is a file, such as a video trailer or a game demo, you can download the file. Internet Explorer provides extensive security warnings and guidance to make sure that you recognize inherent risks associated with downloading a file (such as viruses and spyware) and that you agree to allow the download to continue. If the item that you want to collect is a picture or text, you can copy and paste it to a document on your computer. From there, you can save or print it. When you copy information from a Web page, you should make sure that you are not violating any copyright laws.

> When you copy information from a Web page, you should make sure that you are not violating any copyright laws.

## Save Pictures or Text from a Web Page

Because the Web is a graphical interface, you will often find pictures, clip art, or other graphics that are of interest. If the item is not copyrighted, you can collect it for use in another project, such as for inclusion in a newsletter that you are preparing. First, open the Web page that contains the graphic. Right-click the graphic and select Save Picture As. Select the drive and folder in which you plan to save the picture and change the file name if desired. Click Save.

You can also copy text from a Web page. Perhaps you are working with the local chapter of the Red Cross and have found an article concerning CPR that you want to pass along to colleagues. Open the Web page containing the article and select (click and drag) the article. Right-click the selected text, and then select Copy, as shown in Figure 1.15. Open a Word document, click where you want the text to appear, and then use the Paste command to paste a copy of the selected text in your document.

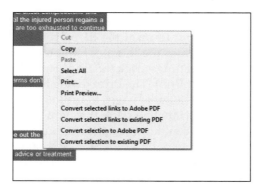

**Figure 1.15** Copy Text from the Web

### Download Files from the Web

Several Web sites, such as *www.download.com* and *www.zdnet.com*, offer files and programs to download. Before downloading anything, however, you should be certain that your computer's antivirus software and spyware remover is current. A downloaded file might appear legitimate, when, in truth, it is disguising a virus or other harmful program.

When you find a program or file to download, locate the download link. A well-designed Web page will display a link, perhaps *Download Now,* or simply *Download,* in a prominent location. Click the link to begin the download, and then click Save. Indicate where the file should be saved. An information box similar to that shown in Figure 1.16 might give details such as the time required for the download and the file size. When the download is complete, click Open or Run to install the program, or click Close if you plan to install the downloaded program later. If you want to install the program but do not see a dialog box, you will need to use My Computer to navigate to the downloaded file and double-click the file to begin the installation (if it is a program file) or to open it (if it is a data file).

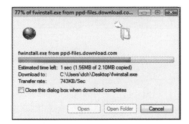

**Figure 1.16** Download Dialog Box

# Toolbar Menus | Reference

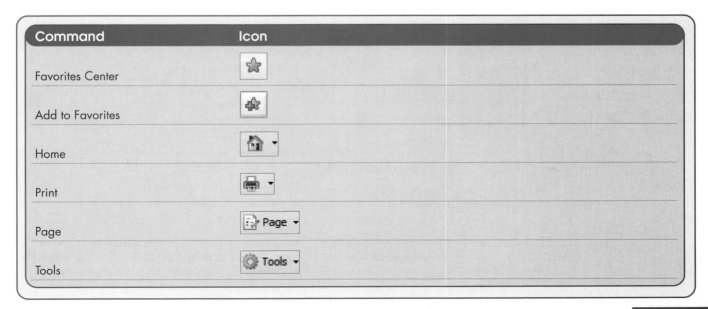

| Command | Icon |
|---|---|
| Favorites Center | ☆ |
| Add to Favorites | ✦ |
| Home | 🏠 ▾ |
| Print | 🖨 ▾ |
| Page | 📄 Page ▾ |
| Tools | ⚙ Tools ▾ |

## 1 | Browsing World Wide Web Sites

**Skills covered: 1.** Access a Web Site **2.** Use Hyperlinks **3.** Refresh a Web Page **4.** Use the Zoom Tool **5.** Browse with Tabs **6.** Save a Picture **7.** Print a Web Page

---

### Step 1
#### Access a Web Site

Refer to Figure 1.17 as you complete Step 1.

**a.** Open Internet Explorer using one of the methods given below:

- Double-click the **Internet Explorer icon** on the desktop.
- Click **Start** and click **Internet**.
- Click **Start**, select **All Programs**, and click **Internet Explorer**.
- Click **Internet Explorer** in the Quick Launch toolbar.

You will see your browser's home page.

**b.** Click in the **Address bar** and type **www.weather.gov**. Press **Enter**.

Your window should appear, as shown in Figure 1.17.

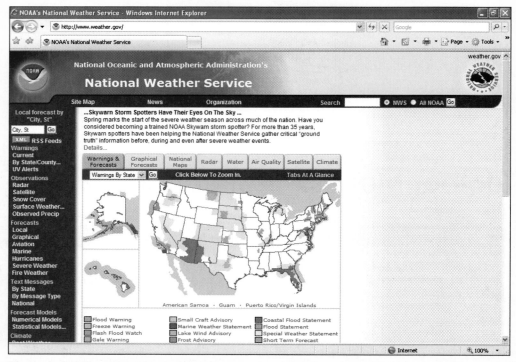

**Figure 1.17** A Weather Web Site

**c.** Click in the **Address bar** and type *www.weather.gov/forecasts/graphical/sectors*. Press **Enter**.

If you know the address of the Web page, you can type the entire address, as you have done here. You could have clicked appropriate links from a Web site's home page, as well, to arrive at a destination (without typing a lengthy Web address), which you will do in the next step.

Refer to Figure 1.18 as you complete Step 2.

**a.** Click in the **Address bar** and type **www.usa.gov**. Press **Enter**.

**b.** Move the pointer around the page, identifying hyperlinks (usually areas where the pointer becomes a pointing hand).

Notice that this home page contains both text and graphic links. At the top of the page are tabs, which are links to other areas on the Web site.

**c.** Position the pointer over one of the graphic links, as shown in Figure 1.18. Click to move to the linked page or resource.

**Figure 1.18** Hyperlinks

**d.** Click the **Back button** or press **Backspace** to return to the USA home page.

**e.** Position the pointer over one of the text links. Click to move to the linked page or resource.

The page that displays after you click a link might not be part of the USA Web site. A hyperlink can direct your display to any site on the Web.

**f.** Click the **Back button** or press **Backspace** to return to the USA home page. Click the **Forward button** to retrace your steps.

**g.** Click the **Back button** to return to the USA home page. Scroll down slightly, if necessary, and place the pointer over the Family, Home, and Community link (or another link if that one is unavailable). Right-click the link, and then select **Open in New Window**.

Instead of leaving the current Web page, your linked page will open in a new window. Thus, you will have both the current page and the new page open at the same time.

**h.** Close the new Internet window. You should see the USA home page.

<table>
<tr><td>

## Step 3
### Refresh a Web Page
</td><td>

**a.** Click in the **Address bar** and type **www.weather.gov**. Press **Enter**.

**b.** Click **Radar** (under **Observations**).

**c.** Click the **Refresh button** to refresh the Web page.

If the Web page remains on your monitor for a little while, the Radar image might change when you refresh the Web page. That is because the radar scan might actually change, showing moving weather fronts. When you refresh the Web page, it displays the most current radar image.
</td></tr>
<tr><td>

## Step 4
### Use the Zoom Tool
</td><td>

Refer to Figure 1.19 as you complete Step 4.

**a.** Click in the **Address bar** and type **prenhall**. Press and hold **Ctrl** while pressing **Enter**.

When typing a business address, such as *www.prenhall.com*, you have to type only the business name. Then press Ctrl and Enter to complete the rest of the address automatically.

**b.** Click in the **Keyword box** and type **Microsoft Word 2007**. Press **Enter**.

**c.** Click the **Zoom Options arrow** at the bottom right of the browser window. Change the zoom to **200**%, as shown in Figure 1.19.
</td></tr>
</table>

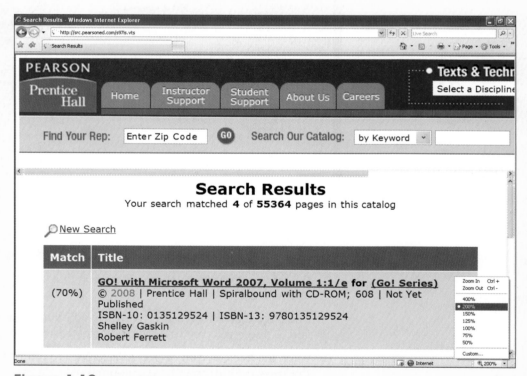

**Figure 1.19** Zoom Options

**d.** Press and hold **Ctrl** while you press the plus key (+) repeatedly to increase the zoom. Press and hold **Ctrl** while you press the minus key (−) repeatedly to decrease the zoom. To return to 100%, press and hold **Ctrl** while you press the zero key (0).

**e.** Click the **Page arrow** in the toolbar. Point to **Zoom**. Click **Custom**, type **500** in the box, and click **OK**.

**f.** Click the **Page button**, point to **Zoom**, and click **100**%.

Refer to Figure 1.20 as you complete Step 5.

**a.** Click in the **Address bar** and type **www.consumer.gov**. Press **Enter**.

**b.** Hold down **Ctrl** and click the **Food** link. Release **Ctrl**. Your display should be similar to Figure 1.20.

You have created two tabs, one for the Consumer home page, and another for the Food page. You can switch between the pages by clicking the identifying tab.

**Figure 1.20** Working with Tabs

**c.** Click the **Consumer.gov** tab. Press **Ctrl** and click the **Children** link.

**d.** Click the **Quick Tabs button** to view a thumbnail of all open tabs. Click the third thumbnail to make it the active page.

**e.** Close the open tab by clicking the **Close button** on the tab.

**f.** Click the **Add to Favorites button** and click **Add Tab Group to Favorites**. Type a name for the group, perhaps **Consumer.gov**. Click **Add**.

The Consumer.gov tab group is now saved.

**g.** Right-click the **Consumer.gov tab** and select **Close Other Tabs**.

**a.** Click in the **Address bar** and type **www.avery.com**. Press **Enter**.

**b.** Point to the Software/Templates tab and click **Clip Art Collection**.

**c.** Click the **Nature and Animals link**. Click **Flowers**.

**d.** Right-click a flower graphic and select **Save Picture As.**

**e.** Click **Desktop**. Accept the file name as is and click **Save**.

Refer to Figure 1.21 as you complete Step 7.

**a.** Click in the **Address bar** and type **www.loc.gov**. Press **Enter**.

**b.** Click the **Print arrow** and click **Page Setup**.

**c.** Click in the **Header box** and remove any current text. (Press **Backspace** to delete characters to the left of the insertion point or **Delete** to remove characters to the right of the insertion point.) Type your first and last name. Leave the footer as is.

**d.** Select **Landscape**. Your display should be similar to Figure 1.21. Click **OK**.

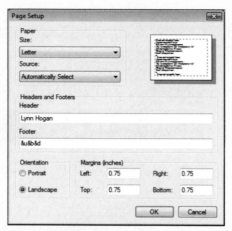

**Figure 1.21**  Page Setup

**e.** Click the **Print arrow** and click **Print Preview**.

**f.** Click the **Print button** on the Print Preview toolbar. Click **Print** to print the Web page.

**g.** Click the **Close button** to close Print Preview.

**h.** Click the **Close button** to close Internet Explorer. Click Print to print the Web page.

**i.** Close any open windows. At the Desktop, right-click the **Flower graphic** and select **Delete**. Confirm the deletion.

# Browser Options and Internet Searches

Internet Explorer is more than simply a software tool through which you navigate the Internet. It also includes features that enable you to effectively search for information on just about any topic imaginable. When you identify favorite Web pages that you might want to visit later, you can *bookmark* those pages for ready access at any time. In a similar manner, you can maintain a *history* list of previously visited Web pages, even those that you might have worked with several weeks ago. By managing security settings, you can control pop-up windows (usually promoting a product or service), phishing attempts, and cookies. *Phishing* is an e-mail scam in which someone attempts to convince you to provide personal information or account numbers. The sender tries to frighten you by suggesting that one of your financial accounts or credit card accounts is possibly compromised. Pretending to be a legitimate financial institution, the sender suggests that you provide personal information so that he can address the problem. A *cookie* is a text file that is sometimes saved to your computer when you visit a Web site, identifying you as a return visitor when you revisit the site later, perhaps presenting a personalized page or remembering your site password for you.

> **Phishing** is the act of sending fraudulent e-mail in an attempt to collect personal information by pretending to be a legitimate enterprise.
>
> A **cookie** is a text file saved on your computer by a Web site that you visited.

In this section, you will learn to create a list of favorite Web sites so that you can easily return to them later. Using a history list, you can even return to sites that you might have visited several weeks ago. Searching the Internet is an easy process when you learn how to effectively phrase keywords. You will also be able to manage browser settings, such as cookies, security levels, the browser home page, and Windows updates (downloads that enhance the security or usability of your operating system).

## Working with Favorites and the History List

As you enjoy the Internet, you will identify Web pages that are favorites—those to which you often return. Especially if the address of a favorite Web page is lengthy, you will appreciate a shortcut to typing the URL each time you want to visit the site. Such a shortcut is called a *favorite*, or sometimes a *bookmark*.

> A **favorite**, or **bookmark**, is a marker that identifies a Web page so that you can quickly display the page later.

Internet Explorer provides a Favorites Center, from which you can keep track of favorite sites, adding, deleting, and renaming the references whenever you like. If your list of favorites grows long, you will want to delete some that you no longer find helpful or possibly move some into folders. The Favorites Center button, shown in Figure 1.22, is the starting point to managing your favorites.

> ( Internet Explorer provides a Favorites Center, from which you can keep track of favorite sites, adding, deleting, and renaming the references whenever you like. )

Suppose that as a grants administrator for a local university, you often locate information on the availability of National Science Foundation grants. In fact, you are such a frequent visitor that you find it extremely repetitive to type the URL each time. You know that you can add the URL to your list of favorites so that, in the future, you can simply open your favorites list and click the NSF link to quickly display the site. To do that, first display the NSF Web site (*http://www.nsf.gov*). Then click the Add to Favorites button, as shown in Figure 1.22. Click Add to Favorites. Type the name for the site or agree to the default name provided. Click the Create In drop-down arrow (see Figure 1.23) and select a folder from the Favorites menu. Instead of using a Favorites folder, you can click New Folder, type a folder name, and indicate the location in which to place the folder in the Favorites folder structure. Finally, click Add.

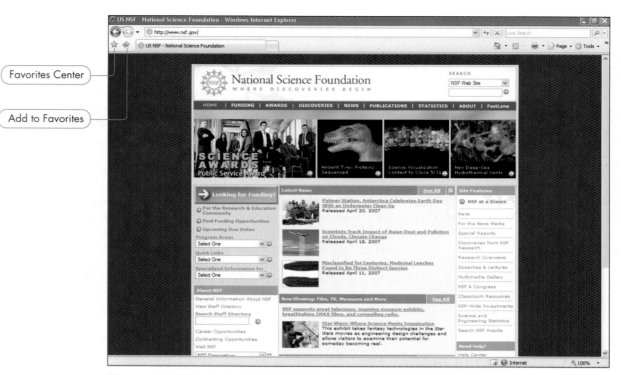

**Figure 1.22** Working with Favorites

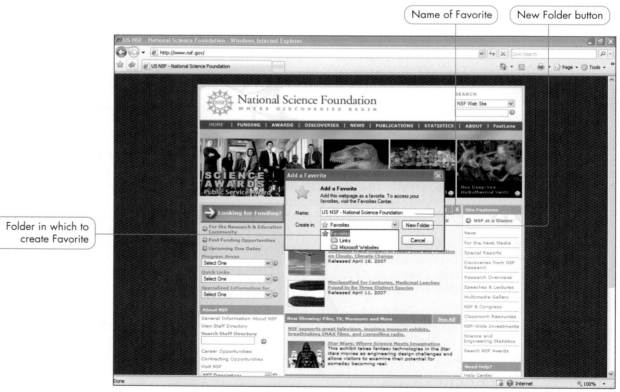

**Figure 1.23** Add a Favorite Dialog Box

## TIP Adding a Favorite

When you display a Web page that you want to make a favorite, press Ctrl+D to display the Add to Favorites dialog box. Press Alt+C to open the Favorites Center.

The next time you want to display the NSF site (which is now one of your favorites), click the Favorites Center button, as shown in Figure 1.22. The Favorites Center pane appears. Click Favorites to view your Favorites folders. Figure 1.24 shows the Favorites pane. Click a folder, if necessary. Click the NSF favorite. The Web page is displayed.

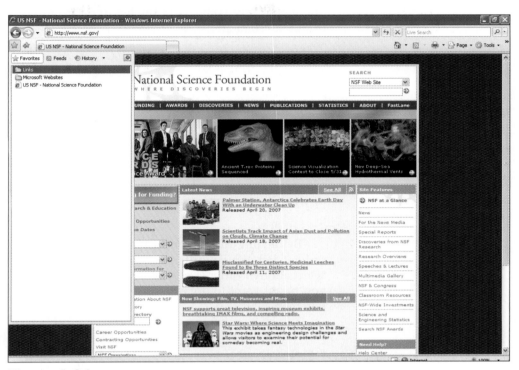

**Figure 1.24**  Favorites Pane

As your list of favorites grows, you might want to organize similar favorites into appropriately named folders. Organizing your favorites into folders helps you find related favorite Web sites faster. Click the Add to Favorites button (see Figure 1.22). Click Organize Favorites. The dialog box shown in Figure 1.25 is displayed. If you want to create a new folder in which to place one or more favorites, click New Folder, type the folder name, and press Enter. Then locate and click a favorite. Click Move. Navigate to the new folder, click it, and click OK. The favorite is moved into the folder. To access the folder, click the folder name. All favorites (and subfolders) in the folder should appear. As you can see from Figure 1.25, you can also move, rename, or delete favorites or folders from the dialog box.

**Figure 1.25**  Organize Favorites Dialog Box

At times, you may want to revisit a Web site that you viewed a few days or weeks ago, but you cannot remember the URL. If you did not make the site a favorite, you can use the History feature, which keeps track of the sites you visited, in order by date, site, most visited, or order visited today. To access the History list, click Favorites Center (see Figure 1.22). Click the History button, as shown in Figure 1.26. Then click a day or week in the pane to expand the list of sites visited. From that point, click any Web site in the list to return to it, or make an additional selection from a subsequent list.

**Figure 1.26** History List

By default, the History list is displayed by Date. However, you can change the order. Click the Favorites Center button. Click the History drop-down arrow and select another order (Date, Site, Most Visited, or Order Visited Today). For example, you might want to organize the history so that the most visited sites are displayed together.

The History list can occupy a great deal of hard drive space if it is not managed. Internet Explorer deletes the History list periodically, according to settings that you specify. To specify the number of days that pages are retained in the History list, click Tools and click Internet Options, as shown in Figure 1.27. Click the General tab. Click Settings in the *Browsing history* section. Specify the number of days to maintain history. Click OK. Click OK. To clear the History list, click Tools, and then click Delete Browsing History, as shown in Figure 1.27. Click Delete History and click Yes. Click Close.

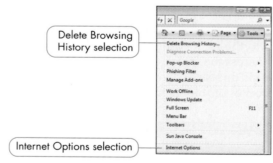

**Figure 1.27** Tools Menu

## Managing Internet Options

Because you will most likely spend a great deal of time accessing the Internet, you will want to make sure that your browser is configured to be as secure as possible. You might also want to customize the browser to suit your style and work requirements. Internet Explorer includes provisions for blocking pop-up advertisements, avoiding phishing scams, managing temporary files and cookies, and changing the home page.

## Understand and Control Cookies

If you shop online, you are aware that you are often required to provide or create personal information, such as a user name and password, for ease of access later. Similarly, online classes in which you might be enrolled, or the online financial entity with which you do business, might require identifying information. Usually that information is saved in small text files (called cookies) and placed on your hard drive. That way, when you return to the Web site, you might not even have to remember your password (because the cookie transparently provides it). You might even be greeted with a Welcome message including your name. The basic purpose of cookies is to make your life easier by remembering such items as login information and shopping preferences. At that level, nothing is wrong with cookies and you have no reason to be suspicious of them. Some advertisers, however, use *tracking cookies* to record your browsing history so that you can be targeted with advertising. If you prefer a bit more privacy than that, you will want to control the way cookies are allowed onto your computer.

To manage the way Internet Explorer deals with cookies, click Tools, Internet Options. Click the Privacy tab. The dialog box shown in Figure 1.28 is displayed. Click and drag the Settings slider to select a greater or lesser degree of cookie access. No matter where you choose to place the slider, you should make sure that you always block third-party cookies, which could come from spying advertisers. To delete all existing cookies (those that have already been copied to your computer), click Tools, Delete Browsing History, and Delete Cookies. Click Yes to confirm the deletion, and then click Close.

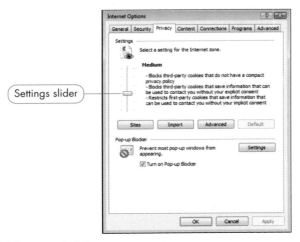

**Figure 1.28**   Privacy Settings

## Change the Home Page

The Web page that appears when you open Internet Explorer, or when you click the Home button (as shown in Figure 1.29), is the home page. If you prefer another home page, you can easily change it. Internet Explorer even enables you to select several home pages, grouping them in a tab group. Open the desired home page in a tab or tab group. Click the Home arrow and select Add or Change Home Page (see Figure 1.29). Choose either *Use this Web page as your only home page* or *Add this Web page to your home page tabs*. Click Yes.

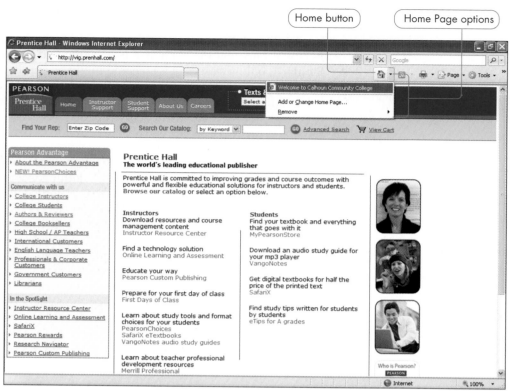

**Figure 1.29** Home Page Options

To remove one of your home pages, click the Home arrow, point to Remove, and then click the page that you want to remove. Click Yes. If you want to restore the home page to the default (the one used when Internet Explorer was installed), click Tools, Internet Options. Click the General tab. Select *Use current* or *Use blank*. The advantage to selecting a blank page for your home page is that you will not have to wait for a page to load each time you open Internet Explorer.

## Delete Temporary Internet Files

Each time you visit a Web page, Internet Explorer stores, or *caches* (pronounced "cashes"), a copy of the page on your hard drive. Then, when you revisit the page, IE is able to display the page very quickly because it opens the page from your hard drive instead of the Web server (the computer on which the Web page is actually stored). The only problem with that is that if you do not manage those temporary Internet files, they can collect in great number on your hard drive, taking up valuable storage space. To delete temporary files, click Tools, Delete Browsing History. Click Delete Files, beside Temporary Internet Files. Click Yes to confirm the deletion. Click Close. To control the amount of disk space allotted to temporary files, click Tools, Internet Options. Click Settings (in the Browsing history section). Change the amount of reserved disk space, as shown in Figure 1.30, and click OK.

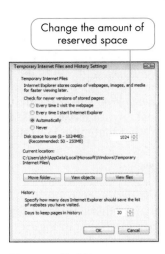

Change the amount of reserved space

**Figure 1.30** Temporary Internet File Settings

## Control Pop-Up Advertisements

A ***pop-up*** is an uninvited browser window that appears in front of an active browser window.

A ***pop-under*** is an uninvited browser window that appears when an active browser window is closed.

Pop-up and pop-under ads are windows that appear without any action on your part. They are usually advertising windows, attempting to sell a product or service. A ***pop-up*** is an advertisement that displays above the current browser window, while ***pop-under*** (sometimes called pop-behind) ads display when you close the browser window. You have to stop what you are doing and close them if you want them to go away. Although not threatening to your privacy or security, pop-up ads are usually annoying. Some pop-ups, however, might be useful, showing small help windows or enabling a chat window, for example. Internet Explorer includes a Pop-up Blocker that is turned on by default. However, you can turn it off or customize its settings so that certain pop-ups are allowed.

To check whether the Pop-up Blocker is turned on, click Tools and point to Pop-up Blocker. If necessary, click Turn On Pop-up Blocker, and then click Yes. You can click Turn off Pop-up Blocker to reverse the setting. At times, you might want to temporarily allow pop-ups. Suppose, for example, that while shopping for an item of clothing, you click a link to display a close-up of the fabric. Normally, the close-up appears in a pop-up window, which might be disallowed by Pop-up Blocker. To temporarily allow the pop-up, click the Information bar (the yellow bar that will appear at the top of Internet Explorer, providing information on an attempted action). Click Temporarily Allow Pop-Ups.

If you know of a specific Web site from which you always want to allow pop-ups—perhaps the Web site of the online class in which you are enrolled—click Tools and point to Pop-up Blocker. Click Pop-up Blocker Settings. Click in the Address of Web site to Allow box and type the address of the Web site (from which you want to allow pop-ups). Click Add. From the same dialog box, you can remove any previously allowed sites. Click Close.

## Avoid Phishing Attempts

Although it is impossible to completely protect yourself from phishing attempts (legitimate-looking e-mail messages attempting to trick you into revealing personal or financial information), Internet Explorer provides a Phishing Filter tool that helps detect known phishing sites. When you visit a known phishing site, the filter warns you with color-coded alerts in the Address bar. To check a currently displayed Web site against Microsoft's list of known phishing sites, click Tools and point to Phishing Filter. Click Check This Website. From the same menu, you can also report a possible phishing site or turn off automatic Web site checking.

# Using Search Engines

One reason to use the Internet is to find information. As you plan a trip to another country, you can use the Internet to learn more about your destination. Or perhaps your doctor has prescribed a certain drug and you wonder about the side effects. Using a *search engine*, which is a Web site specializing in searching the Internet, you can find information on almost any topic. The trick in assuring valid search results is to phrase search *keywords* so that matching Web sites are as relevant as possible.

> A *search engine* is a Web site that provides search tools so that you can find information on a topic.
>
> A *keyword* is a word or phrase that describe information that you want to retrieve.

## Select a Search Engine

Major search engines, also called search portals, include Google, Yahoo, Lycos, Windows Live Search, and many others. Internet Explorer includes a Windows Live Search box on the Address bar, as shown in Figure 1.31, which makes searching the Internet as simple as typing one or more keywords in the Search box and pressing Enter. Although your choices of search engines are many, you will probably find that you gravitate to one or the other because you appreciate a particular search engine's interface or the way it displays results to a search. Many people prefer Google, due to its fast, accurate, and comprehensive search results in order of keyword frequency. Others like Yahoo's approach to presenting major subject categories. You will find Google at *www.google.com*, whereas Yahoo is accessed at *www.yahoo.com*. Search engines review different lists of Internet content, so it is likely that searching two or more search engines using the same keywords will return different results. A comprehensive search, then, might involve more than one search engine.

> Using a search engine, which is a Web site specializing in searching the Internet, you can find information on almost any topic.

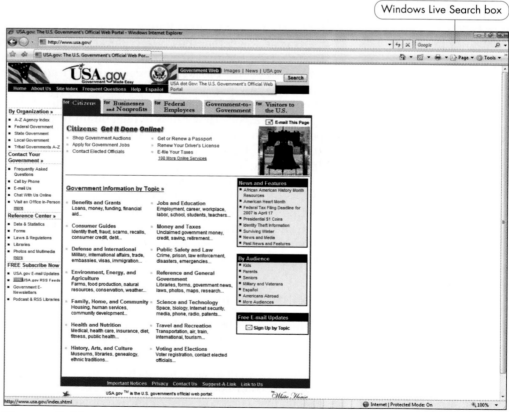

**Figure 1.31** Windows Live Search

## Phrase a Search

Regardless of which search engine you choose, your first task is to phrase keywords in such a way as to return the most relevant Web site matches. The more specific you are, the better. For example, if you are seeking information on purchasing a Dell computer, you could type the word *Dell* in a search or keyword area. However, probably thousands of Web sites related to the Dell Corporation exist. Instead, you might phrase your search, *Purchasing a Dell computer*. The number of sites returned will likely be far fewer but more relevant.

As you work with search engines, you will probably develop a preference for one site or tool that seems to work well for you. Perhaps you enjoy the ease with which you can get immediate results through Windows Live Search. Or maybe you like the way Google differentiates results that are sponsored links (those paid for by advertisers) from those that are not sponsored. Although search engine sites are very similar in the way they act on your keywords, minor differences exist, especially in the phrasing of more complex searches. If you return to the same search site frequently, you will become familiar with its unique search rules and will learn to effectively initiate searches. You can usually find a *Help* menu item or link that will provide information on how to work with the particular search site.

When phrasing keywords, you should consider using several keywords. For example, if you want to get suggestions on how to prepare an effective resume, you should be as specific as possible in your selection of keywords—*tips for preparing a resume* will return more relevant results than simply *resume*. Advanced search phrasing, using AND, OR, and NOT terms, is an option with most search sites. Also, you can place search keywords between quotation marks if you want to identify only those Web sites containing the keywords in that particular order. The keyword phrase *"Ancient Rome"* will only show sites containing both keywords in that order, whereas the keywords *Ancient Rome*, without quotation marks, will list sites containing either the word *Ancient* or *Rome*. It is usually true, however, that sites containing both keywords, in any order, will be shown first.

If a search is successful, you will see a list of sites matching the search keyword criteria. Each resulting site will contain a short summary and an underlined link. Click the link to open the site. Click the Back button to return to the results so that you can click to view another site.

# Hands-On Exercises

## 2 | Exploring Browser Options and Searching the Web

**Skills covered: 1.** Create Favorites **2.** Control Cookies and Temporary Internet Files **3.** Manage the History List
**4.** Search the Web

---

<table>
<tr>
<td valign="top">

**Step 1**

**Create Favorites**

</td>
<td valign="top">

Refer to Figure 1.32 as you complete Step 1.

**a.** Open Internet Explorer and visit **http://www.sba.gov**.

You plan to start a small business and want to be fully informed of possibilities as well as risks. A good place to start is the U.S. Small Business Administration Web site.

**b.** Click **Local Resources**.

You think it would be helpful to find what assistance may be available in your area of the country.

**c.** Click your state on the map provided.

**d.** Click the **Add to Favorites button** and click **Add to Favorites**. Accept the Name provided.

**e.** Click the **New Folder button**. Type **Business Information** in the **Folder Name** box. Make sure **Favorites** is displayed in the **Create in** box, as shown in Figure 1.32. Click **Create**, and then click **Add**.

</td>
</tr>
</table>

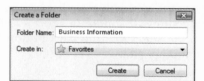

**Figure 1.32** Creating a Favorite

**f.** Visit **www.entrepreneur.com**.

You have learned about a Web site dedicated to the principles of business success, called Entrepreneur.com.

**g.** Click the **Add to Favorites button**. Click **Add to Favorites**. If Business Information does not appear in the Create in area, click the **drop-down arrow** to the right and click **Business Information**.

**h.** Click in the **Name box** and replace the current contents with **Entrepreneur.com**. Click **Add**.

**i.** Click the **Favorites Center button**, and then click **Favorites**. Click the **Business Information folder**. Click **Small Business Administration** to return to the SBA page.

**j.** Click the **Add to Favorites button**, and then click **Organize Favorites**. Click the **Business Information folder** and click **Delete**. Click **Yes** to confirm the deletion, and then click **Close**.

Since you are probably working in a public computer lab, you will remove the Business Information folder.

---

## Step 2
### Control Cookies and Temporary Internet Files

Refer to Figure 1.33 as you complete Step 2.

**a.** Click **Tools**. Click **Internet Options.**

**b.** Click the **Privacy tab**, as shown in Figure 1.33.

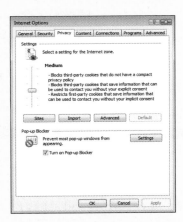

**Figure 1.33** Manage Privacy Settings

**c.** Click and drag the Settings tab to **High**.

This will block all cookies that save information about you without your written consent.

**d.** Click the **Turn off (or Turn on) Pop-up Blocker check box**. Click the check box again to return the setting to its original state. Click **Cancel**.

Since you are most likely in a public computer lab, you will not actually make any changes to the privacy settings.

**e.** Click **Tools**, and then click **Delete Browsing History**.

Before completing Step f, check with your instructor to be certain that you are allowed to delete temporary Internet files.

**f.** Click **Delete Files** (beside Temporary Internet Files). Click **Yes**.

**g.** Click **Close**.

Refer to Figure 1.34 as you complete Step 3.

**a.** Click the **Favorites Center button** (see Figure 1.34).

**b.** Click **History.**

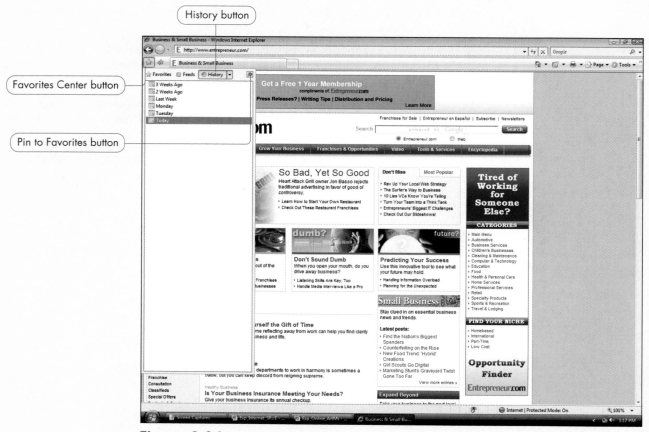

**Figure 1.34** Manage the History List

**c.** Click the **History drop-down arrow** and select **By Site**.

**d.** Click the **History drop-down arrow** and select **By Most Visited**.

**e.** Click the **History drop-down arrow** and select **By Order Visited Today**.

**f.** Click the **green arrow** to the right of the History list (see Figure 1.34) to pin the list to the toolbar.

**g.** Click the **Close button** at the top right of the History list to close it.

**h.** Click **Tools**. Before completing Step i, check with your instructor to see if you are permitted to delete the History log.

**i.** Click **Delete Browsing History**.

**j.** Click **Delete History** (beside History).

**k.** Click **Yes**, and then click **Close**.

**a.** Visit **www.rif.org**.

As a volunteer with a local literacy program, you are going to work with elementary school children in encouraging reading. The elementary school to which you are assigned has a large number of Hispanic children, so you will research tools that will help you reach children of all backgrounds.

**b.** Click a Volunteer link to learn how to volunteer with Reading Is Fundamental.

**c.** Click the **Back button** to return to the RIF home page.

**d.** Click in the **Windows Live Search box**.

**e.** Type keywords related to literacy tools for teaching English as a second language (perhaps *teaching English as a second language*). Click the **Search button** (magnifying glass). You should see several resulting Web sites.

**f.** Visit **www.yahoo.com**.

**g.** Repeat step (e), but use Yahoo's keyword **area**.

Using the Yahoo search engine, did you find any sources that were different from those you found when using Windows Live Search?

**h.** Close Internet Explorer.

# Online Communication

Communicating with others online, primarily through *e-mail*, has become a way of life for many people. Windows Vista includes the **Windows Mail** e-mail program, which enables you to send and receive e-mail, whereas **Windows Contacts** can be used to manage your contacts (people or companies with whom you communicate electronically).

In this section, you learn how to work with Windows Mail, composing e-mail messages, receiving e-mail, and managing a contacts list. You will also learn about instant messaging and blogs.

**E-mail** is the transmission of messages over a communication network.

**Windows Mail** is an e-mail program included with Windows Vista.

**Windows Contacts** is a Windows Vista feature that stores information about people with whom you communicate electronically.

## Communicating Through Windows Mail

Many people often cite e-mail as the primary reason for purchasing a computer. E-mail is a form of electronic communication that enables you to send and receive messages and files. Most workplaces now use e-mail extensively to communicate with employees, conducting business and passing along company communiqués. Indeed, e-mail communication worldwide between people of all backgrounds, ages, and employment status is now the norm—so much so that a new form of grammar seems to have emerged. Acronyms, such as TTYL (talk to you later) and IMO (in my opinion), are commonly used shortcuts in very informal e-mail messages. Although e-mail communication is quick and easy, you should remain aware of the need to communicate effectively, avoiding grammatical and spelling errors and always remembering that a person is at the other end your message.

( Windows Mail enables you to communicate with anyone who has an e-mail account. )

Windows Vista includes an e-mail program called Windows Mail, which replaces Outlook Express (an e-mail program included with earlier versions of IE). Windows Mail enables you to communicate with anyone who has an e-mail account. It also includes provisions for attachments, filtering junk mail, identifying possible phishing attempts, and personalization.

### Create E-mail

Creating and sending an e-mail message is, in many ways, similar to sending a letter through the postal service. The postal stations through which a letter would travel are analogous to e-mail servers (computers) through which your e-mail message will pass on its way to the recipient. To use e-mail, you must have access to the Internet and must have an e-mail account with an e-mail provider. Some accounts, such as those that you can set up with Yahoo (*www.yahoo.com*) and Google (*www.google.com*), are free, but to use your e-mail account, you must still connect to the Internet, either through an Internet Service Provider (ISP) or through a public computer facility. Anyone with an e-mail account has a unique e-mail address composed of a user id, the @ sign, and the e-mail server. For example, if your ISP is America Online, and your AOL user id is pthornton38799, then your e-mail address is pthornton38799@aol.com. Just as you cannot send an unaddressed letter through the mail, you cannot send an e-mail message without addressing it first.

Before using Windows Mail, you will need your account name, password, e-mail server type, and the names of your incoming and outgoing e-mail servers from your ISP or network administrator. To access Windows Mail, click Start, Windows Mail. Follow the steps provided by the Connect to the Internet wizard to set up your e-mail account. During the e-mail setup process, you will provide your display name (simply your name) and the e-mail address from your ISP (for example, pthornton38799@aol.com). You will also be asked for e-mail server information, which is the information provided by your ISP about its mail servers. When the setup process is complete, you will be able to send and receive e-mail through Windows Mail. The Windows Mail window is shown in Figure 1.35.

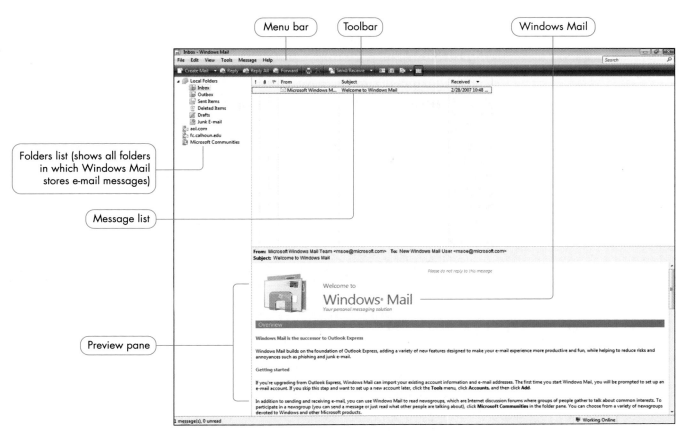

**Figure 1.35** Windows Mail

When you want to send a message, open Windows Mail and click Create Mail on the toolbar. A new message window appears, as shown in Figure 1.36. Type the recipient's e-mail address in the To area. You must type a complete address, including *@server*. For example, if you are sending a message to Patricia Thornton, you might type pthornton38799@aol.com in the To box. To send a message to more than one address, separate addresses with a semicolon (;). If you want to send a copy of the e-mail to others, type additional addresses in the carbon copy (Cc) area. Although you are not required to include an entry in the Subject line, it is a good idea to do so. Click in the Message area (large white box) and type the e-mail contents.

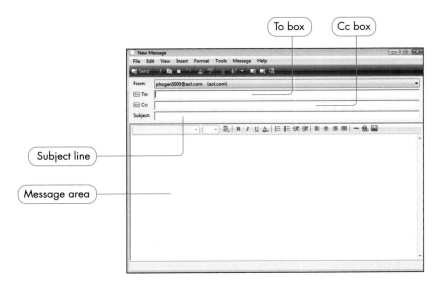

**Figure 1.36** Composing an E-mail

When sending an e-mail message to several people, you might consider using the bcc (blind carbon copy) area. Bcc recipients do not see the addresses of other recipients. Therefore, it is a good way to maintain the privacy of your friends' e-mail addresses. Professors often use bcc to send e-mail to all the students in their classes so that the students don't see each other's e-mail addresses. It also keeps recipients from having to scroll through a long list of names in the To area before reading the message content. To see the bcc box, click View, All Headers.

Although composing an e-mail is usually quick and easy, you should give thought to wording and spelling. To check spelling, click Tools, Spelling. The spelling check is only available if Microsoft Office is installed on your computer. Of course, you should also proofread each e-mail message yourself, because the spell check might not catch all incorrect word usages. Because the recipient cannot see your face or interpret your body language, proper wording is very important.

> ## TIP   Including an E-mail Subject
>
> It is a good idea to also fill in the Subject line of an e-mail message, because that gives your recipient an idea of why you are writing. Briefly, the subject line should summarize the body of your message. It should relate directly to your message, not have a generic plea like *Urgent* or *Very Important*. Although many senders neglect to use it, the subject line is particularly important if you want to make sure your message is read. Almost everyone receives large amounts of junk mail. By inserting a subject line in your message you give the reader an incentive to open, not delete, your message.

## Check Spelling Automatically

You might want to have your e-mail messages spell-checked automatically before sending them. To have Windows Mail automatically check your spelling, click Tools. Click Options. Click the Spelling tab and select *Always check spelling before sending*. Click OK.

To be an effective e-mail communicator, you should be aware of commonly recognized suggestions for electronic communication, commonly called *netiquette*.

- Always type in upper and lowercase (not ALL CAPS). Capital letters have the effect of shouting in your e-mail.

- Be concise and to the point.

- Use proper spelling and punctuation. It is not cute to be informal and sloppy.

- Answer e-mails as quickly as possible. As a medium designed for speed, e-mail has raised expectations for quick response.

- Consider not forwarding chain e-mails. A chain e-mail is a message that suggests that you forward it to others to promote a cause or to pass along news, rumors, or jokes. Those who use e-mail for work-related purposes might not appreciate the glut that chain letters cause in an inbox.

- Never send an e-mail when you are angry. E-mail is anything but confidential and can be forwarded to many people in very short order.

- Avoid using words like "Urgent" and "Important." These create a false sense of urgency and imply that your message is somehow more important than others.

**TIP** Creating a Signature

Instead of typing your name at the end of every e-mail message, you can create a signature file that is automatically added to each e-mail that you send. Click Tools. Click Options. Click the Signatures tab. Click New. Type your signature information—perhaps your name, title, and contact information. Click Set as Default. If necessary, click to select Add signature to all outgoing messages. Click OK.

## Assess E-mail Privacy

It is natural to assume that sending an e-mail is much like using the U.S. Postal Service to send a letter. You compose your message, put it in an (electronic or paper) envelope, and send it on its way to your desired recipient. When that person receives your e-mail, he or she opens and reads it in private. This expectation is reasonable when it comes to a post office letter. It is highly unlikely that anyone will steam open your sealed envelope, read its contents, then reseal and send it on its way.

In the case of Internet e-mail, however, this expectation is totally misguided. To be blunt: e-mail privacy is not guaranteed. When an e-mail message traverses the Internet, it moves from e-mail server to e-mail server across a network that encompasses tens of thousands of other networks. Its path is determined by routers and is based on traffic patterns in different network areas. Because of this very open route, it is almost impossible to protect an e-mail message from snooping. In addition, because the message might make stops on many servers, copies of your e-mail could exist in places you never intended for it to go. As you can readily see, privacy is not guaranteed. So, the best policy is to never put anything in an e-mail that you do not want others to see.

## Attach Files

An ***attachment*** is a file that is sent along with an e-mail message.

Occasionally, you might want to use e-mail to share a file, such as a photograph or newsletter. The file that is sent along with an e-mail message is called an ***attachment***. When the e-mail arrives, the recipient must open the file in the program that created it or in another compatible program. Although it is sometimes necessary to send attachments, especially in the workplace, several problems are associated with them. They could be large files, taking up a good bit of space in the recipient's inbox. Most e-mail providers limit the size of allowable attachments so that they do not monopolize e-mail server space. Attachments are also a primary vehicle for the transmission of viruses. A virus is an annoying or destructive program that is often disguised as an attachment. You should only send attachments when absolutely necessary.

To attach a file, first compose a message. Then click the Attach File to Message button on the toolbar (Figure 1.37). Navigate through the folder structure to locate the file to attach. Click to select the file, as shown in Figure 1.38. Click Open and then click Send to send the file.

Attach File to Message button

**Figure 1.37** Attaching a File

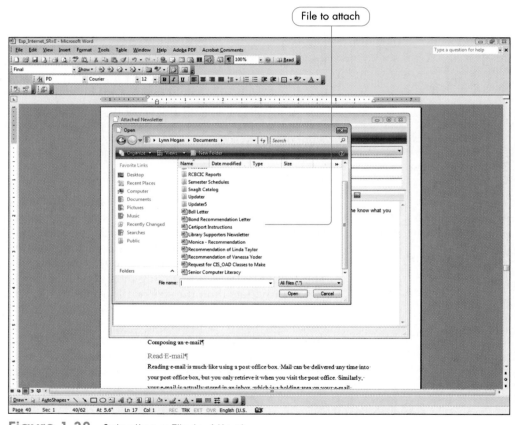

File to attach

**Figure 1.38** Selecting a File to Attach

## Read E-mail

Reading e-mail is much like using a post office box. Mail can be delivered any time into your post office box, but you only retrieve it when you visit the post office. Similarly, your e-mail is actually stored in an inbox, which is a holding area on your e-mail provider's server. To read your e-mail, you actually access the server's inbox, but the e-mail is not saved on your computer unless you specify that it should be. Windows Mail will check for new mail messages each time you open the program, and periodically thereafter while the program is open. Messages in boldface are new messages. Flags or paperclips beside messages indicate a certain priority or the presence of an attachment.

To open your inbox and read mail, click the Inbox icon in the folder list for your e-mail account (see Figure 1.39). To preview a message, single-click the message in the inbox. To open a message so that you can reply to the sender or forward the message to others, double-click it in the inbox.

**Figure 1.39**  Display Contents of Inbox

After reading an e-mail, you can reply to the sender, reply to everyone who originally received the e-mail, or forward the e-mail on to others. Figure 1.40 shows the Reply, Reply All, and Forward buttons. Click Reply to send a response to the sender. Similarly, clicking Reply All will send your response to everyone who received the original message. You can easily send the message to others by clicking Forward. A new message opens, containing the original message. Type the e-mail addresses of the new recipients in the To box. Change the Subject line and edit the message contents, if you like. Click Send.

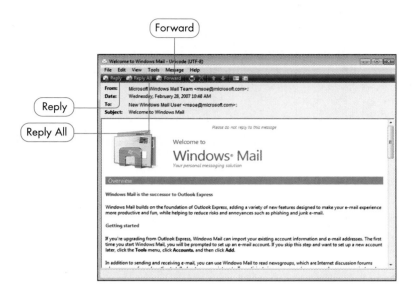

**Figure 1.40** Reply or Forward Options

**TIP** Watch for Phishing

Phishing attempts usually come through e-mail. Windows Mail can help minimize phishing. Click Tools and click Junk E-mail Options. Click the Phishing tab. Select Protect my Inbox from messages with potential Phishing links. Select Move phishing E-mail to the Junk Mail folder. Click OK.

## Receive Attachments

If someone has sent you an e-mail with an attachment, you will see a paperclip beside the message in your inbox. You can either open the attachment or save it to your hard drive for later access. To open the attachment, double-click the file icon in the Attach area (see Figure 1.41). To save an attachment, click the paperclip icon in the header and choose Save Attachments.

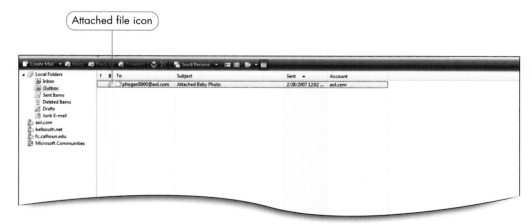

**Figure 1.41** Open an Attachment

## Use Windows Contacts

A feature of Windows Vista, Windows Contacts enables you to store contact information about people or organizations to which you regularly send e-mail. Such information can include mailing addresses, phone numbers, e-mail addresses, job titles, cell phone numbers, and Web page addresses. You can organize your contacts into groups so that you can easily address e-mail messages to several contacts at once.

To enter a Contact, click the Contacts button on the toolbar, as shown in Figure 1.42. You can also click the Start button, point to All Programs, and click Windows Contacts. If needed, click a folder that has your e-mail address as its name, and then click a WindowsLiveContact (file extension) in that folder. Click the New Contact button on the toolbar. Enter the contact's name and e-mail address. Click Add. Click any other tabs to add additional information, as shown in Figure 1.43. Click OK. Click Close.

**Figure 1.42**  Create a Contact

To create a Contact Group, click the Contacts button on the toolbar, as shown in Figure 1.42. Click the New Contact Group button. Type a name for the new group. Click Add to Contact Group. This displays a list of current contacts. Click a contact that you want to add to the group. To select multiple contacts, press and hold Ctrl while clicking additional contacts. Click Add. Click OK, and then click Close.

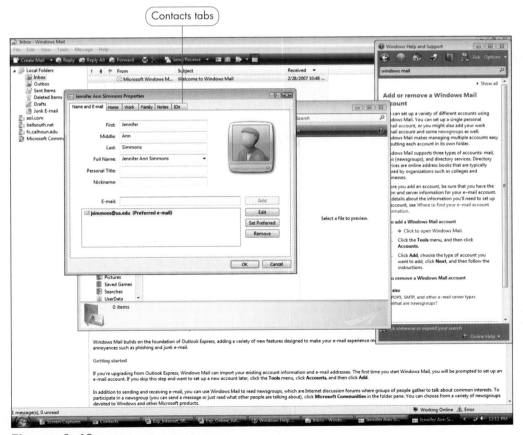

**Figure 1.43**  Add a Contact

# Communicating Through Instant Messages and Blogs

An ***instant message*** is a form of online communication that enables you to type messages to and receive messages from others who are online at the same time.

A ***blog*** is a personal journal entry that is posted online.

Although e-mail is probably the most common type of online communication, you certainly have other choices. Many people enjoy creating ***instant messages***—communicating in real time with others by simply typing messages and receiving immediate responses. Gaining immense popularity is the use of ***blogs*** (short for *Web Log*), which is the online equivalent of personal journal entries. As is the case with e-mail, privacy is not guaranteed, and a small amount of risk exists with instant messaging and blogging. Viruses can be passed through instant messages, and blogs have been subject to abuse by online predators. Nevertheless, both instant messaging and blogging are very popular forms of communication in the online community.

## Use Instant Messaging

The use of instant messages is so widespread that the term is now both a noun and verb. An instant message is a message that you type and send to a friend who is online at the same time that you are. When you send the message, you are said to be *instant messaging* (or *IMing*, for short). To participate in instant messaging, you must first download an IM client, such as Windows Live Messenger or America Online's Instant Messenger (AIM). In addition, you will set up a list of online *buddies*, with whom you plan to communicate. That list is called your Buddy List. You can add or remove buddies at any time. When both you and a buddy are online at the same time, you can send instant messages to each other.

When a buddy is online, you are notified. If you want to chat, you can send an instant message. Your buddy can either accept or reject the communication. You can even chat with more than one person through a custom IM chat room. Unlike regular chat rooms, an IM is designed to be private communication, typically between two people who are online at the same time. Remember, however, that no form of online communication can be guaranteed private.

Although instant messaging is most often used as a method of online communication between friends or business associates, you can also use it to receive updates on daily news, weather, or stock quotes. Because no standard instant messaging protocol exists, you can only communicate with those who are using the same IM service that you are.

Instant messages can be used to communicate both text and attachments. Because attachments are a major vehicle for transmitting viruses, it is possible that an instant message could infect your computer. Therefore, you should make sure that your antivirus software is current and updated regularly. Many businesses are not too fond of instant messaging, viewing the practice as both a virus risk and a waste of employee time and company resources. Instant messaging is not appropriate for all communication; at times, the discussion topic is best understood with personal interaction, where your body language is understood, emotion is conveyed, and the inflection of your voice makes a point.

## Use Blogs

A blog (short for Web Log) is an online journal entry. People who record blogs do so because they want to share their thoughts in a form that is accessible by others. Blogs are not necessarily private. Unless your blog is protected with a password, anyone with access to the Internet can read a posted blog. Even a password is no guarantee of absolute privacy. Blogs can be a lot of fun, but be aware that they are also public statements. In the past, students have been charged with criminal activity when they posted threats against their school or classmates. Blogs have also been misused by predators who learn a lot about their possible victims through blogging sites.

Blogs are simple to create and easy to manage. Visit a site such as *www.livejournal.com* to create a blog for free. For an annual fee, you can also include pictures or subpages. Figure 1.44 displays a blog entry.

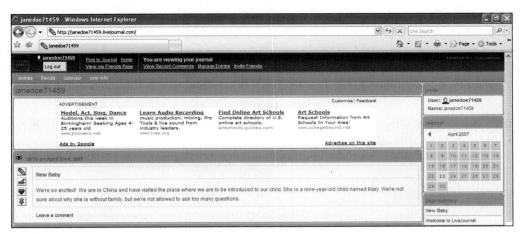

**Figure 1.44** A Blog

# Hands-On Exercises

## 3 | Communicating Online

**Skills covered: 1.** Create E-mail **2.** Attach a File **3.** Use Windows Contacts **4.** Use Phishing Filter **5.** Create a Blog

---

**Step 1**
**Create E-mail**

Refer to Figure 1.45 as you complete Step 1.

**a.** Click **Start**, position the mouse over **All Programs**, and click **Windows Mail**.

Check with your instructor before completing this hands-on exercise. Because you are most likely working in a public computer lab, you should only complete this hands-on exercise at your home. Above all, you will not want to enter your private e-mail identification in a public computer lab.

**b.** Follow all prompts to create a Windows Mail account (unless you already have an account).

Before creating an account, you must be aware of your ISP e-mail server name (both incoming and outgoing) and any login information, such as your password.

**c.** Click **Create Mail**.

**d.** Click in the **To box**, as shown in Figure 1.45, and enter an e-mail address (perhaps a friend's or instructor's).

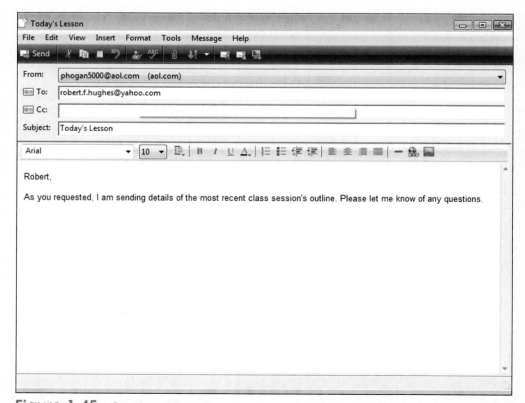

**Figure 1.45** Create an E-mail

**e.** Click in the **Subject box** and type an appropriate subject line.

**f.** Click in the **Message area** and type a message.

**g.** Click **Send**.

**h.** Close Windows Mail.

**Step 2**
**Attach a File**

Refer to Figure 1.46 as you complete Step 2.

**a.** Click **Start**, position the mouse over **All Programs**, click **Accessories**, and click **WordPad**.

**b.** Type a list of supplies that would be expected of a student in a beginning computer class (flash drive, textbook, package of CDs).

**c.** Select **File**, and then select **Save As**.

**d.** Type **chap1_ho3_supplies** in the file name area.

**e.** Click **Browse Folders** (in the left pane) and click **Desktop**.

**f.** Click **Save**. Close WordPad.

**g.** Open Windows Mail.

**h.** Click **Create Mail**.

**i.** Follow Steps 1d, 1e, and 1f to create an e-mail giving information about the Supplies attachment that you plan to send to a fellow student who missed class the first day.

**j.** Click the **Attach File to Message button**, as shown in Figure 1.46.

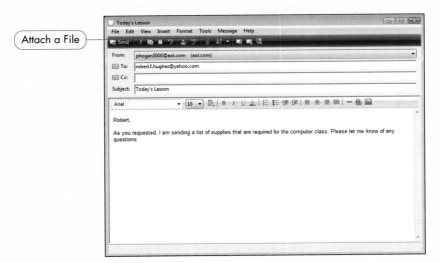

**Figure 1.46** Attach a File

**k.** Click **Desktop** in the left pane.

> **TROUBLESHOOTING:** If you do not see Desktop in the left pane, click Folders.

**l.** Scroll down in the right pane to find *chap1_ho3_supplies*.

**m.** Double-click the file.

**n.** Click **Send**.

Refer to Figure 1.47 as you complete Step 3.

a. Click the folder named as your e-mail address, click a WindowsLiveContact (file extension) in that folder, and click the **Contacts button** on the toolbar.

b. Click **New Contact**.

c. Type contact information for a friend or fictitious person, as shown in Figure 1.47.

**Figure 1.47** Add a Contact

d. Click **Add** and add two more contacts.

e. Click **New Contact Group**.

f. Type a name for the group—**Class Contacts**.

g. Click **Add to Contact Group**.

h. Click a contact.

i. Click **Add**.

j. Add the other two contacts to the group.

k. Click **OK**.

l. Click **Close**.

a. Click **Tools**.

b. Click **Junk E-mail Options**.

c. Click the **Phishing tab**.

d. If it is not already selected, click to select **Protect my Inbox from messages with potential Phishing links**.

e. If it is not already selected, click to select **Move phishing e-mail to the Junk Mail folder**.

f. Click **OK**.

g. Close Windows Mail.

Refer to Figure 1.48 as you complete Step 5.

a. Open Internet Explorer. Click in the **Address bar**, type **www.livejournal.com**, and press **Enter**.

b. Click **Create an Account**.

c. Fill in the form, creating a username and password. If you do not want to supply your e-mail address, you can create a separate e-mail account in *www.hotmail.com* and use that e-mail address on the LiveJournal form. If you do not want to receive e-mail from LiveJournal, click to deselect "Yes, occasionally e-mail me LiveJournal updates." Click to agree to the Terms of Service (read the terms, first).

d. Click **Create Account**.

e. Click the box below Basic (to select the basic free service).

f. Edit your profile, as requested, only providing information that you feel comfortable with.

g. Click **Save and Continue**.

h. Click **Ready for more!**

i. Point to **Journal** and click **Post an Entry**.

j. Click in the **Subject box** and type a subject for your blog (something related to a recent or dreamed of vacation).

k. Click in the large white area and type a blog entry describing the vacation event.

Use this blog as a learning exercise only. Under no circumstances should you provide identifying information such as your name, address, or phone number.

**Figure 1.48** Create a Blog

l. Scroll to the bottom of the Web page and click the **Show this entry to drop-down arrow**. Click **Just Me (Private)**.

m. Click **Post to** *your username*.

n. Click **View the entry**.

o. Click **Logout**.

p. Close Internet Explorer.

# Summary

1. **Understand the World Wide Web.** The World Wide Web is a set of interconnected networks that is accessible to anyone with an Internet connection. Certain rules, or protocol, govern the way that Web pages are displayed and accessed. A Web site is a collection of one or more Web pages. To access a Web site, you can type the address in the Address bar of a browser, such as Internet Explorer 7.

2. **Access and navigate a Web site.** To access a Web site, you must either type a URL in the browser Address bar or click a hyperlink on a Web page. A URL is composed of several parts, including the protocol, company or entity name, and a top-level domain. A hyperlink can be either graphic or text.

3. **Print Web pages.** Although Web pages are not necessarily designed to be printed, you can print a Web page using Print settings provided by Internet Explorer. You can preview a page first and change print settings to modify the page orientation and add headers and footers.

4. **Download information and graphics.** The Web is rich with resources, some of which you can download to your computer. Files or programs are often available as downloads from Web sites. In addition, you can collect graphics, such as photographs and clip art from the Web.

5. **Work with Favorites and the History lists.** Two ways of finding sites you have previously visited are the History and Favorites lists. The History list includes sites visited during the past several weeks, although you can control the number of days or weeks the history is kept. The Favorites list is an area to which you can add links to your favorite, or often visited, Web sites.

6. **Manage Internet options.** You can easily customize certain browser settings, specifically those that deal with your privacy and security. Cookies, which are small identifying text files copied to your computer when you visit Web pages, are most often not harmful. However, you can delete them if you like. Internet Explorer includes a Phishing Filter and Pop-up Blocker that help protect your privacy and keep annoying pop-up ads to a minimum. You can also change your browser's home page.

7. **Use search engines.** The Web is a valuable source of information. Using a search resource, such as Google or Windows Live Search, you can provide keywords that return information on just about any topic imaginable. You will learn to select keywords that narrow the search so that you are presented with relevant information.

8. **Communicate through Windows Mail.** Windows Mail is a program provided with Windows Vista. Using Windows Mail, you can view and manage e-mail from your ISP account. Windows Mail works in conjunction with Windows Contacts, a program that stores information on those people or organizations with which you regularly communicate.

9. **Communicate through instant messages and blogs.** Online communication also includes instant messages and blogs. An instant message is a personal typewritten conversation between two or more people who are online at the same time. A blog is a personal online journal in which you can record and post anything. Be aware that neither blogs nor instant messages are necessarily private. Several Web sites provide free blogging space, and you can easily download free software that facilitates instant messaging.

# Key Terms

# Multiple Choice

1. A unique address for a Web site or Web resource is a(n):

   (a) Browser address
   (b) ISP
   (c) Uniform Resource Locator
   (d) Hyperlink

2. Phishing is:

   (a) Sending what appears to be legitimate e-mail, but attempting to fraudulently acquire personal identification
   (b) Seeking another person's e-mail address through a Web site such as *www.whowhatwhere.com*
   (c) Saving a small text file on another person's computer so that they can be targeted with advertising
   (d) Sending chain e-mails

3. This program is an e-mail component of Windows Vista:

   (a) Outlook Express
   (b) Windows Mail
   (c) Outlook
   (d) Windows Addresses

4. Which of the following domain types is most likely associated with a "for profit" entity?

   (a) .com
   (b) .edu
   (c) .gov
   (d) .org

5. Links on Web pages

   (a) Direct you to other pages on the same Web site, but never to another Web site
   (b) Are always identified by a graphic image
   (c) Open the Help menu for the Web page
   (d) Are usually identified by a pointing hand (as the mouse pointer)

6. Windows Mail

   (a) Can only be used if you do not have another e-mail account
   (b) Is no longer available—it was a component of Internet Explorer 6
   (c) Includes an address book feature called Windows Contacts
   (d) Takes a predetermined route to its destination

7. Cookies are small data files

   (a) Placed on your computer by a Web server
   (b) That help IE maintain your History list
   (c) That make your downloads go faster
   (d) That compress photos into the .jpg format

8. Internet Explorer's search box is called:

   (a) Google
   (b) Browser Search
   (c) Yahoo
   (d) Windows Live Search

9. The Favorites list:

   (a) Reflects those sites that you have visited most often
   (b) Depends on you to add sites you want to remember
   (c) Is determined by a vote of Web users
   (d) Needs to be updated after a specified number of days

10. To adjust your computer's privacy setting,

    (a) Click Tools, Privacy
    (b) Click Tools, Settings, Privacy
    (c) Click Tools, Internet Options, Privacy
    (d) Click Tools, Privacy, Settings

11. The reason that Web pages sometimes display more quickly when you press the Back button than they did when you first viewed them is that they

    (a) Remain in RAM indefinitely
    (b) Are saved locally on the hard drive, from which they can be retrieved quickly
    (c) Are automatically saved as Favorites
    (d) Are only scanned for viruses once, when they are first displayed

12. When viewing a Web page, such as local weather or national news headlines, you might want to refresh the page. Which function key enables you to quickly refresh the view?

    (a) F1
    (b) F3
    (c) F5
    (d) F7

**13.** One concern that businesses have with employees using instant messaging at work is

  (a) The use of company time and resources for non-work-related activities

  (b) The subscription cost for instant messaging

  (c) The hardware requirements for instant messaging

  (d) Computer downtime caused by spyware-riddled instant messages

**14.** A personal journal, maintained online, is called a

  (a) Blog

  (b) Instant Message

  (c) Windows Contact

  (d) Sidebar

**15.** Which of the following services provides instant messaging?

  (a) Windows Live Messenger

  (b) Google Sidekick

  (c) Vista Today

  (d) AIG (America Online Instant Greeting)

# Practice Exercises

As you near college graduation, you look forward to increasing your earnings with a new career. You plan not only to enjoy your income, but to save or invest a substantial portion. Several of your friends have asked you to join them in beginning an investment club, and although the idea sounds interesting, you want to do a little research before you agree. You are aware that the National Association of Investors Corporation (NAIC) has guidelines for running a successful investment club, so you begin your research there.

a. Open Internet Explorer. Visit **www.better-investing.org**. Under Benefits of Membership, click **Learn More** (you might have to scroll down slightly to find the link). Scroll to the bottom of the next Web page to view several items and training that you receive as a Better Investing member. What products and services would you receive?

b. Scroll to the top of the Web page and click the **About Us** link, and then click **Our Mission** to discover the mission of Better Investing. What is the mission?

c. Click the **Home** link on the Our Mission page to return to the home page.

d. Press and hold **Ctrl** while you click the **Personal Finance Tips** link in the Learn Something New group. You should see a tab for the Home page and a tab for the Tools and Resources page.

e. In similar fashion, create a tab for the **Online Discussions and Forums** link in the Benefits of Membership group. You should have three tabs. Click each tab to cycle among the tabbed pages.

f. Right-click the **Home page tab** and select **Close Other Tabs**. All tabs, with the exception of the Home page, should close.

g. Click a graphic link on the Home page. Click the **Back button** to return to the home page.

h. Find and click a link on the Home page to identify the monthly magazine that you could receive as a Better Investing member. What is the magazine? If several magazines are listed, list them all.

i. Close Internet Explorer.

j. Click **Start**, position the mouse over **All Programs**, click **Accessories**, and then click **WordPad**. At the top of the page, type your name and class. Answer the following questions:

- What products and services would you receive as a Better Investing member?
- What is the mission of Better Investing?
- What is the magazine or magazines that you could receive as a Better Investing member?

k. Save the report as **chap1_prac1_investing**.

l. Print a copy of the report.

m. Close WordPad.

Your language arts instructor has asked you to serve as student editor of the college newspaper, *The Voice*. Several student reporters use one computer for Internet research and article development, and as the editor, you are concerned about the security, privacy, and smooth operation of the computer. You want to make sure the History list and cookies are periodically deleted and that temporary Internet files are removed. You also want to be certain that the computer is protected against spyware. Although you will not make changes to the school computer, you will prepare a report for your instructor giving step-by-step instructions on how to manage privacy settings. You will also make a recommendation for antispyware software. You will use Internet Explorer to manage privacy settings and to research antispyware options.

a. Open Internet Explorer.

b. Click **Favorites Center** and then click **History**. The History list probably displays by date. To view it in another order, click the **History drop-down arrow** and click **By Most Visited**. Change the view back to **By Date**.

...continued on Next Page

c. In preparation for your report, follow these steps to delete the History list. Click **Tools** and click **Delete Browsing History**. Note that you could click Delete history, as shown in Figure 1.49, to delete the current History list. Do not delete the History—just make note of the steps to follow. Click **No.**

d. Similarly, follow the steps to delete cookies. Click **Tools** and click **Delete Browsing History**. Note that you could click Delete cookies beside Cookies. Do not delete Cookies, but make note of the steps to follow. Click **No.**

e. Follow the steps to delete temporary Internet files. Click **Tools** and click **Delete Browsing History**. Note that you could click Delete files beside Temporary Internet Files. Do not delete Temporary Internet Files, but make note of the steps to follow. Click **No.** Click **Close.**

f. Click in the **Address bar**, type **www.google.com**, and press **Enter**. The insertion point should be blinking in the keyword area. Type **antispyware software review** and press **Enter**.

g. Click any interesting links to help determine a good choice for antispyware software. Note the availability and cost of the software that you will recommend. Remember to click the Back button (repeatedly, if necessary) to return to the results so that you can visit another linked site.

h. Close Internet Explorer.

i. Click **Start**, position the mouse over **All Programs**, click **Accessories**, and then click **WordPad**. Type your name and class. Compose a report giving instructions on how to delete the History list, Cookies, and Temporary Internet files. Include in the report your recommendation for antispyware software. Give reasons why you believe that your choice of antispyware software is appropriate. Be sure to include cost and availability.

j. Save the report as **chap1_prac2_privacy**.

k. Print a copy of the report.

l. Close WordPad.

**Figure 1.49** Deleting History, Cookies, and Temporary Internet Files

## 3 Local News

It is called the World Wide Web for a reason: This network of networks enables you to find information about almost every city and country in the world. You might be amazed at how much information you can find about your hometown or a locale near your home. Items such as population, attractions, and homes for sale are available at many sites on the Web. In this exercise you will find information about your community.

a. Open Internet Explorer.

b. Click in the Address bar and type **www.google.com**. Click in the keyword area, if necessary, and type your zip code and the name of your hometown. Press **Enter**. The result is a wealth of information from weather to store shopping coupons, library hours, maps, attractions, and recreational information. Click a few links to enjoy the information.

...continued on Next Page

c. Click in the Address bar. Type **www.noaa.gov** and press **Enter**. Click in the box under Today's Weather and type your city and state, separated by a comma. Click **Go**. You will see a detailed description of upcoming weather for your area.

d. Click the **Add to Favorites button**, and then and click **Add to Favorites**. Create a new folder to contain sites related to local information. Click **New Folder**, type **Local Information**, and click **Create**. Accept the suggested Favorite name and click **Add**.

e. Click in the Address bar and type **realestate.yahoo.com/*your state***, replacing the words *your state* with your state (such as Arizona). Be sure to capitalize the state. Press **Enter**.

f. Click the **Add to Favorites button**, and then click **Add to Favorites**. Accept the suggested name and click the Local Information folder. Click **Save**.

g. Click in the Search bar and type the city and state from which you would like to see a real estate listing. If you like, you can enter your price range, as well. Click **Search**.

h. Click in the Address bar and type **www.cia.gov/cia/publications/factbook/index.html**. Press **Enter**. Instead of local information, you might want to learn about another country. An excellent Web resource is the CIA factbook, which you can access from this Web site. Think of a country in which you have an interest and click it in the **Select a Country or Location drop-down list**.

i. Click the **Add to Favorites button**, and then click **Organize Favorites**. Click the **Local Information folder**. Click **Delete**. Confirm the deletion. Click **Close**.

j. Close Internet Explorer.

## 4 Traveling Abroad

You are employed with a company involved in acquiring agricultural products, often on a worldwide scale. Your company is particularly interested in importing sugar, orange juice, and coffee from Brazil. You are fairly fluent in Spanish, and you have a degree in International Business, so your company is sending you to Rio de Janeiro to identify business opportunities. There is much to do before you leave for South America, including getting a physical exam and vaccinations, packing appropriate attire, and understanding the monetary exchange rate. You can gain information on all of those things through Internet research.

a. Open Internet Explorer.

b. Click in the Address bar and type **www.google.com**. Press **Enter.** Click in the keyword area, if necessary, and type **exchange rate dollar to real.** Since the currency of Brazil is the real, you want to know how much the American dollar is currently worth in Brazil. Click **Google Search.** Click a resulting link to determine the exchange rate. If the Web site does not return the required information, click the Back button (repeatedly, if necessary) to return to the Google page. Try another link. How many Brazilian real does one U.S. dollar convert to?

c. Click in the Address bar and type **www.google.com**. Press **Enter**. You will be traveling to Brazil in June and need to know what the weather is like so that you can pack appropriately. Click in the keyword area, if necessary, and type **Rio de Janeiro weather June.** Click **Google Search.** Click a resulting link to find the average temperature in Rio de Janeiro in June. If the Web site does not return the required information, click the Back button (repeatedly, if necessary) to return to the Google page. Try another link.

d. Click in the Address bar, type **www.google.com**, and press **Enter**. You will use the Internet to identify required (or recommended) vaccinations for travel to Brazil. Click in the keyword area, if necessary, and type **required vaccinations Brazil** and click **Google Search.** Peruse the resulting links to find required, or recommended, vaccinations for travel to South America.

e. Click in the Address bar and type **http://travel.state.gov/travel/tips/brochures/brochures_1229.html**. Press **Enter.** You will identify paperwork required by the United States for travel to Brazil. Click the letter **B** in the alphabet listing to navigate to the Brazil page. Exactly what paperwork is required, and how far in advance of your travel?

f. Close Internet Explorer.

...continued on Next Page

g. Click **Start**, position the mouse over **All Programs**, click **Accessories**, and then click **WordPad**. Type your name and class. Create a summary of your findings with respect to travel to Brazil. Include the current exchange rate for dollar to real, the average high and low temperatures for Rio de Janeiro in June, recommended vaccinations and any other health preparations, and passport requirements.

h. Save the report as **chap1_prac4_travel**.

i. Print a copy of the report.

j. Close WordPad.

# Mid-Level Exercises

## 1 Labor News

As a class assignment, your economics instructor has asked that you become familiar with the U.S. Department of Labor Web site and prepare a short report on a few findings.

a. Select a search engine or use Windows Live Search to locate the Web site for the U.S. Department of Labor.

b. Using links on the Labor Department home page, identify the current Secretary of Labor. What is the minimum wage?

c. Visit the Department of Labor newsroom and summarize at least one recent news item.

d. Using a search engine or the Search box on the Department of Labor home page, find the current national unemployment rate.

e. Visit **www.census.gov** and find the current United States population. Also, find the current population of your state.

f. Open WordPad and prepare a report, giving the following:

- Current Secretary of Labor

- Current minimum wage

- Short summary of a recent Department of Labor news item

- Current national unemployment rate

- Current United States population

- Current population of your state

g. Save the report as **chap1_mid1_labor**.

h. Print a copy of the report.

## 2 Environmental Affairs

You are a volunteer for a nonprofit environmental group. You are gathering information to include in a newsletter. Although you will not type the newsletter, you will supply information for the public relations office. You will identify appropriate clip art or photographs that could support the topics of widespread logging, global warming, and increased fuel emissions. Because you, or the authors of the newsletter, are likely to return to the Web sites that you identify, you will create a Favorites folder for the group of environmental Web sites.

a. Search the Web for appropriate clip art or photographs (for the environmental group's newsletter). Determine how to download the items so that you can give directions to the newsletter staff.

b. Create a Favorites folder titled **Environment** and place any Web pages that contain usable content in the Environment folder.

c. As you identify Web sites, create tabs for them so that you can move among them with ease. Use Quick Tabs to view a thumbnail of each Web site.

d. Familiarize yourself with at least one type of existing or proposed federal legislation concerning fuel emissions.

e. Use WordPad to create a summary of your research, listing all Web sites that are in your Favorites list, identifying specific sites from which you can download graphics.

...continued on Next Page

Because the person developing the newsletter staff is new to the job, provide a detailed description of how he is to download any graphics that he wants to use. Your report should also cite at least one item of existing or proposed federal legislation on fuel emissions.

f. Save the report as **chap1_mid2_environment**.

g. Print a copy of the report.

## 3 Vacation Time

You are planning a vacation to Disney World. Assume that you live in Chattanooga, Tennessee, and are uncertain of whether to fly or to drive. If you drive, it will take longer, but your family might enjoy an overnight stop at the beach along the way. You will use the Web to investigate costs and a driving route, and then decide whether to drive or to fly.

a. Visit **www.mapquest.com** and get driving directions from Chattanooga to Disney World (Orlando, Florida). You will not enter a starting address—just use the city of Chattanooga, Tennessee. Next, go to **www.yahoo.com** and use the Maps feature to get driving directions from Chattanooga to Disney World. Do the driving directions from the two Web sites differ?

b. Check on air fare, possibly at a site like **www.travelocity.com** or **www.expedia.com**. If you fly, you will leave on October 16 of the current year and return on October 20. Investigate potential flights and note the one that you will select if you choose to fly.

c. As you consider driving, which route would you select and how many miles is it? If your car gets 24 miles to the gallon, how much would gas cost (at the estimated average price per gallon)?

d. If you drive, you will stop overnight at Panama City, Florida. Check online for accommodations at Panama City and make a selection, noting the cost. Develop a realistic estimate of food costs per day for travel. Unless you spend time at the beach, you will reach Disney World in two days of driving time.

e. Check online for rates and availability at Disney World. Where would you make reservations and what will it cost? Consider the cost of Disney World admission for the three days that you will be there. Also, estimate the cost per day for food and other items.

f. Finally, determine the total trip cost if you fly and the total trip cost if you drive. Which would you choose to do?

g. Develop a report giving the cost breakdown for flying and for driving to Disney World. In your report, list the Web sites that you visited in determining costs and a route.

h. Save the report as **chap1_mid3_vacation**.

i. Print a copy of the report.

# Capstone Exercise

*You are employed as a co-op student with the National Park Service and are currently assigned to a new museum in Sequoyah, Oklahoma. As part of your job duties, and to satisfy the requirements of your history major, you will not only assist with the museum, but will record details of your summer job in a blog. The museum has a large wing dedicated to the history of Native Americans. You are involved with the design of a display giving information on the Trail of Tears. The Trail of Tears was the forced march of Native Americans from their homelands during 1838–1839. Your task is to identify Web resources giving information on the march.*

## Conduct Internet Research

You must search the Internet for a graphical representation of the Trail of Tears route. In addition, you will find at least ten Web sites with historical information related to the Trail of Tears.

a. Create a Favorites folder, titled **Trail of Tears**. In the folder, place at least ten links to Web sites that will be useful for preparation of a report on the Trail of Tears.

b. Identify a Web site that contains a suitable graphical representation of the Trail of Tears route. Include the Web site as a link in the Trail of Tears Favorites folder.

## Clear Temporary Internet Files, and Set and Print a Home Page

You have listed relevant Web sites in a Trail of Tears Favorites folder. In order to maintain an orderly hard drive, you will now remove Temporary Internet files.

a. Use Internet Explorer to delete the browser history.

b. Click the Home button on your browser. Write down the current home page address so that you can reset it in a few minutes.

c. Select a Web site that is rich in Native American history (specifically Trail of Tears information). Make it your home page.

d. Print the new home page.

e. Return the home page to the original setting (the address that you jotted down in Step b).

## Download an Internet File

You will download the map of the Trail of Tears (recently saved as a Favorite) so that you can include it in a report.

a. Access your Favorites list and revisit the Web site containing the map of the Trail of Tears.

b. Download the map to your flash drive.

## Explore Instant Messages and Blogs

You will create a blog account (or use the one that you created in Hands-On Exercise 3) to record a fictitious week at the museum. You will also identify possible sources for instant messaging software.

a. Visit **www.livejournal.com** and create an account—or log into one that you previously created.

b. Create at least two blog entries recording your activities at the museum during one fictitious week. Make the blog entries public, so do not include any personal information. Use completely fictitious events and names.

c. Search the Internet for free Instant Message services. Explore features of each, and make a selection of the one that you would use if you wanted to participate in instant messaging. Record the reasons for your selection for inclusion in a later report.

## Develop a Contacts List

You will be responsible for communicating with other Native American museums, so use the Internet to collect contact information on at least three museums.

a. List the contacts (including mailing address, telephone, and e-mail address) on paper.

## Prepare a Report

Use Microsoft Word to prepare a report outlining your Internet research and accompanying information, such as the contacts list and the downloaded graphic.

a. Open Microsoft Word and type a report, including the following:

- A list of all Web addresses of sites included in your Favorites folder (regarding Trail of Tears information).

- The URL of the site containing the clip art that you downloaded.

- Directions on how to include your contacts in Windows Mail. Assume that you are leaving directions for a clerical assistant who is not familiar with Windows Mail.

- The downloaded clip art (insert it into your document) in any location.

- Information on the instant messaging service that you selected. Provide detail on the product features, procedure for downloading, and why you selected the service.

- At least one-half page of typewritten facts pertaining to the Trail of Tears. Make it a short summary of the events leading up to the march and the actual event.

b. Save the report as **chap1_capstone_trail.**

c. Print the report.

# Mini Cases

*Use the rubric following the case as a guide to evaluate your work, but keep in mind that your instructor may impose additional grading criteria or use a different standard to judge your work.*

## The Outlook for Windows Mail

GENERAL CASE

Windows Mail is an e-mail program included with Windows Vista. Outlook is a much more comprehensive personal information management software package, including not only e-mail, but also appointment scheduling and task management, among other things. Using your Web search skills, compare the two software packages, giving advantages and disadvantages (if any) of each. Include any cost associated with either software. Give reasons why you would prefer one over the other and include a description of how you would obtain the product and how you would learn to use it. Save your findings in a WordPad report titled **chap1_mc1_mail**. Print a copy of the report.

| Performance Elements | Exceeds Expectations | Meets Expectations | Below Expectations |
|---|---|---|---|
| **Organization** | The report is well researched, addressing all required topics. Its length is appropriate. | Although the basic required elements of the report are included, they are not presented in a coherent fashion. The report is shorter than is required, with obvious effort at lengthening the report by filling it with disjointed ideas. | The report is very short, with an obvious lack of preparation. The report contains little or no coverage of required topics. |
| **Visual aspects** | The report is well developed, with appropriate paragraph divisions and no typos. | The report contains a few mistakes, but the basic elements are presented in a readable manner. | The report contains little or no paragraph structure and it is difficult to identify the major points of the report. Obvious mistakes detract from the subject matter. |
| **Mechanics** | The report was developed with Word or WordPad. All required elements are addressed in the report. | The report was developed with Word or WordPad. However, the file contains several spelling and formatting mistakes and/or the file is not named as required. | The report contains multiple mistakes and is very poorly prepared with regard to sentence and paragraph structure. |

## Robotics Education

RESEARCH CASE

As a student assistant, you are helping your computer science instructor prepare for a series of workshops for visiting high school students. The workshops will introduce students to 3D modeling and robotics. Your task is twofold: (1) Clear the lab computers of all History files, Temporary Internet files, and Cookies so that unnecessary files are removed from the hard drives and the Internet history is clear; and (2) Assist in locating software and teaching plans for a high school robotics seminar and also for a 3D modeling seminar. Develop a one- to two-page report covering the following topics and answering several questions:

1. Give a step-by-step plan for removing cookies, Temporary Internet files, and the History list. Because you are likely to be in a public computer lab, you will not actually remove the items, but will provide directions on how to do so.

2. What does Lego have to offer in the way of robotics education? What kits and lesson plans are available from Lego or other companies? What is the cost of the software and any lesson plans? What are the system requirements for a robotics kit (possibly from Lego)?

3. What 3D modeling software would be appropriate for a camp or seminar for high school students? What is the cost? What are the system requirements for the modeling software?

4. Summarize your findings in a WordPad report. Save the report as **chap1_mc2_seminar**. Print a copy of the report.

| Performance Elements | Exceeds Expectations | Meets Expectations | Below Expectations |
|---|---|---|---|
| **Organization** | The report is well researched, addressing all required topics. Its length is appropriate. | Although the basic required elements of the report are included, they are not presented in a coherent fashion. The report is shorter than is required, with obvious effort at lengthening the report by filling it with disjointed ideas. | The report is very short, with an obvious lack of preparation. The report contains little or no coverage of required topics. |
| **Visual aspects** | The report is well developed, with appropriate paragraph divisions and no typos. | The report contains a few mistakes, but the basic elements are presented in a readable manner. | The report contains little or no paragraph structure and it is difficult to identify the major points of the report. Obvious mistakes detract from the subject matter. |
| **Mechanics** | The report was developed with Word or WordPad. All required elements are addressed in the report. | The report was developed with Word or WordPad. However, the file contains several spelling and formatting mistakes and/or the file is not named as required. | The report contains multiple mistakes and is very poorly prepared with regard to sentence and paragraph structure. |

## Identity Theft

DISASTER RECOVERY

In business for yourself as a commercial landscape architect, you often have lunch with clients. After one such lunch today, you realize that you left your wallet at the restaurant table. Although you quickly rush back to recover the wallet, you are too late. It is missing and has not been turned in. Along with a debit card, you lost a small amount of cash, your driver's license, and three credit cards. You quickly call the bank and cancel the debit card until a new one can be issued. You know that your credit cards included Discover, Chase, and Bank of America, but you do not know the account numbers. You are also concerned about the liability associated with misuse of the credit cards. If you report the loss, how much money will you be responsible for? Finally, so that you are better prepared in the future, you want to have more complete information at hand (including account numbers and phone numbers). To assist with that, you will select a money management software program that will maintain credit and debit card information. For this exercise, use the Internet to:

1. Find the telephone numbers for customer support for Discover, Chase, and Bank of America. Record both the telephone numbers and the URLs at which you found the information.

2. Find information related to personal liability for a stolen credit card. Is there a dollar amount for which you are responsible if a credit card is stolen?

3. Locate suggestions from the FDIC on safe online banking. The theft has made you aware of the need to closely monitor debit and credit card activity, but you wonder if online banking is safe. Record the URL at which you found the FDIC information and summarize the suggestions.

4. Compare Microsoft Money and Quicken. From this point forward, you want to maintain accurate records of financial accounts, including account numbers and balances. You have heard that both software programs are excellent, but you want to select the best one for your situation. Be sure to consider your budget and computer equipment when making your selection. Include information on how to purchase or download the product, basic product features, and required computer specifications.

5. Summarize your findings in a one- to two-page WordPad report. Save the report as **chap1_mc3_theft**. Print a copy of the report.

| Performance Elements | Exceeds Expectations | Meets Expectations | Below Expectations |
| --- | --- | --- | --- |
| **Organization** | The report is well researched, addressing all required topics. Its length is appropriate. | Although the basic required elements of the report are included, they are not presented in a coherent fashion. The report is shorter than is required, with obvious effort at lengthening the report by filling it with disjointed ideas. | The report is very short, with an obvious lack of preparation. The report contains little or no coverage of required topics. |
| **Visual aspects** | The report is well developed, with appropriate paragraph divisions and no typos. | The report contains a few mistakes, but the basic elements are presented in a readable manner. | The report contains little or no paragraph structure and it is difficult to identify the major points of the report. Obvious mistakes detract from the subject matter. |
| **Mechanics** | The report was developed with Word or WordPad. All required elements are addressed in the report. | The report was developed with Word or WordPad. However, the file contains several spelling and formatting mistakes and/or the file is not named as required. | The report contains multiple mistakes and is very poorly prepared with regard to sentence and paragraph structure. |

#  Glossary

All key terms appearing in this book (in bold italic) are listed alphabetically in this Glossary for easy reference. If you want to learn more about a feature or concept, use the Index to find the term's other significant occurrences.

**Attachment** A file that is sent along with an e-mail message.

**Blog** A personal journal entry that is posted online; short for *Web Log*.

**Bookmark** See *favorite*.

**Browser** A software application used to display Web pages, access Web resources, and search the Web.

**Cookie** A text file that is sometimes saved to your computer when you visit a Web site, identifying you as a return visitor when you revisit the site later.

**Domain** A name for the resources that make up an organization's Web site.

**E-commerce** Conducting online business through advertising, selling, and buying products.

**E-mail** The transmission of online messages over a communication network.

**Favorite** A marker that identifies a Web page so that you can quickly display the page later, also called a *bookmark*.

**File transfer protocol (ftp)** Used for uploading, storing, and downloading sharable files over the Internet.

**Frame** A boxed area, usually located at the side or top of a Web page, containing links and additional information.

**Home page** The Web page that displays when you open Internet Explorer. Also refers to the main Web page for an organization's Web site.

**Hyperlink (link)** A text or graphical element that, when clicked, displays another area of the same Web page or displays another Web page or resource.

**HyperText Markup Language (HTML)** Widely used authoring language to create Web pages; defines structure and formatting throughout with HTML tags.

**HyperText Transfer Protocol (HTTP)** A set of rules that dictates how Web pages are formatted and how data must be transmitted across the Web.

**Instant message** A form of online communication that enables you to send messages to and receive messages from others who are online at the same time.

**Internet** A global information network comprised of millions of interconnected computers to disseminate information and communicate with other people around the world.

**Internet Explorer 7 (IE)** The newest version of Microsoft's browser.

**Internet Service Provider (ISP)** A company that provides access to the Internet.

**Keyword** A word or phrase that describes information that you want to find on the Internet.

**Phishing** The act of sending fraudulent e-mail in an attempt to collect personal information by pretending to be a legitimate enterprise.

**Pop-under** An uninvited browser window that appears when an active browser window is closed; usually an advertisement.

**Pop-up** An uninvited browser window that appears in front of an active browser window; usually an advertisement.

**Protocol** A set of rules that govern data formats and transmission.

**Search engine** A Web site that provides search tools so that you can find information on a topic.

**Temporary Internet file** A copy of a Web page that is saved onto your hard drive for ease of access later.

**Top-level domain** A suffix that identifies the type of organization sponsoring a Web site.

**Uniform Resource Locator (URL)** The specific address of a World Wide Web file.

**Web page** A single document formatted to be used on the Web, typically consisting of text, graphics, animation, and/or sound

**Web server** A computer that contains Web pages, has server software installed, and is connected to the Internet.

**Web site** A collection of related Web pages maintained by an organization or entity.

**Windows Contacts** A feature of Windows Vista that stores and organizes information about people with which you communicate electronically.

**Windows Mail** An e-mail program included with Windows Vista; enables you to send and receive messages.

**World Wide Web** A subset of the Internet that supports point-and-click navigation to information and resources.

**The Online Experience, Chapter 1**

1.  c
2.  a
3.  b
4.  a
5.  d
6.  c
7.  a
8.  d
9.  b
10. c
11. b
12. c
13. a
14. a
15. a

# Index

Hyperlinks, 3, 5. *See also* Links
  graphic, 7, 8
  text, 7, 8
  use of, 19
  in Web pages, 7, 8
HyperText Markup Language (HTML), 4
HyperText Transfer Protocol (HTTP), 3

# I

Icon
  Add to Favorites, 17
  attached file, 42
  Favorites Center, 17
  Home, 17
  Inbox, 41
  Page, 17
  Print, 17
  Tools, 17
Identity theft exercise, 61–62
IE. *See* Internet Explorer
Images, 16. *See also* Pictures
  clip art, 2
IMing. *See* Instant messaging
Inbox icon, 41
Instant messages, 44, 50
  exercise with, 59
  privacy and, 44
Instant messaging (IMing), 44
Instant Messenger, America Online (AIM), 44
Interconnected networks, 3, 50
Internet, 3. *See also* Web
  addresses, 5
  business on, 3
  development of, 3
  search engines, 30, 35, 50
  security and, 3
  surfing of, 7
  traffic, 8
Internet connections, 4, 50
  broadband, 8
  cable, 4, 8
  dial-up, 8
  DSL, 8
  high-speed, 8
  T-3, 8
Internet Explorer (IE) 7, 4
  browser window, 4
  download, 4
  full screen mode, 4
  options, 26–29, 50
  reference for, 17
  security and, 16, 23, 50
  Vista and, 4

Internet Service Providers (ISPs), 4, 36
Investment exercise, 53
ISPs. *See* Internet Service Providers

# J

Junk e-mail, 36, 38. *See also* E-mail
  options, 42, 48

# K

Keys
  F4, 6
  F5, 10
Keywords, 30
  phrasing of, 31

# L

Links, 3, 5. *See also* Hyperlinks
  response time of, 8
Lycos, 30

# M

Mail. *See* E-mail; Windows Mail
Margin adjust handle, 15
Microsoft Outlook, 60
  contacts list in, 2
  Windows Mail *v.,* 60
Microsoft Outlook Express, 36. *See also* Windows Mail
.mil, 5
Multiple choice test, 50–51

# N

Navigation, of Web sites, 5–13, 50
.net, 5
Netiquette, 38
Networks, 3. *See also* E-mail; Internet
  administrators, 6, 36
  e-mail and, 36, 39
  global information, 3
  interconnected, 3, 50
  network of, 54

# O

Online
  communication, 36–49
  experience, 1–62
Options
  forward, 42
  home page, 28